To my mother,

ENID THACKERY,

and to the memory of my father,

JOHN T. THACKERY, JR.

A LIGHT AND

UNCERTAIN HOLD

A Light

A HISTORY OF THE SIXTY-SIXTH

and Uncertain

OHIO VOLUNTEER INFANTRY

Hold

DAVID T. THACKERY

THE KENT STATE UNIVERSITY PRESS

KENT, OHIO, & LONDON

© 1999 by The Kent State University Press,
Kent, Ohio 44242
All rights reserved
Library of Congress Catalog Card Number 98-31317
ISBN 0-87338-609-4
Manufactured in the United States of America

05 04 03 02 01 00 99   5 4 3 2 1

Frontis photo: The stained-glass window honoring the
Sixty-sixth Ohio Volunteer Infantry, Woodstock Community
Church, Woodstock, Ohio. *Photo by Brenda Burns. Courtesy
of the Woodstock Community Church.*

Library of Congress Cataloging-in-Publication Data
Thackery, David T.
A light and uncertain hold : a history of the Sixty-sixth Ohio
Volunteer Infantry / David T. Thackery.
p.   cm.
Includes bibliographical references and index.
ISBN 0-87338-609-4 (cloth : alk. paper) ∞
1. United States. Army. Ohio Infantry Regiment, 66th
(1861–1865).   2. United States—History—Civil War, 1861–1865
—Regimental histories.   3. Ohio—History—Civil War, 1861–
1865—Regimental histories.
E525.5 66th.T47   1999
973.7'471—dc21   98-31317

British Library Cataloging-in-Publication data are available.

Contents

Maps

Preface

*O*nce, as a boy, exploring a collection of old photographs and family heirlooms, I came upon two poems, published as broadsides. The poet was my great-great-grandmother. Her first poem recounted the pride and anxiety of a young woman as she witnessed her brother going off to fight in the war to save the Union. It was followed by the grief and resignation of her second poem, which told the story of his death in battle. The soldier was Levi Gladden, who had joined the Sixty-sixth Ohio Volunteer Infantry, a local regiment regarded by many as the premier regiment of Champaign County, Ohio. Its first battle was at Port Republic, Virginia, on June 9, 1862, and it was there that young Levi was shot in the forehead and killed.

These sentimental poems were unusual documents, and I appreciated them for their poignancy and rarity. The events they described also beckoned. As the years passed, I became curious about the circumstances surrounding Levi Gladden's death and about the regiment he had joined. Joining the staff of the Newberry Library in 1982, I began to explore the extensive Civil War holdings and discovered that the Sixty-sixth Ohio, though revered in the memory of my county, was not blessed with a published regimental history. The absence of such a history contrasted with many other Union regiments, for which there was at least one published history, sometimes more. There were also published diaries or the collected letters of men who had served in Union regiments, but at that time none from the Sixty-sixth.

If there had been such a history or even a memoir in print, it is possible that my curiosity would have been satisfied by reading it. But as there was no such book, I sought out contemporary accounts of the battle of Port Republic in the local newspaper and compared them with what I could find in the *Official Records* and in the secondary literature available to me. I was captured by the drama of that sharp little battle, but I was also struck with the difficulties of reconciling and integrating everything I was reading; in fact, a few nagging questions remained unanswered about Port Republic until the publication of Robert Krick's authoritative *Conquering the Valley* in 1996. It was my introduction to the challenge of military scholarship.

My curiosity gradually extended beyond the battle in which my kinsman lost his life. What experiences did the Sixty-sixth have prior to Port Republic? What came after? As a genealogist and as the curator of one of the country's foremost local and family history collections, I was led to focus on the individuals who served in the regiment and on their communities as well. I began compiling an annotated roster of the regiment based on the listings in the Ohio adjutant general's *Report,* supplementing that source with information garnered from county histories, pension records, cemeteries, newspapers, and the like. I passed many hours at the Champaign County Public Library, in my hometown of Urbana, Ohio, scanning the microfilm of local newspapers. I was fascinated by what I found in those pages; ultimately, it was reading the newspapers that provoked my desire to write an account of the Sixty-sixth, an account that would be rooted in the history of my community as well as in the combat and field experiences of my distant uncle's regiment.

My annotated roster grew as I received a trickle of photocopies of service and pension records from the National Archives, unearthed biographical sketches from county histories, and discovered articles and obituaries in newspapers. I am not sure when I came to the realization that I was writing a book, but the process was a gradual one; the research and writing of the Sixty-sixth's history extended over at least ten years.

One of this book's goals is to present an accurate record of the Sixty-sixth's military experiences. For many engagements the various primary and secondary sources are not in complete agreement. The official reports are sometimes self-serving, sometimes confused, sometimes contradictory, and often all too brief. The value of letters and diaries is mitigated by the limitations of a single soldier's viewpoint as he tried to comprehend one small corner of the violence and chaos. Scholarly campaign histories and battle accounts are helpful in making sense of larger events, but they often lack the detail I needed to recount fully the Sixty-sixth's part in a battle. As a result, I have not achieved 100 percent certitude in my accounts of some of the engagements in which the Sixty-sixth took part; however, I hope that the careful reader will come away from this book with a reasonably clear sense of what happened. I hope also that this work will also be of some assistance to future writers and historians as the process of clarifying the historical record continues.

As a genealogist and a sympathizer with modern social history (which, until recent years, appears to have kept military history at arm's length), I want this book to be more than the story of a group of anonymous men in blue uniforms marching about the landscape amid exploding shells and musket volleys. Whenever possible I have employed the words and stories of individual soldiers (with original spelling and punctuation retained) in an effort to give depth and substance to the regiment's experience. This is hardly a new approach: Bell Irvin Wiley showed the way over half a century ago; Ken Burns took this approach on television in 1990, and so have many writers of campaign and regimental histories in recent years. This perspective need not be confined to the combat experience; it can and should be applied to issues of organization and morale. The efforts made to keep spirits up in a single Federal regiment stationed in Virginia during the first months of 1863 can tell us much about the Army of the Potomac and the Union war effort as a whole, even as the campaign to reenlist veterans at the close of that year might afford insight into the thoughts and feelings of Union soldiers in the Western army fresh from its triumphs in the Chattanooga campaign.

These men were also extensions of their communities, communities to which many of them would return. If the narrative was to place, however loosely, the Sixty-sixth's story within the framework of community history, it could not be contained within the years 1861 through 1865. The Underground Railroad and antebellum political conflicts were, it seemed, as rightfully a part of this story as the battles at Gettysburg and Lookout Mountain—likewise, postwar Republican hegemony in Champaign County, the activities of veterans' organizations, the pension process, and even to some extent failed race relations. The inclusion of antebellum and postbellum events in this narrative will, I hope, be seen not as gratuitous or distracting but rather as context for its central events.

Following Wiley's lead of five decades ago, recent scholarship has concerned itself with motivation and morale in Civil War armies. These were important issues for me as I researched this book. The question "Why did they fight?" is an important one. There is no simple answer; there was a wide range of experience and attitude during the war. It would be unfair and false to discount the patriotic idealism that motivated many Northern volunteers in 1861, but it would also be unrealistic to assert that such sentiments were the motivating factors for all volunteers or that these convictions were held consistently throughout the conflict. Peer pressure and local hoopla—bordering, it would appear, on hysteria—could also play a role in sending young men to the recruiting officer. Neither was there any shortage of naïveté, for few of the enlistees had any conception of what they would be facing, and nor did their families.

The great dividing line was the introduction to combat. It was the most important catalyst in the creation of regimental pride and identification—assuming that the experience was not too devastating and that the regiment acquitted itself well. In the case of the Sixty-sixth, its first combat experience was Port Republic, which probably figured more strongly in the postwar memories of its survivors than did any other battle. Such an experience set the men of a Civil War apart from the civilian world, whose structures and protections were no longer relevant or effective. The new veterans were divorced from the security of their civilian lives and could rely only on one another, in matters that were truly life and death.

Only a statistical handful of the Civil War enlistees had seen combat in the Mexican War or in fighting with the Indians. Few could have anticipated the horrors to which they were committing themselves. Once the dangers of military life were revealed, idealism might persist, but idealism by itself was not enough to ensure good morale, which could depend on a number of factors, some of them seemingly mundane. Taking into account the doubts and fears of these men does not dishonor their sacrifices or heroism. By acknowledging the soldiers' humanity we do the men of the Sixty-sixth a greater honor than would any amount of flag waving. I have not glossed over the horrors and ambiguities of combat and military life. Yet, I have tried not to detract from the strength of character demonstrated by so many of these men. The commonplace that war brings out the best and worst in humanity is no less true for being threadbare.

I incurred numerous debts of gratitude in the research and writing of this book, but as the research process unfolded over a long period of time, I fear that I may not acknowledge everyone to whom acknowledgment is due. My debts are indeed many. In particular, my fellow Urbana High School graduate Kyle Kelch was very helpful in sharing his knowledge of local Civil War lore, allowing me to consult his manuscript and photograph collections, and alerting me to other sources that I probably would not have discovered without his help. Pat Stickley, another Champaign Countian and an indefatigable researcher into the history and genealogies of the county, also kept an eye out for materials on the Sixty-sixth and its veterans and shared many important finds with me. Tom Pope of Saint Paris, Ohio, also alerted me to several helpful sources. I am especially grateful to William Russell, for allowing me to use the letters of Robert H. Russell, as I am to Robert Pennoyer, for allowing me to quote at length from his edited publication of John Houtz's diary. I should also express my appreciation to the Champaign County Public Library, not only for granting me permission to quote and cite from the W. A. Brand G.A.R. post's memoir book but also for providing a pleasant haven for research over the last decade or more. Likewise a "thank you" to the Champaign County Historical Society for making available to me the Sixty-sixth's reunion association records and the scrapbooks and records of the W. A. Brand G.A.R. post and for allowing me to include in this book photographs from its holdings. I am also grateful to the Ohio Historical Society for allowing me to quote from materials in its manuscript collection, and to Gary Arnold for facilitating my research there. Duke University also merits special thanks for making copies of Joseph Diltz's letters available to me and for allowing me to quote from them. The United States Army Military History Institute at Carlisle Barracks, Pennsylvania, also has my gratitude for providing copies from its photograph collection; I would like to note especially my appreciation to the staff of its manuscript division, where I spent a very pleasant three days in research. The military service and pension records held by the National Archives have been an invaluable resource, and I can only add my fervent prayer to those of thousands of historians and genealogists that the Archives will be able to continue to preserve these records and make them available to the public. The Newberry Library of Chicago, my employer for the last fifteen years, served as a base for researching and writing this book (though of course the work was done on my own time); without access to its collections, this book would have taken much longer to write and would likely not have been as thoroughly researched.

I would also like to thank my mother, for her encouragement over the years and for accompanying me on my several expeditions into the countryside looking for the graves of Sixty-sixth veterans. Finally, I wish to acknowledge my father, whose interest in family history started me on the road that culminated in this book. I only regret that he is not here today to see it.

A LIGHT AND

UNCERTAIN HOLD

Prologue

On a warm August afternoon in 1887, nine middle-aged men made their way to a photographer's studio in Urbana, Ohio. They were businessmen and farmers, also a schoolteacher and a former sheriff. All were veterans, having served in the Sixty-sixth Ohio Volunteer Infantry during the Civil War. They had just returned from a regimental reunion. John T. Mitchell, once an officer of the regiment and now a dry goods merchant, had decided upon this detour to the photographer's studio. But before going back to Columbus their image would be preserved for posterity. They had with them the Sixty-sixth's two colors, on loan from the state capitol.

Between them, the flags had been carried in a dozen battles and numerous skirmishes. On one were emblazoned the names of some of these battles—many of them famous, such as Gettysburg and Antietam, and others, such as Port Republic and Cedar Mountain, not so well known. In the photographer's studio the banners were crossed, a medallion bearing the designation 66th O.V.I. (Ohio Volunteer Infantry) held up between them. The field and stars of one banner had been almost entirely shot away. Both flags exhibited holes and tears. A local newspa-

The Sixty-sixth Ohio Volunteer Infantry's regimental colors, photographed in 1887. *Kyle Kelch Collection.*

per observed: "Most gently and tenderly were the ragged folds unrolled. And it was needful they should be"—for the "scarred and rent banners hung to their staffs by a very light and uncertain hold."[1]

Both flags had been purchased and presented to the regiment by the people of Urbana. The first left town with the regiment one chilly January evening in 1862, the day the Sixty-sixth boarded a train taking them to the mountains of western Virginia. For two years the banner remained with them, a silent witness to shortening roll calls as disease and combat took their toll. The Urbana citizenry presented the second flag to the regiment in January 1864, when the soldiers were home on furlough. Upon this flag were emblazoned the names of the battles through which the first had been carried. It would accompany the regiment through Sherman's Atlanta campaign and the March to the Sea.

The flags and the men who followed them form a small part of a larger national saga. They are part also of a story which includes the soldiers' families, friends, and neighbors in the towns and farms of west-central Ohio, a story that need not be limited to the years 1861 through 1865. So it is that we begin this account four years before the fall of Fort Sumter, in an Ohio village well known for its views on slavery.

1

Udney Hyde and Addison White

It was the evening of April 20, 1857. An enclosed carriage drove into the village of Mechanicsburg, ten miles east of Urbana. It halted in an alleyway not far from the home of Charles Taylor. A man left the carriage, walked to Taylor's door, and knocked. Taylor opened the door, and the visitor asked to be directed to the residence of a black man named Addison White. White's wife was in the carriage, claimed the visitor, and wished to see her husband.

White was a runaway slave, one of many who had made their way into the village on their way to the nearby town of Delaware and ultimately Canada and freedom. Unlike most of them, though, White had made it to Mechanicsburg without the good offices of the Underground Railroad, although he had now elected to remain with Udney Hyde, probably the most active operative of the Railroad in the Mechanicsburg area, to help with farm chores while Hyde recovered from a foot injury. That both White and Hyde apparently felt comfortable with such an arrangement is a fair indication of the strength of abolitionist sentiments in the village and surrounding area. With the assistance of Charles Taylor, the escaped slave had sent a letter to his wife, who was still in Kentucky. The letter had been sent in a manner that was supposed to preclude discovery of its origins. But now here was this stranger at Taylor's door.

Suspicious, Taylor told the man that White could not be reached for two or three days. In the interim, perhaps Addison's wife could be housed at Taylor's until the couple could be reunited? No, that would not do, was the reply; the stranger returned to the carriage and left the way he had come. Taylor followed, catching up with the carriage in the village square. Might it be possible to speak to Mrs. White? From inside the darkened carriage came a response, in the falsetto of a man unsuccessfully attempting to imitate a woman's voice. Taylor's suspicions had been justified.

Despite this incident, which indicated that his whereabouts had been discovered, Addison White remained with Hyde. The town was, after all, a major abolitionist center. But even such a stronghold as Mechanicsburg could be subject to invasion. The Fugitive Slave Act, which mandated the return to their masters of escaped slaves found in the North, was the law of the land, and that land included Mechanicsburg, Ohio. It also included Flemingsburg, Kentucky, the home of White's erstwhile owner, who aimed to see the law of the land enforced and who by one account had been in the carriage which came to Taylor's door that spring night. So it was that in the early morning hours of May 15 nine men might have been seen making their way by carriage through Mechanicsburg toward the Hyde farm, two miles to the southeast. Two of the men were deputy federal marshals; the other seven formed a posse.

They came to the farm just as Hyde, still suffering from his foot injury, was painfully drawing on his boots. White, also inside, spied the nine men advancing upon the house. Springing to a ladder, he found refuge in the loft just as the posse came through the door. Hyde allowed to the lawmen that White was in the loft but told them that the escaped slave would not come down and that he, Hyde, would offer them no assistance. One of the deputies climbed up the ladder, but White had a pistol and fired it at the lawman. Fortunately for the deputy, the bullet was deflected by his gun barrel, inflicting only a small wound to his ear. He fell from the ladder and fled the house, with the rest of his comrades.

The result was a standoff. Addison White would not come down. The posse would not leave. Hyde, a Vermont Yankee noted for his cursing abilities, shouted abuse at the men outside his home while he sought means to alert friends in Mechanicsburg to his situation. He sent his daughter Amanda outside, ostensibly to feed the chickens. She made a break for it, provoking one of the officers to draw his gun and shout, "Stop, you little hell-cat," to which Amanda, very much her father's child, retorted, "Shoot and be damned!" She soon arrived at the nearby home of Russell Hyde, one of Udney's sons; he in turn summoned Hyde's friends and sympathizers. Soon the posse was outnumbered by angry villagers armed with clubs, rakes, and carpet beaters (but apparently no firearms), intent upon rescuing Addison White from his would-be captors. Sensing failure, if not danger, the posse left the scene.

That day Addison White's journey to Canada was resumed, while Udney Hyde found refuge at the home of a neighbor and then a nearby swamp. He remained in hiding for nine months. The following week the party of marshals reappeared in Urbana, with the intention of proceeding to Mechanicsburg to arrest various villagers for resisting federal officers and violating the Fugitive Slave Act. Joseph Carter Brand, an Urbana attorney and abolitionist, rode to Mechanicsburg to inform the villagers of the marshals' imminent arrival, but some of those targeted for arrest opted not to flee or hide.

When the marshals rode into the village, they were able to find Charles Taylor, Russell Hyde, and two other citizens who had assisted White. These four were arrested and told that they would be transported to Urbana, where the marshals would obtain a writ of habeas corpus. The prisoners were deposited in a wagon, and as they awaited departure, a townsman approached and assured them, "You needn't go unless you want to. Just say the word and we will let you free." He was overheard by one of the deputies, who exclaimed, "By God, that's talk!" Even so, the lawmen were able to depart the village with their prisoners.

Suspicious, two Mechanicsburg men rode after the wagon and were alarmed to see the party turn south halfway to Urbana. Where were they going? The pair rode up to the marshals, who threatened to shoot them as well as the prisoners. Word soon spread that the four Mechanicsburg men were being transported south to points unknown. Samuel Baldwin, the Champaign County probate judge, quickly issued a writ of habeas corpus for the four, conveying it to the sheriff of Champaign County as well as to the sheriffs of Clark and Greene Counties to the south.

There followed a frantic pursuit through three counties, with the respective county sheriffs and various parties of citizenry attempting to head off the federal lawmen and rescue the four Mechanicsburg men from the uncertain fate awaiting them should they be conveyed across the Ohio River into Kentucky. Before it was over, the federal marshals had beaten the sheriff of Clark County, and a warrant had been issued for their arrest. The deputy marshals were captured and thrown in jail, charged with assault with intent to kill, and their prisoners were brought back to Urbana, where Judge Baldwin released them.

Not surprisingly, the incident spawned much legal activity, which was eventually resolved when a group of Urbana and Mechanicsburg citizens raised the money to purchase Addison White from his owner in Kentucky. White remained in Ontario at first but later returned to Mechanicsburg. Udney Hyde came out of hiding and resumed his activities in the Underground Railroad, eventually running up an impressive tally of 513 escaped slaves assisted on their way north. This particular case was over, but the tensions it reflected were national and would eventually affect more than abolitionists, escaped slaves, and lawmen.[1]

2

A Splendid Banner

Champaign County, located in west-central Ohio, was primarily agricultural, its largest town being the county seat of Urbana, located in its center. On the eve of the Civil War the county had 21,910 residents; the greatest population concentration, 3,429, was in the township of the county seat. Several small villages punctuated the landscape of farmland and woodlots between Urbana and the boundaries of the county.[1]

To the west of Urbana flows Mad River, since those years rendered placid by the Army Corps of Engineers. Its waters rise in Logan County to the north of Champaign and flow south, defining a trough through a large portion of the country, and eventually join the Miami River and then the Ohio. On either side of the river is farmland, its soil at that time enriched by the frequent occasions on which the stream overflowed its banks. This stretch of good agricultural land takes up much of Champaign; however, one encounters rolling hills and tablelands in the eastern and western portions of the county.

In the 1850s the frontier had long since receded in Champaign County. Its first white settler had been a quasi-mythical French trapper named Pierre Dugan, who had a brief tenure in an area later known as Pretty Prairie, northeast of the future site of Urbana. A Kentuckian, William

Owens, followed him into the area in 1797. He and a steady trickle of upland Southerners began to settle the bottomlands around Mad River. Urbana was laid out in 1805, and in the War of 1812 it was the staging area for the ill-fated expedition to take Detroit. Urbana's most famous early citizen was Simon Kenton, an Indian fighter and associate of Daniel Boone. He spent his final days in Champaign County and was buried in Urbana's cemetery.

The county's earliest settlers were largely backcountry folk of Scots-Irish descent traveling north up the Miami River valley. Later settlement was from points more easterly, along the National Road, which ran to the south of Champaign County and brought many migrants from the Mid-Atlantic states. The great majority of white families in the county had their roots in the upland South or the Mid-Atlantic region, but there were other strands as well. There was a strong Yankee presence in the eastern portion of the county, and free blacks made up a surprising 10 percent of Urbana's population. In 1860 the foreign born accounted for a little over 6 percent of the population, the largest segment apparently the Irish of Urbana, although a significant pocket of Yorkshire immigrants had established themselves to the southeast along the line with neighboring Clark County.

Religiously, Baptists and Methodists predominated, the latter especially in Urbana. Inhabitants of German heritage established Lutheran congregations in some parts of the county, and there was a Mennonite presence along the line with Logan County to the north. In Urbana there were also adherents—some of them among the town's elite—of the Swedish mystic Emanuel Swedenborg, and it was the Swedenborgian Church that established Urbana University in 1850.[2]

The patterns of antebellum political attitudes in Champaign County and later of support for or opposition to the war effort were intertwined with the regional backgrounds of its inhabitants. Resistance to the Fugitive Slave Act, for instance, was far from universal. Urbana's Democratic newspaper, the *Ohio State Democrat,* fulminated in its issue for June 4, 1857: "The question shall the laws of the United States be executed? is one that with the exception of a few half-crazed fanatics, and nearly an equal number of aspiring demagogues who hope by raising the whirlwind that they will be enable to direct the storm which is to blow them into office, all our citizens, no matter what their party predilections, will answer in the affirmative." On the same page the editorialist informed his readership that the "black Republican" party was not concerned with the interests of the foreign born but was intent rather on the enslavement of the Germans and Irish and the elevation of blacks.[3] This was the Democratic line of the late 1850s, designed to appeal to Southerners and immigrants.

When the election rolled around in the fall of 1857, it revealed clear divisions. The townships that had been settled by Southerners turned out for the Democracy, while the areas, fewer in number, settled by New Englanders were just as strong in their support of Republican candidates. Areas without a preponderance of either fell in between. Two townships were mirror images of one another: Goshen Township, in which was abolitionist Mechanicsburg, polled 258 votes for Salmon Chase, the Republican gubernatorial candidate, and 74 for Henry Payne, the Democrat; while Mad River Township, holding the highest proportion of Southern-born in the county, gave 78 votes to Chase and 240 for Payne. In most county races the totals were generally in the range of 1,720 to 1,750 for the Republican candidate and 1,430 to 1,480 for the Democrat, with an ineffectual third-party candidate perhaps drawing off a few votes. Among those elected was Samuel Baldwin, who had played an important role in the Addison White affair and was later to become the county's probate judge.[4]

In the 1857 elections the Republicans maintained their sway in Champaign County. Three years later came the most fateful election in United States history, and they were ready to do their part in electing Abraham Lincoln as the country's first Republican president. Like others across the Midwest, groups of young Republican men organized themselves as "Wide Awakes" and held torchlight parades in Mechanicsburg, Urbana, and other county towns. In the fall of 1860 Urbana's Republican newspaper, the *Urbana Citizen and Gazette,* reported these events with regularity. Local orators, among them a young attorney named Charles Fulton, much noted for his eloquence, entertained the crowds with their speeches, which were followed by fireworks and bonfires. The young ladies of the area bestowed wreaths and other such tokens upon the men "drilling" in the town square. One such rally in Mechanicsburg included two hundred Wide Awakes. "Goshen township is the stronghold of Republicanism in Champaign and will roll up a big majority for Honest Old Abe in the 6th of November," noted the *Citizen and Gazette* approvingly.[5]

Champaign County's final rally was held on October 26 in Urbana. The *Citizen and Gazette* trumpeted an announcement of the great event:

Champaign County, Ohio.

GRAND TORCHLIGHT PROCESSION of WIDE AWAKES; and it is proposed by the Ladies of Urbana, to give to the best drilled company of not less than THIRTY MEMBERS, a SPLENDID BANNER!!!
A committee of Ladies will be appointed to review the drill, decide who is entitled to the Banner, and present the same. The Urbana WIDE AWAKES will be in procession, but not contend for the prize.[6]

The next issue did not record the decision of the "Ladies"; however, the November numbers of the newspaper (it was a weekly) reported the news of Lincoln's election on November 6 and the subsequent observances of his victory in Champaign County, which was carried by the Republicans. It would appear, though, that by this time, after all the torchlight parades and speeches, the political emotions of Urbana were "played out." The *Citizen and Gazette* noted the lack of celebration, observing somewhat petulantly, "We are truly sorry to find so disinterested a set of Republicans in this goodly town of Urbana." Joseph Brand, the lawyer who had ridden to Mechanicsburg to warn of the approaching posse in the Addison White affair, was one of the few to mount a display in his home: in two windows were transparencies inscribed with "Freedom, Justice and the Constitution" and "Republicanism Triumphant. Vox populi, Vox Dei." The window panes in the law office of his son, William Augustus Brand (son-in-law of the newspaper's editor), were also especially illuminated.

Perhaps in addition to emotional exhaustion there was unease. Would the South secede? Would there be war? The newspapers in November and December carried supposedly authoritative stories and letters from the South discounting the likelihood of such a course of events. One such letter, from a Southerner to a Cincinnati man, was reprinted in Ohio newspapers:

The election is over and we breathe freer. It is now noon and the Union is not dissolved. I do hope if South Carolina gets her back up that no one will pay any attention to her. If it did not scare the timid so much, South Carolina would be a benefit to the country as a means of working off surplus humours. I have always regarded South Carolina as a boil on the posterior of the country, very annoying, but on the whole healthful.[7]

The boil became life threatening when South Carolina seceded on December 20, followed in January by Mississippi, Florida, Alabama, Georgia, and Louisiana, with Texas joining the Confederacy on February 1. With the fall of Fort Sumter on April 14 there was widespread excitement throughout the Northern states. "War meetings" were called to declare the unionist sympathies of local citizens and to recruit soldiers for what was anticipated to be a short war in which national integrity would be restored.

Following Sumter's surrender, a young saddler named Michael Shiery wrote from Portsmouth, Ohio, to his wife in Clark County, Champaign County's neighbor to the south:

> As I am now writing the streets are throng with men with fife and drum and young and old are enlisting for the war and what the end will be God only knows but as long as I live O may the Star Spangle Baner wave over the land of the free and the home of the brave. . . . You can not forme any idea of the exsitement that is hear. Men Wimen and Children are on tipto of exsitement it Raind all day yesterday and to day but no one caired for rain or mud or any thing else the streets are full from morning untill night enquireing what is the news.[8]

Champaign County was also excited. The *Free Press,* the Democratic successor to the *Ohio State Democrat,* joined the *Citizen and Gazette* in declaring the necessity of putting down the Southern rebellion. The Democrats were faced with a challenging task. Whereas the Republicans, having elected the president, were the party of loyalism, the Democrats, whose now-shattered coalition had included the Southern "slaveocracy," had now to arrive at a position that preserved their political identity but put their former allies at a distance. The Democrats were unable to escape their political conundrum for the duration of the conflict.

But a war required soldiers in addition to editorials. Champaign County dutifully raised a company under William Baldwin, a local lawyer in his midtwenties. The company was attached to the 2d Ohio Volunteer Infantry, and it was soon embroiled in regimental politics, emerging the worse for it. In a system that found its origins in the practices of colonial militia, the officers of a regiment usually came to their commissions through elections, which could be organized in a variety of ways. According to disgruntled Champaign County recruits, a Clark County man named Rodney Mason had become lieutenant colonel with the support of the Champaign County officers but then bestowed noncommissioned officer positions upon Clark County and Cincinnati men, leaving the Champaign Countians in the lurch. Mason's power was further enhanced when the regiment's colonel resigned his commission, putting the lieutenant colonel in charge of the 2d.

The thirty-seven-year-old Mason was a lawyer and a son of a lawyer. His father, Samson Mason, had attained prominence in the legal profession as well as the rank of major general in the state militia, perhaps explaining the ease with which son Rodney attained the lieutenant colonelcy. Not too surprisingly, another of Samson Mason's sons also received a commission in the 2d Ohio. This was the twenty-one-year-old Edwin C. Mason, who became captain of Company F and was to finish out the war with the rank of brevet brigadier general.[9]

Lieutenant Colonel Mason, it was said, had launched a campaign of persecution against Baldwin's Champaign County company, apparently in response to their complaints over the distribution of noncommissioned officer positions. It was later reported that shortly after the regiment's arrival at Washington he ordered the Champaign County men to dig a trench three hundred yards long and three feet deep following a twenty-four-hour stint on guard duty. The *Citizen and Gazette* sputtered that Mason "has pursued the Champaign Company with such indignities, and the imposition of much of the menial servitude of the camp until 'patience ceases to be a virtue' and we think it just and proper to speak out plainly upon this matter."[10]

3

Let Us Do No Man Injustice

*B*ut the behavior of Colonel Mason toward local recruits was not all that was vexing the residents of Champaign County, which, like many counties in central and southern Ohio, was not of one mind concerning the war. Disagreement reflected divisions of party as well as of regional origin. The county's largest group consisted of people of Southern ancestry, followed closely by settlers from the Mid-Atlantic states and far more distantly by those with New England roots.[1] Although Southern origins did not automatically mean antiwar sentiment (some, like Joseph Brand, had left the South precisely because of their opposition to slavery), such opinions particularly manifested themselves in areas of heavy Southern settlement. Conversely, especially strong pro-war sentiments could be expected from the townships which, like Goshen, had a significant Yankee presence.

Mad River Township, in the western part of the county, had the strongest Southern representation of all the townships, and it was frequently excoriated by the Republican press as a hotbed of secessionist sympathies. At the opposite end of the county, the two easternmost townships, Rush and Goshen, had the highest level of Yankee settlement and were particularly noted for their support of the war. The village of Woodstock in Rush Township made the highest per capita contribution of volunteers to the war of any community in the county, while the abolitionist sentiments of Mechanicsburg in Goshen Township served as a good predictor for high rates of volunteerism and support for the war.

The pages of the *Urbana Citizen and Gazette* attest to the sentiments to be found in Mad River Township. A letter writer identifying himself only as "PHI" wrote, "The epithet of 'Southern sympathizers' at this day, during this hell-born, and hell-doomed rebellion, should be, and will be, resented by every *true* patriot. But I am sorry to say there are persons in Champaign County and *most* in Madriver Township, who, if measured by this standard of a patriot, fall far short. Not only do they not resent the epithet, but openly acknowledge this sympathy." One week later, an apparent Mad River Township resident signing himself "ENEGO" wrote to assert that if the township did in fact contain any friends of secession, then "all the sympathy which traitors will get in some portions of it is that which may be extracted from hemp or rifles." The writer continued: "If traitors abroad deserve death, much more do traitors at home merit death and eternal infamy. Let us ascertain the truth of this matter. Let us do no man injustice, but if there is a traitor among us, let him meet the fate he deserves."[2]

The *Citizen and Gazette* carried a short account of a Democratic meeting held in Mad River Township on August 10, 1861, reporting that its speakers had rejoiced in the prospect of Union defeat and had even voiced the hope that the Confederate army would take Washington and kill Lincoln and his cabinet. The story concluded, "This nest of disunion Democrats in Mad River are making a reputation for themselves that will consign them to a *traitor's* grave. They will be closely watched and remembered."[3]

But the source of the Mad River secessionism, if there was such, is difficult to locate. Urbana's Democratic newspaper, the *Free Press,* adopted a careful War Democrat line and so could not welcome or indulge the sentiments attributed to the Democrats living in the countryside west and southwest of the county seat. That there was resentment of the war—or at least of the Republican prosecution of the war—in the western part of the county would be borne out by future events; nonetheless, the depth of this resentment and the exact nature of the political sentiments informing it in 1861 cannot be reliably inferred from the words of its opponents, as represented by the correspondents (who used pseudonyms) for and letter writers in the *Urbana Citizen and Gazette*. The Democrats of the countryside would never get the final word, at least not in the Republican newspaper, which carried a story purportedly obtained from the *Free Press* to the effect that two unnamed young men from Mad River Township had journeyed south to join the Confederate forces. (As several issues of the *Press* are not extant, the story's provenance cannot be confirmed.) The Republican newspaper also made the predictable assertion that there "are a few more of the same sort in that township, who, to be consistent with their professions, ought to do the same thing."[4]

Divisions could even extend into the families of the most dedicated Republican abolitionists. Joseph Carter Brand, who had figured prominently in the Addison White affair and was to be a force in local military affairs, had left Bourbon County, Kentucky, as a young man. His wife was a Virginian. His grandson later recalled a story of family division, probably dating from early in the war:

> The situation was made all the more poignant because the great issue had separated the family, and there were brothers and cousins on the other side, though one of these, in the person of Aunt Lucretia, chose that inauspicious time to come over from the other side all the way from Virginia, to pay a visit, and celebrated the report of a Confederate victory by parading up-town with a butternut badge on her bosom. She sailed several times about the Square, with her head held high and her crinolines rustling and standing out, and her butternut badge in evidence, and was rescued by my grandmother, who, hearing of her temerity, went uptown in desperation and in fear that she might arrive too late.[5]

Meanwhile, to the south, in Clark County, a Democratic lawyer of recent English extraction, George Spence, reportedly received his comeuppance when he was thrashed by a Judge Litter for declaring that "Abe Lincoln and people who elected him, were as great traitors as Jeff. Davis and his followers." The *Citizen and Gazette* felt that "Spence probably deserved all he got, and we hope it will make him a wiser and better man."[6] The Union was everywhere threatened, but vigilant men of strength and conviction were on hand to support it.

4

Leave the Corn upon the Stalk, John

*C*hampaign County's pride was offended by the treatment of its 2d O.V.I. company at the hands of Colonel Mason and his Clark County associates. After the First Battle of Bull Run and the realization that regiments with a service commitment longer than ninety days would be required, county leaders understood that they would be called upon to provide more than a company or two for the war effort. Given the likelihood of greater recruiting demands and the threat of a draft, it seemed wiser to focus on the organization of a regiment within Champaign County rather than recruit one or two companies at a time and send them off to be subsumed in a regiment raised largely in another county. Aside from the local pride, such a move would ensure fair treatment for the county's recruits. In addition, it was probably not lost on those with recruiting commissions that their own chances for leadership positions and advancement would also be better under such circumstances. As one historian has noted, recruiting was "an inherently political process."[1]

Ohio's regiments were organized from military recruiting districts, into which the counties were grouped. The recipient of a commission to raise a regiment would form the majority of his ten companies from his home county, adding three or four companies raised elsewhere in the district.

A potential candidate for the position of raising a predominantly Champaign County regiment was the prominent Urbana entrepreneur and politician Col. John H. James, an old Whig who had done much to forward the cause of railroads and commerce in Ohio. James Dye, a Mechanicsburg businessman, had offered to forbear seeking a commission in favor of James, who, although not an admirer of Lincoln, was a strong Unionist. Colonel James, however, was well into his fifties, and his ability to see facts clearly—a trait that underlay his business success—ultimately prevented him from seeking a military commission. While still toying with the possibility, he refused a carriage ride one day and decided to proceed to his destination on foot, thinking that "a Colonel should walk." He was on crutches the next day.[2] As other county residents were pursuing commissions, James saw that regimental leadership was not a realistic option.

So it was that on September 28, 1862, James H. Dye of Mechanicsburg received from the governor his commission as lieutenant colonel to direct recruitment of the Sixty-sixth Ohio Volunteer Infantry.[3] The regiment was to be organized near the Champaign County fairgrounds in Urbana, at what was to become Camp McArthur, named after Duncan McArthur, a general in the War of 1812 and an Ohio governor. Joshua Palmer, an Urbana dentist, was already raising a company; now his labors were to be part of a larger effort. A few weeks later the *Urbana Citizen and Gazette* observed, "Champaign County, we know, has suffered in reputation, inconsequence of her boys enlisting in foreign companies. Now that we are raising a regiment in our midst, we hope this game will be blocked, and that the Champaign boys will, for the credit of their own county, enlist in some of the 'home companies' now forming for the new regiment."[4]

Indeed, the local Republican newspaper was a major organ for the Sixty-sixth's recruiting efforts. The activities of the recruiting officers were closely reported as the rolls of the regiment filled. Advertisements promising volunteers pay of thirteen to twenty-four dollars per month, together with free clothing, subsistence, and medical care, were carried regularly. Editorial encouragement was also provided in good measure, primarily from the columnist "Spectacles"—whose real name was Squire H. Wallace and who was, in addition to a newspaper columnist, a deputy U.S. marshal. Under the frenzied headline "War! War! War!" his column for October 10, 1861, inveighed: "For shame's sake, get up, shake off the dust of do-nothing-ness, and go to some recruiting officer and enlist. Let us raise a regiment in Champaign County that will be a credit not only to ourselves, but to the State. Let us do so by volunteering, and not lay back and compel the authorities to resort to the practice of drafting." To his credit, Wallace was not content simply to encourage others; he himself enlisted, receiving the temporary commission of second lieutenant, in which capacity he endeavored to assist in the recruiting process. Married and with five children, he was not a typical volunteer. He was also thirty-seven, which, while not old, was still on the high side for a soldier.[5] And so he proclaimed that

> We have therefore . . . laid down pen and entered upon the service, with powers from the authorities of the War Department. . . . Forsake father, mother, wife and little ones and fly to the rescue, and let your battle cry be death to the traitors! . . . Young man will you go? Now you have an opportunity to enroll your name among the great ones of the earth. We know many in this county whose imperative duty it is to shoulder their muskets and do valiant service for their country. There are many who have no excuse, but a disinclination to present themselves as target for the enemy, or to endure the duties and inconveniences of camp life. Their parents are wealthy and able to take care of themselves; the very reason why they, before a poor man, should go to war. We have in our mind's eye *many* whose names will sink into oblivion if they let this opportunity pass unembraced.[6]

Women were called on to do their part in several ways, not the least of which was playing the suasive role. In an open letter to his fellow recruiter Joshua Palmer, "Spectacles" lamented the fact that "unlike the mothers of the Revolution," some women were discouraging their men from enlisting. This, proclaimed "Spectacles," was far from proper: "Let the mothers, wives and sisters say to their sons, husbands and brothers GO; and let the girls say to their loving Philanders, *go to war*—show yourself a man—bring me some trophy nobly won from the secesh."

The newspaper reported a patriotic meeting at the fairgrounds and that "a good omen of this meeting was that the ladies were out in their strength." The announcement of a similar meeting to be held at Concord Chapel noted that "the ladies are especially invited to attend."[7] One newspaper letter writer suggested that women take over the role of schoolteacher, a position at this time largely filled by men: "Two persons would thus be serving their country, where, otherwise, only one would be engaged—the young man fighting for a free country, without which free schools cannot be sustained—the young lady teaching, thus giving her labor to the glorious cause of human progress."[8]

A few women expressed in verse their dedication to the Union as well as their pride in loved ones who had enlisted. A poem by a local girl, Sarah E. Gladden, was published as a broadside upon the occasion of her twenty-year-old brother Levi's enlistment in Company A and eventual departure with the regiment:

> Our brother dear has gone away,
>   The rebellion to subdue;
> The constitution to preserve,
>   And quell the rebel crew.
>
> Our brother dear has gone from us,
>   'Twas hard for us to part,
> And when I think of bygone days,
>   It draws like cords around my heart.
>
> He was all the company we had;
>   Oh! cruel war, do tell,
> How soon will he return to us,
>   The one we love so well.
>
> Our brother dear has gone to war,
>   With brave and noble men,
> May God protect those honest hearts
>   Till they return again.
>
> We are not the only ones that miss
>   Their brother's smiling face,
> For thousand youths as young as he
>   Are running the same race.
>
> Some aged fathers have gone forth
>   To battle in the strife;
> They have left their weeping children,
>   And have left their mourning wives.

If on the battlefield you fall,
    Or on your lonely couch you lie,
Dear brother, my thoughts are with you there,
    Although my form cannot stand by.

Dear brother, my prayers will always be,
    While you from home doth roam,
May peace and joy return with thee,
    Unto your once loved home.[9]

Most of the men who enlisted were like young Levi. They were in their late teens to midtwenties. Few were married. Some were under eighteen and required the permission of a parent or guardian for their enlistment. The underage enlistee might lie about his age, for which he could be discharged and remanded into the hands of local authorities. Perhaps the youngest lad in Champaign County to attempt enlistment was fourteen-year-old James Swisher of Wayne Township. He was big and husky for his age and so succeeded in his deception until his father found him at camp two days after his disappearance and brought him home.[10]

Another such instance acquired some local notoriety. Young Casper Mouser enlisted in Company G on December 8, 1861. His grandfather and uncle, learning of his enlistment, informed local officials he was not yet eighteen, and young Mouser's enlistment was invalidated. The young man refused to return to his relatives, who reacted by placing an advertisement in the *Citizen and Gazette* disavowing any debts incurred by the runaway and offering a reward of five cents for his return. The former enlistee in turn wrote a letter to the newspaper, which concluded: "I am thankful to get away from their knock down arguments with as little stigma as that is; and I dare my patriotic Uncle to shoulder his musket and stand beside the runaway until this rebellion is put down. If he will, I will guarantee him the five cents will be paid back with interest; if he should ever have it to pay for my apprehension."[11] One might wonder if the young Mouser was sole author of this missive (the style and tone are suspiciously reminiscent of the "Spectacles" columns). Notwithstanding, the sentiments were genuine: young Mouser promptly reenlisted in the Sixty-sixth once he was of age.

Not all the recruits were unmarried men; many left wives and children behind. Some undoubtedly did so out of patriotic conviction. Some, especially those who had hopes of becoming officers, perhaps saw some

Levi Gladden. *Author's Collection.*

hope of advancement after the war by virtue of their service. Others, those who could make their living only as a farmhand or unskilled laborer, may even have seen a soldier's pay of thirteen dollars per month as something more regular and dependable than they were already earning. These considerations were balanced against the possibility of death in service and the loss of a family's breadwinner, a possibility somewhat offset by a still widely held belief that the war might not last much longer, even though the extravagant optimism which held sway prior to the Battle of Bull Run had dissipated. The conflict also gave wives the opportunity to prove their patriotism, which was some consolation for soldier husbands concerned over abandoning their families. Champaign County recruits in another regiment raised a few months later heard the following song while in camp at Columbus:

> Don't stop a moment to think, John,
> Our country calls, then go;
>> Don't fear for me nor the children, John,
>> I'll care for them, you know.
> Leave the corn upon the stalk, John,
> The fruit upon the tree,
> And all our little cares, John,
>> Yes, leave them all to me.
> CHORUS: Then take your gun and go,
>> Yes, take your gun and go,
>> For Ruth can drive the oxen, John,
>> And I can use the hoe.[12]

There were also many recruits who were past the optimal age for military service. Many of these would be the first to succumb to the rigors of military life. The presence of these volunteers in their forties and fifties may surprise us today; however, they were enlisting as part of a militia tradition, a practice of the frontier, not so distant, in which it was the duty of every able-bodied man to take up the musket in times of emergency. Of these, the oldest in Champaign County to enlist was undoubtedly Virginia-born William Sullivan, a potter from Mutual. Although the adjutant general's report listed him as fifty years old when he enlisted on October 11, 1861, other accounts put his age at around seventy-two.[13]

There were also the recruiters themselves, and the more recruits one could lay credit to, the better one's chances for position in the regiment. The perceptive Colonel James wrote to his son, who was himself in service, that "as the commission of the lieutenants and captains depend upon the number they raise, the quality is of little importance if they can be squeezed in at first muster: if they break down in a month after, that is one of the fruits of service."[14]

By the end of October the regiment was recruiting well, with the *Citizen and Gazette* noting that about four hundred men were in camp. Earlier in the month the newspaper had approvingly noted the aggregate weight and height of thirty-two recruits brought into town by Lt. Versalius Horr of Mechanicsburg: 4,172 pounds, standing at a little over 154 feet, with an average of 154 pounds and five feet eight and a half inches in height. "This is a pretty good showing of the men who are filling up the regiment," concluded the newspaper account.[15]

Although the Sixty-sixth was largely considered a Champaign County regiment, some of its ten companies were raised from the other counties in the recruiting district. As often as not the recruiting officer would be commissioned captain of the company he raised, but in many instances more than one person was credited for enlisting a company's recruits. These other recruiters often became officers of lesser rank in the same or other companies.

Company A was raised under the leadership of the young lawyer Charles E. Fulton, whose Republican orations had attracted widespread attention in the county. He became its captain. Its ranks were largely filled within Champaign County by recruits from the rural townships in the central portion of the county.

Company B was raised by the Urbana dentist Joshua G. Palmer, who became its captain. A native New Yorker, he entered the service at age thirty-two and was unmarried. His company was raised partly in Urbana, with a large contingent of men from the vicinity of Terre Haute (locally pronounced "Terry Hut") in Mad River Township. Two younger men also helped to organize the company.[16] One, James Robert Murdoch, was only eighteen, and although he did not become an officer in Company B, by March of 1862 he was a second lieutenant in Company G. The other, William A. Sampson, a twenty-one-year-old Urbana printer, funneled recruits initially intended for Company B into Company K, where he secured a lieutenancy.

Samuel T. McMorran was the force behind Company C. He was a thirty-year-old attorney from Saint Paris, a village in the western portion of the county known for the manufacture of pony carts. Most of his recruits came from that vicinity. Also participating in the raising of this company, although his contribution appears to have been minimal, was Squire H. "Spectacles" Wallace, who was mustered in as a private on January 28, 1862. The company also had the regiment's largest concentration of Irishmen, as well as its two most exotic recruits: an Italian named Sebastian Riboli and the French-born Celestian Saintignon.

Company D was raised in Logan County, to the north of Urbana, by the fifty-five-year-old Robert Crockett. Born in Kentucky in 1807, he had been elected sheriff of Logan County on the Republican ticket in 1856. He was not to lead the company he raised, but was commissioned first lieutenant. Instead, the honor went to Pennsylvania-born Alvin Clark, whose son John found a place in the regimental band.

Company E came from Delaware County and was raised by Thomas J. Buxton, who became its captain. Although much of the recruiting seems to have centered in the county seat of Delaware, a sizeable contingent came from the Welsh settlement in Radnor Township.

Company F was raised by the fifty-nine-year-old John Cassill in Union County, which was also home to most of its recruits. There Cassill had filled various political offices, in addition to being editor of the *Marysville Argus*.[17] He was the first captain of the company, but like many of the older men who organized or officered the companies of 1861, he was not destined for a long military career.

Company G was also recruited in Champaign County; it was primarily raised by the thirty-two-year-old county surveyor, James Q. Baird. One of his men attempted to celebrate the company in verse, writing in his diary:

> James Q. Baird was capt of this little band
> Which he gathered up while tilling the land
> The county savaior [surveyor] elected as easy as nix
> Then left it and joined the bloody 66.[18]

The rolls of the company were filled by men from the eastern and central portions of the county, as well as from neighboring Clark County.

The first captain of Company H was William McAdams, a prosperous forty-seven-year-old stock trader of Lewisburg, located in Rush Township in the northeastern corner of Champaign County. Most of the company's recruits came from the vicinity of Lewisburg or from around the neighboring village of Woodstock.

James Q. Baird. *Richard K. Tibbals Collection, USAMHI.*

From Goshen Township in the southeastern corner of the county came Company I, raised in part in abolitionist Mechanicsburg by Versalius Horr, who became captain of the company. The company was also partly mustered in by Andrew H. Yeazel, who was commissioned first lieutenant the same day Horr became captain.

Originally intended for another regiment, Company K was largely credited to Delaware County; however, a large proportion of its enlistees—possibly as many as fifty-eight—were from Marion County, with Waldo as a recruiting center.[19] Joseph Van Deman was captain.

We are afforded a glimpse into the politics behind the selection of officers through the letter of Robert H. Russell, a Company G recruit, to his parents. As its principal recruiter, James Q. Baird was assured the captaincy of Company G, but the first and second lieutenancies were still open as of December 12, when a Springfield man, Lt. James Christie, arrived with seventeen Clark County recruits, among them the saddler Michael Shiery, who had written the excited letter to his wife after Fort Sumter's fall. According to Russell, Company G was not quite "filled up" and was in need of more men. In fact, the situation had worsened the previous night, when two underage recruits were dismissed from service. The appearance of Christie's squad promised to alleviate the company's manpower shortage. In exchange for signing them onto the company rolls, Christie obtained the first lieutenancy, apparently without much, if any, debate. There was nevertheless an election for the second lieutenancy, with three candidates. In the second round of balloting a twenty-one-year-old coachmaker named Charles Rhodes was victorious.[20] While captains were usually older and more experienced men with standing in the community, lieutenancies often went to youths whose only qualification was popularity; however, other considerations, such as Christie's seventeen men, could also command effective leverage. William Sampson, the Urbana printer and erstwhile recruiter for Company B, pulled off a similar maneuver when he brought in eight men (five men from Champaign and three from other counties) to Company K. Even though Sampson had been recruiting for Company B, and Company K was made up of Marion and Delaware County recruits, Sampson was able to obtain a commission in exchange for providing men to this "foreign" company.[21]

The regiment's first lieutenant colonel, James H. Dye of Mechanicsburg, was born in Lebanon, Ohio, in 1806 and had come to Champaign County in 1827. There he had pursued a number of callings, including cabinetmaking, farming and stock breeding, and the management of a sawmill and a woolens manufactory. The variety of occupations may seem unsettling from a modern perspective, but it was far from atypical for the time and place. He was approximately fifty-five at the time of the regiment's organization, and there are intimations that he had had at least one major bout of illness prior to that time.[22] This early organizer of the Sixty-sixth would share few of its trials.

Assisting Dye was Eugene Powell, a twenty-five-year-old native of Delaware, Ohio. Powell had entered the 4th Ohio Volunteer Infantry in June, rising through the ranks to a captaincy by October. Soon thereafter he was commissioned major in the Sixty-sixth and was dispatched to Camp McArthur. His appointment was probably motivated in large part by political considerations: the Sixty-sixth could not be entirely dominated by Champaign Countians, and a veteran officer, albeit a veteran of four months' service, from Delaware County would provide a good balance. Delaware County had after all provided most of the recruits for one company (E) and a considerable portion for another (K). But even if the appointment had been political, future events would confirm it as a good one. Powell later recalled that when he arrived at Camp McArthur in early November, Lieutenant Colonel Dye, "being a civilian, without any military experience, gave the direction of affairs virtually to me."[23]

Another local citizen prominent in the organization of the regiment was the fifty-one-year-old Joseph Carter Brand; he would become its quartermaster. Shortly after his arrival in Urbana from Kentucky, at age twenty, Brand had found work in his uncle's drug store. Thereafter he had gone into a merchant partnership in Mechanicsburg with Obed Horr, probably of the same family as Versalius Horr, who would become captain of Company I. But Brand gave up merchandising and returned to Urbana to practice law. He was also an abolitionist, active in the Underground Railroad. He had enjoyed the greatest political success of anyone associated with the regiment, having filled the positions of clerk of court and state senator. With the death of Samuel Baldwin in office, Brand filled out the remainder of his term as probate court judge from September through November 1861. His appointment followed a vigorous lobbying campaign in which a large number of his fellow citizens wrote on his behalf to Governor Tod, helping Brand beat out two other supplicants, including Baldwin's son. Brand was indeed a political force to reckon with in Champaign County.[24]

J. C. Brand's son William Augustus, also an attorney, enlisted as a private in Company G. W. A. Brand enjoyed a position of influence with the *Citizen and Gazette,* having married Frances, the daughter of Joshua Saxton, founder and editor of that newspaper. His dispatches from the regiment under the sobriquet "D. N. Arbaw" ("W. A. Brand" in reverse) would be published with fair regularity.[25]

Of greater importance was the post of commanding officer, which would be filled by a colonel. Although some locals may have aspired to the position, none of the regiment's officers had much, if any, previous military experience. The appointment was ultimately the governor's decision, and the choice was susceptible to political manipulation; however, there is no evidence in this case of lobbying by local politicos. After much anticipation, the decision was finally made public: The colonelcy would go to a regular army man (though not a West Pointer) named Charles Candy, who received his commission from the governor as colonel of volunteers on November 25.

Candy's military background was solid enough, though somewhat checkered and not especially stellar. If anything, his career is a good illustration of the opportunities created by the war for anyone with military experience. Born in 1831 in Lexington, Kentucky, the son of English parents, Candy enlisted in the army in 1850. The enlistment record describes him as having blue eyes, dark hair, a fair complexion, and a height of five feet, nine inches. He was ascribed the occupation of carpenter. He joined the First Dragoons and was promoted to corporal on March 31, 1853, and to sergeant on May 25 of the same year. He was became a first sergeant on February 1, 1854, but was returned to the rank of sergeant on June 1, 1854, and was further reduced to private on July 30, 1854, for reasons unknown. He was discharged on May 14, 1855, in New Mexico but reenlisted in January 1856 at Newport Barracks, Kentucky, where he was assigned to a permanent detachment and promoted to sergeant in May of the same year. Thereafter he transferred to the 1st U.S. Infantry.[26]

Having attained the rank of sergeant major, Candy left the 1st Infantry in Texas when his term of service expired on January 1, 1861. Upon Lincoln's first call for volunteers in 1861 Candy offered his services to Ohio's governor and assisted in the organization of the state's military efforts. Shortly thereafter the governor recommended him to George McClellan, then a major general; Candy served on his staff as chief clerk from May to September of 1861. On McClellan's recommendation Candy was promoted to captain, and as assistant adjutant general served on the staff of Gen. F. W. Lander, seeing action at the Battle of Ball's Bluff on October 21. He was then offered his own regiment and accepted appointment as colonel of the Sixty-sixth.[27] His photograph reveals a full-bearded officer with narrow, handsome features, and a patrician nose. The eyes have a clear and intelligent gaze.

Although Candy was not considered a local man, there is strong evidence for a prior association with Urbana, which would provide further rationale for the appointment. Papers in his pension file state that a son from his first marriage died in Urbana in 1858. In addition, the 1860 census for Urbana contains a listing for a fifty-two-year-old John Candy, an English native with two children born in Kentucky. This was probably Charles Candy's father.[28]

Powell relinquished his virtual "direction of affairs" to the new colonel, who at once commenced a thorough inspection of the Sixty-sixth. According to Powell, Candy "established schools for the officers and noncommissioned officers, and was prepared himself to act as Instructor. With him there was no commanding by proxy."[29]

Candy's command style came under the scrutiny of Pvt. William Henry Harrison Tallman of Company E, from Delaware, Ohio. He apparently had some college education, and he would be detached for clerical duties and other tasks throughout his military career with the Sixty-sixth. In Tallman's opinion Candy made a point of giving the older officers a hard time out of the conviction that they "were to [sic] old for campaigning or making well disciplined and well drilled companies out of their men." Lieutenant Colonel Dye seemed a particular target. On one occasion Candy had him take the regiment out for drill, at which time the embarrassed lieutenant colonel maneuvered the regiment into a hollow square position but then did not know the proper sequence of orders to get the men back into a straight line. Captain Cassill, Marysville newspaper editor turned military man, apparently had difficulty in arranging his men in a straight line on dress parade. He would entreat his men, "Come out there in the middle, come out there in the middle," earning a loud rebuke from Candy to the effect that there was no "middle" in military drill.[30]

County residents were generous in their support of the Sixty-sixth, at its base at Camp McArthur on the southern outskirts of Urbana. Ladies relief societies began to organize and send to the camp blankets, clothing, and other helpful articles; inventories were duly carried in the *Citizen and Gazette,* which also featured stories on food contributions from local farmers. For example, one Gabriel Kenton of Concord Township brought in a wagonload of "most excellent turnips" in late November. The physicians of Urbana and Mechanicsburg pledged uncompensated service for the families of volunteers.[31]

Bringing young men together in the recruiting camps, especially if the recruits were from rural areas, was an invitation to disease. There was little understanding of sanitation, and the many recruits who had not already experienced childhood diseases were vulnerable to the mumps and measles. A large contingent of the Sixty-sixth came down with measles at Camp McArthur.

However, the regiment's first death was due to another "plague" of camp life. Reuben Huffman, a thirty-four-year-old volunteer from Saint Paris, suffered a death that, as the *Citizen and Gazette* put it, "was superinduced by intemperance." His remains were accompanied to the train depot by a large body of men from the regiment. The newspaper report noted that "the music of the muffled drum was impressive," concluding with the wish that "the death of this man will be a warning to his comrades who are travelling the same dangerous path."[32]

As the men of the Sixty-sixth were to learn shortly, military life was fraught with "dangerous paths."

5

So We Are Sure to Go

*C*ivil War regiments did not linger long at their place of organization once their officers were in place. The need for new regiments was too great to brook much delay in deployment. In addition, since most regiments were organized not far from the soldiers' homes, a prolonged stay at the base camp, in close proximity to family and friends, could work against the establishment of unit identity. It could also encourage absenteeism, as was the case when five men from Captain Van Deman's Company K left the regiment one night without permission. They made their way to the nearby village of Cable, intending to board a train the following morning for some destination outside Champaign County (Company K contained a number of "foreigners"). Preparing to board a passenger car the next day, they were unpleasantly surprised by the sight of Captain Van Deman, who had followed them to Cable. Their dreams of "irregular leave" shattered, they returned to Camp McArthur with their captain.[1]

They would not remain there long. Troops were needed on several fronts—even in midwinter—and the Sixty-sixth was not accomplishing much for the war effort in Urbana. So it may not have come as much of a surprise to his parents when Pvt. Robert Russell hurriedly wrote them from Camp McArthur on Sunday, January 11 (in what by present-day military standards would be a clear breach of security): "We are going to leave for Romney, Va. on monday or tuesday certain. The Colonel got marching orders about an hour ago. So we are sure to go. . . . Tell everybody we are bound for Romney Va. monday tuesday certain, and if they have anything for any of the boys bring it right-along."[2]

The regiment was destined for departure that week, but it was not until the wee hours of the morning of Friday, January 17, that the train carrying the Sixty-sixth pulled away from the Urbana station. The regiment had marched from Camp McArthur Thursday in the damp and chilly January night to board the cars; it was seen off by what the *Citizen and Gazette* described as a crowd of "several thousand" people.[3] Such a large number of well-wishers may at first seem surprising for a small town and its environs; however, the family members, friends, and sweethearts of the six hundred or so Champaign County men in the regiment would easily add up to such a throng. All of these people would now scan the newspapers for word of the regiment's movements and keep anxious watch for casualty lists after its engagements.

Some of the family men in the Sixty-sixth took the precaution of drawing up a last will and testament, as did Sgt. Stephen Baxter of Company I, who was forty-five years old and had a wife and son. His will was witnessed by Captain Horr on January 16.[4]

Notwithstanding the crowd at the station, word of the Sixty-sixth's departure had not penetrated thoroughly into the countryside. Mary Diltz, the wife of Pvt. Joseph Diltz of Company I, wrote him later that month, "I wanted to see you so bad before you went away. I did not know that you was going till you was gone or I would have come in if I would have had to walked every step of the way." For his part, Joseph wrote, "I never felt so bad in my life befoure I could not get to see you befour I started. The morning befour I started I broke out and started home and thought perhaps I mite not get back in time and I went back to camp."[5]

In fact, many in the regiment were left behind. To begin with, approximately forty men were still in camp hospital. Most were victims of the measles epidemic. One of these, Leonard Stithem of Company F, a "foreigner" from Union County, succumbed the following week. The most notable stay-behind, however, was Lieutenant Colonel Dye, who was suffering from the effects of a freak accident two days before the regiment's departure. The unfortunate officer had been overseeing regimental drill when his horse was spooked. The animal had suddenly sprung forward, lost its footing, and gone down on its knees. Dye had fallen to the ground, the hilt of his sword smashing into his side. He had fractured three ribs and incurred a spinal injury. He would not be boarding the train the following night.[6]

There were also enlistees who did not board the train for the front for other reasons. Close to thirty had deserted from camp, some on their day of enlistment. Three were listed as deserting the day the Sixty-sixth decamped for Virginia.[7]

The Ladies Relief Society sent two boxes with the regiment. The contents were inventoried in exquisite detail and faithfully reported in the *Citizen and Gazette* as follows:

> 1 carpet blanket, 22 quart cans of fruit, 12 pair of drawers, 14 sheets, 24 pair of pillow slips, 312 handkerchiefs, 12 night shirts, 1 bundle of linen rags, 2 bundles of cotton rags, 31 bandages 2 and a half yards long, 32 bandages 4 yards long, 14 bandages 2 yards long, 5 bandages 3 yards long, 1 bandage 4 yards long, 1 washbasin, 7 wooden buckets, 3 double wrappers, 1 bundle of flannel, 27 pair of socks, 12 flannel shirts, 2 bundles of lint, 2 bottles of catsup, 1 jar of peaches, 2 bottles of wine, 2 jars of jelly, 4 bowls of jelly, 3 tumblers of jelly, 1 jar of cherries, 3 bed ticks, 16 muslin sheets, 6 comforts, 16 towels, 1 quilt, 2 bowls of fruit, 2 pillows, 1 pair of slippers.[8]

The train proceeded to Columbus and from there eastward on the Central Ohio Railroad to Bellaire, Ohio, at which point it crossed the Ohio River. The trip was not without incident. Four or five miles north of Bellaire the train's last two cars derailed, killing two men and injuring five. Eugene Powell was in one of the cars affected:

> The first intimation I had of the danger was feeling the car in which I happened to be stationed fly the track, and was being drawn, or impelled by its momentum, every instant pounding and tearing itself on the ties and rocks, as if it were to be dashed to pieces. All our lights were out in an instant. Seats, windows, soldiers, arms and equipments were dashed about in the wildest confusion. Now, a desperate *thud!* and all was over. Our car was clear of the train, off the track, and landed against a ledge of rocks.[9]

Arrangements were made for the dead to be returned to their families, and the regiment resumed its journey.

Crossing the river into the Virginia—soon to be West Virginia—

panhandle, the troops boarded freight cars at Benwood for the south-ward journey that would bring them to the Baltimore and Ohio Railroad. One letter writer complained that several of the cars "proved bad protection against the rain which was then falling." The rain continued, and when the regiment arrived the next day at Newbury it was delayed by a washed-out embankment eight miles down the line. The men settled in for the night, some in the houses of Newbury, others having to remain in the cars. Not wishing to risk the regiment's sobriety and good order, Candy posted guards at a local tavern. To make matters even more certain, he dispatched the regiment's adjutant, axe in hand, to the scene, where he split open three barrels of "Jersey lightning." It is not recorded whether the tavern keeper received any compensation for the destruction of his wares.[10]

On the following day news came that the line had been repaired, and the regiment resumed its journey, bound for New Creek Station, near Paddytown at a bend in the North Fork of the Potomac River. Along the way their train encountered another obstacle, described by Joseph Diltz in letter to a friend back home: "The cars run onto a stone that would weigh 500 lbs it was put on the track by rebels it was just whair the track runs close to the river if the engen had not bin so hevy we would hav all went to hell in a pile or some other seaport."[11] At New Creek the Sixty-sixth joined two infantry regiments, the 39th Illinois and 5th Ohio, to form the nucleus of the Third Brigade of Frederick Lander's division of the Army of the Potomac. They would have a brief association with the 39th, but the Sixty-sixth and the 5th would be together till the war's end. General Lander, a Massachusetts man, had worked as a railroad surveyor for the government and had been sent on a secret mission to Texas governor Sam Houston when the latter was resisting his state's secession movement. More recently, Lander had been seriously wounded in a skirmish at Edwards Ferry on October 22, one day after the disastrous Federal defeat at Ball's Bluff. He was now charged with overseeing the protection and repair of the Baltimore and Ohio Railroad. This translated to keeping Thomas "Stonewall" Jackson at bay, and, if practicable in the cold weather, eliminating any Confederate forces stationed too close to the railroad.

The Sixty-sixth came under the brigade command of Erastus B. Tyler, colonel of the 7th Ohio, which now joined the Sixty-sixth, the 39th, and the 5th. The 7th Ohio would also have a long association with the Sixty-sixth. Tyler, a native of New York and just shy of forty, was a college-educated man who had entered into a commercial career. In fact, his business activities had to some extent prepared him for the first days of his command: he had been engaged in hunting and fur trading in the mountains of western Virginia, and he now found himself on familiar ground.

Some of the men were already feeling homesick, and the importance of letters, a constant theme of camp life throughout the war, became apparent. Joseph Diltz wrote his wife on January 24: "I have cum to the conclusion you have forgat me intierly. I have rote you 10 or 12 letters and have not got but 2 letter from you." Toward the end of the letter he implored, "Dear mary pleas send me your minature. I want to see you so bad I dont no what to do."[12]

The regiment encamped at New Creek Station for two weeks, christening the place "Camp Candy" in honor of their colonel. Life there was not easy. In a letter to a friend Private Diltz had already concluded that "soldiering is a hard business." The quality of their rations was already a problem, engendering criticism of Quartermaster Brand. Diltz continued to his friend that "our quartermaster [is] a damd old raskel. We drew meat last night that was so damd full of skippers [maggots] that it could move alone. Some of them is stout ennuf to cary a musket." He also noted that many men were sick, some with the measles, the epidemic having apparently traveled with them from Ohio.[13] Even so, the men were fairly comfortable, under the circumstances. They slept in large, conical Sibley tents, which could accommodate a dozen or more men and even a stove. Pvt. Augustus Tanner of Company I remarked, "We have tents to sleep in just as the sircus men have. . . . We sleep just as warm as any one need too."[14]

Their stay at New Creek was largely uneventful, although on the night of January 29 a Confederate raiding party attempted to take and burn a nearby railroad bridge. The enemy drove the Union pickets in, but the garrison was called out soon enough to thwart the threat.[15] According to one account, further excitement was generated when a second lieutenant raised a false alarm, misidentifying a herd of cattle as another Confederate raiding party. It cost him his commission.[16]

On the night of February 4 the regiment left New Creek for Patterson's Creek; there they received orders to proceed to French's Store, where they arrived the following afternoon. Sometimes referred to as South Branch Station, French's Store was located on the Baltimore and Ohio just east of the confluence of the north and south forks of the Potomac. W. A. Brand described it as "a hard place with a dilapidated ware-house, storehouse and church owned by a Mr. French, a secessionist, said to be very wealthy." French himself had been put under house arrest and his cattle confiscated.[17]

Upon its arrival, the Sixty-sixth received orders to draw four days' rations. The men would soon be on the move again, but they were tired from their journey and lay down to sleep—only to be awakened at ten o'clock that night with orders to join a column that Lander was dispatching toward Romney. The purpose of the expedition is unclear in retrospect, as there is evidence that the Federals already knew that Romney had been abandoned by the Confederates. Robert Russell wrote to his father on February 5 (noting somewhat wistfully that the Sixty-sixth would not be allowed to bring any of its stoves along) that "the 'secesh' have left Romney and we are going to follow them up."[18] If a newly arrived private knew as much, it is safe to assume that General Lander knew that he was not going to confront the Confederates at Romney.

It was a hard march, following the Little Cacapon River for fifteen miles, wading through the cold waters of the creeks feeding into the river. At dawn it was sleeting as the column came to a halt at the Winchester Road. Some of the Sixty-sixth did not make it that far. The regiment had little marching experience, especially under such circumstances. Tired and cold, some had fallen out of line and returned to French's Store. The historian of another regiment in the march notes that some of the men were so tired by the time they reached the road that they sank down and fell asleep, their clothing freezing to the ground.[19] As some of their comrades still straggled in one direction or another along the river, the Federal troops waited on the Winchester Road while a cavalry force was dispatched to Romney to ascertain the whereabouts of the Confederates. There was no enemy present; forewarned, the Confederates at Romney had withdrawn to Winchester four or five days earlier. The Sixty-sixth would continue to wait for its first engagement.

Although Lander's advance (or its preparations) had likely precipitated the enemy's departure, the expedition seems somewhat questionable; in light of the apparently known absence of surprise, one might wonder at the purpose of a march made by tired troops in the middle of the night through inclement weather. It might have been to offer added protection for the Baltimore and Ohio Railroad from Romney, notwithstanding that in the dead of winter major expeditions were problematic for both sides in this rugged and mountainous terrain. It is also possible that Lander hoped to catch the Confederates on the road to

Winchester; if so, the details of the hoped-for interception of a force that had departed several days before are lost to us.

The Federal expedition partially retraced its steps. Encamping at a farm near Winchester Road, the soldiers dispersed two ricks of unthreshed wheat to serve as bedding for the night. Writing to a cousin, Cpl. Nathan Baker of Company B reported that some of the men created a hot drink with what was at hand: "we . . . rubed out the wheat and browned it on our pans and ground it between to stones and maid some wheat coffy."[20] Company G's Pvt. Samuel B. Briggs wrote in his diary that he had enjoyed a dinner of pork soup and sassafras tea.[21]

The next day they made their way upland to a small plateau, where they set up camp after a fashion. Almost a foot of snow fell that night. Deprived of tents, the men were on short rations and had few blankets or cooking utensils. One such night was bad enough, but as fate and Lander would have it, they were to remain there for almost a week. But even these circumstances provided the opportunity for drill. Erastus Tyler was anxious to get his brigade into shape. Major Powell recalled that their new commander "was determined that his soldiers should not stand idly around fires, and while at the bivouac he caused the Regiments constituting the Brigade, to assemble for Brigade drill, and other evolutions, the soldiers moving in execution of his orders through snow over their shoe-tops." Another soldier from the brigade, noting that Tyler was comfortably ensconced in a nearby farmhouse, reported that this drill in the snow "only vexed the command without accomplishing any good."[22]

When not being drilled by Tyler, the men made the best of the situation by constructing rude shelters from pine and cedar boughs (what Private Briggs referred to as "our playhouses") and collecting wood to build fires, which were kept at a high blaze during the cold nights. Aaron Riker, a private of Company G, summed up the situation in a letter dated February 12: "We have been laying in this camp several days expecting every hour to be ordered forward, and why we are here so long without tents, or anything to shelter us from winter's blasts, save the pine brush which we have gathered from neighboring hills to make us shelter, is more than I know."[23]

No one else seemed to know either, and the one person who might have been able to shed light on the situation was not much longer for this earth. The day after Riker wrote his letter, the Sixty-sixth and the rest of the Romney expedition decamped for Paw Paw. On the same day Lander set out from Paw Paw for a "reconnaissance in force" to Bloomery

Gap, where the restless general personally led a charge that netted several prisoners, including a colonel captured by Lander himself. Lander became seriously ill not long after his return to Paw Paw and telegraphed McClellan that his health was "too much broken to do any severe work" and asked that he be relieved.[24] McClellan discouraged him from giving up his command, telling him to rest at Cumberland.[25] Lander died of pneumonia at Paw Paw on March 2.

Lander was a brave man but energetic to the point of recklessness. Like many commanders, especially near the beginning of the war, he was impatient to prove himself and perhaps overly willing to sacrifice both his men's and his own health in unnecessary maneuvers. The Sixty-sixth was probably better off not continuing under his command. In reply to the congratulations of Secretary of War Edwin M. Stanton for his Romney and Bloomery Gap expeditions, the surveyor-and-explorer-turned-general had praised the "earnestness and energy of the Western troops under my command" but had been quick to claim that "nothing but my experience in mountain life has caused this army to move in the way it has."[26] A surgeon of the 1st Minnesota recalled attempting to treat Lander shortly after his wounding at Edwards Ferry in October: "He swore à blue streak, and vowed he would go on to the ferry before having anything done. I was rather glad to get him off my hands. He was restless and intractable at all times, and by his independent conduct after this wound brought on a septic fever from which he died."[27] Although the surgeon's diagnosis was not correct, such behavior, for better or worse, was in keeping with the commander of the Romney and Bloomery Gap expeditions. Despite their suffering under his command, some of his men voiced their regrets at his passing, Aaron Riker noting in his diary that "in Looseing Landers we had lost a bold and fearless Leader."[28]

However, we also have the testimony of a Pennsylvania cavalryman, John W. Elwood, who had been Lander's orderly for a time. Elwood recalled that "while he was perhaps a brave man, and no doubt could handle troops, he was one of the wickedest men I ever met." News of Lander's death came to Elwood's comrades in the first stages of yet another perhaps ill-considered winter offensive: "Finally the word was passed down the line that General Lander was dead: he had passed away a few moments before. This put a stop to what would, in all probability, have been the destruction of Lander's entire army."[29]

Following Lander's death, the division's base of operations was transferred to Paw Paw, otherwise known as Camp Chase, where a wildly twisting Potomac River flowed northeast around a series of small mountain ranges angling toward the southwest. The divisional quartermaster intoned: "It is noted that a very extraordinary amount of baggage is in the possession of the regiments composing this division. Should this extra baggage be found in the wagons on a march, it will not only be at once thrown out, but the Quartermaster in whose train it is found will be reported." W. A. Brand, whose father as regimental quartermaster was directly affected by the order, noted that there "certainly never was a regiment that started for Virginia with better preparations to settle the country and go to house keeping immediately than was the 66th O.V.I."[30] The "extra baggage" was packed up and dispatched to Cumberland until called for.

Even so, provisions continued to arrive, courtesy of the Ladies Aid Society of Urbana. It is likely, though, that much of what was sent was intended less for the regiment as such than for the Urbana and Champaign County men of the regiment. The smaller contingents from other counties had their own conduits of local support. For instance, the Ladies Aid Society of Delaware once sent thirty pairs of mittens to Captain Van Deman of Company K for distribution to the men of his unit, which had been recruited in large part from Delaware County. While at Camp Chase, Van Deman wrote to the society's president that while his men "are off among the mountains of western Virginia, the cold & bleak winds whistling around their benumbed bodies, yet they have one bright & warm spot in their remembrance for their kind Lady friends of Delaware." If the ladies could have "seen their grateful countenances & have heard their hearty cheer as those mittens were distributed to those who had been grasping *cold gun barrels* with *naked hands,* their heart might have been (like mine) too full for utterance."[31]

Shortly after its arrival at Paw Paw, the regiment was assigned as provost guard, and Colonel Candy was made provost marshal. A squad from the Sixty-sixth was detached to escort forty-eight prisoners back to Ohio. Pvt. William Sayre of Company K reported to his father on their assignment as provost guard: "That is something that the boys do not like for they will haft to stand gard so mutch the more." He went on to report on his health, which was good, but added that "the water is quite bad here on account of so many horses a waiding around." Not surprisingly, widespread dysentery was soon being reported in the Sixty-sixth. Notwithstanding, their quarters were an improvement over recent experience. Joseph Diltz wrote home, "We are very comfortable here now. . . . We have a good plank flore in our bunks."[32]

The regiment attempted to recoup its strength. Approximately one hundred sick and disabled soldiers had been left behind or dispatched to New Creek, where they were under the care of the regimental surgeon, Thomas Bond, and the command of Lieutenant Colonel Dye, who had returned to the regiment about the time of the Romney expedition. By mid-March the regimental aggregate had fallen to 892 men, of whom 730 were available for service.[33] Dye himself had not recovered from his parade-ground injuries but was determined to resume some of his duties; at this point they were limited to overseeing the welfare of the sick, many of whom had been broken down by the Romney expedition. Those who could not soon return to the regiment at Paw Paw were transferred to more comfortable quarters at Cumberland. At least two of the ailing soldiers died there in February. Meanwhile the Ladies Aid Society in Urbana dispatched four stoves and clothing to the regimental hospital. John Gump, an Urbana baker, sent twenty barrels of gingerbread and crackers.[34]

The division now came under the command of James Shields. Although he had served in the Mexican War, Shields was neither West Point nor regular army. He was instead a "political general," and a Democrat at that, whose appointment, like that of Illinois's John Logan, was important in helping to create the appearance of a united front in the North. The Irish-born Shields had served as governor of Oregon and of Minnesota and had reportedly once challenged Congressman Lincoln to a duel (although the misunderstanding that led to the challenge was defused without bloodshed).

The regiment left Camp Chase, now also known as Camp Lander, the morning of March 7. It traveled eastward by rail, initially proceeding four or five miles, at which point the train came to a halt until sundown, when it set out again, not stopping until it reached Sleepy Creek at four in the morning. Robert Russell complained of his own situation: "Our car is crowded awfully, having 45 in a common freight car, so you might bet 'twas poor sleep that any of us got." Russell and a friend roused themselves, though, and went hunting for food at daylight, procuring two huckleberry pies for a quarter.[35]

The train then crossed Sleepy Creek, where the bridge had only just been rebuilt after being burned the previous year. The train continued a short distance, stopping at a large house owned by an avowed Union man who gave breakfast to some of the soldiers for a dime apiece. W. A. Brand, who tended to the tongue-in-cheek bordering on the callous when it came to Southern civilians, described what was perhaps the regiment's first attempt at "foraging": "The spot we 'fixed upon' had not been visited by the soldiery before, except to pass by, and we had good 'pickings.' A fine string of fence was soon leveled to the ground, and put into stoves on board the cars, and on bonfires. Chickens and geese *flew* into the cars rather accommodatingly, and some of the boys say 'they tasted very nice.'"[36]

After satisfying their hunger in one fashion or another, the men reboarded the train, which proceeded for a short distance to Back Creek and halted. The railroad bridge there had been blown up the previous June. (Private Russell reported that it was being rebuilt, supposedly by the party responsible.) In any case, the men had to cross the creek the following day on a makeshift rope-and-plank suspension bridge. It was four feet wide, stretching forty feet above the water at one point. Only one man could cross it at a time.[37]

Assembling on the east side of Back Creek, the Sixty-sixth left the Baltimore and Ohio and marched to Martinsburg by another route, arriving there at ten o'clock that evening. Russell was again not in the best of shape: "Oh! how tired I was. I blistered my feet & my knapsack cut my shoulders until I could hardly get along at all. The distance was not so very great but then we went so fast and such a big load to carry." William Sayre observed of the regiment, "a tiredr set you never saw than what we was"; he claimed that half the regiment had dropped out of the line of march and were continuing to straggle in the following morning.[38]

At Martinsburg the troops reconnected with the Baltimore and Ohio Railroad, and on it an incredible sight awaited them. Fifty or more engines and tenders had been run together and burned on the tracks by the Confederates, and another thirteen engines had been run onto a bridge that had then been set ablaze, tumbling the engines into the local stream. William Sayre reported that the engines had been "burnt all to smash," concluding: "I think that looks hard for my part. you folks there at home know nothing at all a bout these things. you have no idea what has been done here by the rascals."[39]

The next day Shields arrived at Martinsburg to assume command of the division, which in turn was assimilated into the army of Nathaniel P. Banks, another Union political general who had served in Congress and as governor of Massachusetts. The Sixty-sixth retained its role of provost guard in the town, where it was to remain, guarding the division's baggage and supplies, as Shields led his force south to Winchester.

Doubtless many in the regiment were happy not to be going with him. The season could still make for difficult campaigning: as Captain Horr of Company I noted, "Comfortable weather is unknown and unheard of, and will never be experienced by any army in the mountains of Virginia."[40] The regiment settled in for a routine of unloading supplies from railroad cars and transferring them to wagons to follow Shields's army.

The hiatus of garrison duty at Martinsburg also afforded the men an opportunity to reinstitute practices with which they had been familiar in Ohio. The Masons in the regiment met in the local lodge room to organize the "Candy Lodge" of the Free and Accepted Masons, under a special dispensation of the Grand Master of Masons of Ohio. Meanwhile, Lieutenant Sampson put his printing skills to use and published a regimental newspaper called the *Ohio Boys' Bulletin*. This was accomplished on the press of the local newspaper, the *Virginia Republican*, whose editor (most likely *not* a Republican) had been arrested for Confederate sympathies.[41]

The regiment remained at Martinsburg until noon on March 24, when it began the march to Winchester. En route it bivouacked at an abandoned mansion. On one of its walls one of the men inscribed, "A cure for Secession—lead pills well powdered—the compliments of the 66th O.V.I."[42]

6

Distance Lends Enchantment

The Sixty-sixth arrived at Winchester too late to take part in the battle that had occurred on March 23, 1862, just south of that place, at Kernstown. With the telegraph wires down, an order to rejoin the division was sent on March 21 by hand, but it had somehow not found its way to Colonel Candy, else the regiment would then have experienced its first battle.

As it was, its absence was not felt. Thinking that Shields was in retreat and commanding a smaller force than was actually the case, Jackson had attacked. Adequate reconnaissance would have revealed to him that he was outnumbered three to one. Not surprisingly, the Confederates suffered higher casualties than their opponents and were repulsed, leaving many of their dead and wounded on the field.

Several men from the Sixty-sixth went out to inspect the battlefield. W. A. Brand counted it a scene "calculated to cause serious reflection." The citizens of Winchester were burying the Confederate dead, many of whom were area residents. There were more than eighty left on the field, and an additional two hundred or more were discovered in nearby buildings. Robert Russell wrote to his father, "When I was on the field their dead was all unburied and it certainly was a horrible sight to see so many dead men, some had a leg shot off, others an arm, and some again were shot right through the breast, the hole so big that you could see through them. I saw one poor fellow—an artilleryman—that had all the top of his head blown off from his eyes up by a cannon ball." Russell's horror at these sights did not, however, prevent him from gathering up assorted souvenirs from the Confederate dead, including a pistol, a scabbard, and an officer's sash—in addition to an unexploded nine-pound Union percussion shell. The officer's sash he sent on to his father. What he did with the nine-pound shell is unrecorded.[1]

A detachment from the Sixty-sixth was assigned the task of burying the Union dead. The job took the better part of two days. Russell noted that one of the men buried a total of forty-eight bodies. Joseph Diltz wrote his wife, "We ust to think that it was hard to see one person dead but Mary I was passing down [the] street the other day and I looked in a window. I was mutch surprised to see 40 ded soldiers union and rebels piled up together like so many hogs."[2]

The regiment's staff officers were headquartered in the mansion of Col. Angus McDonald, who was with Jackson's cavalry. This put Candy on a collision course with the lady of the house, Colonel McDonald's wife, Cornelia. She was abruptly made aware of her home's occupation upon her return from a walk in town: the Stars and Stripes were flying over the McDonald portico, and an orderly was sitting on the steps below it. She entered the house to find that Candy had taken possession of her husband's study. In a postwar memoir (in which Candy is referred to as "Colonel Candeé") she recalled asking if it might not be possible for him to find quarters elsewhere, to which he replied quietly that his presence would probably act as a protection and that he required but one room.

Seeing that she had no choice in the matter, she still found the flag unacceptable and said as much: "You will confer a favor on me Colonel Candeé if you will have that flag removed from the front door if you must remain, as while it is there, I shall be obliged to enter at the back of the house." This request precipitated the laughter of several onlooking officers, but Candy did not respond immediately. He finally replied, "I will do all in my power, Madam, to make our stay here as little unpleasant to you as possible." Later that day Mrs. McDonald noticed that the flag had been removed from the house.[3]

Relations between Mrs. McDonald and "Colonel Candeé" remained relatively cordial, although she frequently complained to him about the soldiers milking her cows. She later claimed to have done this in order to annoy him in the hope that it might drive him from the house. On one occasion a soldier was caught in the act and became therefore liable to punishment; soon after, she glanced out the front door on her way to breakfast to see the culprit standing on a barrel, hands tied behind his back. The sight disturbed her and caused this otherwise determined Rebel some self-reproach. She knocked on the study door and Candy himself opened it. "How long, Colonel Candeé, do you intend to keep that poor man on that barrel?" Candy replied, "Until justice is satisfied, Madam." "Do let him go. He may have all the milk rather than have him standing on that barrel any longer." "As you please, Madam, if you are contented, he may go." After this incident, she no longer reported the illicit milking of her cows.[4]

The female population of Winchester seems generally to have done their best to make the Yankees feel unwelcome. Captain McAdams was walking in the street not far behind two women when he heard one loudly proclaim, "If one of these Yankees should speak to me I would spit in his face." McAdams confronted her in short order and said, "Madam, if you should spit in my face I would give you a good spanking."[5]

Quartermaster Brand set up his storehouse in the home of James M. Mason, the Confederate diplomat whose capture with John Slidell aboard the British mail steamer *Trent* had almost provoked war between the United States and Great Britain the previous November. Private Russell noted that the grounds were spacious and grand. Ever curious and investigative, he speculated that Mason must be "a very hard drinker from the amount of brandy, gin, wine and whisky bottles, at least twelve or fifteen hundred of them." He also observed a large quantity of papers in Mason's garret, from which he inferred that he must be something of a businessman as well.[6] The Sixty-sixth later sponsored a "hoe down" in Mason's parlor for some of the "contraband" slaves who had attached themselves to the regiment. W. A. Brand reported that these "sable sons of Africa" put on an energetic show.[7]

The problem of "contrabands," the euphemism for slaves belonging to Confederate adherents, was not a new one to the Sixty-sixth. While foraging out of French's Store almost two months previous, William McClean Gwynne, the regimental adjutant, had encountered a farm with a dozen or so slaves whose owner had fled. They professed a willingness to go with the regiment, but Candy refused to be burdened with them. Now that the regiment was making its way into a more populated and prosperous area, the problem was constant. Brand noted that the

> slaves of absent rebels . . . are becoming more "migratory" in their habits, as the army progresses southward. Some very fine, active boys have come to our camp seeking employment, and all who need servants take them when they ascertain to certainty that their masters were in the rebel army, if these boys continue to do as good service as at present, they will be taken to Ohio, upon the return of the army.[8]

The men still awaited their pay and were experiencing hardship. William Sayre came directly to the point in writing to his father: "I want you to send me some Money as soon as you get this if it be mutch or little and if it does not come through safe and if it gets lost i will pay you back anyhow." To more certainly make his point he continued, "Now i want you to be sure and send me some because you have now idea how bad i nead it." He reported that many of his comrades had made similar requests home and that the much-needed cash had arrived safely.[9]

The men were coming to know their colonel, who gradually acquired a reputation as a efficient, fair, and observant officer. Augustus Tanner wrote his father that he had been offered the position of the colonel's orderly. He had expressed surprise at the offer to his corporal, who replied that Candy "took notice of any one that kept themselves clean & looked well." Despite the honor, Tanner declined, explaining, "I should board with him & live good but I do not like to be so much alone."[10]

Relations between the Federal occupiers and the citizens of Winchester continued to be strained. Many of the citizens knew Confederate soldiers killed at Kernstown; Squire "Spectacles" Wallace observed that the whole town seemed to be in mourning. He recounted one incident in which an ambulance pulled up before a house and a young woman came rushing out with tears in her eyes. A Union cavalryman was observing the scene and inquired the cause; the sobbing girl replied that her father had been killed in the recent battle. The trooper asked which army, and upon hearing the reply "Jackson's" he told her not to cry, as her father's being killed saved him being hanged, "as all damned rebels deserve to be." More restrained and philosophical than he had been in his editorial days, Wallace mused, "We passed on inwardly sanctioning the sentiment, but forcibly impressed with the demoralizing influence of war, hardening the heart, blunting the sensibilities, and drying up the fountains of human sympathy."[11]

Without money, the men were not averse to foraging in the yards and gardens of the area (or milking Mrs. McDonald's cows). One nurseryman and gardener, disturbed at the loss of his onions, requested a guard from Colonel Candy. Candy observed that a guard would not be necessary if he would but fly the United States flag over his property. This brought an indignant response from the man, who blustered that he would never do such a thing. Candy replied that he would never dispatch his men to guard the property of anyone who would not fly the Stars and Stripes. Not all was hostility, however, for the town did contain some loyal citizens. These were serenaded on at least one occasion by the regimental band. Colonel Candy even requested that the band strike up "Dixie" for Mrs. McDonald, who nevertheless complained later that it was "spoiled by introducing parts of other pieces, for fear that we, I suppose, should enjoy our rebellious pleasure unalloyed."[12]

Cornelia McDonald also reported on another member of the Sixty-sixth. Adj. William McLean Gwynne, a young man in his early twenties, was the nephew of John McLean, an associate justice of the Supreme Court. One evening he called on Mrs. McDonald, bringing with him letters of introduction from the judge to various local citizens. She was kindly disposed to Gwynne, as he often provided fruits and other delicacies for her sick children. He inquired if it might be proper for him to present these letters to his uncle's friends in Winchester. She replied, "They would not see you, coming with this army, and with that uniform on. If you had come a year ago, as Judge McLean's nephew, you would have met with a hearty welcome." Gwynne pursued the point: "Is it possible that they can carry their political prejudices so far as to refuse to see me because I am on the Union side?" "Not a brother or a son would be received if he came with enemies" was the reply.[13] Gwynne had not yet seen his first battle, and it was still possible for him to equate the war with the political contests of 1856, 1858, and 1860, when opponents might disagree but still made social calls on one another.

Many of the men had family members in the area. A private in Company G had a sister living in nearby Front Royal and thought to visit her. He was able to do so, but he was captured by the Confederates on his return visit, garnering him a stint in a Confederate prison.[14]

The Sixty-sixth's stay in Winchester was brief; the division embarked on a forty-two-mile march to Strasburg on April 5. Candy and his staff thanked Mrs. McDonald for her hospitality and offered their hands, which she was not sure she should take "but could not be rude enough to refuse." She did, however, manage one parting shot: "I shall be very glad to see you Colonel Candeé on your way back if you have time to stop."[15]

The division reached Strasburg the following day. Once again the Sixty-sixth was assigned provost duty. By now the paymaster had found the men, who became frustrated at finding so little on which to spend their money. W. A. Brand noted that there was no grocery or dry goods store in the town, and but one sutler present to sell special food items and supplies such as writing paper to the men. The soldiers were blessed with a profusion of twenty-dollar bills but little in the way of smaller denominations, quarters, or dimes, so that the sutler could not make change for the soldiers' purchases. This state of affairs inspired feelings bordering on mutiny, according to Brand, who sometimes shared the era's propensity for overstatement.[16]

Much of the excess cash went back to Ohio. Robert Russell's uncle, John Russell, came to Strasburg for a visit and left on April 13 with money to be disbursed to the soldiers' families in the Champaign County area. William Sayre wrote his father that "John Rusel and another man from Urbana was here for the Purpose to taking home a lot of Money home for the Boys. they took my money and gave me a receipt for it. John Rusel says he knows you and that if you want to get it all you have to do is to come after it."[17] Trust was granted to anyone with good home credentials. Such a method of money transfer could also be preferable to the mails. Anyone returning to Ohio could act as cash courier.

Even so, the mails were apparently reliable when it came to the delivery of the letters so important to the men. A letter from his wife told Joseph Diltz of life at home: "You have no idea how bad i want to see you. I would give this world to see you. Emma [their daughter] puts on her shall [shawl] every day and says good by Mary i am going to see Joey and he will shakehands when he coms. She kisses your minature evry time she sees it & she holds up her new dress before it and says look here Joey at my new dress."[18]

Squire Wallace reported that "some of the boys are 'spoiling for a fight'" but that there were others of the Sixty-sixth who, after working on burial detail at the Winchester battlefield, were "not quite so keen." He continued, "They say, like the Poet, that 'Distance lends enchantment to the view.' Many of them think that the honor would hardly compensate for the loss of a leg or arm or broken head, although all express themselves ready for the conflict when necessity calls them to action."[19]

The first small taste of necessity soon came for Captain Baird's Company G, when it was sent to watch over the rebuilding of a nearby bridge spanning the Shenandoah River. On April 12 the company came under fire from Confederate cavalry on the river's opposite bank. The exchange lasted ten minutes. Although the men of Company G were unable to cross the river to make sure, the consensus was that the only casualty they may have inflicted on the enemy was the loss of a horse. The Ohioans sustained no casualties themselves. A ball hit a tree three feet above Russell's head during the fight. Ever one for souvenirs, Russell climbed up to extract it and sent it home with Uncle John.[20]

The regiment left Strasburg for New Market in the Shenandoah Valley (to be distinguished from the New Market located in the Bull Run battlefield area) on April 28, arriving there two days later and remaining almost two weeks. While at New Market a private from Company G again came under fire: Oliver P. Taylor was shot and wounded after issuing a challenge while on picket duty. His assailants were not Confederates but a scouting party from the 5th New York Cavalry.[21] This incident aside, the regiment's stay in New Market was relatively uneventful. The collective health of the men, many of whom were still suffering from the effects of the Romney expedition, was still not the best. Many were in camp hospital.

The Union's grand strategy—or more properly, the grand strategy of George McClellan—entailed a new mission for Shields's division and the Sixty-sixth. A movement against Richmond was afoot. Federal forces in the Shenandoah Valley would be needed in the concentration against the Confederate capital. The Sixty-sixth was ordered east.

And so the Sixty-sixth, along with the rest of the division, set out on May 12 for Fredericksburg. The march lasted ten days and took them east through the Masanutten mountain range to Luray, north up the South Fork of the Shenandoah River to Front Royal, and from there via Manassas Gap to Warrenton and then Falmouth, opposite Fredericksburg. The order came down that the men were to carry their knapsacks, the intention being to toughen the soldiers up by adding to their burden during the long march. Colonel Candy thought the order unnecessary, but being a professional soldier he saw no choice but to comply. His solution to the problem was to have the men wrap their blankets and extra clothing in their rubber ponchos and stash them on the company supply wagons. The men marched with their knapsacks strapped on, but the packs were empty.[22]

Regimental officers estimated it as a 120-mile march. Despite the empty knapsacks it was hard on some of the men, but many of the unfit recruits were no longer with the regiment. William Sayre wrote to his father from Manassas Gap, "Well you may think there was some tired Boys but there was not. The boys any of them almost could fall out to play Ball in one hour after we got here." Company K's Captain Van Deman wrote to his wife that on one day the regiment marched twenty-two miles "and many were the blistered feet which met us on the way. Your own humble servant pulling the skin off his feet about the size of a silver dollar, and then marching on though at quite a sacrifice of good feeling I assure you. . . . I now feel very smart, in fact I feel better since I made this march than I have for some weeks back."[23]

When Shields's division arrived at Falmouth on May 22 it joined an army of thirty thousand men, the main force of the newly created Department of the Rappahannock, under the command of Irvin McDowell. The positioning of this army was something of an insurance policy: as McClellan concentrated on the peninsula between the York and James Rivers for an attack on Richmond, McDowell would be able to strike the rear of any Confederate force that might threaten Washington. He was also close enough to Richmond to join McClellan's offensive against the enemy capital.

The newly arrived soldiers of Tyler's brigade, many of them in tattered uniforms, could not help but contrast their condition with what they found. The regimental historian of the 7th Ohio recounted the vision that greeted them: "When Shields's division, after its all-winter campaign at and from Romney . . . reached the Department of the Rappahannock under Major General McDowell, it found a body of 30,000 men who had been quartered in large tents, in perfectly arranged camps, with neat, clean uniforms and guns and accouterments upon which no storm ever beat, the very picture of a perfect soldiery." Captain Van Deman observed that the officers had "as much furniture in their tents as we have at home, dressed all the time in the very best clothes. To go soldiering that way is not bad." The contrast was all too obvious to McDowell's men, who took to calling the new arrivals "Shields's bushwhackers" and "Shields's conscripts." Even so, this was the largest force with which the Sixty-sixth had yet been joined, impressing Joseph Diltz, who wrote his wife, "We have big times out here. Their is so many together it looks like a great city."[24]

The Sixty-sixth's appearance reflected a hard reality that went beyond soiled uniforms and the lack of tents. Poor sanitation, exposure, and exhaustion had wrecked the health of many in the regiment. Eighteen had died of disease, and twenty-two had been discharged on disability, totaling a 4 percent loss to the regiment even before it had fired its first volley on the battlefield.

The spiritual health of the Sixty-sixth was also a matter of concern for the religious, among whom was Sgt. John B. McGowen of Company G. One of the older recruits (he was forty-three), McGowen was a sometime plasterer, sometime music teacher, and a lay preacher in Urbana's Methodist church. He wrote to the mother of one of his messmates, Abraham Hefflebower, "Oh how much wickedness there is in the army. I pray God for the safety of our men, and for their eternal salvation. . . . I often see [Hefflebower] with his mother's Bible in his hand reading. These things have their influence upon the mind. I speak a friendly word too, upon the subject of religion—the importance of reading the Bible and of prayer."[25]

The day following their arrival, President Lincoln visited Falmouth to review the troops. Sixteen years later a remaining veteran claimed that his inspection of the Sixty-sixth and the rest of Tyler's brigade was delayed until dusk so that their ragged uniforms would not perhaps be as noticeable. Some of the men were even without shoes.[26]

The camp was in a high state of anticipation over the movement south. Robert Russell wrote his father on May 24, "We have just got orders for Onward to Richmond to start at six in the morning. There is a large force of rebels in possession of the bridge 4 miles beyond Fredericksburg which we will have to whip on our way there."[27]

Shields's division moved out the next day and did indeed cross the Rappahannock (Russell's "large force" had apparently dissipated); however, it stopped abruptly after crossing, when new orders arrived. Instead of pressing "on to Richmond," it would be returning to the Shenandoah Valley by forced march. Washington had received news that a force of seventeen thousand under Jackson had overwhelmed the Federal garrison at Front Royal. Outnumbered, Banks had abandoned Strasburg and retreated to Winchester, whose delighted citizens, Cornelia McDonald perhaps among them, were treated to the spectacle of blue uniforms chased through the streets by screeching Confederate soldiers. A number of Federals were captured at Winchester, including some of the Sixty-sixth who were still in hospital there. What remained of Banks's army was dashing for the refuge of the Potomac's north bank. To the

John B. McGowen.
*Janice Cotroneo
Collection, USAMHI.*

great disappointment of McClellan and McDowell, Lincoln immediately suspended the movement south from Fredericksburg and ordered two of McDowell's divisions to the Shenandoah Valley to contain—and perhaps destroy—a resurgent Jackson, who was even then threatening Harpers Ferry.

It was for that reason that McDowell dispatched Shields's division, including the Sixty-sixth, back whence it came, following up with a division that he commanded himself. Still outfitted in shabby uniforms, the Sixty-sixth would have to retrace its steps; the prospect was demoralizing. Pvt. Aaron Riker recalled that "the Heart sunk under its load of disappoinment and with feelings that Can not be described we turned our Faces and started Back on the Road which we had But so recently passed over then with spirits Buoyant we over Came the obsticles in our way but now that we must go back it seamed that every thing went wrong. The Mud seemed deeper and it was all the Men Could do to drag along."[28] Meanwhile an army under John Charles "Pathfinder" Frémont was ordered to advance out of the Alleghenies against Jackson. With Banks still to the north, Shields moving in from the east, and Frémont from the west, perhaps Jackson would be trapped.

Shields's division returned to the Valley, retracing the route taken in the march to Fredericksburg. His lead brigade retook Front Royal on

May 30, reversing Jackson's victory there the prior week. The colonel of the Georgia regiment garrisoning the town fled and left behind his men, of whom 156 were taken prisoner. The Federals also liberated twenty-four of their comrades who had been captured the previous week.

The next day Tyler's brigade was at Front Royal and discovered a mill with a great supply of flour. Federal quartermasters offered government receipts to the mill owner for his flour, but they were stoutly refused. The men themselves, who had been paid recently, offered greenbacks, but the miller still refused, proclaiming that he would accept only Confederate currency. The miller, though, was unaware of the presence of "note brokers" accompanying the Federal forces; these enterprising individuals kept on hand a large quantity of counterfeit Confederate bills for just such occasions, selling them at one cent on the dollar. The miller accepted these notes gladly, and soon there was a line of soldiers "with sacks of flour upon their shoulders, much like a stream of ants, wending their way from mill to camps." Observing this procession, Tyler rode to its source to investigate, for in this early stage of the war there was still some concern in the Federal army for the protection of Southern private property. He arrived to find the transactions taking place with the miller, who was still declaring his preference for Confederate scrip. Tyler smiled "childlike and bland" and departed; his men feasted that night on griddle cakes, thickened soups, and dumplings.[29] After the war, Tyler was fond of recounting the story, adding that the miller had later attempted to qualify for official reparations stemming from this episode, only to be thwarted by Tyler's testimony.[30]

7

Port Republic:
And They Say
the Battle Raged

Lincoln's plan for trapping Jackson in the Shenandoah Valley was not succeeding, due less to deficiencies in the plan than to the exertions of the Confederates and the incompetence of Federal commanders. Having eluded both Frémont and Banks, Jackson in the first week of June was driving rapidly up the Shenandoah Valley (that is, moving south), with Frémont's army in pursuit. Jackson was able to give his troops a rest on June 3 after they crossed a bridge spanning the North Fork of the Shenandoah River; burning the bridge, they left Frémont's advance guard on the opposite bank.

Frémont was not Jackson's only worry. Paralleling Frémont's pursuit on the other side of the Massanutten range, Shields was moving up the Luray Valley, through which flowed the South Fork of the Shenandoah River. The Sixty-sixth was in Shields's vanguard, a force consisting of the Third and Fourth Brigades, under Tyler and Col. Samuel S. Carroll respectively, with Tyler exercising overall command.

After the rest afforded him by the burned bridge, Jackson continued his movement up the Valley. In a maneuver noted as a brilliant exploitation of the terrain, Stonewall advanced to Port Republic, a village located just south of the Massanuttens at the point where the North and South Rivers joined to form the South Fork of the Shenandoah. From this strategic point he proposed to defeat his pursuers in detail before they could combine their forces against him.

The village was located within the angle formed by the North and South Rivers. The North River was the deeper of the two and was spanned by a covered bridge; the less formidable South River could be crossed by fording. To the east of the town were the spurs of the Blue Ridge mountain range, and down them woods thick with mountain laurel and scrub oak extended to a road from Port Republic paralleling the South Branch and leading to Conrad's Store to the north. About two miles up this road was an elevated "coaling" (where a local family had produced charcoal).

On June 8 Jackson had his headquarters in Port Republic, and forces under his subordinate Richard S. Ewell were engaging Frémont to the north. That morning Carroll crossed the South River with a detachment of cavalry and artillery in a surprise attack on the town that almost captured Jackson; however, the force was too small, and the attack was repulsed. Learning of these events, Tyler hurried toward Port Republic with his own brigade, which he positioned in the woods. With the two brigades brought together, Tyler had eight infantry regiments, three artillery batteries, and Carroll's cavalry at his disposal. W. A. Brand later wrote that "during the afternoon we were frequently moved about through the woods and over the mountain which ran parallel to the river; and finally were brought to a line in ambush."[1]

At this point Ewell was engaging Frémont at Cross Keys. Ewell would defeat the Pathfinder, but for now Jackson's army was divided. Had Carroll succeeded in burning the bridge on the North River, Ewell would have had difficulty rejoining Jackson, even as Jackson would have been in danger of being pinned against the North River by Tyler. But Carroll had not burned the bridge. (As it turned out, Shields had ordered him not to, but Carroll was later condemned by Shields for following his orders.)[2]

Upon Tyler's arrival, Col. Philip Daum, who was in charge of the artillery on the scene, urged a renewal of the attack: perhaps the bridge could still be destroyed. By now, however, Jackson's army was on guard against attacks from across the South River. Seeing that the Confederates at Port Republic outnumbered his two brigades and were well positioned, Tyler determined that the enemy was situated "to defy an army of 50,000 men" and that an assault against them "would result in the destruction of our little force."[3]

Even so, Tyler's "little force" of about three thousand was strong enough to contest Jackson's departure from Port Republic; it might even delay him long enough for Frémont or Shields—or both—to arrive and close the noose. Jackson for his part could not allow Tyler to remain in his rear as he attempted to break out of the Valley through Brown's Gap to the south. Brand's initial characterization of their placement as an "ambush" was not exactly correct, but Tyler's force presented Jackson with serious problems. A battle would have to be fought.

Tyler's position was a strong one. His left was anchored by the coaling, upon which he placed much of his artillery. A ravine curved in from the coaling's rear and left into its front, and beyond the ravine were the thick woods. Tyler's right was anchored by the South Fork. The 1,275-yard line between the coaling and the river, largely defined by the Lewiston Lane, could be covered easily by the forces Tyler had on hand. On the evening of June 8, though, most of Tyler's men were in the woods behind the coaling.

The next day at dawn a thick fog rose from the river. Tyler and Carroll went out to the picket lines at four; there were no reports of Confederate activity. The Sixty-sixth drew its morning rations at sunrise but did not have time to cook breakfast before Jackson pushed artillery across the South River and began to shell the vicinity of the coaling. Colonel Daum's guns were quick to reply, and an artillery duel ensued. A few regiments of Confederate infantry under Charles S. Winder also crossed and began to advance across the fields to the right and front of the coaling batteries, which were able to inflict great damage upon them.

Tyler sent his regiments fanning out toward what would soon become the Lewiston Lane battle line. Carroll's 7th Indiana, together with artillery, went as far as the river. Falling in on the 7th's left were the 29th, 7th, and 5th Ohio from Tyler's brigade, followed by the 1st (West) Virginia. The Sixty-sixth was placed to the rear of the 7th and 5th Ohio, but eventually it would be shifted to the left and behind the coaling batteries. The 84th and 110th Pennsylvania were placed with the Sixty-sixth in a supporting position. The Sixty-sixth's Company B was stationed in the wooded high ground behind and to the left of the batteries, thus, it was thought, affording further protection against a flanking movement. A company from the 5th Ohio joined Company B but would

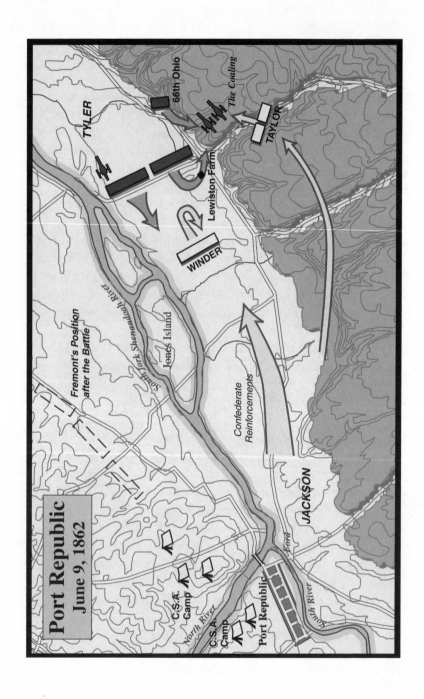

Port Republic
June 9, 1862

TYLER

66th Ohio

The Coaling

TAYLOR

Lewiston Farm

WINDER

Jones Island

South Fork Shenandoah River

Fremont's Position after the Battle

Confederate Reinforcements

C.S.A. Camp

North River

C.S.A. Camp

Port Republic

Ford

JACKSON

South River

later be withdrawn. W. A. Brand described the ground as follows:

> Immediately on the left [of the batteries], and bending around to the right in front, and running nearly directly back, was a mountain covered with timber, brush and bushes. Near the battery was a thick undergrowth of laurel and scrub oak. A deep ravine ran up into the mountain from behind the battery and in front was a deep depression into the side of the hill. On the right and a little in front was a stone or brick house surrounded by numerous small buildings. Beyond and around the house were open fields running forward toward the river.[4]

The house and outbuildings (known collectively as Lewiston) and the wheatfields made up the General Lewis farm, which was soon to be the scene of the most hotly contested battle of the Shenandoah Valley campaign.

While the Confederates drew Tyler's attention to his immediate front, they attempted a flanking movement on the Federal left. It was premature and lacking in strength, consisting of only two Virginia regiments, no more than five hundred men, from the Stonewall Brigade. They advanced through the thick brush to within a hundred yards of the battery. Seeing the Sixty-sixth and perhaps the two Pennsylvania regiments in support of the battery closest to them, the Confederates did not feel up to an assault that could expose them to artillery fire as they attempted to traverse the ravine. A few desultory shots earned the Virginians only several volleys of canister, further convincing them of the folly of an assault on the battery.

The attack the Union line faced along its front was also ineffective. Jackson was having difficulties getting his forces across the South River, and they were being thrown piecemeal into the battle. The Confederate advance across the wheat field stalled under the combined effect of Federal infantry and artillery fire, and many of Jackson's troops fell back to seek the scanty cover of a rail fence. The Federal fire upon the Confederates was intense. The Rebels, who were running out of ammunition and suffering high casualties, broke before a Union charge. The two Pennsylvania regiments positioned with the Sixty-sixth in support of the coaling batteries were also thrown into the action, on the right.

Some of the soldiers of the Sixty-sixth observed the rout of the enemy, not realizing that the threat from their left and rear would soon rematerialize. The withdrawal of the two Pennsylvania regiments made them more vulnerable to a Confederate attack out of the woods. This was forthcoming when Richard Taylor's brigade (minus one regiment) of Louisiana "Tigers," which had followed the two Virginia regiments into the woods, burst with a great shout out of the laurel, down and through the ravine, and up toward the Federal guns. The attack surprised the artillerists, who were neither able to depress their guns sufficiently to fire into the ravine nor to turn them quickly enough in the direction from which the Tigers were attacking. Confederates made it up to the opposing lip of the ravine and began to fire into the batteries, killing and wounding many artillerists, as well as horses.

The artillerists did not give up their guns easily; they fought the Tigers hand to hand. The Sixty-sixth was the only Federal infantry that could help, and it was not well positioned; the regiment faced the river so that only its left was at first engaged in the attempt to push back the Tigers. Tyler later reported that everything was riding on the Sixty-sixth at this juncture, for "had they given way, the command must have been lost."[5] The regiment wheeled about to face the coaling, keeping its left stationary ("marching by left flank"), but at this point some of the artillery horses, still hitched to caissons and wagons, broke to the rear in fright, careening through the ranks. Surprised by the Rebel assault and by the stampede of artillery horses, some of the Sixty-sixth began to give way, but they were steadied by the regiment's officers.[6]

Also, help was on the way. The 5th and 7th Ohio broke off pursuit of the Confederates in the wheatfield, changed front, and advanced on the coaling to join the Sixty-sixth. The three regiments sent a destructive fire into the Louisianians, who had taken most of the guns but were unable to turn them upon the Federals, so exacting were the Ohioans' volleys. Sensing that they would be forced from the guns, the Tigers slaughtered the battery horses; one of the officers cut their throats with a Bowie knife, while enlisted men shot others in the head at point-blank range.[7]

The three Ohio regiments rushed upon the Tigers, driving them from the guns. So thickly were the Confederate dead and wounded piled around the cannons that the Ohioans could not avoid running upon the bodies as they rushed in pursuit of the enemy, most of whom were retreating back across the ravine and into the woods. The Federals found the artillery pieces loaded with canister and fired them into the backs of the retreating Confederates. They also pursued some of the Rebels into the outbuildings of the Lewis farm, where they shot at the Confederates through slats and cracks in the structures.[8]

An anonymous and somewhat breathless account published in 1865 recounted that the Sixty-sixth's initial attack was "thrown back as a clenched fist might be thrown back from a wall of India rubber." At this juncture Pvt. Calvin Irwin of Company I and a few other like-minded souls rallied and called out to their comrades to go back for another try: "Give them another dash! another one, boys, and they'll break!" The narrator continued, "There was the same terrible collision, the same volleys, the same clashing and plunging of bayonets; there were more shouts, and hurrahs, and screams, and dying groans, and gasps; but the regiment was not thrown back this time like a clenched fist from a wall of India rubber." Irwin was shot three times in the legs and was hobbling rearwards when Captain Horr pointed him out to Candy: "Look here, Colonel, he's one of my men, and has three balls in him, but isn't dead yet." "You'll do my brave boy," said Candy, who would have grasped Irwin's hand had not the soldier at that moment fainted to the ground.[9]

Driven back across the ravine, the Louisianians fired on the battery from the woods, making it impossible for the surviving artillery officers, already hampered by a shortage of horses, to remove their pieces. The Louisianians again charged through the ravine, and were again repulsed with heavy casualties. The Tigers also suffered from the fire of the Sixty-sixth's skirmishers positioned above them on the other side of the ravine.

Back at Port Republic, Confederate forces were struggling across the South River in small increments. Jackson was still hampered by his inability to bring all his forces to bear in a timely fashion. The initial movements against Tyler's position were made in small numbers and could not have succeeded; however, these first efforts had distracted the Union commander from his left, allowing Taylor to attack the coaling against only the Sixty-sixth guarding the batteries. Now that Tyler was focused on what was, after all, the key to the battlefield, more Confederate forces were massing on his front. The Federals were clearly outnumbered; Tyler's position began to unravel.

The three Ohio regiments gave way to a third assault on the coaling but continued to fire upon the Confederates, who were once again in possession of the guns. But the fight soon went out of the Ohioans: not only did they have to contend with the Tigers, but they now saw advancing toward them the rallied survivors of the enemy regiments routed earlier in the battle, augmented by reinforcements that had at last made it across the South River. Brand observed, "They were in great numbers—indeed whole fields seemed covered with them."[10] The Federal position had become untenable. Tyler ordered a retreat.

The two brigades were not pursued in force, although Confederate cavalry shadowed them and picked off a few stragglers. Among these stragglers was Pvt. Robert Simpson of the Sixty-sixth's Company H. Hospitalized with a severe cold caught after fording a stream a few weeks before, Simpson had rejoined the regiment just before the battle but lacked the strength to keep up with the retreat. He collapsed a mile from the battlefield and was taken prisoner.[11] The retreat did not seem so desperate to at least one soldier. About two miles into the withdrawal, Cpl. Charles Turner of Company K decided to stop and boil water for coffee. Despite a warning from an officer that the enemy was not far behind, Turner coolly remarked that he would have "a tin of coffee first." The coffee carried a high price: Turner was soon captured.[12]

The retreating Federals were under enemy artillery fire, including shot and shell from the guns they had defended on the coaling. Tyler's force followed the road toward Conrad's Store, but before reaching that point it encountered Shields's main body advancing to its aid.

Behind them, the Lewis farm and coaling was a scene of extraordinary carnage. Taylor, the Tigers' commander, would recall that he had "never seen so many dead and wounded in the same limited space."[13] The battle had not been kind to the artillery horses, either; one Confederate estimated that eighty or ninety of them lay dead over the space of less than an acre.[14]

The Federals' stand had been made at a high price. Tyler stated in his official report that his two brigades suffered total casualties of 1,018 killed, wounded, and captured or missing—approximately one-third of the force engaged at Port Republic. With twenty killed, seventy-five wounded, and 110 captured or missing, the Sixty-sixth suffered the second-highest number of casualties out of the eight Federal infantry regiments engaged. Having gone into the battle with approximately four hundred men, already much reduced by illness and heavy marching, the Sixty-sixth suffered a 50 percent casualty rate at Port Republic.[15]

In fact, the damage of Port Republic went beyond the immediate casualty figures. An examination of all available sources indicates that the number of wounded in the official report was probably accurate but that the actual number of dead was higher: thirty-seven men from the Sixty-sixth were either killed in action or died of their wounds shortly after the battle. Of the 110 listed as missing, most were prisoners; an account of one of the captured men set the number of prisoners from the Sixty-sixth at 112.[16] Some of the wounded were among these prisoners. Seven of the captured soldiers were to die in captivity or expire shortly after release. In addition, at least twenty-one men were discharged or resigned their commissions because of wounds received at Port Republic or as a result of imprisonment. Thus the permanent loss to the regiment as a result of Port Republic would be sixty-five men.

Company A's Levi Gladden, whose sister Sarah had written and published a patriotic poem upon his enlistment, was among those killed in action; he was shot in the head above the left eye early in the battle. He died from the wound, and his body was left on the field.[17] Sarah Gladden wrote another poem, this one mourning his death; like the previous one, it was published as a broadside:

> They tell me that my brother's lying
> Far upon Virginia's soil;
> That he fell while nobly fighting
> Upon the field of blood and toil.
>
> And they say the battle raged
> At the morning rising sun,
> And the last words that he uttered
> Were brave comrades do not run.
>
> Is it so, my dearest brother,
> That you lay so far from home—
> That no sister hand can plant,
> A white rose by your (silent) tomb.
>
> Yes, fighting nobly did he fall,
> While the smoke was curling high—
> Shot by a fatal musket ball
> While dying only heard a sigh.
>
> When I think of bygone pleasure,
> And the times passed pleasantly;
> And they tell me I ne'er shall see him
> It seems to me it cannot be.
>
> I long to see his face once more,
> And hear his welcome voice—
> It would arouse our drooping hearts
> And cause us to rejoice.

> We will miss you dearest brother,
>   When the boy's bright face we see;
>   When your schoolmates gather around us
>   Then we'll sigh and think of thee.
>
> Our family circle by death is broken,
>   For our brother Levi's gone—
> He left us in the prime of life,
>   But found an early tomb.[18]

Port Republic also occasioned other expressions of grief. Sergeant McGowen, the music teacher and moral guardian of Abraham Hefflebower, was killed in action, mourned by his church and community. His sister submitted two memorial poems to the local newspaper, which were duly published: "The kind and loving breast, was pierced by rebel balls. And Jesus took his soul to rest where all is peace and joy."[19] His last moments were recounted by Quartermaster Brand in a letter to McGowen's wife:

> He fell quite near me, from a musket ball in his breast. I was fearful it was fatal and after he was taken back some ten steps from the line of battle, I dismounted to see him. I found him dying. He recognized me, was calm, quiet, and died without a groan or struggle. I asked him if he was wounded badly. He put his hand upon his breast, and I opened his bosom, saw it was fatal; and so told him. He moved his head, as much as to say that he was conscious of it. I took him by the hand and he pressed my hand. I bade him farewell, told him he was dying in a good cause; that he had discharged his duty nobly and all would be well with him soon. He was sinking rapidly, and as I turned to leave him his eyes gradually closed in death.[20]

Although some Federal accounts describe Tyler's retreat as well ordered, the large number of unwounded prisoners from the Sixty-sixth seems to indicate something different. The ranks of the Federal regiments were probably intermixed, perhaps accounting for the seemingly contradictory assertions that five separate regiments, among them the Sixty-sixth, acted as rear guard during the retreat.[21]

Lt. John Rathbun of Company F probably got it right when he wrote to his wife that "you never heard of such a time in your life men running in all directions to save themselves." Another veteran of the Sixty-sixth later recalled that "the 66th being a new regiment had not yet learned how to retreat in face of the foe. When they found the battle was lost they left the immediate field, preserving not a semblance of regimental or company organization."[22]

One account claims that a group of about one hundred men from all the regiments of the Third Brigade were cut off from the main body and retreated into the mountains, where they remained during the night.[23] The fate of Company B, which had been sent into the sloping woods north of the ravine as skirmishers, was unknown to the rest of the regiment immediately following the battle; most of its members, as it turned out, were captured. Even so, Tyler was able to bring some order to his command before rejoining Shields. W. A. Brand recounted that the remnants of the various regiments halted in a field about two miles from the battle site and formed in line, brought up the two guns they had managed to retain, and fired at the Confederate cavalry pursuing them.[24]

The officers of the Sixty-sixth were not spared, although none was killed. Captain Horr (apparently some time after lauding Calvin Irwin) and Sgt. Harrison Davis of Company H hid in a pile of driftwood on the riverbank for the better part of two days, after which the two of them made their way to the mountains and from there eventually rejoined the Sixty-sixth. Other captains were wounded, among them Company F's John Cassill, who was nearing his sixtieth year and soon after resigned his commission. Company C's Capt. Samuel McMorran sustained a neck wound that would plague him the rest of his life. James Q. Baird, of Company G, was wounded in the arm (but suffered no lasting effects from the injury). A few other officers were taken prisoner, among them Capt. Thomas Buxton of Company E, as well as lieutenants from Companies B, E, and K.[25]

Many of the wounded were taken prisoner. Following the battle, Confederate stretcher bearers and medical teams first removed their own wounded from the field and had started to attend to those of the Federal forces when the tardy Frémont began to shell the field from across the river, possibly killing or further injuring the wounded Union soldiers lying there. The Confederate forces suspended their operations in the field until Frémont's gunners, presumably understanding the situation at last, ceased fire. The brick house of the General Lewis farm was converted into a field hospital, where Confederate and Federal wounded were treated. Some of the Federal wounded had to wait two or three days for medical attention. Sgt. Stephen Baxter, who had made out his last will and testament the day before leaving Urbana, was taken to a log stable in front of the coaling and thence on June 12 to the brick house, where his leg was amputated. He died the next day.[26]

A postwar account states that many of the dead from both sides remained unburied for several days. Local citizens, aided by soldiers dispatched back to the battlefield, attempted to do right by the dead but could bring themselves only to shovel dirt on top of the corpses. Hogs, now unencumbered by fences knocked down during the battle, had free range of the field and rooted up many of the bodies again.[27]

The battle of Port Republic was given various interpretations. Jackson rejoiced in his victory, attributing it to divine favor, seeming to ignore the fact that the piecemeal advance of his superior forces had almost cost him the battle and had increased his casualties. Still, the result for Stonewall was a victorious coda to his Valley campaign. For his part, Shields criticized Tyler for failing to destroy the Port Republic bridge and then making what he characterized as a doomed and unnecessary stand. Tyler, of course, defended himself. All the commanders cited the bravery and determination of their men. The enlisted men had their own view of matters, as seen in the diary of Company G's Frank Parker: "Monday, June 9. Port Republic. The rebels open fire at half past six o'clock. We give them hell until ten and then left them to work out their own salvation with fear and trembling."[28]

8

Prisoners of War: I Have Just Been to See a Man Die

*I*n any conflict a prisoner of war's fate is uncertain and unenviable. The Confederacy's prisons were often makeshift and lacked adequate shelter. By war's end the breakdown of the parole and exchange system had resulted in the overcrowding of already substandard facilities, the horrors of Andersonville being among the better-known consequences. The belligerents had arrived at a parole and exchange agreement only on July 22, 1862, over a month after Port Republic, so that Federal prisoners from the Shenandoah had no clear prospect of return to their comrades and families.

The experience of the Sixty-sixth's soldiers taken prisoner at Port Republic was chronicled in a journal kept by Pvt. David Merrill Humes of Company A. His journal was later published serially in the *Urbana Citizen and Gazette,* where his account would supplement those of other prisoners whose letters home had been printed in the summer and fall of 1862.[1]

The Federal prisoners from Port Republic were detained in the vicinity of the battlefield for about two days. They received their first meal as prisoners on the night of June 10, and at five o'clock the next morning all but the seriously wounded were marched eighteen miles south to a railroad depot. From there the sick and wounded prisoners were transported by rail to Charlottesville, leaving the able-bodied to march the seven miles to that city. The prisoners were confined in the court house yard, where they were an object of great curiosity to the townspeople. Locals asked the soldiers if they thought the war would soon be over; some berated them for desecrating the soil of Virginia. A few ladies brought them baskets of provisions, and one woman, a Mrs. Morgan, particularly earned the Ohioans' gratitude for her attention to the sick and wounded. A few of the men gave her small presents as tokens of their appreciation.

At eight o'clock on the night of June 12 they were crammed into railway cars, spending a sleepless night before the train left Charlottesville the next morning for Lynchburg, almost ninety miles to the south. They arrived at four in the afternoon, detrained, and were ushered into a prison camp already containing 1,600 men—in a space estimated by Humes to be no more than an acre and a half. They also ate their first prison meal, half rations of salt beef and crackers.

The prisoners were subjected to a torrential storm during the afternoon of June 15. Having no shelter, they took a drenching. The air became cool, but with neither blankets nor firewood they stood all night rather than attempt to sleep in the mud. Sleep was almost as impossible the next night, although some of the men attempted it in groups huddled together on the wet ground.

The prisoners were transferred on June 17 to the Lynchburg fairgrounds, reckoned at first glance to be a healthier location, though inconvenient to water. Many of the Port Republic prisoners were already lice infested. Sickness from exposure and malnutrition was already manifesting itself.

Three days later the Sixty-sixth's officers were transported to Salisbury, North Carolina. June 20 was also notable for the distribution of four kettles and four mess pans to the over one hundred prisoners of the regiment, although without sufficient kindling the advantage of such utensils was questionable. "Why don't old Abraham exchange us? Think he would if he knew what we had to suffer," mused Humes.[2] The treatment of the officers at Salisbury was little better than that afforded the enlisted men. Thomas Buxton, captain of Company E, later recalled that he had "neither blanket or wrap of any kind to protect myself from exposure and was never supplied with either during my term of imprisonment."[3]

Rations at Lynchburg were adequate for the next several days, and they were supplemented by better food, including such delicacies as fresh fruit—which could be purchased from prison camp sutlers, albeit at high prices. Tents were issued on June 24.

A few days later the prisoners of the Sixty-sixth welcomed two more of their number, Granville Smith and Jacob Messer of Company A. They had been out foraging when importuned by some Virginia householders to enter their home for a hot meal. The two soldiers agreed, but while seated at the table they were suddenly surrounded by seven Confederate soldiers. Messer later recalled that there had been nothing to do but hold up his hands.[4]

More prisoners continued to arrive, until on July 1 the camp held 2,320 Federals. Although tents continued to provide rudimentary shelter, a rainstorm meant that the men, who were still without blankets, would have to lie on wet ground if they hoped to sleep. Sickness and death were constantly at hand. The authorities maintained a camp hospital in large shelter tents just outside the perimeter, but there was a shortage of medicine.

Prisoners were anxious that loved ones should learn of their fate, and they were allowed to send letters. Some letters apparently found their way to Ohio, and some prisoners even received replies. Home was much on their minds, and food played a large role in their fantasies. On the Fourth of July Humes wrote:

How our minds go back to the "fourth's of July" of other years, when it was our right and privilege to celebrate this day in feasting and pleasure, as they always do in old Champaign. Wonder if they are having any "4th" at Urbana today. If they are not, they should have, and we would like to be with them and enjoy a feast of good things in regular Pic-Nic style. But no, I must content myself to *feast* on *fat meat*, cooked with *flour* to my taste.... Such food is too mean for a felon in his dungeon.[5]

Water was a chronic problem. When it came as precipitation, the men were deprived of their sleep; otherwise, there was barely enough to slake their thirsts on the hot summer afternoons, and not enough for them to wash their clothes or their bodies. What was left of their uniforms became greasy and foul smelling. By mid-July many of the prisoners had simply thrown away their shirts. At month's end the officer of the day marched the prisoners to a nearby stream for a much needed bath—just in time to draw the attention of a Confederate colonel who rebuked the men for stripping off their clothes where ladies could see them. He had the prisoners marched back to the fairgrounds without having their bath. Humes smoldered in his journal: "There is no more honor in a Rebel than there is in a highway robber They are as full of *lies* as their satanic majesty could well stuff them. When I believe a rebel, it will be when I am crazy."[6] Tension mounted through late June and into July. Arguments, theft, and violence among the prisoners became frequent. A Massachusetts man picked the pocket of an Indiana soldier and was found out; he was turned over to the authorities but was returned to the camp, where he was severely beaten. On July 12 the guards "bucked" and gagged some of the prisoners outside the perimeter for refusing to work. A crowd of prisoners gathered, and one threw a rock among the guards. Later that day, when the prisoners were presenting themselves for the evening count, one of the guards fired on them (but hurt no one).

Marquis Bower, of the Sixty-sixth's Company E, was shot dead on the morning on July 22. The incident was recorded by Humes: "Among the many sad accidents and incidents which have happened to the 66th, the most painful one I have witnessed happened last night. Bower, Company E, was shot through by a guard, when the villain, without halting him, when he was not within four feet of the lines, raised his piece and shot him dead. It happened about three o'clock this morning—never shall forget it."[7] Bower had been from Delaware, Ohio. In its report of the incident the *Delaware Gazette* referred to him as "Maroot" Bower, "one of our German citizens," who had "stepped a few feet beyond the limits prescribed to the prisoners to procure a bucket of water."[8]

The Sixty-sixth also lost three other men that month. John W. Kettles of Company G was the first; he was seen walking about the camp around midnight on July 9 and was found dead the next morning. John J. Swisher of Company B succumbed to illness on July 24, followed by Harvey Vinyard of the same company the next day. A minister came to camp to pick up the bodies, asking the prisoners to be sure to tell the families of the dead that the deceased had received a decent Christian burial. Indeed, each dead comrade was borne from camp in a coffin— but it seemed to the prisoners that the same coffin always returned for the next corpse.

Another soldier of the Sixty-sixth died on August 2, but the prison ranks of the regiment were augmented two days later, when two or three wounded comrades from Port Republic were brought into camp. Each had lost a leg.

The heat of August became increasingly oppressive, but soon there was good news. On August 7, using the "bread basket" of a prone Jacob Messer for a writing desk, Humes recorded the joyful tidings that they were to be sent home. "The idea of getting away from this awful dirty prison makes me feel so good that I can hardly compose myself sufficiently to make a note in my journal," he wrote. "Besides Jake is so tickled he can't lie still any longer—so I'll quit until tomorrow."[9]

That night they drew rations and stayed up until morning cooking them. The following afternoon the prisoners were on the train to Richmond, although probably none of them realized that the train was taking them to yet another prison, where they were to be further detained. They were going to Belle Isle.

Located in the James River, Belle Isle faced Richmond's Tredegar Ironworks on the north bank and the depot of the Richmond Danville Railroad on the south bank; the only bridge to the island came from the latter side. The approximately eighty-acre island extended from sandy beaches at the water's edge to an upland area rising almost a hundred feet in the center. It was located near the James River's fall line, where the strong currents would discourage escape attempts.[10]

The prisoners arrived at Belle Isle on the evening of August 9 and soon discovered that they were in much worse circumstances than at Lynchburg. Prisoners from McClellan's unsuccessful Peninsula campaign had swelled the island's population to five thousand.[11] Rations were much reduced. On one occasion the men received only a quarter loaf of bread for the day. Additional fare consisted of a thin pea or bean soup, crackers, and beef (usually spoiled and unsalted). Many of the men became faint from hunger after being on the island for only a few days. Some who were seriously ill were transferred to the hospital at Libby Prison. Death came frequently, although none of the prisoners from the Sixty-sixth were lost at Belle Isle. Most of the men found shelter in Sibley tents, which were, however, crowded to more than double the intended occupancy.

As at Lynchburg, there were prison sutlers at Belle Isle. Their prices, however, were exorbitant. On August 23 the prisoners took matters into their own hands and mobbed the sutlers, robbing them of all their goods. Apparently the prison authorities were unable or unwilling to provide any protection for the peddlers.[12] The prisoners' discontent was no doubt provoked by food shortages and the deaths of comrades from malnutrition. An excerpt from Humes's diary for August 26, three days after the attack on the sutlers, attests to the island camp's dreadful conditions:

> I have just been to see a man die. Saw two or three more who will die today. They are starving to death. . . . Can mortal man imagine what a horrid place this is to be sick, without he too is here? Just now a man came to our tent begging bread. He is so weak he can scarcely walk, says he is dying of hunger, and if he does not get something to eat very soon he must die. We told him we had nothing at all to eat, or we would give it him. The hungry starving soldier sank down in his tracks, and he was carried back to his bunk. How humiliating to think we must turn away one who was dying with hunger, and only asked of us a crumb of bread that he might not die, but live; but we had nothing to give him, not even a piece of bread, which was all he asked and he *died,* of *what?* of starvation. Tonight hundreds are begging bread, and as many must go without finding it. And when the rays of tomorrow's sun shall fall on this starving multitude, it will fall on many *dead,* who are now living.

Five days later a heavy rain began at daybreak and lasted two hours. Following the storm, Humes decided to take a walk but had only taken a few steps from his tent when he came upon a man lying upon the ground. He had apparently collapsed there the night before and had not been able to rise even when the storm fell upon him. Humes observed that his face was "red as scarlet and looked *raw.*"[13] He did what he could for the man, but he found others in similar circumstances as he walked the camp that morning.

These conditions continued into the first week of September. The men of the Sixty-sixth knew that it would not be long before they too would begin to die if they remained on the island, but on September 6 their good news finally arrived: they had been exchanged on parole and were to prepare for departure the following morning. All was excitement that night, as the men gathered together their few belongings and excitedly speculated upon their prospects. As Humes penned the welcome tidings in his journal, a group of men were standing nearby singing "Home, Sweet Home."[14]

Early the next morning the men were lined up at the appointed hour and marched across the bridge into Richmond, then south along the James River for about seventeen miles. At length, as they rounded a hill they saw the flag of the United States flying from a ship anchored in the river at Aiken's Landing: it was the ironclad *Eastern City,* which was to be their transport to Union lines and, they hoped, home. The transport was carrying Confederate prisoners who passed through the ranks of the starving Federals: "They all had their haversacks filled with Uncle Sam's crackers and beef. They all looked fat and hearty. When they saw us their hearts were touched with pity and they gave us some of their rations."[15]

Shortly after midnight the vessel shoved off from the landing. The journey was then largely uneventful. Passing the wreck of the *Cumberland,* sunk by the CSS *Virginia* in March, the *Eastern City* proceeded to Fort Monroe, at the tip of the York Peninsula. They arrived there the same day and then steamed north toward the Potomac. The *Eastern City* stopped just short of Washington at Alexandria the following evening and remained at anchor there for the better part of two days.

At this point began a particularly demoralizing episode in the experience of the released prisoners. They had begun to run low on both food and water but were not allowed to go ashore. Once again they felt the onset of hunger, only now they were within sight of the nation's capital. Their boat finally left Alexandria on the afternoon of September 11, but due to a storm the ship had again to drop anchor. The next day the *Eastern City* again set forth but within an hour's time was grounded on a sandbar for four days. Still low on food and water, the men remained on board until another ship, the *Spaulding,* arrived, took them aboard, and proceeded back downriver to Fort Monroe, which they reached on September 16. The *Spaulding* then set out into the Atlantic, eventually depositing its seasick passengers at Fort Delaware, on the New Jersey side of the Delaware River. There the prisoners of the Sixty-sixth remained confined on parole.

They had suffered greatly but were relatively fortunate; Richmond could just as easily have been their initial destination following capture. Indeed, the Richmond authorities had heard rumors that it was to be so.[16] Instead the prisoners had been rerouted to Lynchburg, where conditions were somewhat better than at Belle Isle. Had they been sent to Richmond in mid-June they would have barely preceded the captives from the Army of the Potomac taken prisoner in the Seven Days fighting (June 25–July 1). Had the captives from Port Republic been forced to share the island with this larger group of prisoners as of late June, by August they would have degenerated to the condition in which they found the island's inhabitants upon their arrival from Lynchburg.

Even so, many of the Sixty-sixth who arrived at Fort Monroe were broken men, soon hospitalized. Some never recovered. Among these was Pvt. David M. Humes, who died on October 24, 1862.

9

Regrouping

*E*ven as their comrades were being transported to prison camps in Lynchburg and Salisbury, the remnants of the Sixty-sixth were making their way north down the Shenandoah Valley with the rest of Shields's division. They soon arrived at Luray, where some of the men had the opportunity to compose letters to family and friends in Ohio. Duncan McDonald, a second lieutenant in Company B, reported on his own condition and that of his comrades in a letter to his father:

> I will write a few lines this morning, but it will only be a few, as I have but little time now. . . . I presume that you have heard of our fight, and most likely have had a pretty fair account of it before you receive this. I got out without a scratch but there are still 34 of our company missing yet. I think they are all taken prisoner, and not killed or wounded. Captain Palmer and Lieutenant Ganson, all of our Sergeants, except Wilkins and all of our Corporals except William A. Powell, are missing. . . . We went into the fight with 40 rank and file and but six of us got away.[1]

Leaving Luray, the regiment continued north, arriving at Front Royal on June 16. After resting a few days the Sixty-sixth proceeded to Manassas

Junction, which it reached on June 23, having marched over fifty miles in less than three days.

In addition to the Port Republic casualties, the regiment was also losing men to desertion. After six months' exposure and exhaustion, followed by the slaughter of Port Republic, some determined that a soldier's life was not to their liking. Joseph Diltz wrote to his wife on June 25 that within the past month fifty men had deserted. Two such losses were the Sigman brothers from Company A. John C. and Thomas B. Sigman left camp on June 24 never to return, although John Sigman would later enlist in the 118th O.V.I. under an alias. If they returned to their father's farm in Mad River Township, antiwar sentiment in the area could protect them. In the meantime, the amount owed the army for equipment was dutifully registered in their military records; Thomas Sigman, for example, owed forty cents for a cap box and pick, forty cents for a canteen and cork, and thirty-seven cents for a haversack.[2]

Diltz's estimate of fifty desertions was likely an exaggeration; official records indicate half that number at most. Three men were listed as deserting at Port Republic on June 9, but in these cases it might be difficult to ascertain whether they had slipped away from the field never to return or some misfortune had befallen them.[3] One case of desertion, that of Company B's Pvt. Charles Newcomb, seems to have been fairly straightforward, however; the authorities were still looking for him in November 1863. Urbana's provost marshal wrote to his counterpart in Dubuque, Iowa:

Charles Newcomb a deserter from Co. B, 66th O.V.I. is or was very lately in Dubuque, passing under the name of Henry Berry, John Barry, J. H. Marshall & perhaps others. He is an odd looking genius—hair *very* light—is long, gangling & loose jointed.

He is a cooper by trade & is probably working at that; though on this point, I am not informed. Will be found with low associates.

If you arrest, be sure to notify me, as his arrest would afford great satisfaction in this community.[4]

Some of the men who were carried on the rolls as deserters had returned home to recuperate from illness and failed to go through the proper discharge procedures when they did not recover. Among these was the war-hawk Squire "Spectacles" Wallace, who had left the regiment in May and would eventually require a presidential pardon in 1867 to set the record straight.[5]

After a few days' rest the regiment was again in motion. Its division was ordered on June 27 to join McClellan's army at White House on the York Peninsula, augmenting the forces "Little Mac" had assembled to take Richmond. Traveling by rail that night, the regiment arrived at Alexandria early on the morning of June 28. Later in the day the regiment boarded the ship *North America,* lying at anchor in the Potomac.

They remained on board overnight, fully expecting to find themselves steaming for the Peninsula the next day—only to disembark the following morning at the same location. New orders had been given to Tyler. McClellan was in retreat, his base at White House abandoned; to reinforce the Army of the Potomac, even if one could find a place to land troops, was pointless. There would be other uses for the Port Republic veterans. Company I's Pvt. Frank Parker made a typically brief entry in his diary concerning the day's events: "Saturday, June 28. March down to the river and got on the boat. . . . I am top of the boat writing now. Went up on the upper deck to sleep and all got drunk. Fooled again."[6]

The Sixty-sixth left the Potomac and set up camp on the Centerville Pike just west of Alexandria. Camp was moved five days later to within a half-mile of Fairfax Seminary, site of a military hospital where some of the Sixty-sixth's members were convalescing. The camp itself was considered a good location, being "well supplied with excellent water and great quantities of huckelberries."[7]

The Sixty-sixth was also under a new chain of command. Tyler still commanded their brigade; however, Shields was no longer in charge of the division. He was to be replaced by Christopher Augur, a regular army man and veteran of the Mexican War as well as a former West Point commandant. Although Banks retained control over his command, it was now a corps in John Pope's new Army of Virginia.

The regiment's proximity to Washington provided an opportunity to visit comrades in the several hospitals in and around the capital. The men of the Sixty-sixth were not alone in doing so. In a not unusual display of localism manifesting itself in a war to assert the unity of all United States citizens, the people of Champaign County dispatched representatives to care for their sick and wounded soldiers. The alarming casualty lists from Port Republic must have been the impetus for this move; Champaign County's Samaritans arrived in the Washington area supplied with food, clothing, and generous hearts. Two of these representatives, W. H. Helmick and Jacob Poland, chanced upon the Sixty-sixth as it was boarding the *North America*. Poland remarked in a letter to the *Citizen and Gazette* how sad it was to see the regiment so reduced in numbers and hoping for "an investigation of the disastrous and murderous affair" of Port Republic. He reported that seventy-nine men of the Sixty-sixth were in area hospitals. Ten had just arrived at what was identified as "Mansion House Hospital" in Alexandria (which could have been Robert E. Lee's abandoned home) suffering from disease, sunstroke, and exhaustion.[8]

Champaign's representatives were at times surprisingly solicitous, notwithstanding the logistics of having to visit inmates at several hospitals. W. H. Helmick recounted that

owing to the hospitals being located at such distances from the city, and the men so scattered throughout the different hospitals, they cannot be visited as often as the men would naturally think they should be. The only way in which it can be done is to have a horse and buggy. By the time a person walks three miles with a basket of fruits, and other articels, and spends a short time with each person he visits, (which must be done), and gets back to the city for dinner, (4 o'clock), there is no time to visit another hospital the same day. To show how they charge for what you want done, on Monday evening I ascertained that W. Best, of Co. A, who had lost a leg and was very much reduced, wanted a rocking chair to sit in, having become very tired of the bed. On Tuesday morning I bought one. Being three miles to the hospital, I tried to get a negro to carry it for me, but when he ascertained where it was to go, he had something else to do. An express wagon came along and he wanted *one dollar* to take the chair. I immediately turned negro and carried it myself![9]

Private Best died on July 21 at the Military Asylum Hospital in Washington, but we can imagine that some of his final days were spent in the rocking chair procured by Mr. Helmick at a cost of $1.25—which amount he dutifully entered in his list of expenses submitted to the Ladies Aid Society of Urbana.

The regiment itself was subject to the monotony of camp life and the discomfort of a summer heat wave. The Fourth of July was celebrated without major hoopla, as the division turned out for a 9 A.M. review. The firing of cannons in holiday salute from the forts in the area triggered memories of Port Republic for W. A. Brand.[10]

Days were devoted to drill and nights to attempts at sleep in the oppressive heat. The brigade was summoned on July 9 to General Tyler's headquarters, where it was to be addressed by a delegation of Ohio politicians, including William Dennison, ex-governor of the state. Colonel Candy was placed in charge of marching the brigade to the mansion where Tyler resided. Dennison, however, failed to arrive, so the occasion was taken up by an address from the congressman from whose district the 7th and 29th Ohio regiments had been recruited, followed by comments from Tyler's chaplain, who specifically praised the Sixty-sixth's performance at Port Republic.[11]

As July wore on, the regiment regained some of its strength; the sick and wounded began to trickle back from the hospitals. Even so, as of July 17 the regiment carried the names of 260 men as absent or sick. Presumably this list included the one hundred or so men who were in Confederate prisons, but it also included men who were still in hospital or had deserted. Some had returned to Ohio for convalescence without orders, technically putting them in a state of desertion. That a number of men had opted for this latter course is evidenced by Colonel Candy's order of July 5, addressed to absentees of the Sixty-sixth and published in the *Citizen and Gazette*. Soldiers not with the regiment were to report to duty on pain of court-martial for desertion; those unable to travel were to obtain sworn medical certification of the fact and immediately transmit the documentation to headquarters.[12] Candy also devoted time to the question of promotions, which in this volunteer regiment required the approval of Ohio governor David Tod. The colonel dutifully sent a letter requesting commissions for several men who had distinguished themselves at Port Republic.[13]

Among those recuperating back home was George Milledge, Joseph Diltz's brother-in-law. With surprising candor Diltz wrote his wife, "Tell Gorg to not cum back here if he can help it at all. Tell him he can beg off if he tryes. If I was him I would never cum back to virginia for it is the dams place in the world." Toward the close of the letter, perhaps more fully realizing the gravity of his words, he cautioned her to not "let eny person see this at all not eny person on acount of gorg or about what I sed about him for it would not do for eny body to see it that would let it bee nown."[14]

The Sixty-sixth was not entirely content with developments on the home front. Yet another regiment, the 95th Ohio Volunteer Infantry, was being recruited in Champaign County; its quota of two companies from the county was detracting from efforts to garner new enlistments for the depleted Sixty-sixth. Coincidentally, there were rumors at home questioning the worth and ability of the Sixty-sixth's officers, particularly Colonel Candy, to whom a lack of concern for his men was imputed. In a July 17 dispatch to the *Citizen and Gazette* W. A. Brand observed, "The members of the regiment are wondering just now, why a certain class at home, *interest* themselves so much about our officers. We feel deeply the attempt that is being made by them to crush out what is left of us, by these soreheads who were so disappointed at their failure to procure offices in the organization of the regiment."[15] In a subsequent letter he continued in a similar vein:

> We have been expecting some favorable news from the recruiting business in Champaign but from the manner the Military Committee have called for recruits to fill up the 95th Regiment, it appears the 66th is not much interested in the recruits in the county. The Military Board are certainly or ought to be as much interested in filling up this regiment, as making a new one, unless there is something "behind the bush." I am sure that the general understanding of the people is not that regiments are made up, to give positions to the officers. They generally believe that regiments are gotten up for some other purpose and it is better to keep the regiments already out in the field, in a condition to perform service.[16]

Brand may also have heard of further Urbana shenanigans from his father-in-law, *Citizen and Gazette* editor Joshua Saxton, who had written to Governor Tod to voice his concerns over some local recruiting practices. A local worthy was "taking and uniforming men, some of whom have enlisted in almost every company that has been organized here, and have been *rejected* as unfit for service." He was then apparently billing the government for the uniforms, garnering a small profit in the bargain. "It is no doubt a *swindle* in a small way and should not be allowed," concluded Saxton.[17]

The regiment mobilized itself to refute the attacks on Colonel Candy. Twenty-nine company and staff officers signed an affidavit dated July 3 denouncing as "malicious slander" the imputation that the colonel had anything but the best interests of his regiment at heart, concluding that it was "a compliment to his worth that the only whisper to the contrary can only bespoken hundreds of miles from where he can know of it." The statement was published in the *Citizen and Gazette* together with a corroborating testimonial from Brigadier General Tyler. On the same page was a letter from the captain of Company I, Versalius Horr, who had returned to his home in Mechanicsburg only to find scurrilous rumors circulating as to his behavior at Port Republic—perhaps questioning how he came to be hiding in the river at the conclusion of the battle. These reports Horr denounced as originating with "cowards who are content to remain at a great distance from the smell of the enemy's powder" as well as "enemies of the Union." An affidavit of support was appended signed by Colonel Candy and eleven other officers of the Sixty-sixth.[18]

Meanwhile, camp life continued with drills and the occasional special event. Lincoln was expected on July 23; however, the president was not present for the planned review, which continued without him. On the morning following the review the Sixty-sixth received orders to prepare three days' rations and be ready to move at noon with the rest of Banks's force. Noon came and went without further orders; finally, at 5:00 P.M. the soldiers learned that they were to board the freight cars the following afternoon for Warrenton. This they did on July 25, but they made only indifferent progress on the railroad, not reaching Warrenton until early the next morning.

The brigade made camp on the outskirts of town and began preparations for an overland march. Each regiment was provided with fifteen wagons and the mules to pull them, but provisions beyond the usual rationed fare were scarce. General Pope had banished sutlers from his army, and so hardtack became the unvarying staple for many soldiers.

The Sixty-sixth left Warrenton early in the morning on July 31, crossing the Rappahannock at the village of Waterloo. Here the men noticed the absence of the woolens factory whose English owners had professed both poverty and Union sympathies the last time the regiment had passed through the village. In the interim other Federal troops had discovered Confederate uniforms at the factory and burned it to the ground.[19] In the afternoon the troops set up camp at Amissville, setting out the next morning for Little Washington, Virginia, which they reached the same day. There they were once again within sight of the Blue Ridge Mountains, running north and south on the western horizon.

W. A. Brand noted an incident that, while not involving a man from the Sixty-sixth, was apparently the talk of the brigade. A soldier from the 5th Ohio and a slave, caught attempting to steal chickens, had been ordered by General Tyler to be tied to a tree face to face. This tree was located only a few feet from a porch upon which were seated General

Tyler and two "secesh ladies," whose property he was protecting. Brand hotly proclaimed that when Tyler "insults the honor of a private's position, and debases his manhood, by lashing him to a negro he oversteps his bounds."[20] It was an irony of the war that to be tied to a slave would be considered especially insulting by the white soldiers whose efforts and suffering—indeed, whose deaths—would contribute to the emancipation of the African race.

Tyler was not to be with the brigade much longer. Shortly after arriving at Little Washington, he and his staff reported to Washington for a new assignment. The Sixty-sixth was thereupon folded into a new brigade, with their old companions in the 5th, 7th, and 29th, together with the 28th Pennsylvania. Brigade command was given to John White Geary, the original colonel of the Pennsylvania regiment. If Brand's comments on this turn of events may be taken as representative, the Ohio troops were not likely to have relished coming under the command of a newcomer to the brigade—and an easterner at that:

> Again we are brought under the command of an Eastern man, who has no sympathy whatever with Western troops. The Western men will fight bravely under an officer whom they like, and in whom they have confidence, but to seek a General in Pennsylvania, of all the States, does not accord with their ideas at all. We have seen too many Pennsylvania troops already, for our confidence in their fighting abilities.[21]

Brand's objections were understandable, influenced though they were by sectional bias. Even so, Geary was a formidable man, standing at six feet five inches and weighing over two hundred pounds. He had seen combat in the Mexican War at the head of a Pennsylvania regiment. He had accepted the governorship of Kansas, working to bring order out of the chaos then prevailing in that unfortunate territory, adopting an antislavery stance even though it put his life in jeopardy. Upon the fall of Sumter, he had immediately tendered his services to the government and was given authority to raise a regiment. Such was the regard in which he was held by his fellow Pennsylvanians that sixty-six companies were said to have sent applications to serve under him. So it was that his regiment, the 28th Pennsylvania, was allowed fifteen companies. Through much of the early war period the 28th had a gargantuan appearance and was sometimes mistaken for a brigade. For its own part, the Sixty-sixth would have a long association with Geary.[22]

John W. Geary. *Massachusetts Commandery Military Order of the Loyal Legion and USAMHI.*

General Tyler made his final farewells, personally addressing each of the Ohio regiments in turn. Although his discipline had been sometimes thought too harsh, none questioned his bravery.

While at Little Washington, some of the Sixty-sixth were detached to guard Banks's cattle herd. Among these were Company K's Pvt. William Sayre, who wrote with some satisfaction to his father on August 6 that "if we stay in this business we will draw extry Pay. . . . All we haft to do is to stand gard one day out of ten and when we are not on gard we Can go and Come when we please."[23]

But the men of the Sixty-sixth had not been recruited as cattle drovers. They were now seasoned veterans, and their job was to put down the Southern rebellion, a task that involved killing and being killed. Their old nemesis Stonewall Jackson was nearby.

10

Cedar Mountain: Thy Work and Thy Warfare Done

*R*obert E. Lee had flung his army at McClellan on the Peninsula and pushed the Federals to Harrison's Landing. Having disposed of McClellan for the time being, Lee focused on John Pope's Army of Virginia. Lee was especially indignant over Pope's order mandating the expulsion of civilians outside Federal lines unless they took the oath of allegiance, and also over his command to seize provisions from Southern civilians without reimbursement. In mid-July this coarse Northerner was roaming about Lee's beloved Virginia with an army of forty-five thousand, possibly threatening Richmond. Lee dispatched Jackson to monitor Pope's activities (though he did not at first allot the Confederate hero of the Shenandoah sufficient forces to offer much of a fight). Lee sent reinforcements to Jackson in late July, voicing the hope that Jackson would help to "suppress" Pope. With the arrival of these reinforcements, Stonewall, if presented with the opportunity, might be able to mangle a portion or portions of Pope's army, even if he could not take on the entire Army of Virginia. Jackson established his headquarters at Gordonsville.

His old adversary Banks, whose army was approximately thirty-five miles north of Gordonsville, moved south, separated from the rest of Pope's army. The Sixty-sixth struck its tents on August 6 and marched from Little Washington with the rest of Banks's corps for Culpeper, which it reached the evening of August 8. Having determined that Banks was on his own, Jackson advanced north to offer battle. The Confederate force outnumbered Banks twenty-two thousand to twelve thousand, but Banks, who did not count timidity among his faults, appeared willing to accept the challenge.[1]

The morning of August 9 found the men of the Sixty-sixth cooking breakfast and speculating as to whether they would once again be pitted against Jackson. The answer came soon. They were ordered to pitch their tents and line up in formation for roll call; at noon they began their march through Culpeper south toward Cedar Mountain.

They marched four miles, which put them, after passing through a wooded area, within sight of Cedar Mountain to their left and front. It was about half past one. Federal batteries were already dueling with the enemy artillery in their front and on a forward shoulder of the mountain. At about four o'clock the Sixty-sixth formed with the rest of Augur's division east of Mitchell's Station Road, paralleling their front. Beyond the road was a rolling cornfield, on the opposite side of which, a little over half a mile away, were two Confederate infantry brigades.[2]

The 28th Pennsylvania, the largest regiment in Geary's brigade, was detached to reestablish a signaling position at Thoroughfare Mountain from which Federal Signal officers had been driven. This left the four Ohio regiments on their own. To Geary's left was Henry Prince's brigade, made up of the 3d Maryland, the 102d New York, the 109th and 11th Pennsylvania, and the 8th and 12th U.S. Infantry Battalion. This last-named unit of regulars went forward into the cornfield as skirmishers. The tall corn afforded them some concealment as they harried the Confederate infantry and artillery positions before them.

Geary's brigade advanced into the cornfield around five o'clock, the Sixty-sixth and 7th Ohio making up the forward line, the Sixty-sixth on the left. The 5th and the 29th Ohio advanced behind them, the 29th positioned behind the Sixty-sixth. Prince's brigade advanced simultaneously on Geary's left. Although the advancing Federal troops were well screened by the tall corn, they could not escape the artillery fire from the mountain and their front. The shelling became so fierce that the men were ordered to lie down. As the shells played about them, the men of the Sixty-sixth hugged the ground "as closely as circumstances and soil would permit, some even digging holes in the ground to let their faces down." They remained in this position for about an hour and then continued their advance.[3]

The terrain gradually inclined upward to the Confederate position, which was being reinforced by yet another brigade even as the Federals were advancing through the cornfield. The enemy reinforcements positioned themselves on the Southern right and front about where an advanced Confederate battery was shelling the approaching Federals from a cedar grove. The enemy position was augmented on its left by a brigade positioned in an L-shaped formation in an adjacent wood: its short end faced across the cornfield and the open slope leading up to the Confederate lines. Thus the Federal attack faced enfilading fire from its right, near-enfilading fire from its left, and plunging artillery fire from the mountain, in addition to the musketry of the two double-ranked brigades in the immediate front.

Adding to the troops' discomfiture was the extreme heat. Candy later recalled that it was the hottest day he had ever experienced in the field and that he had "never known troops to suffer more for water, and what little we could get had to be strained through our handkerchiefs into our mouths so as to wet our parched lips."[4]

When Geary's brigade resumed its advance, the carnage among the Ohio troops was tremendous. As the Sixty-sixth left more and more casualties in its wake, it closed to the right, and the 5th Ohio moved from behind to take a place on the Sixty-sixth's left. The Ohioans continued forward and, upon emerging from the cornfield, began trading fire with the Confederate line, advancing a few yards and then falling back—repeating the forward and backward movements several times, firing continuously.[5]

Some of the regiment's officers, at least those on staff, went into battle mounted; Colonel Candy had two horses shot out from under him. One officer in particular, however, appeared to attract the attention of many: twenty-year-old 2d Lt. James Robert Murdoch of Company G. Murdoch was acting as regimental adjutant sergeant major and in that capacity seemed practically everywhere on the battlefield. W. A. Brand later recalled that he was "represented as the coolest officer on the field. During the hottest moments when bullets were whizzing past him and shell and grape flying thick and fast all round, he remained seated upon his horse and demeaned himself in a soldierly manner."[6]

Prince's brigade, advancing on the left of Geary's Ohioans, experienced some confusion. Like that of Geary, Prince's advance was in double line, the 3d Maryland and the 11th Pennsylvania to the left of the Ohioans. Prince, however, was advancing en echelon—in other words, the right regiment of the second line was behind the left regiment of the front line. Although the rear regiments had been ordered to fire to the front and left from the corn, thus sparing their comrades immediately before them, their volleys surprised the front-rank soldiers, who thought the fire was coming from unseen hostile forces in their rear. Many thereupon fled.

After the discomfiture and confusion of Prince's men on Geary's left, a Federal charge on his right found a gap in the Confederate line, flanking and dispersing an enemy brigade that had been firing upon the Ohioans from the woods. The flank attack rolled up the Confederate line in front of the Ohioans. For a few minutes it appeared that the outnumbered Federals might turn the tables on Jackson to seize an upset victory, but this was not to be. Jackson himself rallied his retreating men, even as reinforcements arrived to repulse the Federal attack.

The weight of superior Confederate numbers now began to make itself felt. The survivors of the Federal flanking movement made their way back singly and in small groups as a reinvigorated Southern line pushed forward, once again setting up batteries and punishing the Ohioans in its front with shell and grapeshot. At the onset of dusk Candy observed that the Union forces on his right and left were in retreat or nowhere to be seen; he ordered his much diminished regiment, consisting now of little more than sixty men, to withdraw back through the cornfield.[7]

The retreat continued beyond the Sixty-sixth's position at the beginning of the battle, taking what remained of the regiment back across Cedar Run and into woods on the opposite bank. As the regiment retreated Candy remarked on the shells as they passed over and about his men, observing to his officers that this one was not coming their direction or that that one would pass them by. Then came a sputtering shell that Candy diagnosed as an immediate danger: he yelled, "Down boys! There's one coming right at us." He and his staff dived to the ground, and the shell exploded six feet away.[8]

On the edge of the woods Candy found a jumble of survivors from the 5th, 7th, and 29th Ohio regiments and learned that both Geary and Augur had been wounded. Also, Prince had been captured. Finding him-

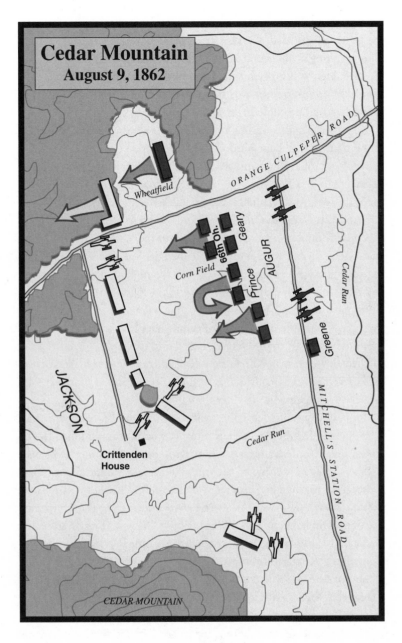

Cedar Mountain
August 9, 1862

self therefore in command of the brigade, Candy led his men out of the
woods and reported personally to Banks, who ordered him to return to
the timber to establish a forward night position. Preceded by Captain
Van Deman and an advance guard of ten or twelve skirmishers, the

Sixty-sixth made its way toward the darkened woods. Van Deman took the center of the road, with his men spread out on either side of him. Upon arriving at the woods' edge, the Ohioans were surprised by calls for surrender. When the men did not throw down their weapons, they were fired upon from the woods by Confederates. Those who were not shot down had no choice but to hide or run. His regiment diminished even further, Candy returned to Banks to report this latest repulse. He found that General Pope himself had arrived upon the scene; the army's commander told him simply to "place [the] men where they could rest for the night."[9] When one of the regiment's supply wagons caught up to the Sixty-sixth that evening, it found only sixteen men; the commissary sergeant distributed the surplus to hungry men in other regiments.

Cedar Mountain exacted a heavy toll on the Sixty-sixth, which had entered the battle with 250 men and concluded the day with little more than a handful present or accounted for. Overnight and during the next day more soldiers found their way back to the Sixty-sixth, but the casualty figures were still bad: ten killed, eighty-one wounded, and three captured.[10] That the number of killed and captured was no higher was attributable in part to the efficient evacuation of the wounded from the battlefield, which spared them capture or further injury. Of the wounded, eight would eventually die, and another thirty would soon leave the service as a consequence of their wounds.

The night ambush cost the regiment some officers. Captain Van Deman, who led the skirmishers into the woods, was wounded by the ambush; the Confederates seized him, with the words, "You are the man we want." (Later, writing to his wife, the captain would take a philosophical approach to his capture: "You must not be low spirited as this is the fate of war and I am no better than others. . . . But you know 'accidents will happen,' and my fate is this." He would resign his commission in early 1863, after his exchange.) Company A's Captain McConnell was separated from his comrades in the darkness but hid in the brush until he could make his way back to the Federal encampment. Captain McMorran of Company C, who had barely recuperated from his Port Republic neck wound, was shot in the right foot; he too would soon have to resign his commission. Two, perhaps three, lieutenants were also wounded. Among these were Company B's Duncan McDonald, who had written to his father of coming through Port Republic "without a scratch." He died from chest wounds six days after Cedar Mountain; his body was shipped back to Urbana and buried in the town cemetery.[11]

Charles Fulton, attorney and Republican activist and now a major, was wounded in his left side. Due to complications from his wound and severe chronic laryngitis, he was to resign his commission in December; in Ohio he would specialize for a time in the submission of pension claims.[12] Also among the wounded was the regiment's oldest enlisted man: William Sullivan, the potter from Mutual, injured by a shell burst. He was discharged for wounds in the groin and the abdomen.

Among those who escaped unscathed was George Milledge, who despite the advice of his brother-in-law Joseph Diltz had returned to the regiment after recuperating from his illness. A spent ball hit him in the chest but did not even break the skin. Diltz himself was sick and remained behind the lines in an ambulance wagon.[13]

Characteristically, the battle provided examples of the curious, if not grotesque, paths a minié ball could take within a human body. James McKittrick of Company F was shot in the neck; the bullet entered just below the left ear lobe, traveled down and beneath the skin, and emerged at about the middle of the chest. E. L. Small, a civilian delegated to look after Champaign County's wounded, later described the wound of Pvt. Stephen Brush of Company B: "Ball entered cheek bone, passed forward under the nose, carrying away the ligaments. . . . Bad for good looks." Both men recovered from their wounds, eventually returning to the regiment.[14]

Not so acting Sgt. Maj. Samuel Clark, who was shot near the ear, the minié ball traveling around the head and coming out near the other ear. He was one of the few wounded from the Sixty-sixth left on the field, where he lay two days before being discovered. By that time Confederate soldiers, perhaps thinking him dead, had stripped him of his clothes. He eventually recovered, but not sufficiently to resume service; he was discharged on disability.

Pvt. David Espy was another soldier of the Sixty-sixth who was left on the field. He had a different experience from Clark, later reporting in his diary, "Rebels al round me, verry kind gave me water sead they were sory I was wounded."[15]

The day after the battle an armistice was declared for the burial of the dead. Quartermaster Brand and Adjutant Murdoch rode out to the battlefield, going as far as the slope occupied by their foes the previous day. There they encountered Jubal Early, who had commanded one of the brigades facing them during the battle, and his staff. Brand and Murdoch attempted a currency exchange, hoping to receive U.S. bills for Confederate notes, but the Confederate officers insisted they held no greenbacks. As was usual in such encounters, the officers debated the causes and outcome of the war, after which they took leave of one another with the exchange of courteous wishes that each be preserved "personally" from harm in future battles.[16]

The two officers also came upon a squad of some twenty Louisiana Tigers, with whom the Sixty-sixth had fought for the coaling battery at Port Republic. Conversation inevitably turned to that battle. The two Ohioans made a point of informing their foes that the abandonment of the battery had been caused by Confederate reinforcements, not the final charge of the Tigers.[17]

With Candy commanding the brigade, Lieutenant Colonel Powell assumed leadership of the Sixty-sixth. This arrangement would stay in place for most of the war. The brigade was reviewed two days after the battle; W. A. Brand observed that no company had enough men to mount a color guard and that Company B was represented by a single private.[18]

The wounded meanwhile were being transported to the hospitals surrounding Washington, where their needs were ministered to by E. L. Small, Champaign County's latest representative in the capital area's hospitals. In an August 19 letter from Alexandria he described the conditions of the Sixty-sixth's wounded of Cedar Mountain, listing Champaign County patients recovering in seven hospitals. He noted that "many of the patients are beginning to smell very bad," that were not most of the hospitals well ventilated "it would be impossible to stay in them." He particularly requested canned fruits for the wounded men; the patients were not, however, wanting for the basic necessities, which were available in great abundance. Even so, he was of the opinion that the nurses provided better treatment to patients whose recuperation was being monitored by outside observers.

In a similar vein, he expressed mild surprise that there was no one there to attend to the Sixty-sixth's wounded from Union or Delaware Counties (to whom he apparently felt no special obligation). The implication of his observation was that if a county's recruits were too small a minority in a regiment, the number of wounded would not be sufficient to generate organized assistance from home—yet another reason to enlist in a "local regiment."[19]

One of those reported on by Small was David Espy, who had been left on the field and received the succor of his foes. He had lost a leg but was given a "fair chance to recover." He did not; in less than a month he was dead. His body was shipped back to Champaign County for burial in Harrison Township, the headstone reading "Died of a wound received at Cedar Mountain while gallantly defending his country." Some months later there appeared a poem in the *Citizen and Gazette* dedicated to his memory:

> Thou didst leave the home in manhood's prime,
>   Thy life to lay at thy country's shrine;
> The pleasures of home were laid aside
>   For those which camp and field combine.
> Far from home thou didst meet thy doom
>   On "Cedar Mountain's" gory field,
> 'Mid battle's roar and cannons' boom,
>   'Twas there thy fate was sealed.
> But yet we hoped for thy return,
>   But O! our hopes were crushed,
> Alas! with sadness did we learn
>   Thy voice in death was hushed.
> Thou art gone! dear loved one—gone,
>   No more shall we behold thee,
> No more await the absent one,
>   Loving arms shall ne'er enfold thee.
> Thy wife in sadness weeps for thee,
>   Thy darling boy still lisps thy name;
> Although thy face he ne'er shall see,
>   He calls for thee! but calls in vain.
> Many friends do miss thee here,
>   Yet why do we repine and grieve?
> Why not suppress the falling tear?
>   And hope thou'rt gone to Heaven to live.
> Dear One! thou hast entered thy rest,
>   Thy work and thy warfare done;
> We hope thou art numbered with the blest,
>   "That the day of thy joy is begun."
> Sleep on, dear David, blessed sleep,
>   From which thou wilt ne'er wake to weep;
> We hope at last in Heaven to meet thee,
>   For 'tis there we hope to greet thee.

The poem was signed simply "Sallie."[20]

11

A Look of Horror and of Desolation

The Sixty-sixth had been seriously battered at Port Republic, and the casualties of Cedar Mountain weakened the regiment even further. Disease continued to deplete its ranks as well. Of these cases the most tragic was that of James Robert Murdoch, who as acting adjutant had so distinguished himself at Cedar Mountain. His father, an Urbana doctor, received word that the young soldier was down with fever and had been transferred to a hospital at Alexandria, Virginia. Doctor Murdoch took the first train east, hoping to attend his son personally, only to be informed upon his arrival that the young man had become delirious and blown out his brains with a revolver. The body was shipped back to Urbana. The Sixty-sixth's chaplain (surnamed Parsons, aptly enough) was on hand to conduct the funeral service.[1]

The mourners may have seen little difference between young Murdoch's death and the slaughter which had claimed the lives of so many local men that summer in Virginia. The Southern rebellion seemed no closer to suppression despite their many sacrifices. McClellan's campaign against Richmond had been in vain; Jackson had outmaneuvered and outfought the armies sent against him in the Shenandoah Valley; and in late August John Pope's Army of Virginia had suffered disaster in a battle fought on the site of the previous summer's engagement at Manassas. Jackson had hoped to catch part of Pope's army and defeat it in detail. He had done so.

After mauling Banks at Cedar Mountain, Jackson had returned to Lee; together they devised a plan for the destruction of Pope's main army. Lee sent Jackson with a Confederate force of twenty-four thousand on a daring envelopment; on August 26 Jackson's troops came down in a forced march on Pope's rear, severing his line of communications and destroying the Federal supply depot at Manassas Junction. Responding to the raid, Pope sought out Jackson's force, hoping to "bag" Stonewall before he could rejoin the rest of Lee's army. Outnumbered, Jackson nevertheless gave battle; Pope assaulted the Confederate position in a series of uncoordinated attacks on August 29 near the Bull Run battlefield of 1861. Victory seemed within Pope's grasp until the next day, when he was confronted with the surprise arrival of the rest of Lee's army, under James Longstreet. The reinforcements hit the Federal left and sent Pope into retreat.

Fortunately for the Sixty-sixth, Banks's corps had little to do with this latest Federal defeat. Following Cedar Mountain, on August 12, his much reduced force had gone into camp at Culpeper Court House. A week later Banks's corps decamped and marched to the Rappahannock, and for the next several days it stayed in the vicinity of the river. Eventually it moved up the Orange and Alexandria Railroad behind Porter's corps to form the extreme left of Pope's army as he attempted to come to grips with Jackson. Nonetheless, when Pope made first contact with Jackson in the opening act of the Second Battle of Manassas, Banks was too far away to take part. The Sixty-sixth, which with the rest of its brigade was assigned to guard the army's wagon trains, was spared participation in yet another Union debacle.

Just before the battle, the brigade had passed through Manassas Junction two or three days after a destructive Confederate raid. W. A. Brand described the scene: "[Railroad] cars, pork barrels, boxes, buttons, dead bodies, and horses were all in promiscious [sic] heaps, and the dull glare of still burning houses and ruins gave the scene a look of horror and of desolation."[2] During the next two days Brand could hear and at times see the progress of the great battle. Pope's defeat and subsequent retreat left Banks cut off from the main army; however, a forced march from Bristoe Station to Fairfax via Brentsville placed the corps out of harm's way.

Although spared another battle, the men of the Sixty-sixth had had a rough time of it. Their diet during the two weeks of marching consisted largely of green corn and green apples. Many were without tents and blankets. There were the usual stragglers, some of whom were scooped up by Confederate patrols. Among them were Company C's French-born Celestian Saintignon, who was subsequently initiated into the mysteries of the newly devised parole system. When applying for a pension many years later (in a necessarily self-interested account) he declared the following:

> I was captured while a member of Co. "C" 66 O.V.I. at Manassas Junc. Va. about Aug. 1862. Was paroled next day, at this time I had no knowledge of the English Language. I did not know to whom I should report. Myself and others who had been paroled went (or I rather followed) first to Harpers Ferry, thence to Cumberland and thence to Columbus, O., came home, and worked on the farm, went where and when I pleased, until arrested by a provost marshal in July 1863.[3]

Saintignon was then transported about between a number of stockades in several states until he broke guard, returned to Ohio, and enlisted in another regiment under an assumed name.

And so the regiment, sans Monsieur Saintignon (and no doubt a few other men), arrived with the rest of the brigade in the vicinity of Fort Richardson north of Alexandria. On September 4 the corps crossed the Potomac and marched to Tenallytown, Maryland, moving on the next day to Rockville.

The Sixty-sixth was now in a much altered chain of command. Pope's defeat had earned him a transfer west to confront the Sioux in Minnesota. Banks's health had failed him, and he had been replaced as corps commander by Alpheus S. Williams (who would command only briefly but would later emerge as one of the Union army's most capable combat leaders). Banks's (now Williams's) corps itself had become the Twelfth Corps of the Army of the Potomac, commanded by George McClellan, whose star had risen once again, in direct proportion to the decline of Pope's. Shortly after the integration of his corps into the Army of the

Potomac, Williams was replaced by the fifty-nine-year-old Joseph K. F. Mansfield, a Connecticut-born regular army man who had been with the military ever since his 1822 graduation from West Point, and for whom corps command satisfied a deep and earnest ambition.

George Sears Greene, a Rhode Island native, was promoted from brigade to division command to replace Augur, wounded at Cedar Mountain. Born in 1801, Greene was one of the Union army's older general officers. He had graduated from West Point in 1823 and in 1836 had left the army for a civil engineer's career. At the outbreak of hostilities he had rejoined the military, and despite having been away from the service for twenty-five years he was still very much a no-nonsense regular. He was also proud of his New England roots and would become active in genealogical circles after the war.

The wounding of Geary at Cedar Mountain had resulted in Colonel Candy's elevation to brigade command, but his health failed him in early September, causing his departure. He was succeeded by Hector Tyndale in charge of what was now designated the First Brigade of the Second Division of the Twelfth Corps of the Army of the Potomac. Tyndale was the commanding officer of the 28th Pennsylvania—which, detached from the brigade before the Battle of Cedar Mountain, had been spared the slaughter of August 9. The Pennsylvania regiment, which had been larger than any of the Ohio regiments before Cedar Mountain, was now larger than all the Buckeye regiments combined.

Tyndale was from a Philadelphia family. His mother was a New Jersey Quaker (upon her account he had declined an appointment to West Point), but his politics were in accord with the increasingly militant tenor of the Northern war effort. He had early identified himself with the Free Soil party, the precursor of the Republicans, and though not a supporter of John Brown's raid, he had escorted Brown's wife south to see her husband at Charlestown and to bring back his body.[4]

In Candy's absence, the Sixty-sixth was under the command of Eugene Powell, who had previously succeeded the unfortunate James Dye (who in turn had left the regiment for good on May 26). Candy was well liked by his men, but Powell apparently did not suffer in comparison. W. A. Brand observed that he "enforces discipline easily, in a peculiar and pleasant way"; though "quiet and unassuming in his manners, everything moves under his control like clockwork." A predictably laudatory biographical sketch in a county "mug book" describes him in a similar vein, adding that he was "scrupulously neat in his personal appearance, it being noticed that when his regiment came in from a long march, tired and eager for rest, he was never too weary to first make himself tidy."[5]

This then was the chain of command for the Sixty-sixth: McClellan, Mansfield, Greene, Tyndale, Powell. It was the chain of command that would see them into yet another bloody encounter with Stonewall Jackson near a Maryland stream called Antietam Creek.

12

Antietam: Just Covered with Dirt and That Is All

*R*obert E. Lee had proven that he was nothing if not daring. Having thoroughly defeated Pope, he was not content to remain in Virginia to await yet another Federal army intent on capturing Richmond; Virginia had sacrificed enough. He would go north instead. The Army of Northern Virginia would invade Maryland and possibly Pennsylvania, where he might garner Northern supplies for his men. Perhaps more Marylanders would be inspired to throw in their lot with the Confederacy. The Union armies around Washington should now be demoralized and ripe for another drubbing, which would leave Baltimore, Philadelphia, or even Washington itself open for capture, possibly leading to European recognition of the Confederacy and the end of the war.

George McClellan had already met Lee before Richmond, where he was repulsed in the series of battles known as the Seven Days. Cautious when Lee was audacious, seeing obstacles everywhere, McClellan was nevertheless possessed of the notion that he was to be the country's savior, and he knew that to save the country he must defeat Lee. Nonetheless, he would not act rashly. He wanted the certitude of a clear strategic advantage.

This certitude was to come to him courtesy of an anonymous, cigar-smoking member of the Confederate general's staff. By the second week of September Lee was threatening an invasion of the north, but his exact whereabouts were unknown. A Federal force was sent west to be in a position to counter Lee; in it was the Twelfth Corps (within which was the Sixty-sixth Ohio). Various estimates survive of the Sixty-sixth's strength as it entered the battle of Antietam, Powell himself providing three different figures at various points in his life; however, in his official report he set the regiment's strength at only 120 men.[1] The Twelfth Corps reached Frederick, Maryland, on September 13, bivouacking on a site occupied by Confederate forces the day before. A soldier of the 27th Indiana discovered what appeared to be a Confederate order wrapped around a packet of cigars. It was conveyed to Alpheus Williams, who was waiting to be relieved of corps command. Headed "Special Orders 191," the document came from Lee's headquarters; it detailed the division of his army as a prelude to the capture of Harpers Ferry. The order was brought to McClellan, who for once was not reluctant to seize an advantage. If he moved quickly, he could attack Lee's force while it was divided and destroy it in detail.

The Federal armies turned west, hoping to catch part of the Confederate army at Hagerstown while the remainder under Jackson was besieging the Harpers Ferry garrison to the south. Standing in the way of the Federal advance was the division of Confederate general D. H. Hill, known for his fighting spirit and deep aversion to Yankees. Hill made his stand at Turner's Gap at South Mountain, holding two Federal corps at bay on September 14 and then withdrawing from the field in the night.

The Twelfth Corps passed over the battlefield the following day—the Harpers Ferry garrison was surrendering to Jackson that very morning—and the men observed the carnage left in the wake of the previous day's fight. The corps proceeded west and bivouacked near Keedysville, a short distance from Antietam Creek. On September 16 the Army of the Potomac continued to concentrate its forces, preparing to attack Lee the following day. McClellan, with the troops he brought up that day, could have defeated Lee, who was still without much of his army. The Confederate commander, however, drew up his forces in battle array as though his entire army were at hand. McClellan hesitated. Once again Lee had bluffed his opponent, allowing more time for the Harpers Ferry expedition to rejoin him.

The men of Tyndale's brigade remained at Keedysville throughout the day, the Army of the Potomac coming up and concentrating all about them. They had the sensation of being a small island surrounded by a swelling blue river. One of the Sixty-sixth's comrades in the 7th Ohio observed: "Everywhere the brigades and divisions of the other corps were going into position. As far as the view extended were regiments, many of them closed en masse on close column by division that looked like solid squares, with their colors in the center. It was a grand, a memorable sight."[2]

At day's end the men ate their evening meal and fell asleep under the stars. At eleven o'clock they were roused and told to fall in. Alpheus Williams recalled the night: it was "so dark, so obscure, so mysterious, so uncertain; with the occasional rapid volleys of pickets and outposts, the low solemn sound of the command as troops came into position, and withal so sleepy that there was a half-dreamy sensation about it all."[3] Noiselessly the brigade marched into the night, crossing a bridge spanning the Antietam. At about two in the morning they arrived at John Poffenberger's farm, their jumping-off point for the next day's battle.

The men were awakened again before daybreak and told to make coffee. As the sun rose, the artillery on both sides opened up, adding smoke to the patches of September fog settling into the low spots of the gently rolling landscape.

A little over a mile to the south of Tyndale's brigade was a low, whitewashed brick structure. It was a church belonging to the German Baptist Brethren, a pacifist sect known as the "Dunkers" for their belief in total baptismal immersion. Their house of worship was to become a focal point of the bloodiest single day in the Civil War. Set on the edge of a copse known in the battle as the West Woods, the church was located on a low plateau overlooking the spot where the Smoketown Road angled in from the northeast to intersect with the Hagerstown Turnpike, running north and south. To the northeast of the church dipped a field of clover and a low pasture, while to the north of these was a cornfield. To the east of the pasture and cornfield was a woodlot, the East Woods.

In and around the West Woods and in front of the Dunker Church were the men of Jackson's corps, some of them tired and only just come up from Harpers Ferry at quick march. The Confederate line was not tightly knit; its elements were positioned in strategic spots to take advantage of the terrain. Between Mansfield's Twelfth Corps and these Confederates were the men of the First Corps, commanded by Joe Hooker, whose headquarters were at a farm owned by another Poffenberger. Hooker was to lead the assault on Jackson, whose men formed the left of the Confederate line.

Hooker's target was clear: the Dunker Church. To take it and the plateau on which it rested could spell the collapse of the Confederate position. The assault began almost at dawn as the First Corps moved south, paralleling the course of the Hagerstown Turnpike. It met determined resistance, with some of the bloodiest fighting surging back and forth through the cornfield. The Confederate line was severely battered, but it held. The men of the Sixty-sixth heard heavy firing, but the rising smoke obscured further what little visibility the misty landscape afforded. Wounded from the First Corps began to trickle back with word that Hooker had been repulsed. Just as some of the men were taking their coffee off the fire, Mansfield rode up and gave the order to fall in without delay. Still clutching coffee cups and blowing on them in an effort to cool them, the soldiers of Tyndale's brigade got into formation and marched south toward the fighting "close column by regiments," the 7th Ohio in the front and the Sixty-sixth behind it. As the brigade advanced it was subjected to skirmishing fire coming out of the East Woods—from the Texans of John Bell Hood, soon to be supported by a brigade of North Carolinians. Tyndale's brigade deployed to the right; the sequence from right to left was the 7th, Sixty-sixth, and 5th Ohio, with the enormous 28th Pennsylvania on the left making up half the brigade's front. The regimental commanders were mounted; Eugene Powell rode to the right of his regiment, advancing side by side with the 7th Ohio's Maj. Orrin Crane, who was riding on his regiment's left.

The two officers chatted as they rode forward, peering into the mist for some clue of the enemy's position. Suddenly to their left and front they saw a line of infantry behind a rail fence not thirty yards away. The line's attention seemed directed to the northwest, not seeing the Ohio troops approaching through the mist on its right. Powell identified them as the enemy and was about to give the command to fire; Crane disagreed, thinking they were Union troops. Powell recalled, "Thus for an instant we struggled, I to get in the first volley, and Crane to convince me that I was mistaken."[4] Powell prevailed, and the Sixty-sixth fired into the mist at the line of men before them. The other Ohio regiments joined in.

Powell's assessment had been correct. It was a Georgia brigade, which amazingly was unaware of the Ohio regiments until it was fired upon. Meanwhile, the 28th Pennsylvania under Tyndale was making its way through the East Woods, scattering the Confederate forces there. When the Pennsylvanians emerged from the trees, they added their fire to the Ohioans', catching the Georgians in the rear. The 6th Georgia, which took the brunt of the assault, would suffer 90 percent casualties by the end of the day. The survivors fled in confusion; many surrendered.

The Sixty-sixth and the rest of the brigade rushed forward. Jubilant at finding themselves in the role of the pursuer for a change, the Ohioans pushed down fence rails as they chased their retreating foes. Powell guided his horse toward one of the breaks in the fence, but the animal resisted passing over the mounds of enemy dead, delaying his progress as the men under his command dashed through the cornfield and into the pasture beyond it.

Their advance brought them to a knoll across the road from the Dunker Church. This high ground, a continuation of the low plateau upon which the church rested, provided some cover for the Federals from artillery fire now being directed against them. Tyndale's force, joined by another brigade from the same division, achieved a lodgment in what had been the Confederate line, but the position was tenuous: the brigades were low on ammunition and needed artillery support. Both were in the offing. Their division commander, the crusty General Greene, had seen the significance of what had been accomplished and was having ammunition brought up; he personally escorted a six-gun battery from his native Rhode Island. The battery arrived on the left of the brigade, and the appearance of Greene, with a bearing "so heroic and knightly," excited the admiration of the troops, who stood and cheered him under fire; Greene responded by rising in his stirrups and lifting his hat. One of the artillerymen shouted, "Hold your place there, boys, and we will stand by you while there is a shot in the locker!"[5]

The battery's arrival was timely. Out of the woods north of the church came a line of Confederate infantry, men of Joseph Kershaw's South Carolina brigade. They were allowed to approach closely before the Union troops rose and fired, their volley joined by the fire of the newly arrived battery. The Confederate line was smashed and retreated into the woods. Soon another enemy brigade dashed out of the woods to attack the Federal position; it was accorded the same reception, with like result. The Union troops pursued into the woods and established a battle line beyond the Dunker Church.

Before the advance into the woods, unidentified Federal troops—perhaps from the Second Corps—had attempted an attack on the woods to the Ohioans' right but had been repulsed. Tyndale, whose horse had been shot out from under him, ordered Powell, the only officer still mounted, to ride over to attempt to rally the retreating troops. Powell tried to do as directed, though he failed to accomplish much; riding back to the brigade, he invited the attention of Rebel marksmen. The well-groomed Powell recalled afterward that the fire cut his cravat from his neck and that two balls passed through his coat collar. (A "cravat" was a leather collar fastened by a buckle, often referred to contemptuously as a "dog collar" and almost never worn by the soldiers.[6] Powell was one of the few soldiers who appears actually to have worn this article.) Eventually a shot took effect, grazing his jaw and neck, just missing the jugular vein. The lieutenant colonel was able to ride back to a field hospital, where a surgeon informed him that "there was the thickness of thin paper between me and eternity."[7]

Powell did not miss much more action on the Union right. Greene's division held its position in the woods until about half past one o'clock, when it became apparent that it was unsupported on both flanks and was threatened by Confederate envelopment. The position was abandoned, and Rebel troops pursued Greene's men back across the meadows south of the cornfield; however, the Federal batteries, still in position, covered the retreating Union troops. Alpheus Williams, acting as corps commander after the wounding of Mansfield earlier in the day, personally directed the fire of one of the batteries; its canister shot stopped the Confederate pursuit in its tracks and contributed yet another layer of corpses to an already bloody field. Greene's men regrouped and marched off to the rear, where they remained in reserve for the rest of the day.

The battle on the Federal right was over, and the fight moved on to the center and left. Although Lee would be hard pressed, the arrival of A. P. Hill's division from Harpers Ferry ultimately saved the Confederate position. The armies faced each other at nightfall with hundreds of dead and wounded lying between their lines.

That night the men of the Sixty-sixth slept on their arms, not knowing whether the fight would be renewed the next day. It was not. Lee lingered defiantly, but McClellan, true to his nature, was not inclined to reopen the contest. After a day of ineffectual posturing, the Army of Northern Virginia left in the night, leaving the field in the possession of McClellan, who was thus able to claim a victory.

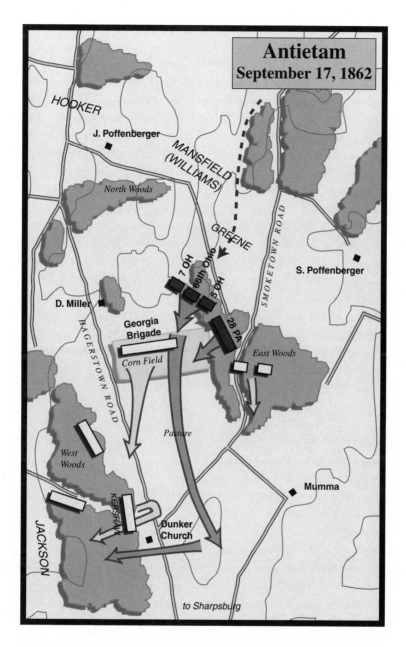

Antietam
September 17, 1862

The Sixty-sixth, which entered the battle with little more than a tenth of its original number, had only two commissioned officers present besides Powell, these being lieutenants from Companies E and I. The other companies were led by noncommissioned officers. Cpl. William Taylor was "senior officer" in Company G; he was wounded in both legs during the battle but would remain with the regiment, eventually attaining the rank of first lieutenant.

The regiment's casualties were not severe. This time the Sixty-sixth Ohio inflicted more damage than it received. Only one enlisted man had been killed in action, and Powell was the only officer wounded. Twenty-two enlisted men were wounded. Of these, seven would within a few months be discharged on account of their wounds, and three would soon die. One of the three was the youthful runaway Casper Mouser, who had defied his uncle in the pages of the *Citizen and Gazette*, challenging him to enlist along with him. He had suffered a leg wound, and it proved fatal.

The battle also exacted a toll on the command structure. Mansfield, the newly appointed corps commander, was shot in the chest at an early stage of the battle. He died the next morning, his longed-for command having spanned all of two days. Tyndale, who had three horses killed under him, had been shot in the head after the retreat from the Dunker Church woods; he would not be leading his brigade of Ohioans and Pennsylvanians again. The wound was at first thought fatal, but he was eventually to pull through. Eugene Powell's neck and face wounds proved superficial and did not deter him from retaining command of the Sixty-sixth, now numbering perhaps no more than one hundred effectives.

Most of the Army of the Potomac remained in place for the next several days, inheriting the task of burying the dead, which numbered well over five thousand. Some were found and buried by comrades, who might erect some identifying marker, but others were discovered by burial details and interred on the spot in unmarked graves. The graves were often shallow, and a stench lingered around the nearby village of Sharpsburg for many weeks.

Joseph Diltz survived the battle, writing afterward to his wife, "Mary, I went in to the fight in good hart but I never want to get in another. It was offal [awful] Mary. You cant form eny idy how it was. The bulets and cannon ball and shells flew as thick as hail."[8] In a letter to his father-in-law he was frank in describing the attitude of the soldiers toward the enemy dead:

> Pap it is very strang how indifernt the soldiers gets for the dead. We dont mind the sight of dead men no more than if they wair dead hogs. . . . Why their at Antietam the rebels was laying over the field bloated up as big as a horse and as black as a negro and the boys run over them and serch their pockets as unconcerned. I

was passing over the field too days after the [battle]. I was going through a cornfield and I ran acros a big grayback as black as the ase of spade. It started me a little at first but I stopd to see what he had but he had bin tended too and so I past on my way rejoicing.[9]

William Sayre wrote to his father from the battlefield that it was "awful to see how many poor felows sufered and died on that day. infact there are men lying within five rod of this place Just covered with dirt and that is all. here is a steep hill right here where there was several poor felows got tore almost to pieces by shell. here lies the remnants of there close [clothes] haversacks Canteens and so on where they have been torn by the shell." He inquired about the 95th Ohio, whether it had in fact as rumored been "cut to pieces in Kentucky" (it had), and closed with a mild rebuke: "Write soon and a little oftener if you please."[10]

13

Stand Off Mr. Secesh

A few days after Antietam, the 12th Corps left the Army of the Potomac and marched to Harpers Ferry. Following Mansfield's death, command of the corps went to Henry Warner Slocum. Born in New York, he was a West Point man who like many Academy graduates had not remained in the army; he had left it in 1856 to practice law and pursue a political career. As colonel commanding the 27th New York Volunteer Infantry, he had been seriously wounded at 1st Bull Run. Upon his recovery he had assumed brigade command, and on May 18, 1862, he received command of the Sixth Corps's First Division, which he led through the Peninsula and Antietam campaigns. He was a capable and intelligent man, if no military genius. Alpheus Williams, having been relieved of command of the corps, was a division commander once again—and perhaps somewhat resentful of the fact, writing after his first meeting with Slocum, "I like our new corps commander very much so far, though he does not strike me as of wonderful capacity."[1]

General Geary had recovered from his Cedar Mountain wounds and had been promoted from brigade command to the Second Division, a position vacated by the plucky old Rhode Island regular George Greene, who now commanded another brigade—the Third—in the Second

Division. Colonel Candy had by mid-October regained his health, and he was now in charge of the Second Division's 1st Brigade (including the Sixty-sixth), thus succeeding the wounded Tyndale. Eugene Powell retained command of the Sixty-sixth.

The men appear to have been satisfied with their commanders, although unsettling rumors continued to circulate of an imminent consolidation of the Sixty-sixth with another regiment. Consequently, returns of comrades from army hospitals or Confederate prison camps not only were occasions for joyful reunions but also decreased the likelihood that the depleted regiment would be a target for consolidation. W. A. Brand again noted with disapproval the practice of forming new regiments (with new officers' commissions) instead of returning veteran regiments to full strength with new recruits. "Soon must our regiment dwindle to nothing, or be consolidated with some worthier regiment of exchanged prisoners, perhaps," he grumbled.[2]

The Sixty-sixth was stationed on Loudoun Heights above Harpers Ferry, where only a few weeks earlier a garrison of over ten thousand Federals had surrendered to Jackson. The atmosphere was bracing, and the men took pleasure in the scenic confluence of the Shenandoah and Potomac Rivers beneath them. From that lofty vantage point a man with good field glasses could see Winchester and Martinsburg and sometimes even Strasburg.

The division commander at one point experimented with another means of obtaining a scenic view—and ostensibly reconnaissance—by ascending in one of Thaddeus Lowe's balloons. The intrepid Geary wrote to his wife that he "experienced no sensations of *giddiness,* and upon the whole if it had not been quite so windy, my aerial voyage would have been a rather pleasant one."[3]

The Sixty-sixth did not remain on Loudoun Heights. Its activity in the Harpers Ferry area consisted of various reconnaissances in force, as well as frequent skirmishing and changes of camp. Conditions in the regiment were improving. The Sixty-sixth was issued new Springfield rifles, replacing the Enfields and Belgian muskets it had received in Ohio. In mid-November the regimental fund purchased a bakery to supply daily fresh bread. Captain Palmer, returned on exchange following his capture at Port Republic, attempted to sink a well for the regiment's use; he struck solid rock at two feet but continued the work with explosive charges, scattering debris about the camp. "Water is predicted—when it rains," remarked a wry Brand.[4]

Another novelty was a feminine presence in camp. With the decreasing likelihood of hard campaigning as autumn deepened into winter, a few officers' wives came to join their husbands. The wife of Quartermaster Brand was one of these. Upon her arrival at the camp of the "good old 66th," she "saw many faces that were familiar at home; and then again I saw many that looked as though they had seen hard service." This was in late November, and the regiment was encamped on the southeastern slope of Bolivar Heights. Increasingly the camp was acquiring a look of permanence, reflecting a hope that the regiment would remain there for the winter. Formidable earthworks were being constructed, duly described by Mrs. Brand: "I saw long lines of earth thrown up, and was told it was rifle pits and fortifications. I also saw many cannon, with their mouths toward the land of Secesh, as much as to say, stand off if you don't want to be hurt Mr. Secesh."[5]

Soldiers constructed dwellings, which tended to be of one of two designs. One was a log cabin with walls four feet high topped by a wedge-tent roof. The other variety had as a base a ring of daubed and plastered pickets, with one of the circular Sibley tents set on top. Some of the officers were even living in small brick houses. Building materials often came from Harpers Ferry structures, supposedly abandoned ones, although according to W. A. Brand many doors and windows disappeared from occupied houses. He recounts one such instance:

> A soldier had taken breakfast with some one in town, and after regaling himself, he was left alone for a moment, when he quietly lifted the plates, cups, &c., off, set them upon the chairs, shouldered the table, and made for camp. But the lady of the house followed him and overtook him before he had reached his quarters. She hollowed lustily for the Colonel, but he was absent, and before she could get her case fairly presented, the soldier was gone— as well as her table.[6]

The regiment was gradually "filling up," making consolidation more and more unlikely in the eyes of the men and thus easing their anxieties. Recruiting in Ohio had garnered over fifty new enlistments for the Sixty-sixth, and some who had been on medical leave returned, as had some of the Sixty-sixth's captured. One of the recent recruits was William Henry Baxter, the son of Stephen Baxter, who had made out his will before departing Urbana in January and was killed at Port Republic. William's diary offers no insight into his decision to join up; certainly there was no expression of a desire for vengeance. His laconic entry for August 5 simply records, "This morning I took a notion to enlist, so in the afternoon I carried it into execution for 3 years."[7]

Candy was concerned with the question of promotions, writing to Governor Tod, "It is rumored that 2d Lieuts. are to be appointed from civil life to command veterans who have served their country since the organization of the Regt. and I am sorry to say that it has caused great dissatisfaction among the men and I am in hopes that it is not so."[8] His fears were groundless, as the Sixty-sixth's officers continued to be promoted through the regimental ranks.

The officers imprisoned in North Carolina had returned by now, but many of the enlisted men were still in parole camp at Fort Delaware. Life was not easy for the parolees. Losing patience with their situation, a few broke guard and found their way back to Ohio, although technically this made them deserters. As of early November some forty men of the Sixty-sixth were still at Fort Delaware. Back in September they had addressed a letter to the *Citizen and Gazette* complaining that they were short of clothing, blankets, and drinking water; conditions, they asserted, were little better than they had experienced in Southern prison camps, scarcely differing from the treatment of Confederate prisoners in Federal facilities. The letter appealed that influence be exerted on their behalf to allow them to be furloughed until their exchanges could be accomplished: "We do not want to be treated like dogs. . . . We know that the Government has the means and are willing to deal justly by us, but there is a screw loose somewhere and we think it is high time that it was tightened."[9]

Their appeal was apparently to no avail, as many of them were still at Fort Delaware in early December, when Pvt. J. Hamilton Armstrong of Company K conveyed a new account of their situation to the *Citizen and Gazette*. Conditions must have improved, as the letter lacked the desperation of the September missive. The parolees—some of whom were seeking transfer into the regular army—had formed a company of "burned-cork Minstrels" to amuse themselves and had even performed for the citizenry outside the camp.[10]

Parole presented problems for the army. Soldiers were usually without their officers in a prisonlike setting for an indefinite duration. Discipline and morale were bound to be affected. A worst-case scenario involved some of the men of the 95th Ohio, many of them recruited in Champaign County; they had been captured en masse at Richmond,

Kentucky. Their confinement in parole camp put them in a rebellious mood; at one point they stormed the camp's guardhouse to liberate a company of the 95th that had been put under arrest.[11]

Fear of rebellious moods in the army was not just a matter of parole camps. In early October the president ordered General McClellan to follow up his victory at Antietam with a major offensive. The general failed to attack Lee, and Lincoln relieved him of command on November 7. There was anxiety both before and after his dismissal that McClellan and the Army of the Potomac would resist the move, possibly producing an attempt to overthrow the government. Indeed McClellan was very popular with much of the army, but his support was not very deep in the Sixty-sixth, which had only served under him in any meaningful fashion at Antietam. The comments of Pvt. David E. Lickliter of Company G, written from hospital on October 16, might be considered representative:

> A month or more of the most favorable weather I ever saw has passed since the fight at Antietam, and the grand army of the Potomac has been lying here as unconcerned as if there was no more fighting to be done, I used to be a McClellan man but unless he moves soon and does something more toward whipping the rebels and putting down the rebellion, I don't care how quick he is removed and his successor appointed.[12]

Not surprisingly, W. A. Brand also had thoughts on the matter; it was, he wrote, rumored that McClellan and his staff thought themselves in a position to "*dictate to* this Government in all things. . . . *He* had no need of superior officers, whilst *riding* on his throne."[13]

The most excitement experienced by the Sixty-sixth while it operated out of Harpers Ferry was a return expedition to Winchester. Geary's division left camp on December 2 for a reconnaissance in force. The first town through which it marched was Charlestown, which the division reached after a minor skirmish. This was the site of John Brown's trial and execution, and the men sang "John Brown's Body" as they marched down the town's only street. As was often the case with Civil War soldiers, the men harbored certain tourist instincts, which were made manifest when some in the column stacked arms and went for an inspection of the courtroom and the field where Brown had been executed.[14]

The march continued down the Berryville Pike, where the Federals encountered Confederate cavalry, which retreated before them. Upon approaching Berryville itself the column discovered another small ene-my force, which dispersed when Geary ordered it shelled. Following another brush with enemy cavalry, the small Federal force continued on to Winchester, reaching it on December 4. Geary demanded the surren-der of the Confederate garrison, but somehow learning of a smallpox epidemic there he did not formally take possession of the town. Even so, the division had by now accumulated 118 prisoners. The Sixty-sixth also managed to recover the trunk of Company I's Lieutenant Yeazel; it had been abandoned when the regiment had left Winchester in March under orders to lighten its baggage.[15]

The division returned to Harpers Ferry on December 6 and shortly afterwards was ordered to break camp. It would be heading east, per-haps to join the Army of the Potomac. Much to the men's chagrin, they would not be wintering in the comfortable cabins they had constructed. The Sixty-sixth left Harpers Ferry on December 10, leaving thirty men behind in hospital. W. A. Brand remained with the convalescents, wor-ried that the troops were carrying only one blanket apiece on the march: "My impression is, that this march will greatly reduce the present strength of the regiment. The weather is very cold, and the ground covered with snow."[16] Even so, accounts of the three-day march to Fairfax Court House do not make it sound arduous. At one point the weather was warm enough to rain instead of snow, although the resulting mud slowed the wagons. The Sixty-sixth was designated rear guard on December 16 for what appeared to be the final leg of the journey, which was to culminate at a town near Quantico Creek's junction with the Potomac. The divi-sion's advance elements made it to Dumfries that day, but the Sixty-sixth had to stay with the wagons, which became stuck in the mud two miles short of town.

The next morning the regiment was commanded to march back the way it came. After three miles the order was countermanded, and the Sixty-sixth, together with the 5th and 7th Ohio, as well as a section of the 1st Maine Battery, started back toward Dumfries. This movement took them across a creek on a rail bridge the Sixty-sixth had construct-ed; here they encountered their former division commander George S. Greene leading his brigade in the opposite direction. Greene rode up to the bridge and claimed precedence for his men, but the soldiers of the Sixty-sixth were already crossing and did not heed him. He directed them to stop; they continued to ignore his commands. It was too much for this strict disciplinarian to tolerate: he rode up to one of the men, apparently to enforce his order in a more compelling fashion. Instead, the bank gave way, and he and his horse tumbled into the creek. Some of the Sixty-sixth fished him out, while the remainder of the regiment passed over. He appeared angry but said no more, perhaps thinking that here was yet another instance of how difficult it was to maintain order in volunteer regiments.[17]

The "Ohio brigade" arrived at Dumfries around noon. Candy set up headquarters in town, and the bulk of his force encamped to the north and west. The position was part of the rear guard of the Army of the Potomac, now under the command of Ambrose Burnside. After its terrible defeat at Fredericksburg on December 13, the army was still encamped on the Rappahannock, poised perhaps for another lunge south against Lee. The men of the Sixty-sixth were fortunate in having avoided the slaughter that had been the battle of Fredericksburg, and they were looking forward to an uneventful stay in their winter bivouac.

Of Dumfries Captain Baird wrote, "What on the face of the earth ever made a sensible man pick out this place in early times for settlement, beats me, for if ever there was a God forsaken looking place it is this." Pvt. Nate Welsh of Company F concurred, writing to a comrade, "Well I will tell you what kind of a dam hole we have got into here it is about . . . the most Godforsaking place in the World I suppose. . . . I heard that you was coming back to the company you are a damn f—l if you do by God your head is not leavel [level]." Once the county seat of Prince William County, Dumfries had lost much of its former glory, so that according to Baird there were "now about 30 dilapidated looking houses, and about 100 dilapidated looking inhabitants." Much of the dilapidation had probably been brought about by Union troops. The most imposing structure remaining was the old courthouse, which had been built of imported brick. A mourning stripe of black had been drawn around the upper walls of the courtroom at the death of George Washington; it was still visible in 1863.[18] Garrisoned in the vicinity with the three Ohio regiments was the section of the 1st Maine Battery that had accompanied them on the recent march, plus detachments from two cavalry regiments, the 12th Illinois and the 1st Maryland.

Although military activity usually decreased in the winter, December 1862 had seen a great deal of action. On December 12, one day before Burnside's disastrous assault at Fredericksburg, a detachment of five hundred Confederate cavalry under Wade Hampton had raided Dumfries, gobbling up (perhaps literally) a wealth of sutler goods and (figuratively) a detachment of Union cavalry that had had the misfortune to be holding the town at the time. Five days later Candy's force had arrived.

Christmas came and went. The depths of winter were approaching, but the season would not have a quiet beginning in Dumfries. Shortly after noon on December 27 the garrison was startled by the sound of cannon fire and of shells shrieking over head. It was J. E. B. Stuart, Lee's audacious cavalry commander, at the head of probably not much more than a thousand men, from the brigades of Fitzgerald "Fitz" Lee and George Washington Custis "Rooney" Lee (Robert E. Lee's nephew and son respectively). Stuart's horse artillery made the first announcement of the Confederate arrival. Perhaps hoping that the town would still be as lightly guarded as Hampton had found it on December 12, Stuart proposed to capture—or at least seriously harass—Dumfries as part of a general effort to unsettle the Yankee rear to the north of Fredericksburg, perhaps in the process capturing enemy stores with which the better to celebrate the New Year.

Candy was not taken entirely by surprise. Before Stuart's men arrived on the banks of Quantico Creek south of Dumfries, he knew something was afoot. A patrol from the 12th Illinois Cavalry on Telegraph Road south of the creek had encountered the raiding party, and most of it had been captured; one man had managed to escape and return with the report of a large body of Confederate cavalry. Candy had dispatched his Maryland troopers to determine the strength of the force and, if possible, rescue the captives.[19]

The 1st Maryland crossed the creek on the Telegraph Road bridge and soon encountered the Confederate raiders. After an exchange of fire the Federals retreated back across the Quantico, followed by a squadron of Rooney Lee's cavalry. They in turn encountered the 7th Ohio, which had advanced to a field south of the town, between it and the creek. By this time Stuart's artillery was in position, and it opened fire in support of Rooney Lee's advance. Despite some casualties from grapeshot, the 7th pushed Lee's men back across the stream, gaining a thicket of pines that provided cover and a position from which to repulse further attacks.

The guns of the Maine battery were placed on the courthouse hill with the 5th Ohio in support, while the Sixty-sixth was divided and shifted about the field as needed. Much of the afternoon was spent skirmishing and changing positions in concert with the 12th Illinois Cavalry, which was fighting dismounted—as were the Confederate troopers. At one point Stuart's men forced a crossing at a ford on Candy's right, but the charge was repulsed by the Sixty-sixth and the 12th. A gun from the Maine battery was shifted to the area to counter the enemy's attempt to flank the Federal force. The skirmishing, maneuvering, and artillery fire continued until nightfall. The next morning Stuart was gone. Dumfries was still in Union hands.

Candy's losses were light, coming to three killed and about twelve wounded. These casualties were largely confined to the 5th and 7th Ohio. Losses to capture came to as many as fifty, including a squad of nine men from the Sixty-sixth who were captured on picket.

William A. Sampson, who was soon to succeed Van Deman as captain of Company K, would later write that the corps commander, General Slocum, arrived at Dumfries the next day with a relief column. Finding that no relief was necessary, Slocum commented that he had been ordered to leave his best troops at Dumfries, and he believed he had done so.[20]

14

I Am Getting Very Tired of Soldiering

*P*vt. Joseph Diltz of Company I was home-sick. It had been almost a year since he had left Champaign County and his wife, Mary, behind. The Sixty-sixth's departure, it may be recalled, had been too quick for them. She had been unable to get to town in time to see him off; he had started for the country but turned back to camp fearing he would miss the regiment at the Urbana railroad station.

He had been a late enlistee, joining up on December 27, 1861, to enter the same company as his younger brother-in-law, the twenty-one-year-old George Milledge. His letters, which survive at Duke University, provide no insight into what motivated his enlistment, but the comparative lateness of his action suggests that he was not caught up in the recruiting fervor sweeping the county in the autumn. The twenty-six-year-old recruit was slightly older than most of the other enlisted men, and he had a wife and two small children, the youngest born perhaps in October.[1] It would have been difficult that autumn to enlist with a wife expecting a child; however, it would seem not much easier to enlist with that child barely two months old. Perhaps in his late enlistment we see the choice of a young family man who wished to preserve the Christmas holiday as a time unsullied by military obligation—but it was also a time of family gatherings, and his brother-in-law George would have been on hand in his uniform, perhaps adding to the pressure to enlist. A farm laborer, Joseph could not claim to have great prospects; neither, however, did he have a farm or business whose running would be disrupted by his departure for the regiment. Enlistment may simply have been "the thing to do," although he did not entertain much enthusiasm for military life. Like most recruits, he planned and hoped for an early end to the conflict.

Certainly his letters contain little patriotic sentiment, but in this respect his correspondence is not unusual. In it misery and homesickness predominate for weeks at a time. He was sick for much of the latter part of 1862, lying in an ambulance wagon during the Battle of Cedar Mountain, although he recovered sufficiently to see combat at Antietam. Like many other soldiers, he had bowel problems, which eventually developed into dysentery. In addition, he did substantial injury to himself: fashioning tent stakes at Loudoun Heights, he smashed the index finger of his left hand with a dull ax. The finger was amputated at the second joint.[2]

By the end of November he was in hospital at Patterson Park, Baltimore. Shortly before his transfer he had written to his wife, "For my part I am getting very tired of soldiering. I wish the war was over for I want to go home and see you all so bad." Writing from hospital on Christmas Day, he was desperate for a discharge, appealing to Mary to have her father seek out the former major—now a civilian—Charles Fulton in Urbana "to send me a recomend for a discharge. . . . [H]e can tell the major that my famley is in a very bad fix and that you ar sick." Diltz apparently felt that Fulton still had enough pull with the regimental surgeon to effect his departure from the service, although how this might have been done is not clear; it was probably just very wishful and naive thinking. "I have got tiard of the war for it is no use to fight it does know good and I am going to get out of it if I can." He continued in this somewhat desperate vein, "I am a going to go home this winter if I have to take a french furlough [absence without leave]." He repeated to his wife five days later his request that she appeal for Fulton's intervention, going so far as to declare, "If I get home I will pay him well for his trubel."[3]

We do not have Mary's replies to his letters, but she apparently sent him something of a rebuke, for in his next letter from hospital he wrote,

"Well Mary you seme to think that you dont want me to run of and leave the army. I did not have eny notion of runing off. When I rote to you last I thought that I would see how patriotic you was but I see that you are true grit."[4] However that may have been, he closed with another request that she have her father approach Fulton.

Joseph Diltz remained in hospital for almost four more months. He repeated his requests to arrange Fulton's intercession, but nothing apparently came of it. Nothing more was said about "french furloughs." He could not have helped but note that many of his fellow patients were receiving discharges, and he seems not to have entertained the possibility that the army might nurse its men back to health so that they could fight again, that a stay in the hospital did not automatically mean a return to civilian life. He continued to question the meaning of all the fighting; he was further troubled by emancipation, writing later that "it is no use to fight for it does no good and this thing of turning the dmd Nigers loos I dont lik."[5]

He was not the only Union soldier with reservations over turning the slaves "loos." The Emancipation Proclamation had been announced against the backdrop of victory at Antietam—or at least as close to victory as the Army of the Potomac had been able to achieve under McClellan. Since then there had been the failure to pursue Lee, followed by the pointless slaughter at Fredericksburg. Morale among Union troops in Virginia was not high as the second year of the war drew to a close. Soldiers who had enlisted—for a quick war, many of them thought—to preserve the Union now found themselves in a seemingly interminable conflict to free the slaves. There seemed to be a danger that soldiers from the Midwest, many of them with Southern ancestry and relations in the Confederate army, might feel they had been sucked into a war of abolition foisted upon them by New Englanders. Certainly there were those in the Confederacy hoping for precisely that attitude.

The Sixty-sixth remained in camp at Dumfries all winter and into the spring. After the excitement of Stuart's raid, life at Dumfries fell into fairly predictable, if unexciting, patterns. With time on their hands, some of the men, like Joseph Diltz in his hospital bed, began to entertain reservations about the war. John Houtz, a private in Company B, confided to his journal in April that "we had better let the rebs go, as they are determined to go. . . . [A]ll the boys are willing to let them go."[6] This entry came more than a month after another letter writer had asserted that the "broken and divided opinion which prevailed a month

John W. Houtz. *Robert T. Pennoyer Collection.*

ago, is now consolidated and firm."[7] Although there is little evidence for serious discontent, the "broken and divided opinion" reference and John Houtz's "let the rebs go" entry are probably of a piece.

Letters from home also began to call the war into question, as can be inferred from an especially revealing missive from a Saint Paris tailor, now a private in Company C, named Charles Poffenberger. A self-proclaimed Democrat, on March 4 he addressed his fellow citizens in a letter to the *Citizen and Gazette,* "having frequently received letters from friends at home, and also read letters addressed to other men in this regiment . . . in which they talk about 'resisting the draft,' opposing the President's Emancipation Proclamation, and that 'soldiers will lay down their arms and go home' if 'Old Abe' don't do thus and so." In the letter he urged obedience to the government, even if that meant support of the Emancipation Proclamation, for which he did not himself evince great enthusiasm: "You don't like his Emancipation scheme—neither do I; but as he is the Governor, and I am the governed, I submit." He went on to lecture his "Copperhead" (antiwar) Democratic brethren: "You need have no fear about the soldiers laying down their arms to go home. We enlisted to defend your homes, your property, and your lives.

. . . And, unlike you, we are not so lost to all sense of honor or duty as to desert the Government in this her time of need." He closed by urging his friends and neighbors, when writing to the soldiers,

> instead of infusing a spirit of disobedience, encourage us by kind words to do our duty, and then when the storm of battle rages, our arms and breasts will be strengthened by a knowledge that our efforts are appreciated at home by friends, who have an interest in our welfare, and who will at least remember us kindly, if we should loose our lives in the great struggle to maintain their independence.[8]

The officers of the Sixty-sixth also felt compelled to produce evidence of a united front. They met on March 6 and appointed a committee consisting of Lieutenant Colonel Powell, Quartermaster Brand, and Joshua Palmer, formerly captain of Company B and now, with Charles Fulton's resignation, promoted to major. Charged to report resolutions for the "consideration of the regiment," the committee presented an eight-part declaration at regimental dress parade the following day. Among its affirmations were: "We yield implicit obedience as soldiers to [the president's] orders and proclamations," and "The treasonable propositions of Northern Traitors for 'peace' . . . merit the contempt and scorn of all loyal citizens and soldiers." The sectional issue was also addressed, by the resolution that the soldiers would "stand by the New England states as long as they stand by the Government . . . and Woe be unto the 'Copperhead' demagogues who may attempt to sever the Northwest from the East."[9] It was reported that the full resolution was adopted unanimously by the men standing in dress parade.

The regiment's resolutions were a response to the efforts of peace Democrats and Confederates to drive a wedge between the Midwest and New England. No reading between the lines was required in the columns of the *Crisis,* a Columbus, Ohio, newspaper opposed to Lincoln and the war: "Shall we sink down as serfs to the heartless speculative Yankee for all time to come—swindled by his tariffs, robbed by his taxes, skinned by his railroad monopolies? The West will demand a Convention of the states, with delegates elected by the people themselves, without intervention of bayonets, and if other States refuse to meet her, she will, through her delegates, consult her own interests."[10] The possibility of a western secession movement was being broached.

By mid-March 1863 the regiment was, as described by W. A. Brand in one of his "D. N. Arbaw" letters, at "full strength" with 326 men.[11] This was one-third the number of men who had left Urbana in January 1862. The two-thirds attrition was due only in small part to deaths resulting from combat, sixty-four men having died in this fashion. Disease, arising in part from Lander's ill-conceived Romney campaign as well as from the effects of imprisonment, had been responsible for slightly more deaths. Of the men captured at Port Republic, all those who were fit had returned to the regiment, although a few who had been captured in Stuart's recent raid may still have been absent. Desertion had also been a problem but was not a major factor in bringing down regimental strength.

In fact, desertion was a somewhat subjective matter in this volunteer army—though whatever the circumstances, the men were still absent. Some men returned home to recover from illness or wounds. Others obtained furloughs and did not return to the regiment when expected. Others "escaped" from parole camp. William J. Constant, a private from Company H, wrote to his lieutenant from Marysville, Ohio, on April 20. He had been captured at Dumfries and paroled a few days later, at which point he had apparently gone home. He opened his letter by deferentially stating the obvious: "Respected friend as you will perceive I am at home and without leave." He, like other soldiers in similar circumstances, professed confusion as to the workings of the parole system. He did not know if he had been "exchanged" yet, and he was wondering what he should do. If it was necessary to report to Columbus or elsewhere, he would do so, "although I would like to stay at home as long as I can that is until I am exchanged." He closed his letter with the assurance that "I am ready to do my duty at all times"—although without an explanation of why he was finally writing almost four months after his parole.[12]

It was discharge for wounds or illness that accounted for most of the attrition in the Sixty-sixth. Many of the men discharged on disability certificates were older soldiers, who were apt to have been less fit than the younger enlistees and probably had no business enlisting in the first place. Disease accounted for most of the discharges, in addition to which from 20 to 30 percent of the wounded in any battle would be eventually discharged. Accidents, such as the train derailment in Bellaire, Ohio, or unintentional discharge of weapons, would account for the occasional death or injury.

The officers' ranks were also in flux. Lieutenant McDonald of Company E, shot at Cedar Mountain, was the only officer to lose his life, although several other officers were wounded in the regiment's three major battles. On the other hand, five of the ten companies lost their captains to medical discharge. The average age of these men was forty-eight, much higher than the regimental average, the oldest being Capt. John ("Come out there in the middle") Cassill of Company F, who had reached or was pushing sixty. Colonel Candy had himself been ill for a time, and before that the regiment had lost James Dye, its first lieutenant colonel, and Charles Fulton, its first major. Replacing Fulton with Company B's Capt. Joshua Palmer created yet another vacancy in the grade of captain.

Opportunities for promotion thus abounded, especially given the discharge or—in the case of McDonald—death of six first and second lieutenants. The advancement of Company H's Harrison Davis is one example. He had enlisted as a private and was promoted to sergeant prior to Port Republic (in the aftermath of which he hid with Captain Horr for two days in the brush along the riverbank). He was made a second lieutenant on November 10 and a first lieutenant on February 19.

Davis had been an unmarried twenty-nine-year-old laborer living near Woodstock at the time of his enlistment.[13] Perhaps his was not the background from which officers would typically have come in 1861, but he had proven himself and was well liked in his community, which celebrated his commission when he went home on furlough. A crowd gathered in the evening of January 30 at the First Universalist Church in Woodstock to present him with a sword, raised by subscription. A local band was even present, to make it a real celebration. (Predictably the *Citizen and Gazette* in its report of the event got in its usual digs on the local Copperheads, who apparently existed even in and around the Yankee enclave of Woodstock: "The Butternuts [a reference to a dye often used in Confederate uniforms] of this place, whose sympathies have lately been aroused by the Emancipation Proclamation, utterly [refused] to subscribe even one cent for the purchase of the Sword.")[14] It was shortly after his return to Dumfries that Davis discovered he had been promoted yet again and would be carrying his sword as a first lieutenant.

As was often the case, the Sixty-sixth had a recruiting detachment in Urbana. It included Sgt. Charles Butts of Delaware, Ohio; however, he apparently busied himself with matters other than recruiting, thereby creating a scandal. In January he visited a hotel in nearby Springfield to keep a rendezvous with a young woman, all of seventeen years old. After his departure from the hotel, she committed suicide. The *Citizen and Gazette* reported the incident in great detail, castigating Butts as "that dirty puppy and infernal scoundrel," quoting an unidentified snippet of verse ("Oh! for a whip, in every hand, / To lash the rascal naked through the land"), and concluding that "such a vile pest as he is unworthy to bear an American musket."[15]

In fact, even such "vile pests" as Butts, and worse, would be more than welcome in the Union army in 1863, which would see carnage equal to, if not greater than, that of 1862.

15

Chancellorsville: I Stood Up to the Rack and Cut the Hay

*T*he Sixty-sixth was readying for departure in mid-April, and for most of the men it was none too soon. The weather had been cold and wet. The ubiquitous ponds of mud meant that the men were seldom brought out for drill (William Baxter noted on March 7 that "Mud is stil almost bottomless, with rain");[1] picket duty, however, was an unpleasant duty shared by all. Nonetheless, the uneventful life at Dumfries following Stuart's raid had given the regiment a chance to consolidate its organization, its health, and its morale. The tedium of garrison life seemed to breed a new determination to complete the suppression of the Southern rebellion. Amidst the perpetual mud of winter, the Ohioans reflected on their experiences of the previous year, and if some, like John Houtz, harbored doubts, they did not express them publicly.

The more committed renewed their faith in the Union. Robert Russell, who like Harrison Davis had advanced rapidly through the ranks, became a first lieutenant on February 3. Two days before his promotion he wrote to his father that "I should like very much to see my friends and relations, but as long as I keep my health and there seems to be *any* prospect of terminating the war I am willing to stay away from home & undergo hardships and trials."[2] Russell did in fact put in for a short furlough, but because Major Palmer, among others, overstayed his leave, Russell was not allowed to return home.

In January, following his defeat at Fredericksburg, Burnside attempted a turning movement across the Rappahannock. It bogged down in rain and sleet—Confederate pickets jeered the Federals from across the river. The offensive was canceled before it had rightly begun; the affair came to be known as "The Mud March." The Army of the Potomac was suffering from low morale, and for good reason. Some of Burnside's officers were lobbying for his removal. With no successes and two failures to his account, Burnside's days were numbered; on January 26 he was replaced by Joseph "Fighting Joe" Hooker, who had commanded the First Corps at Antietam, and who had also been the most active of Burnside's subordinates in seeking the commanding general's removal.

Hooker soon became more popular than his predecessor, inaugurating his command with decisive measures, all of which tended to improve morale and discipline. He reformed the quartermaster organization, making sure his men received regular rations of fresh bread and vegetables. He also introduced a rotating furlough system, which, although it did not always work as it was supposed to, allowed many men to return home that winter and thereby probably reduced desertions. Concurrently, Hooker tightened military discipline, ordering company commanders to report all absences. Russell noted approvingly that Hooker had "been weeding the army of incompetent & inefficient officers, and given those that are left to understand that they must be diligent, faithful & prompt in the discharge of their duties. He has had some thirty Deserters condemned to be shot, and the men seeing that he is in earnest about these things, take courage knowing that full justice will be done to all."[3] Hooker also implemented a corps badge system that persisted in the Army of the Potomac for the remainder of the war: each corps was given a distinctive badge to be worn on the hat and perhaps the shirt or overcoat, with different colors assigned to each of its divisions. The Sixty-sixth was part of the Twelfth Corps and so was assigned a star; being in the Second Division, its men's stars were white. Their identity as "White Stars" was something they clung to proudly for the duration of their service.

It was a reinvigorated "Ohio brigade" that left Dumfries for Aquia Creek on April 20 to join the rest of the Second Division. (Not that its discipline was perfect—the previous evening some of the "boys" had been thwarted in an attempt to rush a sutler's tent, and all of them had been confined to quarters.)[4] The Sixty-sixth also left behind a further diminished Dumfries, whose already dilapidated colonial courthouse had been gradually demolished for its materials, to construct chimneys for the men's winter quarters.

The command structure below Hooker as it applied to the Sixty-sixth was unaltered from the aftermath of Antietam. Slocum retained command of the Twelfth Corps. Geary remained in charge of the Second Division, with the Sixty-sixth's own Colonel Candy still in command of the brigade. Lt. Col. Eugene Powell continued in command of the Sixty-sixth; he had by now, W. A. Brand noted, "by his kind and peculiar government" secured the loyalty of the men.[5]

The brigade itself was largely unaltered. Buckeye units predominated with the 5th, 7th, 29th, and Sixty-sixth Ohio making up four of six regiments. The 28th Pennsylvania, Geary's original regiment, was still brigaded with them but was no longer so gargantuan. Its "surplus" men had been made the nucleus of the 147th Pennsylvania, supplemented by further recruiting in the Keystone State.[6] The Pennsylvania regiments, together with the 29th Ohio, had been stationed at Stafford Court House over the winter, but they would reunite with the Dumfries contingent to form the full brigade for the upcoming campaign.

The march to Aquia Creek was slowed by rain and mud. The troops were also perhaps a bit out of shape after four months of garrison duty, in addition to being weighed down by heavy packs (Hooker having reduced the number of wagons that could accompany a regiment in the field). Progress was apparently no easier for mounted officers; Colonel Candy, who was a veteran cavalryman, fell from his horse in the march. On this first day out of Dumfries the Sixty-sixth covered only three miles, ending the march at Aquia Creek Church, a mid-eighteenth-century structure that provoked the interest and admiration of the men.

Midwestern troops, many of whom had never been far from home, were frequently fascinated by the older buildings and cemeteries they encountered on the eastern seaboard. A common reaction was to record in their journals and letters home the inscriptions they found. In a letter to his family, Robert Russell transcribed the names of the vestrymen listed on a church plaque from the year 1757. Even the less demonstrative John Houtz noted in his diary, "This is a nice church."[7]

Spirits were high. Representative of the turnaround in morale over the previous four months were the almost exultant comments of the previously demoralized Joseph Diltz, who had been released from hospital in Baltimore. Mustering all the forcefulness his creative spelling would allow, he wrote wife that when "fiting Jo hurls his mity forse against old Lee I think that he Will have to back off."[8]

The next day the Ohio troops continued their march, passing Stafford Court House, where Slocum had established corps headquarters. They continued to Aquia Creek Landing, where they were encamped until the morning of April 27. The men passed the time waiting for the paymaster, playing cards, and speculating about the nature of the coming forward movement—hoping that it would not entail another frontal assault on the Fredericksburg heights. Some of the men saw reconnaissance balloons in the distance; they knew the balloons presaged some new movement—but where and when?

Hooker was concentrating his army for a decisive turning movement against Lee's army at Fredericksburg. While a Federal cavalry expedition struck south of the Confederate army and cut Lee's rail link to Richmond, a diversionary force was to cross the Rappahannock east of Fredericksburg. The bulk of Hooker's army would cross much farther upriver—that is, west of Fredericksburg—marching then through a tangled area of second-growth woods and scrub known as the "Wilderness" to take Lee on his left. As the plan had it, the outnumbered and outmaneuvered Lee would then face the choice of attacking a vastly superior force on ground not of his choosing or retreating before that force, with the Federal cavalry in Lee's rear threatening his communications.

That was the plan, and it was a good one. The Sixty-sixth shared the assignment of Slocum's Twelfth Corps, which was one of the three corps entrusted with the upriver turning movement, as Hooker's right wing. The Eleventh, Twelfth, and Fifth Corps crossed the Rappahannock at Kelly's Ford on April 29. The Eleventh and Twelfth Corps then crossed the Rapidan at Germanna Ford, while the Fifth Corps, under George Meade, crossed farther east at Ely's Ford. On April 30 the two forces converged on Chancellorsville—not a town but a large house owned by the Chancellor family, standing at a crossroads clearing in the Wilderness.

Slocum's corps encountered little resistance. Skirmishing with some of Stuart's cavalry produced a few stray casualties but did not appreciably slow the progress of the great turning movement. Arriving at Chancellorsville with the vanguard of his corps, Slocum encountered Meade, whose Fifth Corps was already there; Meade shouted, "Hurrah for old Joe!" He expected their combined forces to continue east, emerging from the Wilderness to fall immediately on Lee's flank.

Hooker had placed Slocum in command of the right wing, originally instructing him, indeed, to continue out of the Wilderness after joining up with Meade at Chancellorsville. Now, however, there was a change in orders, a change that was probably the first step in the unraveling of a promising offensive. Hooker decided that the three corps should consolidate their positions and move out of the Wilderness the following day. Trusting that the Union forces could maintain their initiative, Hooker felt he would still be in a position to "bag" the Army of Northern Virginia.

So it was that a somewhat deflated Meade banished thoughts of marching triumphantly that day out of the Wilderness onto the Confederate left flank. So it was also that on the evening of Thursday, April 30, Candy's brigade was busy entrenching south of the Chancellor house and just west of the Orange Plank Road; the Sixty-sixth was the right most regiment. Candy later recalled that the men of his brigade set themselves to their task with a will. After felling the trees in their front they commenced building a breastwork facing south, "throwing the dirt up with bayonets, swords, tin plates, and many using nothing but their hands."[9] That night groups of officers gathered behind them at the Chancellor house to congratulate one another over the campaign's brilliant opening. It seemed to many in the Federal camp that success was a foregone conclusion.

The next day, May 1, the Union forces resumed their eastward advance. Lee by now was well aware of their presence; however, this knowledge did not mitigate the precariousness of the position in which he found himself. Jackson was put in charge of halting the Federal advance and, being Jackson, decided that although he was outnumbered he would attack the forces marching toward him out of the Wilderness.

Slocum's corps moved southeast down the Orange Plank Road. Geary's division maintained its relative position of the night before, advancing along the right of the road. Candy's men formed a reserve behind the other two brigades of the division; their advance began late in the morning and took them through more dense underbrush and scrub. After advancing a mile or so, Geary's division emerged from the Wilderness onto an open plain, where they encountered Confederate artillery fire and skirmishers.

They remained in position for little more than half an hour. It was then that the Twelfth Corps received the astounding order to fall back to the previous night's position. The order, originating from Hooker himself, surprised many. Hooker dispatched W. A. Roebling (an engineering officer who would in later years preside over the building of the Brooklyn Bridge) to communicate the new directive to an incredulous Slocum, who had just established contact with the enemy. According to Roebling the Twelfth Corps commander exclaimed, "Roebling, you are a damned liar! Nobody but a crazy man would give such an order when we have victory in sight!" He then rode back to remonstrate personally with Hooker.[10] It was to no avail. The Twelfth Corps returned to Chancellorsville in good order; although it had been under fire in the open, it had sustained only ten casualties. Hooker had just handed Lee the initiative. The Sixty-sixth Ohio, together with the rest of Slocum's corps, was fated to fight a defensive battle in the Wilderness.

Returning to the earthworks they had created the night before, the men strengthened them even more, John Houtz remarking in his journal that they were "strong enough to stand sheling."[11] This accorded with Hooker's expectations; he hoped Lee would assault him, thereby reversing the roles at Fredericksburg in December, when Union troops had been slaughtered in a futile attack against strong Confederate positions.

Lee was indeed planning to attack, but not where Hooker was preparing to receive him. To the right of Slocum was Oliver Howard's Eleventh Corps, facing south along the Orange Turnpike and forming the extreme right of Hooker's army. Howard's right was "in the air"—that is, unanchored and unprotected by either topography or friendly forces. It was here that Lee would strike, in the person of Stonewall Jackson, who would by a circuitous route lead half of the Confederate army around Hooker's front to strike Howard on his exposed right flank. All through the following day, Saturday, May 2, there were reports of a large Confederate force moving along the Wilderness roads south of the Federal position, yet the threat was not perceived by the Union high command.

In the waning afternoon hours, Jackson positioned his men in the scrub and underbrush, facing east just beyond Howard's unprotected right. Many of the men in the Eleventh Corps had stacked their arms and were preparing an evening meal when the first ranks of screeching Confederates rushed in upon them. Howard's line rolled up, disintegrating brigade by brigade, division by division; the men of the Eleventh Corps fled in panic. Arriving at Chancellorsville barely ahead of the rout was the Sixty-sixth's Quartermaster Brand, who with his son

William Augustus had led a mule train laden with forage along the Eleventh Corps line just before Jackson's assault; by the time they reached the Chancellor house, which was Hooker's headquarters, shells and solid shot were falling about them.[12] William Flago, a sergeant from the Sixty-sixth's Company B, was also separated from the regiment and was swept up in the confusion. He later reported that the Sixty-sixth had been part of the runaway; the report was in error and would cause him great embarrassment.[13]

It was not long before the rout reached Slocum's position. Because Geary was on Slocum's left and Candy's was the leftmost brigade of Geary's division, the Sixty-sixth did not bear the brunt of the Eleventh Corps stampede. One veteran of the Sixty-sixth wrote fifteen years later (the incident is not mentioned in any other source) that the panic to their right infected some of the men in the Sixty-sixth, causing them to flee: "The shades of night were falling around us, the gloom and darkness of the forest were settling upon us, in each man's face was read doubt and uncertainty. Then came the report that there were no troops to our right, that all had gone, and that the rebels were marching down upon us. Then fear overcame the courage of many, and several companies of the Sixty-sixth broke from their trenches and started to flee for the rear." Their flight was eventually checked by the Sixty-sixth's officers.[14] A number of the retreating men from the Eleventh Corps did reach as far as Candy. His officers appropriated those who still held muskets and positioned them behind the trenches, sending those without arms to the rear. Candy did not mention in his report any of his own troops being caught up in the panic.[15]

Earlier in the day, Rebel troops in Candy's front had given his brigade some attention. The 23d North Carolina had advanced up the Plank Road—perhaps in error—shortly after dawn, coming under the eye of a Pennsylvania battery, which had let loose with grape and canister shot. Four of the Carolinians went down, and the Tarheels drew back; their skirmishers had continued to exchange shots with Candy's men.

At this point something unusual had taken place. His leg shot off, one of the wounded Confederates lay in the road crying for aid. He seems to have been closer to the Ohioans' breastworks than the Carolinians' skirmish lines. Geary had observed this and asked—though one account states it was Hooker—for volunteers to go over to the works to bring him in. Four men from the Sixty-sixth's Company A had volunteered. It is recorded that their commander told them something to the effect of, "The roads are full of rebels, but if you go boldly down unarmed, they will know that you are after a wounded man and will surely not be so inhuman as to fire on you who are bringing relief to one of their own men." The men had thrown off their accoutrements, gone out between the lines, and brought in the wounded man on two army blankets held as a stretcher to the Chancellor house (which was acting as hospital as well as Hooker's headquarters). Some years after the war the four men received the Congressional Medal of Honor for their actions.[16]

The Sixty-sixth had been subjected to enemy fire the entire day, even as Jackson was positioning his troops for the great flank attack. By that evening the works on the Sixty-sixth's right were empty, inviting a brief Confederate incursion barely mentioned in the official reports. As the Sixty-sixth held the brigade's right, it was especially at risk, and as Major Palmer put it, "the enemy commenced pouring in"; the Confederate assault came directly at the Sixty-sixth's portion of the line. Robert Russell, now a lieutenant, wrote that the Confederates "charged right up to our Breastworks & laying their guns on them fired right down upon us. They were so close that the powder stung my face." (Russell had not had an eventless day; Rebel sharpshooters sent four shots whizzing past his head when the young officer left the trenches to answer nature's call.)[17] Peter Mitchell, a private in Company D, wrote in his journal that "one rebel caught the musket of a man standing by my side and asked him what in h—l was firing at, and then climbed on the breastworks and sprang over my head and went to the rear." The Sixty-sixth did not break, and with the help of reinforcements it repelled the incursion, taking several Confederates prisoner. The regiment's stand was part of the coalescence of a new Union line that would halt Jackson's offensive.

With night falling, Jackson's men found that pursuer, like pursued, was subject to disorganization. Confederate units became confused and mixed as Union resistance stiffened. As the assault played out, a mounted Jackson and his staff reconnoitered the ground before the Southern lines. In the darkness and confusion of the Wilderness he was fired upon by his own troops and mortally wounded. The general who had commanded Confederate forces opposing the Sixty-sixth at Port Republic, Cedar Mountain, and Antietam would soon be no more.

That night one man from each company in the Sixty-sixth was sent out for picket duty. One picket, the same veteran who would recount the panic that affected some of the Sixty-sixth earlier in the day, remembered it as a balmy night with a bright moon, but it was a night fraught with peril. The Confederates posed the most obvious danger, although one's comrades could be just as much a threat: "Behind me were our own men in their works whom I feared and dreaded as much as the rebels, for I had had some experience with them during the day, and knew that at the first alarm many of them would shoot without giving a guard a chance to save himself." His solution was to find a good-sized stump; in the event of a nighttime Confederate advance, he would fire a warning shot and then lie down with the stump between him and the Federal lines, allowing the enemy troops to pass over him.[18]

Sporadic firing continued through the night. The morning found many in the Army of the Potomac wondering if they would be prisoners or worse before the next sunrise. They were irredeemably on the defensive. The men in the Sixty-sixth heard some whippoorwills that night and joked that their cry was actually, "We whipped old Joe."[19] The Federals still outnumbered Lee's army, but their position and lowered morale, the terrain, and—one might add—the deficiencies of their commanding general canceled out their numerical advantage. It remained to be seen whether these weaknesses would be enough to allow the Confederates to break the Union position.

Together with the rest of Candy's brigade, the Sixty-sixth remained in its breastworks until the morning. Shortly after dawn the men heard firing to their right and rear. With Jackson wounded, the Confederate command in that sector had shifted to J. E. B. Stuart, who was renewing the offensive. Within half an hour the fighting reached Geary's White Stars. Lee was also committing the forces that had not accompanied Jackson the previous day, launching an assault from the south as Stuart threw his men at the Federal lines from the west. Geary soon found himself under heavy pressure from both the front and the right. The right began to give way, leaving him unsupported. Meanwhile, Confederate artillery fire played heavily upon his lines. It was probably with some relief that Geary obeyed an order to withdraw to form a new line perpendicular to the original breastworks, in the vicinity of the Chancellor house.[20]

No sooner had Geary executed the order than Hooker himself appeared on the scene and told him to return to his original position. In the confusion, however, Geary had "lost" two of his three brigades; the brigades under Greene and Thomas L. Kane had apparently fallen back north of the Chancellor house, leaving him only Candy's First Brigade. Geary nonetheless complied as best he could and advanced to reoccupy the breastworks. The men of the Sixty-sixth found there that Greene had actually left behind two of his New York regiments, the 60th and 102d. By most accounts in the Sixty-sixth, the 60th New York—or at

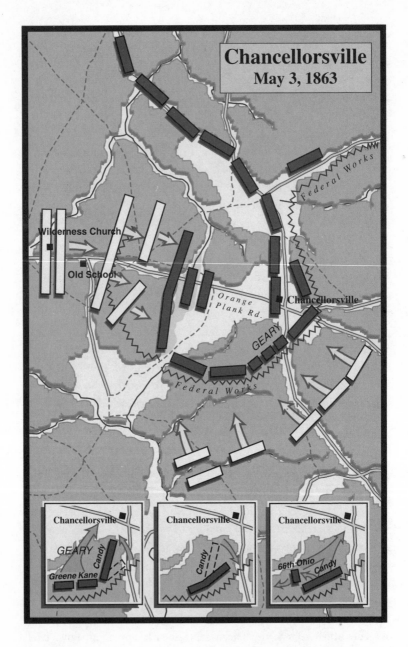

Chancellorsville
May 3, 1863

least a portion of it—had been made prisoners until the Ohioans res-
cued them. As Candy's brigade came down upon them, the New Yorkers turned the tables on their captors and demanded their surrender.
One bewildered Confederate guard turned to Major Palmer and asked

if this meant that he was a prisoner. Wrote Palmer, "My pistol convinced him."[21]

Once repositioned in the trenches, the Sixty-sixth found itself on the division's extreme right. It was ordered to "change front," that is, to turn around to face what had been the rear. Geary himself then commanded the regiment to pivot out to protect the division's flank and engage the enemy, who was advancing through the woods. Eugene Powell recalled (with forgivable hyperbole), "The desperation of the situation now flashes upon me, when a single Regiment has to move forward to meet a column that the evening before routed a corps."[22]

From where it stood, with its left still resting on the trenches, the Sixty-sixth charged unsupported for a short distance through the woods. It soon encountered large bodies of Confederates. It also took fire from enemy batteries. Lieutenant Russell described "this terrible storm of shot and shell," observing that "there was nothing terrible about 'Port Republic' to the side of 'Chancellorsville.'"[23]

The position was clearly untenable and the men slowly fell back, firing as they withdrew. To their left and rear their comrades in the First Brigade had abandoned the works and were in retreat as well. The brigade received the praise of an expansive Geary, who noted in his official report that "Candy's brigade seemed animated by a desire to contest single-handed the possession of the field, and before the deadly aim of our rifles rank after rank of the rebel infantry went down, never to rise again." Pvt. Augustus Tanner of Company I later wrote to his mother that "I was quite certain that some of our times had come to die[.] for my own self I did not think of getting hurt. I was no more frightened I was going to say than I am now. . . . I tell you my gun barrell got as hot as fire. I stood up to the rack and cut the hay without giving an inch." It was at this juncture that the Sixty-sixth suffered the bulk of its Chancellorsville casualties: three men were killed, many more wounded.[24]

Sgt. William Flago, who the day before had erroneously reported the rout of the Sixty-sixth, was back with his regiment, determined, according to Powell, to distinguish himself, having been "intensely mortified at his mistakes and flight." The sergeant resolved to make up for this embarrassment during the third day's fight, in which he fearlessly exposed himself to enemy fire. Major Palmer was near him when Flago was shot through the jugular; the sergeant attempted to speak, but his mouth filled with blood and he fell to the ground. The major had no last words to report when he wrote the sergeant's widow. Flago, a young man barely twenty, if that, had been promoted to second lieutenant the previous month but had not been mustered in at that rank, and now he never would be.[25]

Geary's men fell back slowly to a position north of the Chancellor house, which was in flames. Their resistance helped stall the enemy advance and maintain the integrity of the contracting Federal position. Falling back through the line of the Second Corps behind them, the regiment's cool withdrawal in the face of the enemy was further evidence of their status as veterans.

That night the Sixty-sixth occupied a new position on the Federal left, where it once again dug in. On Monday it again changed position. Lee did not renew his attack, and on Tuesday Hooker's army withdrew in good order across the Rappahannock to occupy its old campsites. W. A. Brand wrote that the men "were all greatly disappointed, when ordered to recross the Rappahannock, as all believed they were able to hold their position—indeed, all knew the enemy had suffered much more severely than we had."

It had been a botched campaign, nothing less than a disaster for the Army of the Potomac. Joseph Diltz's brother-in-law George Milledge had stayed behind, apparently in hospital. He evinced a more jaundiced attitude reminiscent of Diltz several months before, writing to his sister Mary that "i was not in the fight and i am not sorow for it and am not ag[o]ing to fource mi selfein the next one. . . . [F]ighting is plaid out with me there is no fun in it any more."[26]

William Sayre wrote to his father Ziba the same day that "we have been out on a buchering expedition and we Just returned day before yesterday evening to our old camp again. well I cant say that we done much more of that kind of business than what the Rebes done. but there was buchering done on both sides." He reported that the Sixty-sixth had suffered sixty or more casualties and that it was certainly a blow to the much diminished regiment, but "we must not expect to go in a fight and then get out without getting some of our boys killed and wounded."[27]

The casualty returns for the Sixty-sixth reported, besides the three killed in action, a total of forty wounded and thirty missing, for an aggregate loss of seventy-three. Only five of the reported casualties were officers. Thomas McConnell, captain of Company A, was wounded in the shoulder and would be disabled for several months. The official returns listed no officers as missing, but in fact Company K's Capt. William A. Sampson, who had last been seen between the regiment and the advancing enemy kneeling and firing his revolver, was a prisoner. Also, Lt. Elhannon Zook of Company G had been wounded in the leg and taken prisoner. (Prisoners from Chancellorsville were sent to Belle Isle, but most would be paroled and back within Federal lines in two weeks.)[28]

Given the extent of the carnage (521 casualties in the brigade and 1,209 for the division), the Sixty-sixth got off rather lightly.[29] Eugene Powell had reported 360 officers and men present for duty on the morning of May 2, so its casualties came to roughly one in five, far lower than the 50 percent casualties of Port Republic and the 40 percent of Cedar Mountain. Indeed, it is not surprising that some of the Sixty-sixth were disappointed at recrossing the river. In their opinion—and they were probably correct—the Sixty-sixth had inflicted more damage than it had incurred. Although they had fallen back on Sunday, they still occupied a good defensive position and were quite prepared to shoot down any enemy troops brave or foolhardy enough to charge their works.

It had been a confusing fight. Perhaps it is no coincidence that the only two letters that have come to light in which men of the Sixty-sixth enclosed hand-drawn battle maps were both written after Chancellorsville.[30] There were also requests for newspapers so that they could read about the battle, presumably to help them make better sense of what they had been through. William Tallman recalled that "we hardly knew whether we had been whipped or not."[31]

The Sixty-sixth Ohio had fought its second major battle as part of the Army of the Potomac. Antietam had been classified as a victory, though far from decisive. Chancellorsville had been almost as bloody as Antietam, but it was clearly a defeat. In both battles the Federal commanders had been seriously flawed. Soon the Army of the Potomac would have a new commander to lead it through yet another desperate battle, this one on the hillsides on the outskirts of a county seat in southeastern Pennsylvania.

16

Gettysburg: The Enemy Will Simply Swallow You

*D*epending on their position in the Battle of Chancellorsville, many Union soldiers did not have a clear perception of defeat; however, as the outlines of the contest became more certain, it was clear that "Fighting Joe" had not been much of a fighter. The North was in shock. Horace Greeley, editor of the *New York Tribune*, was incredulous, and he perhaps best summed up the popular reaction: "My God, it is horrible. Horrible. And to think of it—130,000 magnificent soldiers so cut to pieces by less than 60,000 half-starved ragamuffins."[1]

Meanwhile the Army of the Potomac created an exceptionally well-ordered camp, almost as if in so doing its men were demonstrating to the world—and maybe to themselves—that they were still a coherent force. They laid out streets and avenues by brigade, regiment, and company and decorated them with evergreen boughs. Lt. Robert Russell, though his jaw sore from two tooth extractions, was nonetheless content with his situation, writing to his parents, "We have such a nice camp here. It is situated on a high ridge & we have set out a lot of fine cedar which makes it cool & shady."[2]

The regiment remained at Aquia Creek for well over a month, spending much of its time in drill as the days lengthened and warmed. John Houtz noted in his diary that division drill took up the better part of ten hours on a particular day, culminating in a review by General Slocum. Two days later there was brigade drill, after which the men were treated to a speech by General Geary. Eugene Powell recalled that in early June the men "had fully recovered from the hardships and exposures of the late campaign and if not as strong in numbers we were under more thorough discipline and organization."[3]

The paymaster visited the regiment, and large consignments of cash were sent to Ohio. If surviving correspondence is any indication, the men had gotten into the habit of sending most of their pay to their families. Husbands posted funds to wives, while the unmarried sent money to parents. A soldier's life was uncertain, and it was better to give loved ones the benefit of their pay than a stranger rifling their pockets should they become a prisoner or a corpse—or for that matter, a hospital patient. Also, inflation was high, increasing the economic hardships of soldiers' families. A private's wages of thirteen dollars a month may not have amounted to much, but three or four months' pay together (for the paymaster could be a stranger for several months at a time) could constitute a helpful windfall for a soldier's family.

The Twelfth Corps received orders to break camp on June 13, and it left Aquia Creek that evening. After marching through the night, the regiment rested briefly at Dumfries. The much-maligned town looked a bit better now that it was spring; John Houtz wrote that "dumfries looks well since the trees around has come out green."[4] The march continued on June 15, and the men arrived at Fairfax Court House the same day. The weather was hot and the march a hard one; several men in Slocum's corps died of sunstroke.

Lee was on the move in the Shenandoah Valley beyond the screen of the Blue Ridge, but Hooker, still commanding the Army of the Potomac, was uncertain of his opponent's whereabouts and ultimate destination. The obvious fear was that Lee would once again cross the Potomac, in which case Hooker would likewise have to move north to stand between the Confederates and Washington or Baltimore—or, should Lee penetrate even farther north, Philadelphia.

The Twelfth Corps remained at Fairfax for a day and then marched to Leesburg, on the south bank of the Potomac and east of the Catoctin

Mountains, arriving there on June 18. The march to Leesburg had been an uncomfortable one in the continuing hot weather. A portion of the route had been over a road strewn with unbroken stones, which were hard on soldiers used to marching on soft dirt roads.[5]

The Sixty-sixth remained in the Leesburg area for a week. In that time the only major event was the execution of three deserters from Alpheus Williams's division. The corps was marched around the three coffins; "It was a hard sight," John Houtz reported. Geary took a predictably sterner attitude towards the event, writing to his wife that "Justice to the living requires some punishment for such a crime, 'Verily the way of the transgressor is hard.'"[6]

The Sixty-sixth remained in Leesburg until the morning of June 26, when the regiment was awakened at one o'clock. A heavy rain was falling, and the tents were heavy with water as the men struck them in preparation for a move across the Potomac. The regiment crossed the river by pontoon bridge with the rest of the corps and advanced a short distance into Maryland. The same night it encamped briefly at Poolesville and remained there for a few hours. On the morning of June 27 the Sixty-sixth crossed the Monocacy River and followed the Baltimore and Ohio Railroad west to Knoxville, about four miles from Harpers Ferry.

By now Hooker was aware that Lee's army was across the Potomac and marching through Pennsylvania. His response was to maneuver the various corps of the Army of the Potomac so as to interpose Union troops between Lee and the nation's capital. Slocum's Twelfth Corps was holding down the army's left, while the First and the Eleventh Corps were advanced into Pennsylvania. They in turn were preceded by Union cavalry under John Buford, feeling out the enemy's position and screening Hooker.

The Twelfth Corps advance now took the Sixty-sixth northeast, away from Harpers Ferry, bringing it just short of Frederick, Maryland, on June 28. A race for position was on. Slocum's men drove north from Fredericksburg, many regiments marching twenty-two miles or more. The Sixty-sixth made its way through Frederick early in the morning of June 29 and ate breakfast two miles beyond. It resumed its march, passing through three or four small towns and stopping in the vicinity of Middlesburg.

Tuesday, June 30, saw fifteen miles of hard marching, ending in Littlestown, Pennsylvania. As the men proceeded north out of Virginia into Maryland and then into Pennsylvania they began to encounter more sympathetic civilians. Having campaigned almost exclusively in Virginia, the soldiers of the Sixty-sixth were not accustomed to meeting friendly citizens while on the march. The patriotic inhabitants of Littlestown greeted the tired troops with buckets of cool water. Despite some nearby skirmishing with Confederate cavalry, the men were happy to rest the night there, for as Sergeant Tallman noted, "we were among our friends and out of Rebeldom." In W. A. Brand's view, "The people seemed to us like a different race from those we had become accustomed to meeting in Virginia. Every one had a kind word or a nod of welcome to the soldiers, and their faces gleamed with pride as they gazed upon those who had come to protect their homes from the invader."[7]

The next day, July 1, the Sixty-sixth took up the march with the rest of the Twelfth Corps for Gettysburg, by way of the Baltimore Pike. Some of the men stopped at farmhouses along the way and bartered for bread and apple butter. William Tallman recalled encountering a cheese "the like of which I had never smelled before." It came in round balls approximating the size of a baseball, and when broken up it "perfumed the air for rods around us." Struck by the novelty of it all, the Ohioans engaged in a food fight while on the march, pelting one another with the cheese balls. Tallman recalled that "the odor in and around our company was dense enough to cut with a knife."[8]

W. A. Brand and his father were meanwhile enjoying hospitality of a more refined nature. A mile to the east they had discovered the residence of Alexander McAllister, whose family was busily preparing food for the Union troops on the road. Brand noted that "often the fair hands of his beautiful daughters Miss Mary and Miss Eliza, distributed the provision to the delighted soldiers." The Brands were invited to stay for supper with the McAllisters, who provided them with "a sumptuous dinner, embracing all the edibles of the season, and were waited on and entertained by Mrs. and the Misses McCallister in a manner that impressed us with the elegance and refinement of the family." Mr. McAllister informed the officers that he had lost a team and nineteen barrels of flour to Rebel cavalry that morning.[9]

Geary's White Stars arrived at Two Taverns around eleven in the morning and encamped west of the road. Some of the men could hear the muffled sounds of artillery in the distance, although no one was apparently aware that a major battle was underway—as in fact one was. Five miles up the road at Gettysburg the First and Eleventh Corps were coming to grips with Confederate forces under Hill and Ewell advancing on Gettysburg from the west and the north. The outnumbered Federals were engaged in a desperate holding action.

Slocum remained at Two Taverns until midafternoon, a delay that later garnered him some probably unjustified criticism. William Tallman recalled that once the decision was made to continue the march the men fell in rapidly and were soon hurrying toward Gettysburg: "The sun was hot. The ground was hot. The breezes that fanned our brows was hot, and the men panted like dogs on the chase and sweat and sweltered through clouds of dust that come back from Knapps Battery in our front. The order was quick march and no halts, but once or twice a stop was made that the horses of the artillery might not give out entirely." After an hour of this they neared the town and encountered fleeing civilians. Tallman recalled his comrades beckoning after them, "Oh come back; we are going to have lots of fun," or "What are you going away from the picnic for?"[10] A more somber mood prevailed when the advancing troops met wounded from the First and Eleventh Corps.

The two Federal corps were forced into retreat but made a stand on Cemetery Hill, south of Gettysburg. Their losses had been high, including the First Corps commander, John F. Reynolds, shot dead by a sniper early in the battle. Slocum's corps came up on the right of the Union line; much of Geary's division was placed in reserve farther to the south, at the base of the 550-foot hill called Little Round Top. The hill was to assume great importance in the next day's fighting, but that would not be the Sixty-sixth's fight. Early the next morning, July 2, the regiment joined the rest of Geary's White Stars on Culp's Hill, located to the east of Cemetery Hill, where the First and Eleventh Corps had made their final stand the previous day.

For a time during the first day's fighting Slocum was in charge of the Union forces at Gettysburg. Upon learning of Reynolds's death he rode ahead of his corps, after turning command over to Alpheus Williams. Geary was still in charge of the First Division, while Candy and Powell continued in brigade and regimental command, respectively.

More importantly, the Army of the Potomac itself was under new management. Hooker had asked for the troops at Harpers Ferry to augment his forces. When his request was refused, he submitted his resignation, which Lincoln had been only too glad to accept. On June 28, George Gordon Meade, commander of the Fifth Corps, had been named Hooker's successor. Meade was a forty-seven-year-old West Pointer with an engineer's methodical mind. For several years prior to the war his military service had consisted primarily of constructing lighthouses and breakwaters. During the war he had risen through the command structure, proving himself a capable brigade and then division commander.

In December he assumed corps command, continuing a reputation for competence and reliability.

Lee seems to have considered Meade superior to Hooker but thought that a change in command at such a critical moment would work in the Confederates' favor. Known for his bad temper and as a terror to his subordinates, Meade was called a "damned old snapping turtle" by some of his men. In charge of an entire army for the first time, the temperamental Meade faced a major battle only three days after taking command.

Candy's brigade assumed a reserve position on Culp's Hill behind the men of George Greene's New York brigade, who were busily entrenching and creating works of logs. Between the hill and Rock Creek to the east the slopes were heavily wooded. Downhill from their works Union troops erected abatis, defenses of felled tree with sharpened stakes, designed to slow any assault by the Confederate troops, who, though unseen, were known to be on the other side of the stream.

The morning of July 2 found the Federal position anchored on the right by Slocum's corps on Culp's Hill, curving at Cemetery Hill and extending south along Cemetery Ridge for a short distance before it bent westward in a salient that culminated in a peach orchard. The Federal line then curved back through a wheatfield and a scrambled collection of boulders called Devil's Den. Overlooking Devil's Den was Little Round Top, beneath which the Sixty-sixth had encamped the night before.

Between the night of July 1 and the morning of July 2 the Federals had considered launching an attack from Cemetery and Culp's Hills, in which eventuality Slocum was to have been the wing commander. Though the plan was abandoned, Slocum persisted in seeing himself in this elevated role, and he was never explicitly contradicted in his assumption by Meade, who had more important matters to consider. Thus command of the Twelfth Corps again reverted to Williams.

Meade was content to adopt a defensive position; he generally found the ground to his liking, though the peach orchard salient had been established contrary to his instructions. The Federal position was largely on high ground, and it had the advantage of interior lines—Meade could easily shift forces back and forth. The only vulnerable point was the salient below Little Round Top. Lee's forces, however, faced an uphill fight. In addition, several miles separated the extreme Confederate left from its extreme right, making reinforcement difficult.

Lee assumed the offensive. He ordered an assault by Longstreet's corps on the Federal left, to strike against Little Round Top, the salient below it, and also the center of the Federal line on Cemetery Ridge. If successful, the attack would gain Little Round Top, which was the end of the Federal line and its anchor; it would roll up the Federal left and center in a series of successive assaults. Ewell's corps, meanwhile, facing the Federal "hook" at Cemetery and Culp's Hills, would exert pressure to prevent Meade from reinforcing his left with men from Slocum's wing. Ewell was given discretionary powers to turn his diversionary activities into something more serious if circumstances warranted.

Longstreet's attack started at four o'clock. The Federals managed to hold Little Round Top, but the peach orchard salient was shattered and the Cemetery Ridge line almost pierced. Ewell's artillery opened up on Slocum's corps as Longstreet began his attack. By half past six the peach orchard salient was disintegrating, and Meade called on Slocum for reinforcements to shore up the Federal left and center. In response, Williams's division (now under the command of Thomas Ruger, with Williams in charge of the corps) marched down the Baltimore Pike and took a right turn on a road that would take it into the heart of the fighting on Cemetery Ridge. Slocum also dispatched Geary with two of his three brigades—Candy's (including the Sixty-sixth) and Thomas Kane's brigades—leaving Greene's thinly stretched New Yorkers to hold Culp's Hill.

The move to reinforce was ineffectual. By the time Ruger's First Division arrived at Cemetery Ridge, the situation had stabilized, while Geary, in one of the great blunders of his military career, missed the right turn and continued south down the Baltimore Pike, out of the battle. Eventually, confused as to where he was and where he was supposed to be, he halted his men at McAllister's Mill, where the pike crossed Rock Creek. His official report later lamented that "when ordered thus to leave my intrenchments, I received no specific instructions as to the object of the move, the direction to be taken, or the point to be reached, beyond the order to . . . follow the First [Ruger's] Division." Ruger's division had been completely out of sight, and Geary had followed stragglers he thought to have been with Ruger's command. So it was not his fault, he argued, that his two brigades found themselves where they could be of little benefit to anyone except (by their absence) the Confederates.[11]

At half past seven Geary received an order to hold his position as far as the creek "at all hazards"—hardly a difficult task. So aside from some stray shells during the mistaken march down the Baltimore Pike, the men of the Sixty-sixth had come through the second day's fighting at Gettysburg without being engaged.

Not so their comrades in Greene's 3d Brigade, which had been left to hold the breastworks on Culp's Hill. Culp's Hill is in fact two hills: an "upper hill," where Greene's men were dug in, and to the south a "lower hill," where the First Division had been entrenched before being called away to the left. As fate would have it, Ewell launched an assault which took his men into the abandoned Federal trenches on the lower hill. Meanwhile, an attack on Greene's position was repulsed at great cost to the Confederates. With the help of reinforcements, the New Yorkers were able to beat back four enemy assaults. Three hours' fighting ended with the Confederates still occupying the lower hill's works, and Greene, having refused (that is, having bent) his line to face the lower hill, still in control of the higher ground.

Slocum and Williams determined that at the earliest opportunity they should retake the breastworks on the lower Culp's Hill. Consequently Geary was relieved of his guard duty at the Rock Creek bridge and was commanded to return with his two brigades to Culp's Hill. Candy's brigade, including the Sixty-sixth, returned to its old position supporting Greene's New Yorkers.

The Sixty-sixth was then ordered, perhaps by Geary, to take an advanced position perpendicular to and on the left front of Greene. It was a daring move, but since Geary did not discuss it in either his reports or correspondence, we do not know his thoughts (if indeed he had directed the movement) on thus placing the Sixty-sixth in what might have been a disastrously exposed position. Upon receiving his orders, Powell led the Sixty-sixth to the top of Culp's Hill and sought out the officer in command—possibly Greene—to inform him of the position the Sixty-sixth had been instructed to take. The other officer responded in astonishment: "My God! If you go out there the enemy will simply swallow you!"[12]

Powell nevertheless had his orders. He obtained a guide "who had been on the outside of the works and knew the lay of the ground." At dawn the two slipped over the Federal works and briefly reconnoitered the rocky slope of Culp's Hill. They were not fired upon, and they returned to their line without incident.[13]

Powell returned to the regiment and called his men to fall in. He did so in a low voice, but he was heard well enough, and the regiment quickly assembled. The Sixty-sixth crossed Greene's lines to assume the ordered position, which would allow it to deliver enfilading fire on the enemy (that is, upon an exposed flank). The Sixty-sixth came under fire itself as soon as it emerged from the Union works; nonetheless, it took the

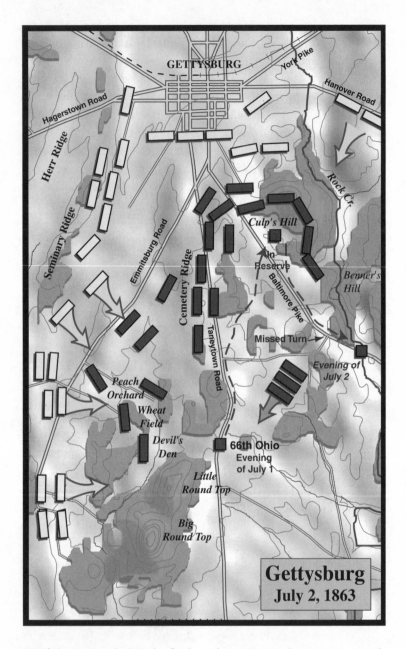

Gettysburg
July 2, 1863

Confederates on their right flank as they attempted once again to advance up Culp's Hill.

The heavily wooded terrain was no doubt confusing. Large boulders, trees, and saplings felled in the previous day's fighting obscured the vision of men on both sides. The Sixty-sixth may also have had a line of fire on the Confederates occupying the abandoned Federal works on the lower hill, although the woods on the slope would probably have kept their shots from having much effect.[14]

Although the Sixty-sixth's left was very much "in the air," the limited visibility afforded by the terrain likely concealed their vulnerability from the advancing Confederates, who were more intent on taking Culp's Hill than in rolling up the concealed regiment firing at them from their right. If the monument and markers the Sixty-sixth's representatives later placed on the site are accurate, its line did not extend very far, probably only about sixty paces down the slope. This was a short distance for a formation of approximately three hundred men, perhaps reflecting reluctance to spread an unanchored line too far. It is very likely that the "line" was a rough one, in which the men were allowed to find cover behind whatever rocks and fallen trees were available.

The regiment's left extended to an outcropping, upon which stood Major Palmer, whose field glasses swept the hazy and tangled landscape to his left, rear, and front. Doubtless he wanted to guard against the possibility that the Sixty-sixth would in fact be "swallowed up" by a Confederate attack on its exposed flank. The major's dutifulness cost him his life; he was shot through the lung and died a week later. Pvt. John Houtz later recalled how he and three other privates from Company B carried the major back to the main line. Upon setting him down, Houtz observed that Palmer was "breathing through the hole the ball had made," and he applied to the wound a silk handkerchief he had wet with canteen water. Palmer said, "Oh, that did me so much good," and then exhorted his men, "Stay with them boys! I will soon be back with you." Houtz returned to the firing line, and together with another man he located and shot the sniper they deemed responsible for the major's wounding. "Brave Major Palmer, how we loved him. He was the soul of honor and brave as steel." Palmer's body was shipped back to his parents for burial in Parma, New York.[15]

The Sixty-sixth was withdrawn from its flanking position at some point during the morning and eventually went into the line on Culp's Hill to take the place of a New York regiment whose ammunition was depleted. The position was a secure one, and apparently the regiment suffered no casualties as it joined in repulsing the Confederates' frontal assaults on the hill.

The Ohioans were probably placed in the center or right of the New Yorkers' entrenched line, and it was here that the Sixty-sixth once again faced Stonewall Jackson's veterans of the Second Corps, now part of

The Sixty-sixth Ohio's monument at Culp's Hill, Gettysburg.

Edward Johnson's division. Jackson, however, was in his grave, and before the day was over many of the troops he had commanded would also be dead. In all there were three assaults that day. Many Confederates huddled behind boulders or in other "dead zones," where the terrain afforded shelter from Federal fire. Some felt themselves in an impossible situation, and rather than risk almost certain death by making a break for the rear they improvised white flags of surrender and went up the hill to become prisoners. These included men of the Stonewall Brigade, who may have been opposite part of the line occupied by the Sixty-sixth. Maj. B. W. Leigh, who was acting as Johnson's adjutant,

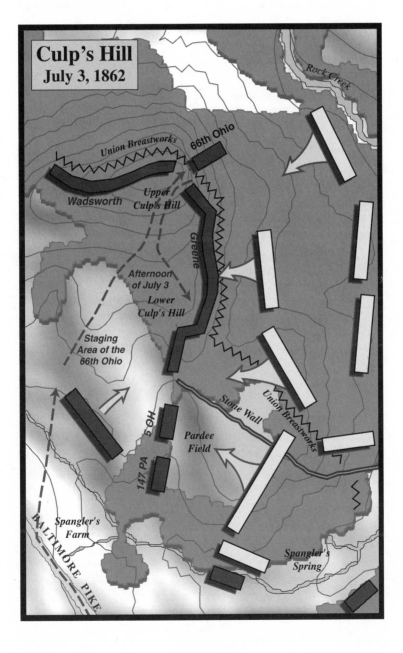

Culp's Hill
July 3, 1862

Rock Creek

Union Breastworks

66th Ohio

Wadsworth

Upper Culp's Hill

Greene

Afternoon of July 3

Lower Culp's Hill

Staging Area of the 66th Ohio

147 PA

5 OH

Pardee Field

Stone Wall

Union Breastworks

Spangler's Farm

BALTIMORE PIKE

Spangler's Spring

rode forward in an attempt to halt the surrenders. Both he and his horse were killed, riddled by Union bullets.

Robert Russell, now captain of Company G, was to claim that Leigh's brave sally brought him to within a hundred yards of the Sixty-sixth, and that it was its fire—no doubt combined with that of other regiments—which brought him down. In a letter describing the battle, Russell, still the souvenir collector, enclosed a piece of Leigh's coat, together with a piece of the 21st Virginia's battle flag and a cutting from an unnamed Confederate officer's sash.[16]

The Sixty-sixth likely inflicted heavy casualties, and it did not incur many in return. An analysis of all sources reveals only one killed in action and nineteen wounded out of 303 men engaged.[17] The toll on commissioned and noncommissioned officers was a bit disproportionate. Company E's Lt. Charles E. Butts, promoted since his scandalous behavior the previous winter, was wounded by a minié ball that passed through his right wrist and into his left thigh, while Lt. John T. Morgan of Company I was wounded in the left thigh. There was also the loss of Major Palmer. Five sergeants were wounded as well.

Probably the most horrific casualty was Sgt. William M. Scott of Company D. Shell fragments from an overhead explosion caught him in the face, taking away the entire upper left jaw and all of his nose. Powell recalled seeing him as he was being taken to the rear: "As he breathed his cheeks seemed to meet, as there was not anything to keep them apart." Miraculously, he survived and was discharged for disabilities. Horribly disfigured and incapable of speech, Scott returned to Logan County, where he lived for many years thereafter. In the 1880s he was part of a committee delegated to select a site for the Sixty-sixth's marker on Culp's Hill.[18]

Following Johnson's assault on Culp's Hill, Lee launched the famous attack known as Pickett's Charge against the Union center on Cemetery Ridge. It was preceded by a furious artillery barrage, a few of the shells flying over Cemetery Ridge and landing in the vicinity of Culp's Hill. William Tallman was serving as assistant to the Sixty-sixth's surgeon and was stationed in a barn off the Baltimore Pike at the time of the shelling. Shells began to explode around the barn, which made staying there "untenable." The wounded were quickly evacuated. Tallman would recall, "I was much more exposed in going to the rear than I would have been with the Regiment in their works. I shall not deny I made fast time in the direction of the rear."[19]

After the artillery barrage, a mile-long line of fifteen thousand Confederates stepped out of the Seminary Ridge woods and advanced across the fields before Cemetery Ridge and up the gentle slopes of the ridge itself. In perhaps the best-known episode of the war, the charge was repulsed, leaving the Army of Northern Virginia defeated on all fronts that day at Gettysburg.

That night the Federals on Culp's Hill did not know whether Lee would renew the fight. There was sporadic firing in the darkness, but in the dawn's light it became apparent that Ewell was gone; the next day would see Lee's entire army in retreat. The defenders of Culp's Hill were free to inspect the ground before their lines. In front of Greene's works there were 391 Confederate dead, with another 150 or so on the other side of the creek. Geary's division also took 130 prisoners and picked up two thousand rifles, most of which had been in Confederate hands.[20]

Tallman returned to the Sixty-sixth early on the morning of July 4 and walked out upon the slope to inspect the carnage of the last two days' fighting. He found the ground "thickly strewn with dead and wounded, of all ages and conditions of men." He noticed one young man and searched his pockets for some sign of identification but found only a letter, without his name or regiment. He sent the letter back to Ohio enclosed in one of his own "intending perhaps to have it sent to the writer at some future time." William Sayre wrote to his family that "the Rebs lay thicker than ever I saw them before. . . . I counted twenty five at least on a spot of grass not over five rods wide." Sayre did not know for a fact whether he had shot anyone, but he could say that he had fired "upwards on ninty rounds at the Rascals." Indeed, Geary claimed that his division expended 277,000 rounds on July 3 alone.[21]

As at Antietam, the task of burying the dead fell to the victors. Burial details placed the Union dead in individual graves, while the Confederate dead, many of them slain two days before and already blackened and swelling, were laid to rest in trenches.

Soldiers not on burial detail occupied themselves with writing letters home and preparing meals. Some of the men were also trying to get the damp powder out of their pieces. It was the custom of the men to drop a live coal down a musket barrel after removing the bullet so that the packed damp powder would "come out with a flash and a fizz," as Tallman recounted one such attempt. A soldier from Company K had performed this ritual, but the "coal did not operate on the spur of the moment and he looked down the muzzle just at the point of explosion and the fellows cap went up in the air and he went backward onto the ground. He thought his end had come, but beyond spoiling his mustache and robbing him of his eyebrows and forelocks no damage was done."[22] Some distance to the left, a regiment discharged its weapons to eliminate the dampened powder. The volley provoked a brief panic; Federal soldiers raced back up the slope and jumped behind their works, shouting that the "Johnnys were coming back."[23]

17

We All Are Anxious to Leave This Place

There were always soldiers separated from the regiment—often a great many men, perhaps more than a third of those carried on the rolls. There were the recovering sick and wounded and those on detached duty. There were also those on furlough. Pvt. Joseph Diltz, now fully recovered from disease and injury, had finally obtained leave in June and was able to return home to his wife. (One result of his visit would be a newborn child in the Diltz household the following March.)

Furlough was up at month's end, and Diltz made his way to Columbus, where he purchased a ticket to Washington. He got as far as Harrisburg on June 27 and found the city in an uproar over Lee's invasion. Harrisburg felt itself threatened—and understandably so. Diltz reported to the provost marshal, who told him to remain in the city until the crisis had passed. Diltz, who was perhaps aware of the executions for desertion within the Army of the Potomac, was not comfortable with the situation, but there was no choice but to obey. He wrote to his wife, "I am a good deal uneasy about not getting on to the regiment but the Provost Marshal told me that it would be all right I would have a good excuse for not getting to the regiment." In the aftermath of Gettysburg it took him three weeks to catch up to the Sixty-sixth.[1]

For several days following the battle, the Sixty-sixth, together with the rest of Twelfth Corps, took part in the pursuit of Lee. As they advanced to the Potomac the regiment passed a clump of trees where W. A. Brand found the corpse of a spy named William Richardson, who had been captured and hanged by General Buford. In a "D. N. Arbaw" letter to the *Citizen and Gazette* he expressed the view that there were few who would "fail to recognize in him, a man who has for nearly two years sold us books, papers, &c."[2] William Tallman corroborated Brand, recalling Richardson as "a peculiar looking man of about 40, who would mount stump or some other convenient elevation, sing Patriotic songs and then offer them for sale, that is printed copies and sometimes in pamphlet form. At the time I never heard any one express any suspicions as to his not being what he seemed, a fellow who wanted to have an easy time, enjoy himself and pick up a few dimes by the wayside."[3]

The attempt to catch and defeat Lee's army before it could cross the Potomac was unsuccessful, but the Army of the Potomac could now claim an unambiguous victory over its old foe. The remainder of the summer was not very eventful for the Sixty-sixth, though over the next month it marched approximately four hundred miles through Maryland and northern Virginia. With the close of the Gettysburg campaign, the Sixty-sixth, together with the rest of the Twelfth Corps, advanced to Harpers Ferry via Frederick. Maneuvering continued, punctuated by a small skirmish at Snickersville, Virginia. The regiment eventually came to rest at Ellis Ford on the Rappahannock River, not far from the Chancellorsville battleground. The enemy was on the other side of the river, but the Ohioans had little contact with them.

The weather in Virginia was hot, and the area around Kelly's Ford was largely devoid of forage, leading General Geary to observe, "This is the hottest weather I ever saw. To call it warm would only burlesque the whole thing. . . . The inhabitants are in a starving condition. The only things that do grow here to any extent are whortleberries, blackberries and snakes." George Milledge, Joseph Diltz's brother-in-law, wrote to his sister that the women he had seen looked as though they "had bin threw [into] a thorn patch rong end first[.] they are starved until they air not thick as mi leg."[4]

The regiment boarded a train to Alexandria on August 16. There the men were to board a steamship for New York City. They would follow other veteran regiments, troops fresh from Gettysburg, to join them in putting down the mid-July draft riots. All was peaceful now, but the draft was soon to go into effect, and the government wanted more troops on hand in the event of further trouble.

The regiment reached Alexandria on July 17 and remained there for several days awaiting the paymaster. If the journal of John Houtz is any indication, discipline was lax. He recorded that he "went to town and saw a great many of the boys drunk and fighting every store keper they came to." The paymaster was slow in getting to the Sixty-sixth. Houtz wrote on July 20, "no pay yet the pay master has been cursed more than a million times since we have been here all the boys want to have a spree before we leave. . . . we all are ancious to leave this place it is the meanest hole in virginia."[5]

The Sixty-sixth was finally paid and soon thereafter boarded the steamer *Baltic*. It was apparently a large vessel, for it took on four other regiments in addition to the Sixty-sixth. The men spent the night on board and got underway at dawn on July 23. The Sixty-sixth renewed its bad luck with water transport. Repeating the experience of the returning *Port Republic* prisoners a year earlier, the *Baltic* became stuck on a sandbar. There it—and its passengers—remained for the next five days. Other vessels attempted unsuccessfully to pull the *Baltic* off, prompting Houtz to record, "some say they may as well try to pul the blue ridge over as to pul of this boat." He also complained that "we cant get any good watter to drink the water here is kept in barles and it dont taste like watter."[6] In an effort to lighten the weight on board, many of the men transferred over to other ships, but still to no avail. Finally on August 27 some tugs with the assistance of a high tide got the *Baltic* off the sandbar.

The journey was not a pleasant one for the Ohioans. The water was very rough, the men unused to ocean travel. Most of them were seasick, including Houtz, who was detailed for guard duty but allowed that he "did not stand much."[7] Meanwhile it was observed that the regimental surgeon "was required to use all his medical skill and persuasions" to convince Lieutenant Colonel Powell "that he was not going to die."[8] The men disembarked from the *Baltic* at Governor's Island, in New York Harbor, on August 30.

The implementation of the draft created no new disturbances in New York City or Brooklyn, and so the troops on Governor's Island remained where they were. They spent their time drilling and touring what points of interest the island offered (including the cemetery—again demonstrating the fascination cemeteries held for many Civil War soldiers). The ocean voyage that returned them to Alexandria commenced on

September 9. It was a smooth transit this time, and the good ship *Baltic*—again employed to transport the men of the Sixty-sixth—managed to avoid sandbars. They disembarked at Alexandria on September 11 and the next day began the march back to the Rappahannock line. Five days later they went into camp at Raccoon Ford on the Rapidan.

The day after its return the Sixty-sixth was assembled to witness the execution of deserters. The unfortunates were two New Yorkers from Greene's brigade. As was the practice, the division was drawn up into a hollow square; in the center of the formation two graves were dug. The blindfolded prisoners were brought out, tied hand and foot, and made to sit on their coffins with their backs to their graves. Two ranks of soldiers, twelve men each, were then positioned fifteen paces away. The volley of the first twelve killed one of the prisoners, but the other remained sitting. The second line then fired; the prisoner, though wounded, remained alive and sitting up. Geary was seen to rush excitedly up to the firing squad's captain, who pulled out his revolver and walked up to the prisoner to deliver the coup de grace. Although only half of the firing squad's rifles had been loaded, it had seemed, William Tallman reported that some of the shots had kicked up dust off to the side of the prisoner. The firing squad was placed under arrest and marched back to headquarters.[9]

John Houtz absented himself from the spectacle and was punished with eight hours' picket duty. The historian of the 7th Ohio recalled, "This was a most unpleasant and trying ordeal under any circumstances, but when the execution, as in this case, was conducted in a bungling and unnecessarily cruel manner, it was horrible in the extreme." There were other executions in the army that day, nineteen in all. Writing to his wife, General Geary concluded, "Thus you see the crime of desertion will no longer go unpunished, when so many expiate their crimes upon the same day."[10]

A few days later the Sixty-sixth and the rest of the White Stars were once again on the march. On September 26 they reached Bealton Station, Virginia, where they boarded a westbound train, having just learned that their destination was to be a different theater of operations. Under the overall command of Joseph Hooker, the Eleventh and Twelfth Corps were being transferred to join the Army of the Cumberland, which was now penned up in Chattanooga, Tennessee, following its defeat at Chickamauga earlier that month.

Their transfer would begin a new phase in the Sixty-sixth's military career. Having been westerners in a predominantly eastern army, they would soon become an Army of the Potomac regiment in an army of westerners. No longer pitted against the Army of Northern Virginia, they would face the Army of Tennessee, under Braxton Bragg. That army had not always been well led, but it had tasted victory at Chickamauga, and at the moment it seemed to have the upper hand.

18

Why, Ain't I Distributing Them?

*T*he cars took the Sixty-sixth over the same tracks that had transported the men east in the winter of 1862. When they reached Bellaire, Ohio, the site of their derailment the previous year, the men seem to have encountered some Copperhead sympathy. W. A. Brand would write that while the citizens of Wheeling exerted themselves preparing coffee and pork for the soldiers when they passed through, "the citizens of Bellaire could not be persuaded to interest themselves on our behalf." Some of the White Stars from the 7th Ohio encountered a surly hotel keeper in town who initially refused them service; they persuaded him to change his mind—rather than see "his house ripped up from top to bottom." A little west of Bellaire, in the town of Cambridge, the returning Ohio troops encountered a group of Democrats returning from a rally in support of Clement L. Vallandigham, a Copperhead Democrat running for governor of Ohio. A dozen or so of the Sixty-sixth's soldiers fired a volley of blanks into them. William Tallman recalled, "They thought they were to be massacred sure." Another practice of the Ohio troops was to get one of their fellows to cry out, "Three cheers for Vallandigham!" on a station platform and then to pelt with stones and pieces of coal anyone who responded affirmatively.[1]

Some of the Sixty-sixth were able to pay a "flying visit" to Urbana on their trip west. They left the troop train, later catching up to it in Indiana or Kentucky by taking civilian transport. Some who had the appropriate political background from before the war were lobbied at the Urbana train station by local Democrats, who wanted them to distribute tickets for the Democratic slate. Having left a packet of tickets with a soldier he had supposed to be a son of the Democracy, the hapless Democratic candidate for probate judge discovered the soldier throwing them to the wind. The candidate rebuked him and reminded the soldier that he had been given the tickets to distribute them. Replied the veteran of the Sixty-sixth: "Why, ain't I distributing them?"[2]

A few men in the Sixty-sixth were already resentful over attempts to put them up for local office on the Democratic ticket. One of these was Theodoric G. Keller, who had been a lawyer before the war and was now the Sixty-sixth's adjutant. He was Maryland-born, perhaps increasing the likelihood that he had entertained Democratic leanings prior to his enlistment. Keller did not mince words on the subject, denouncing "the d——d Butternuts talk about using my name in connection with the office of the Prosecuting Attorney on their ticket. I don't belong to any such infernal, traitorous, treasonable party or clique. . . . I am emphatically for the next President, and the present one, Old Abe; the Union, and for Johnny Brough [the Republican candidate for governor], and the Union."[3]

The divisiveness that had produced the draft riots of New York was not unique to that city. Buoyed by victory at Gettysburg and the Confederate surrender of Vicksburg, the Union cause seemed in the ascendance, but progress had been purchased at a great price in blood. Many who condemned the war were now, with the draft bearing down on them, in danger of being called to fight and die in its prosecution. There were avenues of escape for the well-to-do draftee, but they provided no solace for the poor farmworker or day laborer, who could neither afford the three-hundred-dollar commutation fee nor pay for a substitute. Neither was the Emancipation Proclamation going down well in certain quarters. Many had always believed that the Republicans were at heart the party of abolitionism and that the war had been provoked with just this end in mind. To them the war for the Union was a sham—it was really a war to "free the nigger"—and some immigrants and poor whites (especially those of Southern extraction) in the Midwest wanted no part of it.

The western portion of Champaign County remained disaffected. One center of Copperhead sympathy, in addition to Mad River Township, was Careysville, the only village in Adams Township in the isolated northwestern corner of the county. In what may have been an intentional provocation, a large party of Republicans, most of them from outside the township, staged a rally on August 20 just outside the village. There were the predictable speeches condemning Vallandigham and praising Brough. Afterward, the participants made their way through Careysville in sixteen wagons. When the wagons reached Main Street, their passengers were singing various patriotic and war songs, such as "Rally 'Round the Flag, Boys." They were met by a group of locals, reportedly 150 men and women, who called out to them to cease their singing and began throwing stones at the wagons. The wagons quickened their pace and were pursued by the angry Copperheads. After being chased through the length of the village, the Republicans pulled up their wagons at the outskirts of town; the men collected themselves to resist any further attacks. There was some scuffling, and then shots were exchanged, bringing down a Republican, one George Cummins, who would eventually recover from his wound.

The unionists demanded, reported on the threat of burning down the town, that the "Rebels" surrender Levi Dow, who had fired the shot that had wounded Cummins. There was a brief standoff. It ended when Dow was handed over to the Republicans, who transported him to Urbana, where he was promptly jailed. Apparently the Careysville residents had no stomach for an escalating conflict. The next day a mounted troop of one hundred National Guardsmen arrived in Careysville to arrest the rioters, many of whom had fled into the woods and cornfields; however, six men surrendered themselves, perhaps thinking their apprehension was inevitable. Antiwar disaffection in the county had flared into violence, but it faded quickly enough. The Ohio countryside would not be the scene of guerrilla warfare.[4]

The trains bearing the Sixty-sixth and the other White Stars continued west to Indianapolis, arriving there on October 2. The next day they proceeded south, crossing the Ohio River into Louisville. From there they reached Nashville on October 4 and Tullahoma the following day. Although there were breaks in the journey, it was a long trip with very few, if any, amenities. One soldier later recalled that they were "shipped down to Tennessee in Big Cars like so many hogs."[5]

Upon arrival at Tullahoma, the regiment was pressed into the role of railroad guards. The Sixty-sixth, along with elements of the 7th Ohio, was ordered onto the cars for a train ride north in the middle of the night. The expedition was under the command of the 33d Indiana's Col. John Coburn. He was responsible for that segment of the line, which was threatened from the north by a large force of Confederate raiders. The Federal troops, numbering no more than four hundred, stopped short of Wartrace, which, as it transpired, had fallen into enemy hands. Coburn was reluctant to engage the Confederates, although Powell wanted to alight and defend the railroad bridge spanning the creek just south of town. Coburn declined to do so, placing greater importance on the Duck River bridge further south. The Federals withdrew, followed by Confederate forces, who pressed them, in a tentative fashion, at Duck River. Thereupon the Ohioans were given free rein and advanced north along the tracks, pushing back the Confederate skirmishers. They took no casualties and, it seems, inflicted none.

Candy's brigade had its headquarters at Duck River, while the Sixty-sixth was shuttled about on scouting expeditions for the next several days, occasioning the odd skirmish. Eventually the regiment was stationed at Wartrace Creek, just north of Wartrace. The men constructed shanties to shelter themselves from the rain, which was falling constantly, while Powell organized the men in the building of a small fort to protect the bridge.[6]

On October 13, the regiment voted. Robert Russell fretted that some of the men might vote for Vallandigham: "I am really afraid that a good many in the Sixty-sixth are going to vote for 'Old Val.' If they do they ought to be *courtmartialed!* because Vallandigham is nothing *but a traitor!* They are those that are disaffected or tired of soldiering and are foolish enough to believe that a peace will come sooner by voting for Val." He need not have worried, for only seven votes were cast for Vallandigham—and 198 for Brough! The seven votes were from Marion and Delaware County recruits in Company K, although in reporting this fact, W. A. Brand hastened to note that "Capt. Sampson, however, votes the Union ticket, and is in no way responsible for the vote of his company."[7]

Vallandigham lost in Ohio. In a sharply polarized Champaign County, Brough won by a landslide, chalking up 2,656 votes to Vallandigham's 1,582. The divisions were predictable: Mad River Township voted three to one for the Democracy, while Goshen Township and Mechanicsburg voted 335 to 52 for Brough.[8]

The results of the election were hailed by most of the troops. The men of the Sixty-sixth were beginning to settle in at Wartrace, hoping that they might carry on with railroad garrison duty throughout the winter, but on October 28 they were given an hour's notice to break camp and board the cars for Bridgeport, Alabama. "We had very respectable winter quarters erected and with the good foraging district around us, could have spent the winter quite pleasantly at Wartrace Bridge," lamented W. A. Brand.[9]

The timing was bad in another respect. In an effort to retain its veteran regiments, the government was offering a $402 bonus and a thirty-day furlough to the soldiers whose terms were up in 1864 if they would reenlist for three years or the duration of the war. In addition, if three-quarters of a regiment "veteranized" in this way, it would retain its organization and numerical designation, adding the honorific "Veteran"— for instance, the Sixty-sixth Ohio Volunteer Veteran Infantry. The officers had already mounted a campaign to persuade the men to accept the government's offer. Their task had been made easier by the outlook of garrison duty in quarters that were already substantially begun, but the sudden uprooting to Bridgeport changed all that. Brand noted from Bridgeport that "had we remained at Wartrace Bridge, the veterans would have triumphed gloriously. . . . The more than active life and the less than half rations which the boys are now enduring, may cause them to feel like doing much more, and may be, much less."[10]

Arriving at Bridgeport, Candy's brigade lagged behind the rest of the White Star division. Geary's other two brigades had proceeded as far as Wauhatchie, about twenty-five miles away in the shadow of Lookout Mountain, on the other side of the Sand and Raccoon Mountains. There on the night of October 27 they were attacked by Confederates, who threatened to envelop them with assaults from the east, the north, and the northwest.

The battle lasted well into the morning and cost Geary 216 casualties. Among the wounded was the commander of the Third Brigade, Gen. George Greene, who was shot in the face and would not return to duty until 1865 (although he would survive the war and die at the respectable age of ninety-seven in 1899). Among the dead was Geary's son Edward, a lieutenant in the artillery, recently commissioned a captain. Geary felt the loss keenly, and the experience lent a grim, if not vengeful, determination to his outlook on the war. The loss of Greene was a blow to the division. The Rhode Islander had been a more than competent brigadier and could be relied upon to assume command of the division if circumstances dictated—a role which he had, in fact, filled at Antietam. The Ohioans in the brigade could irritate him (they rather enjoyed getting his goat—Brand reported that they delighted in calling him "Corporal"), but notwithstanding the occasional collisions he had their respect.[11]

Candy's brigade left Bridgeport for Wauhatchie on October 30 and arrived there the next day. The White Stars were now all together, encamped across a stream from Lookout Mountain, the setting for the Sixty-sixth's next engagement—the conclusion of which would be regarded by many as the most dramatic of the war.

19

A Flag on the Mountain

Hooker's two corps fell under the ultimate command of Ulysses S. Grant, whose star was ascendant following his capture of Vicksburg on July 4, falling wonderfully on the heels of the Union victory in Pennsylvania. Grant had demonstrated determination and resourcefulness, some would say brilliance, in the campaign leading to the fall of Vicksburg—a notable contrast to the usual run of Union commanders.

Grant's ascendance coincided with the downfall of William S. Rosecrans, the Army of the Cumberland's commander since the autumn of 1862. Rosecrans's record had been mixed. He had a reputation for slowness, occasioning great exasperation in Washington; however, he had won an important victory at Stones River, Tennessee, at a time when the Union cause was in great need of one. Unfortunately for Rosecrans and the Union cause, he had also presided in September over a disastrous defeat at Chickamauga in northern Georgia. Most of it routed, his army fled north to Chattanooga, where it was now holed up, half-starved and demoralized. The attenuated Bridgeport supply line, now littered with dead mules, was barely able to keep the Union army alive. In fact, Hooker's men had not been dispatched to Chattanooga itself for fear that once there they would become additional candidates for starvation.

Grant was appointed commander of the new Military Division of the Mississippi on October 16, giving him control of the departments of the Ohio, the Cumberland, and the Tennessee. One of his first acts was to relieve Rosecrans. Lincoln had encouraged but not mandated the removal of the unfortunate general, whom he had recently characterized as "confused and stunned like a duck hit on the head" in the wake of Chickamauga. Though suffering from the effects of a riding accident, Grant nevertheless wasted little time in proceeding to Chattanooga to observe the situation himself and assume personal command of a campaign to raise the siege and push Bragg south. Inspecting the lines, Grant speculated that the Confederates "looked upon the garrison of Chattanooga as prisoners of war, feeding or starving themselves, and thought it would be inhuman to kill any of them except in self defense."[1]

Chattanooga was nestled in a curve of the Tennessee River, on its south bank. To the south and east was Missionary Ridge, and to the southwest loomed Lookout Mountain, rising 2,200 feet above sea level. Both these heights were occupied by Confederate forces, who not only held a good position but enjoyed a numerical advantage. One of Grant's first initiatives was to shorten the supply line between Bridgeport and Chattanooga. He accomplished this in part by having Hooker send a force east from Bridgeport through the Raccoon Mountain pass. The movement was successful and accomplished with little bloodshed, despite a nighttime Confederate counterpunch at Wauhatchie.

Having opened up a shorter and more effective supply line, Grant turned his attention to the enemy on Missionary Ridge and Lookout Mountain. The broad strategy was to attack the main Confederate force on Missionary Ridge from the north, ultimately flanking and rolling up Bragg's army along the heights. A second Federal force would be positioned before the ridge to pin down Bragg's army as it was attacked on its right and assault the Confederate center once its flank began to give way. The attack on Missionary Ridge would be accompanied by a movement against Lookout Mountain. That operation would simply be a diversion, but it might also open the way to flank the enemy position from the south.

Hooker was responsible for Union operations on the right, and Geary was given command of the attack on Lookout Mountain. Before Geary could come to grips with the Confederates on the heights above him, however, he had to cross Lookout Creek, running to the west of the mountain to the Tennessee River. Upon receiving his orders Geary summoned Eugene Powell, who as the division's Officer of the Day had recently surveyed the picket line along the stream. A messenger appeared with a summons at Powell's tent in the early morning hours of November 24. Together they rode to division headquarters, where Powell noticed lights in several tents and surmised that a movement was being planned. He entered Geary's command tent and found him seated there with his staff officers and officers from Grant's and Hooker's headquarters. Powell later recalled, "It struck me, as I stepped into Geary's tent, that I had seldom looked upon a more silent, solemn party, but Geary broke the silence by saying, 'Colonel I have sent for you, I have orders to make a demonstration upon Lookout Mountain. I wish to know where and how I can cross that creek with my command.'"[2]

The request reminded Powell that he had seen, protruding above the creek's surface, the "knees" of an unfinished dam near a small gristmill. He described this to Geary, venturing that it would be possible to construct a footbridge to the other side by taking boards from the mill and lashing them to the dam supports. Geary endorsed the plan and ordered Powell to proceed with the project, using the reserve pickets, who happened to be from Geary's old regiment, the 28th Pennsylvania.

Powell returned to the picket line and gathered the men. He told them his orders and explained that he needed volunteers to cross the creek and form a half circle on the other side, so as to draw the fire of the enemy and allow the other men to construct the footbridge in relative security. It was clearly a risky proposition, since there were certainly Confederate pickets on the other side. Powell recalled that "there was a complete silence for a time, when a soldier stated he would go, then another, and it was evident that the whole command would go, so I divided my command as nearly equal as to numbers as I could and directed the right to sling their guns across their shoulders and climb across the knees."[3]

To the surprise of Powell and of his pickets, they were not fired upon, and the footbridge was constructed without opposition. A soldier was positioned upon each knee, and lumber was torn away from the mill and passed down the line. The rude structure was made without hammer, nails, or saw; timbers were lashed down with rope to produce a narrow but sturdy bridge over which Geary's troops could cross in single file. Upon accomplishing his task, Powell returned to the mill to find

Geary, who was much pleased with the project's success. He wasted no time in sending over his division, augmented by a brigade from another corps. By nine in the morning they were all across, and the Federal line arranged itself up the lower western slope of the mountain, facing north. On its immediate right were steep, unscalable cliffs. Geary's line would proceed north, wheeling to the right, ascending the mountain as far as an intermediate "bench" on the northern face, which when gained would position them to advance to the mountaintop itself.

A skirmish line was thrown out, and Geary's men began their advance. The terrain was rough and obscured by a damp mist. Ravines and gullies would suddenly open up in the fog. Candy's brigade was placed on the extreme left. The Sixty-sixth, together with fifty men from the 5th Ohio, were on the left of the brigade, and thus at the end of the Federal line. Geary's troops pushed forward, sweeping away some Mississippi pickets, who were surprised to find Yankees on their left and rear. The Sixty-sixth and Candy's brigade saw little if any action up to this point, although they had overrun the camp of the brigade whose pickets they had encountered, garnering two artillery pieces. Their primary function here was to sweep the lower slope so as to secure a crossing of Lookout Creek by another Federal force farther downstream.

Geary and Candy had a small run-in at this point. Geary was accompanying the brigade when a group of two hundred prisoners was brought in from the right. Geary ordered Thomas McConnell, formerly captain of Company A and now a major, to take charge of the prisoners. Candy was also present and ordered McConnell to stay where he was. Geary shot back, "Colonel Candy, I command this division," to which Candy replied, "General Geary, I command this brigade and if you have any orders for my regiment give them through me." The prisoners were conveyed to the hands of the soldiers of the 5th Ohio who had already assumed the role of guards.[4]

A fair number of Confederates were captured and passed through the lines back to the provost guard. "Our line advances as rapidly as the enemy retires," W. A. Brand reported, "but every tree and every stone shields a rebel and he gladly rushes to the rear as our lines pass him." Also among the prisoners were the mysteriously acquiescent pickets who had allowed the construction of the footbridge across Lookout Creek. Powell reported that twenty pickets

> gave themselves up as prisoners, stating that they saw the force building the foot bridge, but as that force was small they decided

it was surely a scouting party, and they would let us come over, then they would charge and cut us off from the bridge and capture our entire party, so they decided not to fire or molest us; but when the bridge was completed what was their surprise at seeing not the balance of our pickets coming over, but instead Geary's division and on the run.

They had hid in the bushes until they realized they were cut off and that the battle had gone against them, at which point they surrendered.[5]

By one o'clock Candy's brigade had wheeled around to the right and was positioned below Lookout Point, facing the heights from the north. Being on the extreme left of Geary's line, it followed the other three Federal brigades in the ascent up the mountain. Consequently the other brigades, among them Greene's New Yorkers, took the brunt of the punishment in pushing back the Confederates, who attempted a stand in the vicinity of the Craven house on the mountain's bench. Candy's brigade was held in reserve.

The Confederate troops, under the command of Brig. Gen. Edward C. Walthall, were up against more than they could handle, and they were pushed back. At three in the afternoon three companies of the Sixty-sixth (B, G, and K) were sent forward to relieve the 149th New York, under heavy fire. The mist obscured the situation, and the Federal commanders were not sure of the extent of their success. By this time, however, Confederate resistance had dissipated, the fire was nothing more than a rear-guard action, and the three companies were sheltered by the rocky terrain of the mountain; the Sixty-sixth took very few casualties. Major McConnell reported five men wounded by stray shots. As it turned out, Colonel Candy was the only casualty of real note. Between two and three o'clock he fell on the rocks, severely injuring his hip; his injury caused him to relinquish brigade command to Col. William Creighton of the 7th Ohio. Captain Russell also took a tumble; probably after the shooting had stopped, he lost his footing and fell nine or ten feet, landing on his face. He was fortunate not to have broken his neck, although he did lose four front teeth. The collision also slammed his head backward, causing a sprain to his neck and upper back.[6]

At nine in the evening the Sixty-sixth's companies were taken off the line and allowed to go to the rear for their first meal of the day. By the next morning the battle was over, and Lookout Mountain was bereft of Confederates. Soon the Stars and Stripes was planted on Point Lookout, together with the white star banner of Geary's division. During the

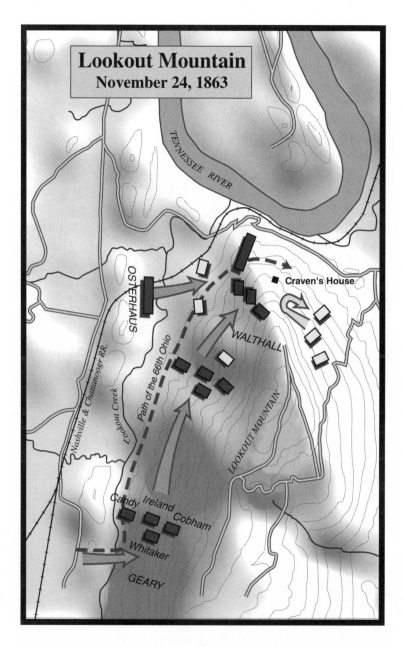

Lookout Mountain
November 24, 1863

TENNESSEE RIVER

OSTERHAUS

Craven's House

Path of the 66th Ohio

WALTHALL

Nashville & Chattanooga RR.

Lookout Creek

LOOKOUT MOUNTAIN

Candy

Ireland

Cobham

Whitaker

GEARY

night Union troops in the valley had seen the flashes of musketry piercing the clouds and mist on the mountain, and they were awaiting some sign of the outcome. When the morning clouds parted to reveal the national flag waving from the peak, great rejoicing broke out. After Chickamauga and the weeks of half-starved confinement in Chattanooga, here was the first indication that their fortunes were changing.

In fact, however, events were not proceeding as Grant had planned. The push against the Confederate right on Missionary Ridge had stalled. Grant's trusted subordinate, William Tecumseh Sherman, had attacked with four Federal divisions to seize what he had thought was the north end of Missionary Ridge. To his chagrin, Sherman discovered that he had in fact captured a separate and distinct hill, set apart by a wide depression from the ridge proper. Sherman had hoped to be in a position on the ridge that might allow him to roll up Bragg's line, but that was not the case. Instead, Hooker's "diversion" on Lookout had been the successful operation of the day. In later years Powell would claim that it had been his discovery of the mill dam crossing that had enabled Geary to transform the demonstration called for by Grant into a full-blown and successful assault.[7]

Grant determined to renew the attack on Missionary Ridge. Even as the White Stars' banner was being planted on Point Lookout, the attack on the Confederate right was about to be renewed. Sherman's troops resumed their assault on northern Missionary Ridge, while the much-maligned Army of the Cumberland moved across the plain before the ridge to engage the first line of Confederate pickets, near its base. The resistance against Sherman was fierce. Meanwhile, the Union troops advancing against the ridge decided to go farther than their orders specified. Having swept aside the first Confederate lines, many of them realized that by halting only partway up the slope they were exposing themselves to enemy fire from above, whereas continuing the ascent would afford many of them shelter in "dead zones," where the Confederate fire could not find them. By pushing on, in fact, they might take the ridge. With the events of Lookout Mountain to inspire them, this was precisely what they did.

Hooker was directed to assault the ridge from the south. Geary's division and two others were sent in, making the offensive against the Rebel line a general one, although the attack did not coincide with the fighting to the north. Hooker's force had to rebuild a bridge over Chattanooga Creek before it could proceed to the base of Missionary Ridge. Once there, the men emulated their comrades on the left and proceeded to climb. By midafternoon they were engaging the enemy, but by then Bragg's army was disintegrating and fleeing down the opposite slope. Once again the Sixty-sixth was spared significant casualties; in fact, it appears to have suffered none.

So, little bloodied on Lookout Mountain and Missionary Ridge, Candy's brigade—now Creighton's—was sent forward the next day with the rest of the White Stars to pursue Bragg's retreating army. Geary's division made its way through the Chickamauga Valley in company with two other divisions, those of Osterhaus (Fifteenth Corps) and Cruft (Third Corps). Geary described the chaos of the Confederate retreat in his official report: "Along the whole route were evidences of the precipitate flight of the enemy; the smoke of his burning trains and supplies, hastily fired by him for want of time for removal, was visible upon all the routes. Our path was strewn with abandoned caissons and limbers filled with ammunition, broken wagons, tents, arms, accouterments, and camp equipage in profusion."[8] The Federals picked up many stragglers on the first day of pursuit, but they did not encounter the main body of Bragg's rear guard. At about eleven o'clock Geary's men, now in Georgia, bivouacked for the night, with the town of Ringgold just four miles down the road.

They were awakened at half past five the next morning to continue the pursuit. Geary's division was in the middle of Hooker's line of advance, Osterhaus in front, and Cruft bringing up the rear. Two hours later the column was approaching a covered bridge spanning South Chickamauga Creek. On the opposite bank was a regiment of Confederate cavalry, supported by a regiment of infantry. They were greatly outnumbered by the oncoming Federals but were in a position to put up a decent fight, if only for a short while. It looked as though the Federals might have to contend for the bridge; however, their foes delivered a single long-distance volley and retreated down the road toward Ringgold. Inexplicably, the Confederates did not fire the bridge, allowing Hooker an unopposed crossing. Beyond Ringgold was a gap in Taylor's Ridge, also known as Pigeon Hills. Through the gap went Chickamauga Creek, the Western and Atlantic Railroad, and the Ringgold Dalton Road—down which Bragg's defeated army was retreating.

The ease with which the bridge guard was brushed aside may have elevated the Federals' confidence. If that was the case, it may have been what Confederate general Patrick Cleburne, whose division was assigned the role of rear guard, intended. Bragg had chosen well: the Irish-born Cleburne was a fighter. His division had held off Sherman's assault on the northern end of Missionary Ridge and had retreated in good order on a day when good order was not typical in the Army of Tennessee. This morning Cleburne selected the best position to stop the Federal pursuit. In and around the gap and at the base of the ridge he concealed his men in ravines and stands of timber.

Hooker saw the geography before him and may have realized the danger, but he did not wish to slow the pursuit by waiting for his artillery to come up. He sent in Osterhaus. The first regiments ventured forward, only to be ambushed by Confederate rifle fire; canister and grapeshot tore holes through their ranks from a battery concealed in a thicket near the gap. An advance against the ridge on the Confederate right was likewise fruitless and led to the rout of the Missouri regiments attempting the attack. More of Osterhaus's regiments were brought up to flank Cleburne's position across the ridge; however, the Confederates were able to bring up fresh regiments, keeping pace with the extension of the Federal line. As new Federal regiments were thrown into the battle, they encountered a well-positioned enemy, whose fire pinned them down or threw them back in disarray.

It was Geary's turn. Four regiments under Creighton marched across the plain before the ridge. Their orders were to scale the ridge and to extend the Federal left, in the continuing effort to outflank the enemy. They advanced in two lines, en echelon. The Sixty-sixth was on the right of the first line, which it shared with the 28th Pennsylvania, the second line consisting of the 7th Ohio and the 147th Pennsylvania.

After a quick advance to the base of the ridge, the four regiments assembled in single line of battle. The Sixty-sixth anchored the right, the order from right to left then being the 28th, the 7th, and the 147th. The Sixty-sixth advanced up the ridge with the rest of the brigade. It was difficult climbing by all accounts. Geary reported that the ascent "was necessarily slow, as it would have been a severe task to have mounted the abrupt acclivity even without opposition."[9]

In light of its sad results, Geary's order to advance up the ridge was occasion for controversy and resentment within the brigade. Powell, who was not with the pursuit force, wrote after the war that the troops had been "clamorous" for an immediate assault. This was perhaps a description of the ritual crowing in which the colonel of the 7th Ohio led his men (the regiment was known in brigade code as "rooster") before advancing forward. Nevertheless, this assertion invited a strong reaction from W. A. Brand, who made some rather serious charges:

> I have never yet heard another man say that "our troops" were clamorous for an assault at Ringgold. Gen. Powell was not there and his information is doubtless derived from Gen. Geary, who

was on confidential terms with Powell and the information was conveyed to Powell for the purpose of shielding Geary from the responsibility of an assault, unordered and impossible of success. Geary, without advice or direction from a superior ordered one Brigade (Candy's) to assault *and carry* a position that was almost insurmountable. . . . When Gen. Hooker rode along . . . he asked Geary "Who ordered this movement?" And Geary with the most astonishing imperturbability replied "*I do not know!*" Hence his desire to shield himself, through the idea that his "troops" were clamorous.[10]

Brand did not state whether he was an eyewitness to that exchange, but one can imagine Geary desiring additional glory after Lookout Mountain. It would also become clear that many of the men in the brigade, particularly in the 7th Ohio, held a grudge against him.

The Sixty-sixth took a position to the left of the 26th Iowa, which was stalled partway up the slope. Some accounts state that, together with the 28th Pennsylvania, the Sixty-sixth may have forced a lodgement close to the crest, but in the absence of major progress elsewhere along the line its advance stalled. The standoff continued until the Ohioans were out of ammunition, at which point they withdrew. The Sixty-sixth sustained a total of fifteen casualties: ten enlisted men wounded and four killed, and one commissioned officer mortally wounded.

The officer was Lt. Harrison Davis, who earlier that year had received his sword at the Universalist Church in Woodstock, Ohio. Captain Sampson wrote a few days later from Chattanooga that Davis "was shot through the body. After he was hit he started down the hill by himself, and I supposed he was only slightly wounded. I was surprised to hear of his death after the fight."[11]

Further to the left on Taylor's Ridge, the Sixty-sixth's comrades in the 7th Ohio were badly mauled. Their advance had brought them to a ravine above which concealed Confederates suddenly emerged to pour down a murderous fire. All but one of their officers was shot. Among these casualties was Lt. Colonel Orrin Crane, in command of the regiment now that Colonel Creighton was leading the brigade. Crane was shot dead, as was Creighton very soon thereafter. In all, the 7th incurred seventy-four casualties at Ringgold (sixteen dead and fifty-eight wounded).[12] If in fact Geary later attempted to dodge responsibility for the failed assault, the blame would then have rested with Creighton, who was dead.

The Federal assault was ultimately unsuccessful and, from the point of view of many of the men, pointless and irresponsible. In the afternoon, after punishing the Yankee attempts to outflank him, Cleburne withdrew. He had gained sufficient time for Bragg to get his wagon trains out of pursuit range; there was no need to linger. Meanwhile, Grant himself came up to Ringgold and called off the chase.

The 7th's decimation saddened many in the Sixty-sixth. The two organizations had fought side by side since Port Republic (Candy had referred to them in command code as "bulldog" and "rooster" respectively). Eugene Powell may have recalled his ride through the Antietam mist with Orrin Crane at his side, and their argument over whether to fire at the half-seen line (of what turned out to be Georgians) before them. Captain Sampson wrote of the 7th's officers: "They were all good friends of mine and I esteemed them highly." William H. H. Tallman testified to similar feelings among the enlisted men, noting that "everyone in the division felt the loss of Cols. Creighton and Crane, for they were both men all the boys loved and respected."[13]

With the success of the scaling attacks on Lookout Mountain and Missionary Ridge behind them, Union commanders may have been prone to minimize the difficulties inherent in uphill assaults. Taylor's Ridge was a reminder that in such circumstances the advantage was usually with the defenders.

Were it not for Taylor's Ridge, the Chattanooga campaign would have cost the Sixty-sixth almost no casualties. Now the regiment had been bloodied, albeit slightly compared to the 7th Ohio, and it had helped take Lookout Mountain. Its men were now part of the western army and its traditions.

In the aftermath of the battle, Geary sent through Ringgold Gap a few scouting expeditions, which ran up against the Confederate rear guard's skirmish line. A few shots were exchanged, but that was all. The Chattanooga campaign was over.

20

Reenlistment and Furlough: Representatives of All That Is Best

*T*he White Stars remained for a few days in Ringgold, where several houses were converted into field hospitals for the more than three hundred wounded. Captain Sampson proceeded on to Chattanooga, thence to Bridgeport, where he shipped north the bodies of Harrison Davis and two Pennsylvania officers. Geary was ordered to burn facilities in the town that could be useful to the Confederate war effort. This he accomplished with gusto, later claiming in a letter to his wife that he had burned the entire town "because the enemy fired upon us from the houses."[1]

The White Stars returned to Wauhatchie, where they continued to grapple with the issue of whether to reenlist. The campaign to veteranize fizzled in the 7th Ohio. Officers were key players in the push to reenlist, and most of the 7th's were dead or incapacitated. In the end there was not a sufficient number of reenlistments in the sadly deci-mated and demoralized 7th Ohio to ensure the further existence of the regiment as a "veteran" unit. A regimental historian would recall, "The severe losses at Ringgold had so depleted the ranks of the 7th that great depression fell upon the few remaining officers and men, which never again seemed to be fully obliterated." Another reported that when Geary, for whom many in the 7th had no fondness, attempted to persuade them to reenlist, the response was negative: "We know the promises of men in authority, and how much care is exercised for the comfort of those under them. We love the society of our friends at home as well as the multitudes of young men who have never spent a day in service. We will take our turn with them."[2]

Not so with the Sixty-sixth. The officers had begun proselytizing at Wartrace in October and once again took up the task, although some of them, perhaps for reasons of health, would not themselves keep their commissions. Since its stay at Wartrace the Sixty-sixth had taken part in three actions and sustained relatively few casualties. The honor of the regiment had been upheld, and its participation in the capture of Look-out Mountain—already hailed as a great triumph of Federal arms—had ensured them a place in wartime legend.

The positives tended to outweigh the negatives in the eyes of most veterans. The $402 bounty itself was an obvious incentive for the Cham-paign County recruits of 1861 and 1862. There is evidence that some of them received a fifty-dollar local bounty at enlistment (presumably in addition to the initial twenty-five-dollar payment ordained by act of Congress);[3] that amount, however, was not much when compared to the money substitutes were collecting, or to the local bounties more re-cent recruits were receiving. Reenlistment therefore provided the older veterans an opportunity for parity. The furlough home was another ma-jor attraction. Many of the veterans had not been back to Ohio for a year or more (not counting their brief visit while en route to Tennessee from the Northeast), and here was a chance to be with friends and fam-ily, perhaps over the holidays. If he did not veteranize, there was a chance that a soldier could die in 1864 without ever seeing home again. (Here we might note that the 7th Ohio had been organized before the Sixty-sixth and that therefore the men of the 7th knew they only had to make it to June to survive the war, whereas the soldiers of the Sixty-sixth were committed through November.) On the other hand, if in fact the war was close to an end, it would be foolish not to pick up the added boun-ty. It might very well transpire that those who veteranized and those who did not would spend the same short amount of time in service (it was easy to be optimistic after Missionary Ridge), except those who had reenlisted would be four hundred dollars richer. William Tallman recalled some of these factors in the decision-making process: "Our late success made us feel that the end was that much nearer and that we could not extend our time very greatly. That to be home about the holidays was a great inducement and often the point that decided many wavering minds."[4]

There was also unit pride and the desire to stick together. (One modern Civil War historian has argued, "Perhaps the best way to understand small-unit cohesion is to think of the company as a substitute family.")[5] As noted, if a sufficient number of men reenlisted, the regiment could remain intact, with its original numerical designation. Certainly the Sixty-sixth could boast of a good record. Although superior enemy numbers had on more than one occasion forced the regiment into retreat, it had never been routed (with the possible exception of Port Republic) and had never lost its colors—no small consideration to a Civil War soldier. The regiment had maintained its honor from Port Republic through Taylor's Ridge. Surely this was a proud tradition, one worth maintaining. The alternative was to be amalgamated like new recruits into other regiments, which would not share their history. A soldier in such a situation would be the odd man out. Even such mundane matters as the identity of one's messmates would be upset. How much better to finish out the war in the company of comrades and under familiar regimental banners!

The major argument against reenlistment was a blend of pessimism and optimism—pessimism in the assumption that the war was in fact fated to last for another year or more and that to reenlist was to expand the window of opportunity for being killed or wounded—optimism in the faith that even were the war to last much longer one could manage to stay alive until one's term of enlistment was up in the fall. Some of the men may have presumed that if enough men reenlisted to veteranize the regiment, soldiers who did not reenlist might be able to stay with their old regiment, thus avoiding the problems of being sent to a new unit while still ensuring their departure from the service before 1865. Even so, there was often great anxiety over the risk of transfer.

The arguments for veteranizing won out in the Sixty-sixth and in many other regiments. As it turned out, on December 15 the Sixty-sixth became the first Ohio regiment to chalk up the required numbers to veteranize.

Once again Private Diltz provides an example of how an enlisted man's thinking might evolve. His opinion of military life had not changed significantly since his days in the Baltimore hospital, although his furlough in June and the improved military situation had helped his outlook somewhat. Apparently his wife, Mary, did not want to see him reenlist, and Diltz was not initially keen on the idea either. On December 4 he wrote to his wife, "Dam the enlisting again I am not so full of War as that." He thought it was time for some of the Copperheads to take their turn, feeling that it must "pleas them too think the old soldiers is a enlisting again"—for presumably each reenlistment could mean one less draftee. Even so, Diltz calculated that the war would not last another year and that the men who reenlisted would be getting a bounty for less than one year's service.[6]

Two days later Diltz wrote again to his wife. He reported that there continued to be much excitement in the Sixty-sixth on the subject of veteranizing. He was still holding to his previous convictions but was beginning to see that his was the minority position; it seemed that he "and a few others will be left to be transfered into some other regiment I will feel lost to see the boys all go home and be left behind but I will do the best I can if it is the cais."[7]

By December 12, three days before the regiment would formally veteranize, Diltz professed confusion over the best course to take, while at the same time allowing the likelihood that he would reenlist. The prospect of being left behind in the ranks of another regiment while his comrades returned to Ohio on their special furlough dismayed him: "Im in the most trubel for a week that ever Was in my life our regiment is all split up sum is going home to stay this Winter and some is to be scatered among other regiments I don't know what to do." He went on to report that his brother-in-law George Milledge had reenlisted, as had most of the Sixty-sixth's original recruits. "Dear Mary you have know idear how I feel about it the thought of being put in some other regiment just the same as a new recruit whair one will [be] imposed on and put rite in front." General Grant himself had told them the other day that he thought the war would be over in June. Now the government was giving a $402 bounty to "the old Soldiers that caim out first that did not get eny"; this would be in addition to an anticipated $100 local bounty, totaling $502: "good pay for one year's sirvis."

He continued to reason the matter out: "You know that I have one year to serve eny way and I am very serten that the war will bee over in less than one year. . . . [T]he regiment is to start home in a few days and if I cum with it dont be suprised for I think it is the best thing I can do and I am shure that I will get out of the sirvis just as soon." Diltz would be on the train home.[8]

The reenlisted veterans arrived in Columbus the day after Christmas. They detrained in the morning and marched to the state capitol grounds. A field piece was fired in salute, and they were addressed by outgoing Governor Tod, who then shook the hand of every man in the regiment. The Champaign County men arrived in Urbana two days later, but their return was apparently late at night, and there were not the throngs turned out to greet them that had been present for their departure two years earlier.

The banner that the women of the town had given the Sixty-sixth was now in tatters. As a symbol of the regiment's trials and indeed as a symbol of the regiment itself, the colors—which at first were put on public display in a local bookstore and later removed to the county auditor's office for safekeeping—were much remarked upon. Many other regiments had lost their colors (a brother regiment, the 5th Ohio, had lost its flag at Port Republic), but not the Sixty-sixth. The banner was ample testimony that local honor had been upheld.[9]

Married men in the Sixty-sixth returned to find that their families had been supported by friends and neighbors. Goshen Township had been especially active. In November a township meeting had been convened to discuss the possible plight of soldiers' families from a shortage of food and fuel during the coming winter. Committees were organized in each school district to round up supplies for soldiers' families in the vicinity. There were estimated to be about forty; approximately a third had lost their breadwinner to combat or disease. November 25 was set for bringing contributions to Mechanicsburg. On the appointed day hundreds of the citizenry converged on the distribution point, bringing with them flour, corn, pork, beef, and 129 cords of wood. The Mechanicsburg ladies prepared a dinner for the contributors, "which repast was duly appreciated and ably discussed by some hundreds of happy guests."

Charles Fulton, the Sixty-sixth's former major, was slated to address them—as he had before the war, when he had been one of the county's more noteworthy Republican orators—but he was still suffering from the effects of his wound and sickness of the previous year. One of the organizers took his place: "Again, let me say to our boys in the field, we will be kind to those you have left behind. You shall know that you have friends at home that will not forget you or yours." Assisting the citizens of Mechanicsburg and Goshen Township was an organization called the

"Saw Buck Rangers," consisting of thirty or more lads aged ten to sixteen, who in addition to learning military drill, split and sawed the donated wood before its distribution to needy families.[10]

Even so, private aid had long since proven inadequate as the sole support of needy families. State and local funds (both through subscription and appropriation) provided aid to the "necessitous" wives and children of Champaign County soldiers. Shortly after the return of the Sixty-sixth, the county commissioners reported that in the previous six months $7,301 had been distributed to eligible families.[11]

Although married recruits were becoming less typical, the promise of official relief and examples of philanthropic activities such as Mechanicsburg's "wood procession" might smooth a family man's path to enlistment, a fact which was probably not lost on the Sixty-sixth's officers, for the regiment's furlough home was doubling as a recruiting trip. A number of men had not reenlisted and would be leaving the Sixty-sixth by the end of 1864, and of course casualties and sickness had depleted—and would continue to deplete—the ranks. More men were needed, and more men were obtained. During their month in Ohio, the Sixty-sixth's veterans garnered over seventy enlistments, of whom all but two reported for duty. Enlistments often followed the demographics of the regiment's original organization; Company C's six recruits, for example, were all Irish.[12]

By this stage in the war, however, recruiting in the North generally had become problematic. Most of the idealists had volunteered in 1861 and 1862, although by 1864 a few young men who had not been of age at the war's commencement entered the service. The great motivator in many cases was money. Capt. William McAdams, who had commanded the Sixty-sixth's Company H before receiving a disability discharge, was occupied with recruiting and would soon be sending substitutes and draftees to the front. According to his friend Col. James, McAdams had arrived at a cynical view of the process, asserting that "money was 'the thing men served.' They demanded high prices for their services as substitutes, then enlisted for bounty and regular pay." The same circumstances prompted the Ohio journalist and historian Whitelaw Reid to observe, "Upon two classes came the whole weight of the war—the most willing and the most purchasable."[13]

Still, the return of a local regiment such as the Sixty-sixth could stir whatever untapped idealism remained, increasing the numbers of the "willing." Some of the January recruits were probably motivated by bounty money, but many were moved as well by the prospect of joining an honored local regiment to fight for the Union's preservation.

The community demonstrated its esteem for the regiment on January 21. At about noon the local companies of the Sixty-sixth formed up in front of the courthouse, with Colonel Candy in his old position of regimental command. It then marched to the public square for ceremonies and speeches. The day was a fair one. There was snow on the ground, but this did not prevent a large number of people from coming into town for the occasion. Urbana's streets were filled with sleighs.

First on the agenda was the presentation of new regimental colors, with the names of the Sixty-sixth's battles and skirmishes embroidered between the stripes. Like the first banner, this one was the gift of the Ladies Aid Society. The presentation speech was made by Milo G. Williams, husband of the president of the society. He expounded on the regiment and the cause in which it fought, taking special note of the many who had not returned.

Wilson Parsons, the regimental chaplain, was on hand to accept the banner and to convey 1862's tattered colors back to the ladies—and presumably Mr. Williams as well. The Sixty-sixth was the representative of this community, he told his listeners, "the representatives of all that is best in American Civilization. The free schools, free labor, churches, and homes of the West." This war was but one stage in a struggle that went back to "Germany and the Reformers—France and the Huguenots—Cromwell and England—The War of the Revolution." (What the Irish Catholics of Company C might have thought of this historical lineage is unrecorded.) Following a brief speech by yet another male representative of the Ladies Aid Society, the Sixty-sixth and its friends, no doubt somewhat chilled by this time, returned to the courthouse for a grand dinner, after which the regiment reassembled to have its photograph taken in front of the offices of Collins's Daguerrean Rooms. Unfortunately, no copy of this photograph has yet been found.[14]

The men of the Sixty-sixth entrained for the South at month's end, leaving behind friends and family who would be praying for their survival in the renewed conflict. The Democratic press, having failed to gain the allegiance of the returning veterans, would say nothing against them, perhaps counting itself fortunate that the soldiers had not ransacked its offices, as had happened in some midwestern communities. The editor of the *Union County Democrat* remarked upon the departure of the Sixty-sixth's Company F from Marysville, "And we thought, as we looked upon the many sad faces and turned away, how long must this be? How long must those who pray for the surcease of this sorrow be the objects of cruel and relentless persecution?" The blame for all this bloodshed, the Democratic newspaperman continued, should be placed on the abolitionists, "bloodstained murderers who profit by the calamities of their country, who brought war and its sorrows upon us, and desire its continuance for mercenary purposes and their love for the negro."[15]

Opinion was still divided on the home front, but the war would continue to be prosecuted vigorously. Ultimately it would fall to the western army, now under Sherman, to maintain the war's momentum. Some in the Sixty-sixth speculated that they might be kept in reserve, perhaps on some sort of garrison duty, while the rest of Sherman's army embarked on the campaign to take Atlanta. But this was not to be. The government had not encouraged the reenlistment of veterans only to keep them out of combat. The Sixty-sixth would see more action.

21

Preparation for Atlanta

While the "veterans" were being feted in Ohio, their comrades who had not reenlisted—forty-two in number—were temporarily posted with the 7th Ohio at Bridgeport. Their garrison duty in Alabama was largely uneventful. Pvt. John Houtz had resisted the call to veteranize and was now concerned with staying warm. General Geary, who remained with his division, found the weather disconcerting, blustering to his wife that "the whole idea of 'Sunny South' is exploded, and much of the poetic idea of Southern beauty is with us fully exploded. It is a humbug and a false-hood and a lie." Geary also continued his efforts to persuade more of the troops in his division to reenlist. These attempts seemed to be focused on the 5th Ohio, which veteranized and returned to Ohio for its special furlough in mid-January.[1]

Houtz's diary entry for January 25 recorded the fact that the names of the soldiers who had not reenlisted were to be published and that noncommissioned officers who had not reenlisted would be reduced in rank, with the comment, "oh how some of those officers will have to watch when they are out of this service." But in addition to being afflicted by boredom and the cold, he was at times lonely for his old comrades.[2]

So he was pleased when the Sixty-sixth returned to the division on February 9 with Colonel Candy, still limping from his Lookout Mountain injury, at its head. Although he remained assigned to the 7th, Houtz spent a great deal of time in the Sixty-sixth's camp. He enjoyed seeing old friends again but he did not let slip the opportunity to rib the veterans for having so long to remain in service. "We can run over there and engoy [enjoy] ourselves plaguing them," he chortled, noting that "a great many of them are down in the mouth and sorry that they did enlist."[3]

In fact, Houtz and some others temporarily in the 7th Ohio had decided that they would rather stay with that regiment. On February 13 he signed a petition to General Slocum requesting permanent transfer to the 7th. The request seems to have been denied, if in fact it was even considered; the nonveteran 7th's term of service would be up before the Sixty-sixth's, in itself sufficient cause to deny the petition. On March 24 the names of all troops from the Sixty-sixth were dropped from the 7th's rolls, and within two days Houtz was back with his old regiment. He recorded his displeasure in returning to the Sixty-sixth: in his opinion, the 7th kept better clothing accounts and was fairer and better organized in assigning guard duty. One morning the Sixty-sixth went out for drill, but Houtz hid under his bed and avoided the exercise.[4]

Meanwhile, a controversy emerged over the payment of the local bounty. The reenlistments of the veterans were credited initially to congressional districts, not to individual counties or townships. Upon the Sixty-sixth's return to Ohio, soldiers outside Champaign County received their bounties and consequently were credited to their home counties and townships; many Champaign County veterans, however, were confronted with bureaucratic difficulties and did not receive their bounty money. After returning to Bridgeport, W. A. Brand, still a quartermaster sergeant, agreed to act on behalf of twenty-five Champaign County veterans in obtaining their local bounties and having their reenlistments credited appropriately. (A soldier from the Sixty-sixth whose reenlistment had not been credited to his home township would not count against the county's enlistment quota; one more draftee from the neighborhood could be the result, possibly engendering local resentment.) To the chagrin of Captain Sampson, who had returned to Urbana for recruiting and was attempting to iron out the matter, the twenty-five veterans received their bounties from counties other than Champaign. "How are you, conscripts?" taunted Brand in a letter home, satirizing the salutation "How are you, veterans?" which had become a popular way to address soldiers who had reenlisted.

Sampson, who was himself an Urbana man, claimed that the crediting to other counties was only a rumor and reported himself "pained" by the incident, worrying that the families of these men would suffer the consequences: "Many who have heard the statement that they 'sold out,' have at once concluded that it was true, and have decided to cut off from favor and assistance the families of the men who have been so misrepresented." Brand replied that the twenty-five reenlistments had in fact been credited outside Champaign County but that the men had been perfectly justified in their course of action, especially in view of the runaround they had received:

> The soldier who is working hard every day and gets shot at occasionally, all for thirteen dollars per month—lives upon Government rations—suffers all the hardships of rapid marches—sleeps on the cold ground—compelled to live without any of the luxuries of civilized life, except at sutler's prices—can perhaps more quickly see the injustice of withholding his "home bounty" than those who are being well paid, and also those who are making fortunes at home in these flush times.

Although Brand did not say as much in his letter, Champaign County was offering only a fifty-dollar bounty, whereas he was able to obtain hundred-dollar payouts for his comrades outside the county.[5]

Meanwhile, in Alabama, Geary was transforming Bridgeport into a bustling transportation center and storehouse for the army. It would be an important link in the chain that was to send supplies and troops to Sherman's army in the field. Not all of Geary's troops, however, were sta-tioned at Bridgeport. Four of the Sixty-sixth's companies had been sent downstream as a picket on the Tennessee River. There they assisted families who were fleeing into Federal lines. Northern Alabama had always had a fair number of Unionist sympathizers, their ranks no doubt swelled by recent Confederate reverses and the introduction of a more stringent conscription act that threatened to draft men up to fifty years old.

Pvt. Joseph Diltz met his downfall in assisting such a family. On March 29 a squad of eight from Company I crossed the river at Caperton Ferry to bring a family over to the Federal side. Apparently there were two boats, each holding four enlisted men; Diltz, who had recently received word of the birth of a son, was in the first. On the far side they were fired upon, and Diltz was one of three captured. His next letter to his wife Mary would be from Andersonville prison. The second boat, with Capt. John Morgan, Lt. John Organ, and two enlisted men, reversed course under fire. Morgan was shot in the thigh and Organ lost a finger, but they made it back to the Federal side of the river.[6]

On April 12, the Sixty-sixth became part of a small expeditionary force sent down the Tennessee River aboard a steamboat. The following day artillery pieces on board shelled the village of Guntersville, dispersing some Confederate cavalry stationed there. Geary then sent ashore a detachment, which captured some mail and destroyed canoes and other small craft. That evening the Federals came to a point about thirteen miles short of Decatur, where they found Confederate artillery and infantry arrayed against them on both sides of the river. Deeming their boat unable to withstand shelling, the Federals steamed back to Bridgeport, arriving there on the evening of April 14.

The Sixty-sixth appears to have been in good spirits at Bridgeport. It was thought that Alpheus Williams's First Division would be sent to the front but that Geary's Second Division would stay behind for garrison duty. This was only fair, some soldiers reasoned, since the White Stars had been sent into the Chattanooga campaign (with four engagements, including the night attack at Wauhatchie), while Williams's men had been kept behind guarding the railroad. W. A. Brand reported at the end of February that the Sixty-sixth was "now well fixed" for staying in Bridgeport for the remainder of the year. "Comfortable quarters have been built by the men, and after several days policing the parades look neat and clean." With the addition of new recruits and the return of recovered wounded and sick, he estimated that the rolls of the Sixty-sixth had swelled to six hundred men.[7]

The immediate chain of command was unaltered. Powell remained in command of the Sixty-sixth, and Candy retained leadership of the First Brigade, consisting of the same four Ohio regiments and two Pennsylvania regiments that had been together since Chancellorsville. Geary was still in divisional command. With Greene of the Third Brigade recovering from his Wauhatchie wounds, Candy assumed command of the White Stars while Geary was away from Bridgeport in January and February, indicating a prospect of advancement for the Sixty-sixth's colonel; as for Geary, however, the rank of major general still eluded him, despite his not inconsiderable skills of self-promotion.

Other things would remain the same as well. Even with the change in army and corps affiliation, Geary's division would continue to use the old Army of the Potomac "White Star" designation. The retention of the symbol was especially appropriate since the division was once more under the command of Joe Hooker, who had introduced the use of corps and division badges in 1863. The badge also called attention to its wearers as newcomers to the Army of the Cumberland. William Tallman recalled, "When we joined the Army of the Cumberland, such a thing as a corp badge was unknown to any Western troops and they was inclined to make fun of our Army of the Potomac ways: they seemed to think us featherbed soldiers. . . . They wanted to know if we were all Brigadier Generals as we all wore stars."[8]

Hooker was in command of the new Twentieth Corps, a combination of the old Eleventh and Twelfth Corps of the Army of the Potomac. Their former commanders, Oliver Howard and Henry Slocum, respectively, did not work well with Hooker and had been reassigned elsewhere. Hooker reported to Gen. George Thomas, commanding the Army of the Cumberland. Grant left in March for Washington, where, promoted to lieutenant general, he assumed control of all Federal armies. He would not return to the west, instead making his headquarters in the field with the Army of the Potomac as it continued to grapple with Lee in Virginia. Sherman was in charge of the western army, set to move south on Atlanta.

Opposing Sherman was Joseph Johnston. Following the debacle of the Chattanooga campaign, President Jefferson Davis had had little choice but to replace Bragg, even though he respected Bragg and loathed Johnston. The change was generally considered a positive one within the Army of Tennessee, whose officers and men had by and large disliked Bragg. Now encamped at Dalton, the army was demoralized following its defeat at Missionary Ridge, but it still had good commanders, such as Cleburne, and its ranks were to be augmented by Leonidas Polk's army, whose theatre of operations had heretofore been Mississippi and Alabama. Although outnumbered by the Federals (approximately seventy thousand men, with Polk's reinforcement, against one hundred thousand in Sherman's army), the Army of Tennessee still had fight in it. Committed by circumstances and temperament to a defensive campaign, Johnston would use this army to good effect.

Sherman's target was Atlanta, a crucial transportation hub. Following Grant's instructions, he would mount his offensive simultaneously with a renewal of the Army of the Potomac's campaign against Lee. Under pressure on both fronts, the weakening Confederacy would no longer be able to reinforce one army from the other. Already cut in two by the loss of the Mississippi River, with the fall of Atlanta the Confederacy would be a significant step closer to being divided yet again. In addition, the loss of Atlanta would damage Southern morale while helping morale in the North, possibly giving a boost to Lincoln in the upcoming presidential election.

Between Sherman and Atlanta was hilly and mountainous terrain, often thickly wooded, with many rivers and streams to ford. At Lookout Mountain, Missionary Ridge, and Taylor Ridge, what was now Sherman's army had been committed to uphill assaults; Joe Johnston could give them more of this. A Confederate defensive campaign was likely to inflict more casualties on the Federals than the South would suffer. However, against an army that was already the larger force, Johnston could not afford long casualty lists, for even if he could repel frontal assaults, Sherman's army would often as not be able to outflank him and force him back. Johnston, who was under strong pressure from the president for a decisive victory, would try to preserve his army and wait for Sherman or one of his corps commanders to make a mistake. Sherman, for his part, was more intent on taking Atlanta and preventing Johnston from reinforcing Lee than in actually knocking out the Army of Tennessee. He was therefore more prone to maneuver than to combat. Even so, Sherman's army, and with it the Sixty-sixth, would be committed to a long series of battles and skirmishes before reaching Atlanta.

22

Oh!

The Sixty-sixth Ohio was not destined for garrison duty. On May 3 the White Stars began their march to the front in northern Georgia. Morale was cautiously optimistic. William Sayre wrote his adoptive father Ziba that "we may expect to have something to do now as old Jo [Joe Hooker] is all for fight," while Geary was "not much behind him."[1] The Confederate army was still at Dalton. Interposed between it and the Federals was mountainous terrain, several miles long, called Rocky Face Ridge, running east to west then south. Sherman's plan was to apply pressure at various points along the ridge, thus pinning down Johnston, while a force under James Birdseye McPherson made its way south along the ridge to pass through Snake Creek Gap into Johnston's rear, there to take Resaca and cut the railroad that was Johnston's supply line.

Geary's men took part in the movement against Rocky Face Ridge. By May 7 they were before the ridge, and the next day Geary marched south to attack a point in the ridge called Dug (sometimes Mill Creek) Gap, located north of Snake Creek Gap. It was a costly and ultimately unsuccessful assault, but one in which the Sixty-sixth was not significantly engaged.

After a strenuous march on a very hot day, the White Stars drew up before Dug Gap in midafternoon. Geary immediately sent forward skirmishers, followed by Cobham's and Candy's brigades. The Sixty-sixth and the 5th Ohio were held in reserve. Perhaps out of consideration for its losses at Ringgold, the depleted 7th Ohio was designated Geary's bodyguard, leaving only the 29th Ohio and the 28th Pennsylvania for the attack. Gen. Jacob Cox supplied a succinct description of the action in his history of the Atlanta campaign: "The skirmishers advanced, scrambling over the rocks and through the undergrowth, till already blown and nearly exhausted they found themselves facing a perpendicular wall with only clefts and crevices leading up through it, the narrow roadway which had been their guide being strongly held by the enemy and intrenched." Repeated assaults were to no avail, even though the Confederates were outnumbered more than four to one. Candy's brigade lost a total of 145 in killed, wounded, and missing, mostly from the 29th Ohio and the 28th Pennsylvania. With the exception of one of its officers, who was wounded while detached to the division's pioneers, the Sixty-sixth suffered no casualties. Geary's total losses came to 357 killed, wounded, and missing.[2]

Nonetheless, Geary felt he could take satisfaction in his labors. McPherson had penetrated through Snake Creek Gap to the south and, for all Geary knew, was busy smashing Johnston's communications at Resaca. If his attack on Dug Gap had helped divert Confederate forces from concentrating against McPherson's essential work, then to some extent he could share in McPherson's accomplishment. Unfortunately, in fact, McPherson became apprehensive after advancing to within sight of Resaca, which was garrisoned by only four thousand men. Had he gone forward, there is little doubt that his force would have taken the town, cut the railroad, and perhaps brought about the destruction of Johnston's army. But he did not go forward. Without a good map or sufficient cavalry to scout the situation, McPherson returned his army to Snake Creek Gap. The lost opportunity, which greatly disappointed Sherman, became one of the Civil War's better-known "might have beens."

McPherson remained at Snake Creek Gap to be reinforced by the rest of Sherman's army for the attack that was to result in the battle of Resaca on May 13–15. Johnston had taken advantage of the time given him by McPherson and had concentrated to meet the Federal threat. After the two sides between them had incurred five to six thousand casualties, the Confederate commander took his army south to find another defensive site. The Sixty-sixth was in reserve for most of the battle, and its casualties amounted to only two slightly wounded.[3]

Following the railroad line, Johnston took his army south and, after further maneuvering, crossed the Etowah River, concentrating his army at Allatoona. At Allatoona Pass the railroad ran through a narrow gorge flanked by high hills. It was highly defensible and just the place for Johnston to seize upon in the hope that Sherman would be so unwise as to attack.

Sherman declined to do so. Instead, the Federal army crossed the Etowah to the west with the intention once again of taking Johnston in the rear with a flanking movement. As part of this maneuver, Candy's brigade was put across the river on May 23. The heat was brutal. Private Houtz recorded in his diary that "the boys gave out like sheep and were scattered on the road." That day the bugles had awakened the Sixty-sixth at three in the morning, but the march had not commenced until eight. The morning of May 24 went differently. "Those Tormenting bugals commenced squealing at 3 o'clock but they did not fool many this time," recorded Houtz; "the boys slept until daylight and then got up and got breakfast in good time to start."[4]

Hooker's corps proceeded east, with Geary's division in the lead. On May 25 Hooker's and Geary's cavalry escort broke up a Confederate attempt to burn the bridge at Pumpkinvine Creek and drove off a small band of enemy cavalry. Geary's division took the road to Dallas, while the rest of Hooker's force advanced by a different route. Candy's brigade led the division, the role of skirmishers filled by the 7th Ohio, until then spared any serious exposure.

The White Stars advanced through extensive and often dense woods. It was not a good place in which to be surprised, and there was a surprise awaiting them. The Union command did not expect to encounter any major concentration of enemy troops for several more miles, not knowing that Johnston's army had transferred its base and formed a line extending from east of Dallas north to a Methodist meetinghouse called New Hope Church. New Hope Church was just ahead of Geary, who was marching into the right wing of Johnston's line. The 7th Ohio began to encounter Confederate skirmishers, and soon it was heavily engaged with a Confederate regiment (the consolidated 32d/58th Alabama) supported by a battalion of Louisiana sharpshooters. The 28th Pennsylvania was brought up to support the 7th Ohio, and the rest of the brigade was placed in line, the Sixty-sixth Ohio holding down the right.

The brigade's line easily overlapped both the right and left flanks of the Alabamians, who were forced to withdraw. Candy's men took prisoners, and from them Geary and Hooker (who had remained with the White Star advance) learned that the Confederate corps of John Bell Hood was to their front. Geary's division was on its own, five miles removed from any other Federal force and in peril of being overwhelmed should Hood decide to advance. Hooker sent an urgent summons for reinforcements and waited; Candy's brigade dug in.

The usually aggressive Hood, perhaps as uncertain of the situation as Hooker, did not attack. At last Geary's savior arrived, in the person of Alpheus Williams, who placed his division to the front of Candy's brigade. The force was also joined by Daniel Butterfield's division, which formed to the left and rear of Geary. Hooker advanced his forces, and within a mile he encountered renewed skirmishing. Williams described the terrain as a "dense woods with considerable underbrush and the ground full of small ravines enclosed in gently swelling hills, which evidently grew higher in front."[5] Williams's men, still to the front of Geary, now began to double-time forward, until they came to an upward slope, where a storm of rifle and artillery fire broke over them.

The slope led up to New Hope Church, and Hood's men were well dug in. The Federals hastily found what cover was available and returned fire. There was little hope of piercing Hood's line and taking the churchyard, where Confederates behind breastworks were shooting through the trees and underbrush. Nonetheless, fire was exchanged until a violent early evening thunderstorm forced an end to the battle. The Federals fell back.

Williams's division was badly mauled, and the 5th Ohio in Candy's brigade had lost its colonel, but the Sixty-sixth had taken few casualties—two enlisted men killed and several wounded. The most notable casualty was Lt. Joseph Hitt, who had been acting as Candy's aide-de-camp. The son of a wealthy Urbana merchant, he was only nineteen, but he was considered an especially promising young officer. At an early stage in the fight, Federal skirmishers, who were being driven in, were endangered when a company in the Sixty-sixth opened fire without orders. Candy dispatched Hitt to Powell to stop the firing. Powell recalled that Hitt "stated he would move forward with me and see the fight begin." In a moment, though, a bullet pierced Hitt's throat, killing him instantly. His last word was simply "Oh!" as he fell from his horse.[6]

Together with the rest of the division, the Sixty-sixth settled into its first experience, lasting a week, of extended trench warfare. The storm ended during the night, and morning found Candy's brigade dug in along a ridge facing Hood's line, which was from eighty to three hundred yards away depending on the curvatures of the positions. A stalemate held while both sides improved their works and kept their enemies under more or less continuous fire. Skirmishers were thrown out between the lines, and sharpshooters on both sides were a constant annoyance. The Confederates attempted at least one major assault, but to no avail.

John Houtz noted on May 27, in a typical run-on journal entry, "The sun rose beautifully and the birds were singing their sweet songs, and behold men stood here the wisest of all creatures shooting each other down such never was known among the wildest beings in the world." That same day George Milledge, Joseph Diltz's brother-in-law, was killed. Mary Diltz now had a husband imprisoned at Andersonville and a brother dead at New Hope Church.

The Sixty-sixth rotated in and out of the breastworks with the 7th and 5th Ohio regiments for the space of a week and continued to take sporadic casualties. During the battle of New Hope Church and the standoff that followed, twenty-two men from the Sixty-sixth were wounded, including two captains and a lieutenant, and five men were killed outright. Two more enlisted men eventually died of their wounds, one of them Pvt. Peter Cox of Company G, who at first looked as though he might pull through. Although the circumstances surrounding his injuries are not clear, he was on the receiving end of Confederate canister or grapeshot. His right arm was broken in two places and had to be amputated, and he was also hit in the face and in both legs. The day following the amputation he was seen on his feet; however, his injuries ultimately killed him as he lay in a Nashville hospital bed.[7]

Near the end of the month Geary decided to straighten the part of his line that was occupied by Candy's brigade. The Sixty-sixth brought up logs in darkness to a new position 140 yards beyond the Union entrenchments. Powell recalled the sometimes grisly details surrounding the dangerous night assignment:

Our route led across a space from which both we and the enemy had been driven as our lines had swayed back and forth in the varying result of the long continued battle. The dead were lying thick along our path and had been exposed to the intense heat . . . and the stench was beyond endurance. As my fatigue parties would in the darkness of the night step upon and stumble over some of these long-neglected, the men would fall with their load and some actually faint at the terrible stench. The enemy hearing the fall of the log would rise above their works and pour volley after volley at random through the woods, thinking that the noise told of an advance on our part, but as the party returned no shot, and as everything was as silent with us as the dead amongst whom we were, the enemy soon ceased firing and fell back to sleep again, we re-commencing our work of building the advanced line of entrenchments, and by moving, to the surprise of the enemy, a strong, well-built field work confronted them at a portion of our line that had heretofore retired abruptly back.[8]

The change in position placed the dead within Federal lines, and they were promptly buried.

It had been a grueling seven days, starting with the first battle on May 25. The Sixty-sixth's casualties had not been especially high, but several more such weeks of steady attrition could seriously reduce the regiment's effectiveness. Geary reported that "my entire division was under fire, without an hour of relief. Owing to the proximity of the lines, and the nature of the ground, no one, whether in front or rear, could rest quietly with any assurance of safety." He also noted "a large increase of sickness" among the White Stars, resulting from exposure, poor diet, and lack of sleep.[9]

So it was with some relief that on June 1 Geary's men were pulled out of the line for a movement to the left. Sherman was shifting his army eastward in order to establish contact once again with the Western and Atlantic rail line, even as he worked to open up the railroad from the Etowah River (where the bridge had to be rebuilt) south to Allatoona (now abandoned by Johnston) and beyond. Battles and skirmishing had occupied both armies in the week that the Sixty-sixth was part of the deadlock at New Hope Church, but neither Sherman nor Johnston was able to score a decisive victory. The style of maneuvering that had characterized the Atlanta campaign thus far continued as Sherman returned to the railroad and made it his line of advance. It was his path to Atlanta and his supply line north. Johnston would continue to block him on that line, watching for a mistake.

The fighting around New Hope Church eventually ceased, as the opposing armies shifted east. Private Houtz summarized it as having been "sometimes hard and sometimes nothing but bushwacking but a great many were picked of[f] by it."[10] Mid-June found Geary's division (now minus the 7th Ohio—its men's enlistments had expired, and they had returned home) before Pine Mountain.

Johnston had established a new line, anchored on the right by Kennesaw Mountain, which commanded the railroad, and extending to Lost Mountain in the west. Pine Mountain was an outpost about midway in the Confederate line, which curved behind it. Johnston's high command was gathered at its summit on June 14 to view the surrounding area, in clear view of the Federal forces assembled before them. Sherman did not know the identities of the officers peering down upon him, but he found their presence audacious and irritating. He ordered them shelled. One of the first projectiles to arch toward the Confederate generals, a solid shot, struck and instantly killed General Polk. Geary later claimed that it was his order and his battery that caused Polk's death.[11]

The next day, June 15, Sherman determined that the Confederates had evacuated the mountain, and he ordered a Federal advance around it. Sherman did not know that the Confederates were still in force beyond the mountain, but he discovered their presence soon enough. At around noon Geary's division, with Butterfield on his right and elements of the Fourth Corps on his left, went forward, moving to the south and west of the mountain, where they encountered Johnston's main line. Candy's brigade led the way for the White Stars and encountered enemy pickets after advancing only a mile. The ground was rough and typical of what had been encountered so far in northern Georgia. Although Geary was supported on both his left and right, he lost contact with the other divisions and seemed to be on his own as his brigades and regiments tried to maintain cohesion while advancing through the heavily wooded hills, ridges, and ravines.

Shortly after encountering Confederate pickets, the division drew up in double line of battle and advanced toward the Confederate position. The fighting began around two in the afternoon and continued until well after dark. The Federals, once again charging up ridges and through woods, eventually drove their foes into strong entrenchments on Pine Knob near Gilgal Church. This was Johnston's main line, connecting Kennesaw with Lost Mountain. The Confederates had been at work for several days, and their entrenchments were well developed, with abatis and chevaux-de-frise before them. They also had artillery, although the Federals were able to silence some of the batteries. Despite best efforts to break the line, it was too strong, and the White Stars suffered heavily in their attempt to take it. Candy's front regiments, the 29th Ohio and the

28th Pennsylvania, got to within thirty yards of the enemy, while the Sixty-sixth and the brigade's other two regiments in the second line threw up breastworks under fire from Confederate sharpshooters.

The following morning the Sixty-sixth and the rest of Candy's second line relieved the 29th and 28th and skirmished for the rest of the day.[12] The Federal skirmish line was about seventy-five yards from Johnston's works. One of the Sixty-sixth's wounded was Pvt. William Sayre, who was shot in the shoulder. Captain Sampson looked at his wound before Sayre was taken to the rear; the ball had entered his right shoulder and apparently traveled down his back. Sampson thought the wound serious but not mortal. He had voiced a similar judgment about Lieutenant Davis's wound at Ringgold and had been wrong; he learned the next day that he was wrong also about Sayre, who had died in hospital.

Writing to Sayre's father, Sampson reported that he had asked his son to act in the capacity of sergeant and had been intending to promote him. Sayre's grave was near the Second Division hospital and "plainly marked." Sherman had prohibited disinterments prior to October 31; after that date the body could be sent home. "If I am spared and can be of any assistance to you at that time I will cheerfully aid you," concluded Sampson.[13]

Indeed, the butcher's bill was relatively high at Pine Knob. Geary's total casualties in the less than two days' fighting came to 519, slightly more than he had suffered at New Hope Church. The Sixty-sixth's casualties were also commensurate with New Hope Church, five killed in action and twenty-three wounded, four of whom would die of their injuries. None of the casualties were officers, which was good for the regiment, as it could ill afford to lose many more. One of the wounded privates was Company E's Elias Kyle; a minié ball had hit the top of his head, plowing a furrow along the skull and tearing away a bit of hair and scalp. The impact had knocked him unconscious, but upon recovering he gathered up the piece of scalp; several years later he still retained it as a combat memento.

The Confederates abandoned their works in the night, and Geary's skirmishers, followed by his entire division, occupied them.[14] For the rest of June and into early July, Geary's men continued with sporadic skirmishing and maneuvering south. Their comrades in Williams's division were involved in a sharp scrap at the battle of Kolb's Farm on June 22, but the White Stars had little to do with it, even though Geary was to claim a significant role and devote substantial space to the engagement in his official report of the campaign.[15]

The positions of the two armies were often in flux. On one occasion Maj. Thomas McConnell, posting pickets, spied blackberries a short distance off. Lured by the prospect of fresh fruit, he made his way to them and was quietly enjoying his berries when he heard a voice say, "Come on boys! this way!" Looking up, he saw two Confederate soldiers walking past. McConnell called out "Halt!" and startled them into surrender, though the major, unbeknownst to them, was unarmed.[16]

On June 27 came Sherman's disastrous assault against Johnston's entrenchments at Kennesaw Mountain, costing the Federals approximately three thousand casualties and gaining them nothing. The Sixty-sixth was spared a major role in this battle, although the 113th Ohio, which contained a large number of Champaign County men (including a few who had also served in the Sixty-sixth), was sent in and sustained horrific casualties. For its part, the Sixty-sixth appears to have been in a support position, taking a few sporadic casualties. The repulse at Kennesaw cheered the Confederacy, and the people of Atlanta had cause to think that Johnston had finally drawn the line beyond which Sherman could not advance. The comparative strengths of the two armies, however, had not altered, and the Federals could still flank Johnston without endangering their supply line. In early July the Federal army crossed the Chattahoochee River above Johnston's right. Although there were still more streams to traverse, the Chattahoochee had been the last major natural obstacle between Sherman and Atlanta; Johnston had to abandon any hope of a defensive line north of it.

Johnston's retreat brought Sherman to within sight of the city. Captain Sampson reported that once camp was pitched every large tree had two or three soldiers in it gazing toward Atlanta's steeples and rooftops.[17] It was the final straw for Jefferson Davis, who on July 17 relieved Johnston and replaced him with John Bell Hood. Hood was a Texan and a fighter; he had distinguished himself as a division commander under Lee and had been transferred to the Army of Tennessee the previous fall. At Chickamauga he had been wounded, losing his right leg. He had been an aggressive corps commander under Johnston—but at the same time he had been maneuvering to undermine his superior. When Davis had asked for Lee's advice on replacing Johnston with Hood, Lee had responded, "Hood is a bold fighter. I am doubtful as to the other qualities necessary."[18]

23

General Sherman Has Taken Atlanta

With Hood commanding the Army of Tennessee, Sherman would not have an easy march into Atlanta. Davis wanted a fight for the city. Hood would provide one. Two days after the change in Confederate commanders the Army of the Cumberland was crossing to the south bank of Peachtree Creek, a steep-banked stream running west into the Chattahoochee. Hood hoped to attack the Yankees after they crossed the stream and before they had a chance to entrench, drive them back to Peachtree Creek, and force their capture or annihilation.

July 20 was another hot day in a string of hot days. The soldiers of the Sixty-sixth, like most of Sherman's army, needed a new issue of clothes. The men were fatigued and lice ridden. Many were undernourished, and some had scurvy, but their goal was before them. After Peachtree Creek there would not be many more streams to ford. They hoped to be marching into Atlanta soon, and with the fall of Atlanta the war would draw closer to an end.

Geary's division continued to advance that morning, with Candy's brigade in the lead, backed by the Second Brigade immediately to its rear, which was followed in turn by the Third Brigade. The Sixty-sixth provided skirmishers for the advance, which traversed two ridges and came to rest on a third. Because it had supplied the division's skirmishers and thus was under strength, the Sixty-sixth had been placed in reserve; however, it moved up to the front line on the brigade's extreme right when Geary ordered Candy to occupy the ridge in a single line. The Second Brigade was placed on the ridge behind Candy but did not extend so far as to support the Sixty-sixth. The New Yorkers' Third Brigade occupied the ridge behind the First and Second Brigades.

Candy's ridge ran roughly east and west, with a road running along it, but there was a pronounced curve toward the front at the western end of the ridge, which was heavily timbered. Consequently the Sixty-sixth's position jutted out from the Federal line. Candy was informed that Williams's division would be arriving on his right and that they should be able to establish a connection; however, Williams had still not come up, so Candy's right—and the Sixty-sixth's—was unsupported. To make the position even more vulnerable, beyond the woods to the right the ridge was broken by a ravine that curved into their rear, thus facilitating an enemy flanking maneuver in the event of an assault.

Geary's position on the ridge was intended to form part of a provisional line, with Williams's division on his right and Ward's division from the Fourth Corps on his left. Although it was a temporary position, Candy's brigade took the precaution of throwing up log and stone breastworks. A battery was brought up on its left, and some of its guns were interspersed along the brigade's line.

Meanwhile, Geary personally reconnoitered the area, after ordering the 33d New Jersey to position itself in front of his main line, on an isolated hill that he thought might hold tactical value. The skirmishers took three prisoners, who volunteered that the main Confederate force was at least two miles distant. All seemed well, but the storm was about to break. As the 33d was establishing itself on the hilltop, Geary sent the skirmishers forward, only to discover that the Confederates were advancing in heavy force to his immediate front and on both sides. To avoid envelopment, the 33d, Geary himself, and many of the skirmishers made rapidly for the ridge behind them, the 33d losing heavily in the process. Powell (who may not have been present) later wrote that the Confederates had charged through the Sixty-sixth's skirmish line "without taking prisoner or returning a shot, and at double-quick swept on beyond our rear to strike our main line." Perhaps "the enemy was so bent on larger game" that they could not be bothered to disarm the Federals and send them back as prisoners; in any case, the Sixty-sixth's skirmishers were somehow able to regain their own lines.[1]

Even before contacting the enemy, however, the skirmishers had not had an easy time. Robert Russell, as brigade "Officer of the Day," was in command. Like Candy, he had taken a tumble on Lookout Mountain and was partially disabled as a result. He was back with the regiment, but he was nonetheless in poor health, and the heat was not helping matters. While on the skirmish line he was prostrated by sunstroke and was carried back to the ridge only minutes before the enemy appeared. Once returned to the regiment, he refused to leave for hospital, though he could barely speak above a whisper. Pvt. John Houtz was sent back after having gotten in among some species of poisonous plant that eventually caused both his legs to swell up "as big as saplins."[2]

The Confederate assault, spreading across the entire Federal line, came at three or four o'clock in the afternoon. The skirmishers who had been able to rejoin the Sixty-sixth were returning to the most vulnerable portion of Candy's line. Enemy troops, shouting at the Ohioans to surrender, attacked them from three directions: from their front, from out of the woods on their right, and from the ravine behind them. The Sixty-sixth may have gotten in a few shots before its position disintegrated and the men began to run across the ridge to their left and downhill to their left and rear. Riding up with the order to fall back (as though a formal command were required), Geary's adjutant was shot and instantly killed. The position continued to roll up as the 29th Ohio, the regiment next in line to the Sixty-sixth's left, also broke.

Officers, among them a somewhat recovered Robert Russell, attempted to rally the fleeing men, while the brigade, with the exception of the 147th Pennsylvania on the extreme left, shifted front to the right in order to meet the attack. Meanwhile, the Second Brigade moved up to the front to come in line with the 147th to help meet the frontal assault, even as the New York brigade on the ridge behind them also changed front so as to link their left with Candy's right, and their right with Williams's left.

Geary later described the attack on his front:

The appearance of the enemy as they charged upon our front was magnificent. Rarely has such a sight been presented in battle. Pouring out from the woods they advanced in immense brown and gray masses (not lines), with flags and banners, many of them new

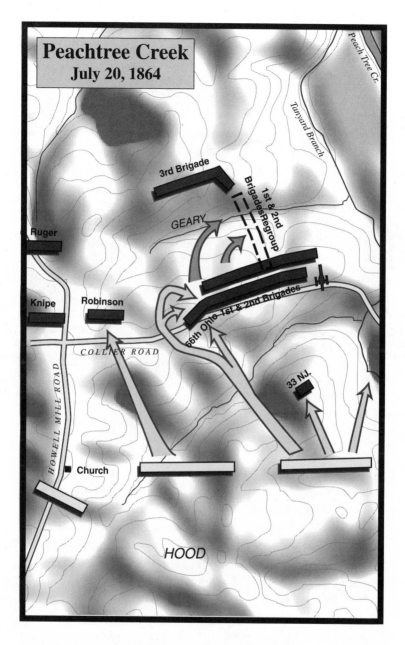

Peachtree Creek
July 20, 1864

Peach Tree Cr.

Tanyard Branch

3rd Brigade

1st & 2nd Brigades Regroup

GEARY

Ruger

Knipe

Robinson

66th Ohio 1st & 2nd Brigades

COLLIER ROAD

HOWELL MILL ROAD

33 N.J.

Church

HOOD

and beautiful, while their general and staff officers were in plain
view, with drawn sabers flashing in the light, galloping here and
there as they urged their troops on to the charge. The Rebel troops
also seemed to rush forward with more than customary nerve and
heartiness in the attack.[3]

Candy did not have the time for an aesthetic appraisal of his opponents. His brigade, no doubt much mixed and disorganized, fell back some three hundred yards, but with the help of the New Yorkers, who fired into the Confederates' left flank, it was able to counterattack. Eventually the attackers were driven off the ridge; the assault, having been unsuccessful along the entire line, was not renewed. It had been a close call for the Ohio men. Hood had lived up to his reputation for combativeness, but he had achieved nothing.

The battle had lasted only an hour, but it had been a costly affair. Had the defenders not been battle-hardened veterans, the results might have been far different. Geary reported eighty-two killed, 229 wounded, and 165 missing from his division (most of the missing likely from the unfortunate 33d New Jersey), for an aggregate loss of 476. The Sixty-sixth had approximately twenty-three casualties, with only two killed. Candy's favorite horse, Bill, which had been with him since leaving Camp McArthur, was among the fatalities.[4]

One of the Sixty-sixth's casualties was Company G's Lt. John R. Organ. He had been only twenty-one years old but nonetheless a capable veteran officer, who had received his commission in January 1863. He had been wounded in the initial assault, a minié ball fracturing his thigh bone above the knee, causing profuse bleeding. He had soon found himself behind the Confederate assault line. To their credit, the Southerners improvised from some rags and Organ's tobacco pipe a tourniquet that the Sixty-sixth's surgeon, Jesse Brock, judged "novel" but "which answered every purpose." Following the Federal counterattack, Organ was again among friends, but he had lost a great deal of blood. Brock attempted to amputate the leg. He was on the surgeon's table for about fifteen minutes; according to the surgeon, Organ was conscious the entire time, praying constantly. Brock's efforts were in vain; the young lieutenant had lost too much blood. He was buried in a marked grave, following an unsuccessful attempt to find embalming fluid. The body was eventually sent home and interred in Urbana's cemetery.[5]

Brock himself came to harm. In the process of treating a soldier's wounded hand, he pricked his finger on some exposed bone. As it turned out, the wound had been gangrenous, and the doctor was in danger of losing his own hand; in the end the amputation of his forefinger was sufficient remedy.[6]

Among the wounded was Company G's William V. Taylor, who as corporal had led his company at Antietam, where he was wounded in both legs. He had sustained a head wound at Gettysburg, and in this latest engagement he had been shot in the hand, arm, and shoulder. Once again he survived.

There had apparently been some hand-to-hand fighting, for an enemy officer had whacked Company E's Lt. James P. Conn on the head with his sword. Conn recovered and was promoted to captain the following April. Following the war, however, he continued to complain of the pain caused by his wound. He eventually became mentally unbalanced and ended his days in the Cleveland Hospital for the Insane.[7]

The Sixty-sixth's losses, not counting those attributable to illness, had come to about eighty since the beginning of the campaign. The regiment was not sustaining Port Republic or Cedar Mountain casualty rates; rather, it was being ground down slowly. In a June 25 letter, a soldier from Company H reported that the regiment was down to 190 men, while W. A. Brand observed in a July 10 letter, "It appears that about nine tenths of the sick and wounded of our regiment who get to the Chattanooga Hospital die."[8] Although draftees and substitutes would soon arrive to fill up its ranks, the Sixty-sixth could not afford to lose its veterans. The loss of competent junior officers such as Hitt at New Hope Church and Organ at Peachtree Creek was especially troubling, at a time when other officers, such as Russell, were succumbing to illness and the heat.

The Battle of Peachtree Creek, however, had been harder on the attackers. The Confederate assault force took, it is estimated, approximately 2,500 casualties, compared to a loss of 1,900 on the Federal side. It was another clear victory for the Army of the Cumberland.[9]

Geary cleaned up what was in front of him, estimating that his fatigue parties buried approximately six hundred Confederate dead on the day of the battle and on the day following. W. A. Brand wrote on July 23 that the woods still contained many Rebel corpses: "the bodies are loathsome and appear fit emblems of their Confederacy." He noted the many pits that served as mass graves, one with a sign reading, "Col. Drake, 33 Miss., and 34 men."[10]

The Sixty-sixth still had Powell, and the brigade still had Candy, but in late July there was a reshuffling of army and corps commanders that placed the White Stars under new, if familiar, leadership. Two days after Peachtree Creek Hood attacked McPherson's Army of Tennessee, which was menacing Atlanta from the east. It was a flank attack, and it enjoyed some initial success. McPherson rode to investigate, encountering

Confederate skirmishers, who called on him to surrender. He ignored their demand and galloped away. He was shot and killed. Sherman chose Oliver Howard to replace McPherson, provoking the wrath of Hooker, who felt the promotion should have gone his way. In protest Hooker resigned his command of the Twentieth Corps, and Slocum, who had been a corps commander over the White Stars at Chancellorsville and Gettysburg, replaced him.

Peachtree Creek was the last battle of the campaign for the Sixty-sixth. Following an ineffectual cavalry raid that failed to break Atlanta's rail link with Macon, Sherman shifted his army south of the city in order to break Hood's communications and thereby force his hand. The Twentieth Corps remained north of Atlanta, maintaining pressure on Hood from that direction and safeguarding Sherman's supply line. The Sixty-sixth was on the skirmishing line within sight of Atlanta for much of August, drawing back to the Chattahoochee once Sherman's army had been shifted to the right and sent south of the city.

The final battles of the Atlanta campaign occurred at Jonesboro on August 31 and September 1. The fighting began with the loss of large numbers of Confederates in a bungled assault on Federal works that had been thrown up to overlook the Macon railroad. On the second day the Confederates barely fended off a Federal counterattack. (A former member of the Sixty-sixth took part in the action around Jonesboro. Celestian Saintignon, who had been captured and paroled in the vicinity of Manassas in August 1862 and subsequently carried on the Sixty-sixth's rolls as a deserter, had reenlisted in the 54th Ohio under the name John Lorain. He was wounded in the shoulder while charging Confederate rifle pits.)[11]

It was clear that Hood could no longer maintain an army at Atlanta. He evacuated the city. Slocum sent detachments from each of his divisions into the city the next day. Two of Geary's White Star regiments, the 111th Pennsylvania and the 60th New York, were the first to make it to the city hall, from which the national and divisional flags were soon flying: as at Lookout Mountain, the White Stars were placing their imprimatur on Union victory. Slocum telegraphed Washington that afternoon, "General Sherman has taken Atlanta."

Hood eventually broke for the north with his army, in the hope—ultimately a vain one—to regain Tennessee for the Confederacy and march his army to the Ohio. Sherman gave chase for a short time but returned to Atlanta. The Twentieth Corps remained behind as the city's garrison. Always quick to make his contribution to the official record, Geary settled down to compose his division report for the campaign. Not surprisingly, Geary's report chronicling the White Stars' activities was longer than Sherman's report for the entire army.[12]

For the time being, Sherman's army had the opportunity to regroup and gather its strength, but the western army would not remain in Atlanta for much longer. Soon it would march to Savannah and the sea.

24

To the Sea
and Victory

*L*ike most of the other Federal regiments at Atlanta, the Sixty-sixth was seriously understrength. It was losing men to the wear and tear of military life even without shots being fired. Accidents happened, and sometimes they were fatal. One of the January recruits, nineteen-year-old Sampson Turner in Company F, was resting under a tree on August 27. Another soldier set his gun against the tree; it slipped and fell, hitting young Turner in the head, somehow killing him instantly. Also, the dutiful Captain Sampson became incapacitated while detailed to the Commissary Department, accompanying a wagon train to Chattanooga. His horse stumbled and fell, pitching him forward so that the pommel caught him in the crotch. He was not well afterward and soon came down with a fever. After three weeks in hospital at Chattanooga he returned to Urbana, where he was treated for an enlarged prostate. He was granted a medical discharge the following January.[1]

Robert Russell's fortunes had not improved. Despite his sunstroke, the young captain was allowed to remain with the regiment. A few days after the battle at Peachtree Creek he was shot by a Confederate sharpshooter in the left instep while overseeing the installation of a brush awning over some earthworks. While not a serious wound, it, together with the lingering aftereffects of his sunstroke, landed him in an officers' hospital—situated, interestingly enough, on Lookout Mountain, where he, like Colonel Candy, had fallen during the "battle above the clouds." He remained there convalescing into October. He had company, as both Candy and Powell were patients. Indeed, it was rumored that Powell would resign due to disability; the story was told that General Thomas had reacted to this possibility with the comment that "Powell was too good an officer to lose" and had accordingly sent him to Lookout Mountain to recover.[2]

The Sixty-sixth was losing another company commander to resignation. John M. Rathbun, of Company C, been promoted captain but had not been well in recent months, although he had managed to stay with his company for most of the Atlanta campaign. That he had been able to do so seems especially remarkable in light of his resignation letter, which opened, "I am a very corpulent man, weighing about two hundred and fifty pounds and even in camp or garrison on account of which any duties & Disabilities are much more severe for me than they would be otherwise." His resignation was approved by General Thomas.[3]

Another hospital inmate was Pvt. Augustus Tanner, who had "stood up to the rack and cut the hay" at Chancellorsville. He would not be cutting much hay now: his left arm had been amputated. Writing to his father, he declared,

> Folks at home does not know the sufferings of a soldier's life. Losing an arm is nothing. Sometimes I feel glad to think I have got out of the field, away from the roar of musketry & the belching of cannon. Those that are not wounded or killed has stood four long months campaign, & three months of this they have not been a day away from the sound of the musket. There is no soldier that could ever find language to express his feelings. All he can do is to drop everything and become like a dumb brute. Obey his superiors, take up your gun and knapsack and forward march . . . into the cannon's mouth.[4]

Nonetheless, Sherman's success was having important consequences, and the sacrifices of men like Tanner were not in vain. Atlanta's fall was a boost to the electoral prospects of the Republican party, which was technically presenting itself under under the unionist label in 1864. Lincoln's opponent was Gen. George McClellan, who was running on a peace platform and was favored to win if the military stalemate of early summer lasted into the fall. With Grant bogged down in Virginia, the only place where a breakthrough might occur in time to make a political difference was Georgia. Fortunately for the Republicans and the Union war effort (the two had for all intents and purposes become synonymous), Sherman was able to deliver.

The importance of Atlanta's fall was not missed in Champaign County, or for that matter, anywhere in the North. When word came of Sherman's triumph, posters went up around Urbana headed "Atlanta has fallen! Victory! Victory! Victory!" A committee soon formed to canvass the town for donations of stray kindling, old wooden boxes, and barrels. Wagonloads of wood were collected in a central place and piled into a thirty-three-foot pyramid that was then doused with coal tar. At seven o'clock in the evening on Thursday, September 8, all the town bells rang to summon the citizenry:

> And as the mingling tones of the bells rolled out their summons on the air, the community seemed at once to be awakened, crowds rushed into the streets; women and children could be seen wending their way to the common and soon scores of people there assembled. At half past 7, the fire was kindled, and in two minutes the flames rolled high and heavenward, and then went up a mighty shout—a shout that was a shout—thousands of happy voices mingling together in one loud hurrah.

A crowd numbered at three thousand lingered to watch the flames and listen to patriotic addresses.[5] In hundreds of Northern communities, Sherman's victory was vigorously celebrated. His triumph in Georgia created the political momentum that would culminate in Lincoln's re-election.

The victory was much needed. Dissension, especially in such places as the western half of Champaign County, continued. The Knights of the Golden Circle, a secret society opposed to the Union war effort, was supposedly gathering strength in the countryside. A county historian would recount how he had discovered records in Columbus listing the names of the disloyal in the county:

> Many are still living who can recall the ruse which effected the capture of a preacher at St. Paris who was industriously engaged in having pistols delivered in baskets by a couple of boys. Not

only was the pistol supply confiscated, but before the St. Paris Southern sympathizers knew what was going on, a detective of Governor Brough had been in the village, enlisted in their organization, learned their secrets and of course, secured a complete list of all their members. This same list is now [1917] on file at Columbus in the adjutant general's office.[6]

The Sixty-sixth was biding its time in Atlanta. Geary was assigned various foraging expeditions in October, but Candy's brigade was not included in them. The Sixty-sixth was assigned to commissary duties.[7]

Also, the regiment was receiving its first infusion of draftees and substitutes (as opposed to new voluntary recruits). Although all were Ohioans, none were Champaign County men—or, with but a handful of possible exceptions, men from any of the other counties from which the Sixty-sixth had been recruited. Whether this was intentional policy or just happenstance is hard to say. On one hand, there was often an understandable tension between veterans and men who had been coerced or "bribed" into service, and such tensions could be accentuated, rather than mitigated, if the draftees were thrown together with veterans from the same community. On the other hand, by virtue of the logistics of organization and transportation, draftees and substitutes from the same area were often processed together, and they often ended up in the same regiments. So, even if draftees and substitutes encountered the cold shoulder from the veterans in their regiment, they might be able to fall back on the support of neighbors, with whom they could share the soldier's life.

The Sixty-sixth was allotted approximately 168 substitutes and 113 draftees in the late summer and early fall of 1864. The first batch of substitutes bound for the Sixty-sixth entered the service in August, but a number of them were bounty jumpers and deserted a few days after enlistment. Perhaps this was why a detail of forty men from the Sixty-sixth was sent north in late September to escort the Sixty-sixth's substitutes and draftees from Ohio to Georgia. The detail returned with its charges—approximately two hundred men, according to John Houtz—on October 29. They were divided into ten groups of twenty and divvied out to each of the companies. In some companies they might have outnumbered enlisted men already present. Houtz spoke with them and found most in good spirits, although "the ones that are drafted goes around camp hanging heads as if sick." A few days later Houtz noted that "the drafted men are learning to drill fast. it is supposed that they will fight well" and that "all is wanted is good officers." In fact, although twenty or more of the Sixty-sixth's substitutes would desert, all but one of its draftees would stay in the ranks until death or discharge.[8]

The Sixty-sixth had only two weeks to turn the draftees and substitutes into soldiers: on November 15 Sherman began his march to the sea. Having ignored Hood's foray into Tennessee, he elected to slice in two the Confederacy east of the Mississippi by cutting a sixty-mile-wide swathe of destruction from Atlanta to Savannah. Supply lines would cease to be a concern; he would live off the land, punishing the civilians of Georgia by consuming whatever crops or livestock his army needed to maintain itself. Anything of military value would be destroyed: "Until we can repopulate Georgia, it is useless to occupy it; but the utter destruction of its roads, houses and people will cripple their military resources. . . . I can make the march, and make Georgia howl!"[9] Assuming a steady source of food was available, Sherman did not think the movement would be much of a military challenge, as the only opposition he faced was cavalry and home guards.

The march was relatively uneventful for the Sixty-sixth, although a few of its men were captured, primarily substitutes and draftees, probably foraging or straggling. There was generally a good supply of pigs, barnyard fowl, and the occasional wild turkey, along with sweet potatoes. Sweet potatoes seemed to be the great staple; Robert Russell, who had returned to the regiment, wrote, "I never saw the like of sweet potatoes in my life, on some plantations there was two and three thousand bushels. . . . In history I think this . . . campaign will be known as 'Gen'l Sherman's Great Sweet Potato Raid.'"[10]

Days were spent marching, tearing up railroad tracks, and burning buildings deemed of military value. Union troops encountered little armed opposition. The freestyle looting and destruction perpetrated by Sherman's troops are well known, but there is little information concerning the Sixty-sixth's participation or lack of it in such activities. Houtz's diary often speaks of his pursuit of chickens and pigs ("I started out after a hog found some and chased them in a swamp followed in and got lost"), but it does not admit to anything more destructive, unless, like tearing up tracks, it had been ordered.[11]

Geary was a strict disciplinarian, and although he nursed vengeful feelings towards the Confederacy, he would probably not have countenanced his men running amok. Indeed, he was often assigned the post of military governor in surrendered Southern cities (Bridgeport, Atlanta, and later Savannah). There is reason to believe that the Sixty-sixth's part in the great march was as disciplined as might be hoped for under the circumstances. The portion of the devastation that was officially sanctioned—Geary's official report for the march is an incredibly detailed catalog of destruction[12]—would likely have been enough to keep the White Stars busy.

Geary's men reached Savannah's defenses on December 11. The First Brigade, now under the command of Arlo Pardee of the 147th Pennsylvania, was ordered to support an assault by the Third Brigade on a portion of the Confederate line early the next morning; however, the attack was called off, and the White Stars settled into a ten-day siege. It was largely uneventful, although the Sixty-sixth sustained casualties on December 19 when a large shell exploded in its ranks, killing three men and wounding three more, one of whom was later to succumb to his wounds.[13]

Early on the morning of December 21 it was determined that the defenders had abandoned their works, and Geary's skirmishers moved in. After dispatching word to Slocum, Geary pushed his whole division toward the city, and at half past four in the morning, just outside the city limits, he encountered the mayor of Savannah and a delegation of city fathers under a flag of truce. The result: "My entire division entered the city of Savannah at early dawn, and before the sun first gilded the morning clouds our National colors, side by side with those of my own division, were unfurled from the dome of the Exchange and over the U.S. custom house." Once again Geary and the White Stars had staked their claim to history. As at Atlanta, Geary was put in charge of the city, leading him to proclaim proudly to his wife, "My eventful career is still upon its everlasting whirl. I am now the Commandante of the City, in honor of its capture by me, and of the surrender to me."[14]

It was a time for celebration on a number of counts. Although Grant was still stalled in front of Richmond and Petersburg, Sherman had continued the war's momentum, and Lincoln had been reelected. Meanwhile, Hood's army, on its quixotic invasion of Tennessee, had been smashed in the battles at Franklin and Nashville. Confederate casualties had been horrific, including several generals—among them Patrick Cleburne, who had savaged the White Stars at Ringgold. The end of the war was in sight. It was in any case very much over for the 1861 enlistees who had not veteranized, among them John Houtz. They were mustered out on December 22, and most left by boat for Hilton Head at month's end. The remaining troops played tourist in Savannah, and many got drunk. Houtz noted that "the boys at the co. is all drunk they pay five dollars a canteen full and just a swilling it down."[15]

One of the officers who mustered out was Robert Russell. He had returned to the regiment and survived the March to the Sea. Although he had not reenlisted, he had done his part by any reasonable measure. Curiously, he elected to remain in Savannah for a few weeks and go into the grocery business (perhaps an investment from his mustering-out pay) in partnership with a German resident of the city. Despite the southern latitudes, it was cold at times, and he needed his overcoat—which was apparently with his parents in Ohio. He wrote repeatedly for it, but the shipment was apparently delayed, along with all other shipments to civilians, which of course was what he was now. He caught cold in mid-February and made plans to return north.[16]

Pvt. William Tallman, who had been absent from the regiment for several months, rejoined it in Savannah. He found a much altered organization, noting of Company E that "so many changes had taken place among officers and men that at first twas like joining a new company." He also voiced regret that he had not been present with the regiment, suspecting that had he been he would now be in line for a promotion. The substantial presence of draftees and substitutes also made a difference, for although they kept the aggregate up, "they could not take the place socially of the Boys killed wounded and discharged."[17]

It was rough going for many of the substitutes and draftees, unaccustomed as they were to military life and the rigors of the march. Tallman recounted the story of two draftees in his company, John and Samuel Albright. They were family men, each owning a farm in Fairfield County. Rather than spend the money (assuming they had it) needed to hire substitutes, they had gone into the service but "found the dangers and hardships very much greater than they thought possible." They became sick and demoralized, and they died within a few days of each other in Savannah. Sounding a more compassionate note than did many veterans when discussing draftees, he mused that he had sometimes thought "how much better it would have been if they had made a sacrifice of their money or property and hired men without families to take their place."[18]

Sherman's army remained in Savannah for a little over a month. There was an option of transporting his troops by sea to link up with Grant in Virginia, where the combined armies would outnumber Lee so overwhelmingly that the Confederate capital would have to be abandoned in short order. Instead, Sherman brought total war to the state that had initiated the conflict. He proposed to march through South Carolina the same way he had marched through Georgia.

So, on January 27 Geary's division began its part in the invasion of the Palmetto State. The White Stars were still under Slocum's command, which made up Sherman's left wing. With Candy still sick, Pardee retained command of the First Brigade, while Powell remained in charge of the Sixty-sixth.

The going was rough. Like the rest of Sherman's army, the White Stars were faced with large expanses of low and swampy ground. From the beginning of the march, Geary's pioneers were busy corduroying (cutting down trees to lay across roads, closely spaced, to make them passable). The Carolinas campaign would be less a combat victory—for the most part Sherman faced little in the way of Confederate opposition—than a triumph of military engineering. Shortly after departing Savannah, the division's road was submerged for two miles; in some places the water was twelve feet deep. On the morning of February 7 the White Stars reached the Coosawhatchie Swamp. Geary reported:

> There was no bridge for even infantry to cross; 600 pioneers and axmen were set at work constructing a foot bridge and corduroying the entrance to the water. By 4 P.M. my command began to cross; the three leading brigades, my artillery, and a good share of the train crossed during the afternoon and night. . . . The bottom of the stream worked into deep holes of a quicksand nature, so that it was necessary frequently during the night to halt the trains, send the pioneers waist deep into the stream and construct corduroy road three or four feet under water, pinning it down to prevent it from floating. In this way about one half of the train crossed during the night, which was dark and rainy, thus adding to the discomforts of the occasion.[19]

The White Stars dealt with such conditions for the better part of the month.

As in Georgia, Sherman's army foreswore a supply line and relied solely on foraging. It also continued to destroy facilities of military value. The burning of cities and towns was not specifically mandated; however, in the atmosphere of destruction and vengeance that pervaded the march, military discipline could and did break down. Such was the case when Federal troops under Oliver O. Howard occupied Columbia, the state capitol. Fires broke out on the night of February 17, while drunken troops and civilians looted and rioted. One-third of the city burned.

The events of February 21 in Winnsborough formed an interesting contrast. Two miles from the town, Geary noticed heavy smoke rising from its direction and ordered Pardee's brigade, including the Sixty-sixth, to advance at the double-quick. They arrived in time to put out the fires and bring the "foragers" from various corps of the Union army under control. Pardee indignantly reported what he found: "These men, in the most unlicensed manner, had plundered the public and nearly all the private residences, and to the same body may be charged the firing of the town."

William Tallman would recall a scene of exceptional chaos. Many of the buildings on the main street were ablaze; women and children of the town were dashing about in every direction with buckets and other vessels filled with water. A hundred or so former slaves—now free people—were standing in the square rejoicing at the advent of "Massa Linkum's soldiers." Also in the square was a vintage fire pump engine, which had become disabled with the first attempt to use it. Pardee's men rounded up all the soldiers not in their brigade, and soon a vacant lot was filled with the Union looters, together with mules, buggies, and carriages laden with food and plunder.[20]

The Sixty-sixth and the rest of the First Brigade under Pardee occupied the town and maintained order, while Geary's other two brigades destroyed nearby track. Guards were placed at every house in town. Wade Hampton, commander of the Confederate cavalry that had vacated Winnsborough, had left a note with the mayor pledging the safety of any Federals who might be left behind to preserve order after the army departed. Geary took Hampton at his word and left behind two mounted men from his provost guard, who organized the citizens of the town and managed to repel some Union stragglers who entered the town with mischief in mind. When a detachment of Confederate cavalry entered the town, it treated Geary's men with courtesy and allowed them to leave, with the acclaim of the citizenry.[21]

Events at Winnsborough underscored Geary's intolerance for disorder. He felt so strongly about foraging that he inserted in his official report recommendations on the subject, concluding that

no foraging parties should be allowed to leave the main body, except those regularly authorized, under command of energetic and faithful officers, who could be relied upon not only to obtain supplies, but to control every man under their command. None but the best soldiers should be mounted for the purpose, and every breach of discipline, by exhibition either by cowardice or cruelty, should be promptly and severely punished. This system should be enforced throughout the entire army to render the plan of subsisting an army upon the country honorable as well as efficient.[22]

Sherman's army crossed into North Carolina. It had encountered very little military opposition in South Carolina. However, in its front Joseph Johnston once again had a command in the field; he was attempting to pull together elements of widely scattered forces to make a final stand. Among the troops he inherited were the sorry remnants of the Army of Tennessee, survivors of its near annihilation under Hood, who had been relieved from command upon his own request.

There was a battle at Bentonville, North Carolina, between March 19 and 21; it cost Sherman 1,455 casualties and Johnston 2,347. Geary's division played no role in the fighting, aside from some skirmishing. Johnston retreated, but Sherman did not pursue. The White Stars moved on to the vicinity of Goldsboro and from there to Raleigh. There they learned of Lincoln's assassination on April 14, even as negotiations were beginning for Johnston's surrender. The men were shocked and outraged: General Geary observed that Lincoln's "untimely loss has created a profound sensation in the entire army, and if we have to fight anymore, woe be to Rebeldom!"[23]

Within a few days Lincoln's funeral train would make its way west to Illinois, proceeding slowly through the cities and towns of the Northeast and Middle West. It passed through Champaign County on the evening of April 29, stopping briefly in Woodstock, Cable, Urbana, and Saint Paris. The train arrived at the platform of the Urbana station at 10:40 P.M.; three thousand people were gathered. Great bonfires were lit, which, according to one account, "made the night light as day." The Ladies Aid Society had constructed a large cross to stand on the platform. It was entwined with evergreens and "colored transparencies." An interfaith choir of forty singers sang the hymn "Go to Thy Rest," and a delegation of ten young women was permitted to enter the car and lay flowers on the bier.[24]

Meanwhile, the fighting was coming to a close. What remained of Confederate forces in North Carolina surrendered to Sherman on April 26, a little over two weeks after Lee had surrendered to Grant at Appomattox. It was over.

25

Honor and Position

The Sixty-sixth's final duty was to march in the Grand Review at Washington, D.C. Its journey to the capital city took the men over several battlefields in Virginia, among them Chancellorsville, where soldiers from Company B sought out and found the grave of Sgt. William Flago, who had been killed at the side of Major Palmer during the final day's fighting. They disinterred his remains and shipped them back to Urbana.[1]

Upon reaching the Washington area, they were issued new uniforms, even down to fresh white flannel stars. This caused some uneasiness among the men, who feared that the new uniforms could augur continued service, perhaps in Texas, where there might still be Confederate resistance.[2] In fact, however, the new outfits were strictly "for show." On May 24 the Sixty-sixth was with Sherman's army when it passed the reviewing stand of President Andrew Johnson and other high-ranking officials, the Army of the Potomac having done likewise the day before. The Sixty-sixth bivouacked for a short time in Bladensburg, Maryland, where the draftees and substitutes were mustered out.

The spring also saw a flurry of promotions as many officers left the army and replacements were found to fill their places until the regiment was formally disbanded. Eugene Powell left the Sixty-sixth, promoted

John T. Mitchell. *Brad L. Pruden Collection.*

to full colonel to take command of the 193d Ohio, which had been organized only in March.[3] On April 8 Capt. John T. Mitchell of Company I was, at age twenty-two, promoted to major—and then four days later to lieutenant colonel! After the war he would be active in regimental reunion activities; he would oversee the photographing of the regiment's colors and participate in determining the site of the regiment's monument at Gettysburg.

On July 15 the Sixty-sixth was mustered out at Louisville, Kentucky. The regiment had served in the war's two major theatres, traveled through thirteen states, and fought in twelve battles, two sieges, and innumerable skirmishes. Casualties came to 101 officers and men killed or mortally wounded, and 144 officers and men succumbing to disease, for a total of 245 deaths in service.[4] These losses were about average for three-year and veteran regiments. The Sixty-sixth's most damaging encounter with the Confederacy had been its first engagement, at Port Republic. Although a few subsequent fights, especially Cedar Mountain, had cost the regiment dearly, the Sixty-sixth in general experienced military campaigning as a slow, grinding process, which would have gradually reduced the regiment's numbers to a handful of men were it not for the influx of new recruits and, later, draftees and substitutes.

Of the one thousand or so original recruits who pulled out of the Urbana train station on January 17, 1862, about two hundred remained with the Sixty-sixth to be mustered out in the spring and summer of 1865. As previously noted, the reduction in numbers was only partially attributable to fatalities. Many—close to three hundred—were wounded so severely or else had their health so broken by disease and exposure that they left the army on disability discharges. Of these, many likely succumbed to untimely deaths after leaving service. Some in the Sixty-sixth transferred to other units, the Veteran Reserve Corps (V.R.C.) accounting for the largest share of these. Forty-six men from the Sixty-sixth, injured badly enough to disqualify them from active campaigning but not enough to merit discharge, played out the rest of their enlistments in the V.R.C. doing garrison duty and other tasks that did not require great physical stamina or even intact limbs.

As was true with most veteran regiments, the Sixty-sixth's ranks were in a state of constant flux throughout the war, but the company officers and noncommissioned officers supplied regimental cohesion. Not surprisingly, the original recruits usually formed a company's nucleus; they provided the regiment with a sense of identity and continuity. Advancement was generally reserved for them, and there were certainly opportunities for advancement—for example, none of the original captains mustered out with their companies. In Company H, of the fifteen original enlistees still in service after Johnston's surrender, twelve were officers or noncommissioned officers. The case of Robert Russell, who entered as a private and left the Sixty-sixth a captain, was not unusual. We might consider Charles Candy another such case: a sergeant in the U.S. Army in 1859, by 1865 he had attained the rank of brevet (that is, temporary) brigadier general.

The prisoners were also coming home. There had been a parole and exchange system during the second and third years of the war, but these conventions broke down by 1864. Instead of relatively brief, though often arduous, experiences in camps such as Belle Isle, captured Yankees in 1864 and 1865 faced an indefinite stay at Andersonville or other prison pens. (Actually, only one soldier of the Sixty-sixth appears to have died at Andersonville.) After the surrenders of Lee and Johnston, prisoners from the regiment who had been captured in the latter phase of the war began to make their way north.

Some had survived imprisonment but were not well. One such case was a substitute named Frank Levelle. A native of Ontario, he had joined up in Wooster, Ohio. Levelle was recorded as deserting at Savannah on January 7, 1865; perhaps he had in fact attempted to do so, but in any event he was captured and imprisoned by Confederate forces. He did not have to wait long for release, but by then he was suffering from chronic diarrhea, an ailment fatal to thousands of Civil War soldiers. Remarks entered on his "Medical Descriptive List" paint a sad picture: "The patient on admission was very much reduced by the effect of the disease from which he had been suffering for about four months. . . . Mentally, he was found much depressed, and remained in this condition until the last, refusing his medicine repeatedly." He died on March 22. Levelle had been single. His personal effects, which were inventoried and recorded for his service record, were sold at auction.[5]

Another released prisoner was Joseph Sherman Diltz. Following his capture at Caperton Ferry, he had been sent to Andersonville but had been transferred to a camp in Florence, South Carolina. By early April he had been liberated and within a few months was back in Ohio. He remained in Champaign County with his family and farmed for the rest of his life. He died in 1910.[6]

Indeed, the "boys" of the Sixty-sixth had been returning home for three years, starting with 1862's invalids from General Lander's ill-conceived Romney expedition and the wounded from Port Republic. Although most would return to a farm or a small-town trade or business, some were discovering that being a veteran, especially a wounded veteran, was a positive advantage when seeking elective office or political appointment. "A Citizen" (so signing himself) wrote a letter to the editor of the *Citizen and Gazette* advising that although the current Urbana postmaster wished to remain in his position, one William W. Wilson, a young veteran who had lost his leg at Port Republic, was interested in the post:

The truth is the people of Champaign county owe a debt to the young men who have made their sacrifices for the country, and they admit it, and talk about it, but they do but little; and many, like a set of ninnies, remain silent while the contest is going on between the men who should in justice, have the positions of profit under the Government, and those who now hold them. All may be equally well qualified, but the crippled soldiers have the best right. . . . Four years ago, when meetings were held to induce young men to enlist, we said to them, through our speakers, "It is true, boys, you may lose three years of your time, and you may not be so well qualified for business when you return, as if you stay at home, but go, boys, and if you fall it will be in a holy cause, and we will mourn you; but if you come back alive you shall never regret having gone, but we will give you honor and position.". . . . Hoping that our Congressman will feel that the wishes of the loyal people of this community should be consulted and carried out, for surely he will acknowledge the true republican idea that he is not to serve his private ends, but the wishes of the people he represents. Let us then have a ballot of the Union men of Urbana township, on the question of Post Master here, and in this way give shape and form to our feelings, and whether we will in honest, earnest and good faith carry out our repeated expressed determinations before and during the war.[7]

Wilson's quest for appointment found him a position as journal clerk in Ohio's House of Representatives in 1866 and 1867. He then became state revenue collector for his district in 1867, a position he held until 1878, at which point he became cashier at a local bank, of which he eventually became president. Wilson's assistant during his stint as revenue collector was John M. Fitzpatrick, a veteran who had lost his arm at Chickamauga. He was elected county auditor in 1868 and reelected five times thereafter.[8]

William V. Taylor's political prospects surely benefited from his veteran status. He had led his company at Antietam (where he was wounded in both legs) while holding the rank of corporal. As a lieutenant, Wilson had been wounded in the head at Gettysburg and shot three times at Peachtree Creek. Perhaps not surprisingly, he opted not to veteranize in 1864. While still in service in the field, he stood for Champaign County sheriff and was elected. He returned home in reasonably good health, although local physicians were still extracting bullet fragments from him several months thereafter. He continued as sheriff for three consecutive terms, after which he was elected to the position of county auditor, succeeding William H. Baxter, a Sixty-sixth veteran (also an amputee) who had concluded his service in the 113th Ohio.[9]

Veterans of the Sixty-sixth, in fact, were frequently elected to office. Most notably, from 1865 to 1889, of the six men who served as county sheriff, five were veterans of the Sixty-sixth; they accounted for all but two of the twelve terms in that twenty-four-year period. Two Sixty-sixth veterans also served consecutively as county recorders for the years 1879 through 1893. A former officer of the Sixty-sixth, Samuel T. McMorran, attained political office shortly after the war. McMorran had helped to raise Company C and had been its captain. He had been wounded in the neck at Port Republic and in the right foot at Cedar Mountain, the latter wound disabling him and causing his resignation. Following the war he served two terms in the Ohio House of Representatives.[10]

The political success enjoyed by Civil War veterans in Champaign County was not unusual, although the attainments of the Sixty-sixth veterans in particular may have been disproportionate. While statewide and urban politics in Ohio brought Democratic victories within a few years after the war, the Republicans remained ascendant in many of the rural counties. In Champaign County they had had the upper hand going into the war; the Union victory further cemented their dominance, and it is not surprising that returning veterans from the county's most celebrated regiment enjoyed a privileged position in a political environment that virtually ruled out Democratic officeholders and appointees. Moreover, as the "Citizen" represented in his letter, the veteran who had lost an arm, a leg, or an eye elicited a strong sense of public debt. Very few of the returning veterans were Democrats. Most subscribed to the political philosophy of a Sixty-sixth veteran who was described in a county history as "an uncompromising Republican, and, to use his own expression, 'believes in voting as he shot.'"[11]

The returning soldier–Republican politician became a ubiquitous fixture on the Ohio and national political scenes. Two Ohio generals, James A. Garfield and Rutherford B. Hayes, went on to become president. One Ohio political insider grumbled, "There is a combination amongst certain officers of the army to monopolize hereafter all civil offices"; while another asserted, "The best offices have become the prize and reward of military service." Even the cynics, however, could not discount the value of a military background, as noted by a political historian of the period: "Service in the Union army was a valuable training ground for politics. It introduced men to discipline, responsibility, and corporate loyalty. . . . Their army experience, in short, was a form of vocational training in political and administrative ability, and these men carried their training back with them into civilian life."[12] Another officer associated with the Sixty-sixth who did quite well politically was its old division commander, John White Geary. Running on the Republican ticket (though previously a Democrat), he was elected governor of Pennsylvania upon returning to his home state in 1866.[13]

Joseph Carter Brand probably enjoyed the greatest success in postwar government and politics of any of the Sixty-sixth's veterans, due largely to a well-established political career prior to the war. He parted company with the Sixty-sixth upon its departure to the western theater, transferring to the Commissary Department of the Army of the Potomac. According to a story he was fond of telling his family, he once visited the president, to whom he was presented by his friend and fellow Ohio politico—and now secretary of the treasury—Salmon P. Chase. During the conversation an aide advised Lincoln that an Indiana regiment was on the White House grounds and desired to see its commander in chief. Lincoln complied and asked Brand to accompany him to the portico. As the regiment cheered, the aide came to Brand's side and informed him, much to his embarrassment, that it would be necessary for him to step back a few paces. The president took in the situation and explained wryly to the major, "You see, Mr. Brand, they might not know which was the President."[14]

Brand was at Appomattox for Lee's surrender—apparently still in the Commissary Department, for he participated in the transfers of large quantities of Union rations to the nearly starving Confederate soldiers. In the words of his grandson, "no act of his life gave him quite as much satisfaction as to have been the first to pour his whole supply of hardtack into the blankets of those whom still and always he remembered as his own blood." He then returned to Washington and sought out his political ally, Chase, who asked what he could do for him; Brand replied that he wished to go home, and he was speedily discharged from service. Later Chase would be instrumental in obtaining Brand's appointment as consul to Nuremburg during the Grant administration; Brand remained in this post for almost three years and then returned to Ohio, where he was elected to four consecutive terms as mayor of Urbana.[15]

His son, William Augustus, the wartime correspondent "D. N. Arbaw," departed the service with the rank of first lieutenant, having succeeded to his father's former position as regimental quartermaster. Upon returning home he purchased half interest in his father-in-law's

Joseph Carter Brand, probably at the time of his appointment by President Grant as consul to Nuremburg. *Champaign County Historical Society.*

newspaper. Not surprisingly, under Brand's and Saxton's direction, the *Citizen and Gazette* continued to serve as an organ of the Republican party. His biography in an 1881 county history observed that "being a Republican by conviction, and feeling that through that party only could be preserved the results of the severe struggles of our armies from 1861 to 1865, he put his whole soul into his political work." Unfortunately his health declined, and while fairly young he gave up his newspaper career for an appointment as Urbana postmaster in 1878. The change did not restore his health, and he died at the age of forty-one. (He was succeeded as postmaster by a veteran of the 2d O.V.I. who had lost his left eye in the service.)[16]

In addition to electing its veterans to office, Champaign County memorialized them in stone and bronze. In the fall of 1865 a small group of former soldiers began to discuss building a soldier's monument in the county. Champaign had lost 578 men, or 14 percent of the county's men of military age, to the war.[17] Such a loss deserved commemoration. The movement grew, culminating in a meeting on January 13, 1866, that decided to raise the sum of ten thousand dollars to erect a monument in the center of Urbana's town square. As might be expected, Joseph C. Brand was elected president of the monument association, and the Sixty-sixth's Major McConnell acted as solicitor and collector.

It proved difficult to raise the entire sum, but the work gradually proceeded; a contract was let for the granite base in 1867 and the limestone foundation was laid in 1869. The following year the association contracted for the monument itself with the National Fine Art Foundry in New York; according to an early twentieth-century county history, "The choice of design was submitted to numbers of known connoisseurs in art matters and resulted in the adoption of the figure of a cavalryman." The cavalry figure, who was dismounted, was perhaps an unlikely choice, given the comparatively small number of cavalry enlistments in the county; nonetheless, the meditative figure with head bowed, facing north for the return home, must rank as one of the more interesting examples of small-town Civil War monumental art. Certainly it contrasts noticeably with the stiff, tin-soldier figures that usually grace the Civil War monuments of cemeteries and courthouse squares, let alone the regimental monuments on many battlefields. The unveiling ceremony took place on December 7, 1871. The colors of local regiments, including the Sixty-sixth, were on display, and Governor Rutherford B. Hayes was among those who addressed the crowd.[18]

The area's cemeteries gradually filled with reminders of the war. Many veterans' families opted for the government-issue tombstone, which bore only the name, rank, company, and regiment of the deceased; however, regimental affiliation was often included on the headstones of veterans whose families could afford the work of local stone carvers. The inscription "66th OVI" appears on the granite and marble markers of many men who died well into the twentieth century. In lifetimes of sixty, seventy, or eighty years, the war had been the defining experience for these

The decorated Civil War monument in the town square in Urbana, Ohio, probably on Memorial Day around the turn of the century. Note the woman on the monument pedestal placing garland on the figure's hat.
Champaign County Historical Society.

veterans. Company F's Cpl. Francis M. Gibson, who died in 1922, had a stone from Culp's Hill placed at the foot of his grave in Marysville, Ohio.

The war devastated many lives and many families in the North. The surviving veterans had not only "lost time" in comparison to their cohorts who had remained at home to pursue civilian careers, but many of them had returned disabled by wounds and sickness, perhaps to live shortened lives. The nation's pension law of 1862 offered federal assistance to veterans suffering from service-related disabilities and to dependent survivors of those killed in the war. The rates ranged from eight to thirty dollars per month, depending on rank and nature of disability.

The requirement that disabilities be service-related in order to be pensionable remained in effect until the Dependent Pension Act of 1890, which granted a pension to any honorably discharged veteran who had served for ninety days and who suffered from any disability incapacitating him from manual labor, regardless of the nature or origin of the disability. Veterans' widows no longer had to prove that a husband's death had been service related. The pension rolls ballooned with the 1890 liberalization; the number of names on the national rolls rose from 537,944 in 1890 to 966,012 in 1893, approaching a proportion of one in sixty for the total U.S. population and accounting for over 40 percent of the total federal budget. By 1902 the number of military-pension recipients, the vast majority of them Civil War veterans or their dependents, had reached a high of 999,446. The 1890 act cost the government between sixty and seventy million dollars per year, and by 1907 the total had come to over a billion dollars.[19] The American Civil War, so often credited with creating a modern nation-state, was thus ultimately responsible for one of the country's first large-scale "entitlement" programs.

Parents of unmarried veterans were eligible for a pension if it could be demonstrated that the son had provided them support, which could simply mean that at one time or another he had sent some of his pay home. Irish-born Thomas Whalen, a corporal of Company C in the Sixty-sixth, died on July 14, 1864, from wounds received at Pine Mountain. Within two weeks of his death his mother, Bridget, who had also suffered the loss of her husband that year, began the pension application process, citing her son's support. She received her first pension payment in December 1866, coming to $144, or eight dollars a month from the date of her son's death.[20] Given a private soldier's pay of thirteen dollars a month, by the standards of the time this was a relatively generous dispensation.

A less timely application was that of Emmor and Eliza Gladden, parents of Levi Gladden, whose enlistment, and death at Port Republic, had inspired the poetic muse in his sister Sarah. They did not apply for aid upon their son's death but waited, perhaps, until severe economic need drove them to find what support was available (although changes in the pension law may also have been a factor). After some additional delay, occasioned in part by an incompetent pension lawyer, a pension of twelve dollars per month was granted in 1889. The pension was formally granted to Eliza, although her husband was still living. Affidavits indicated that Emmor, a farmer born in 1813, was no longer capable of providing for the two of them and had only ten acres of "poor land." In addition, there were the obligatory statements to the effect that Levi had in fact helped to support his parents until his death on June 9, 1862. A neighbor, with perhaps better than average memory, recalled in 1888 that Levi was an "industrious young man [who] worked hard and saved his money and contributed to his mother's support about one half or three quarters of his entire earnings from on or about the month of May or June 1858 . . . up to October 1861." Howard Linville, a comrade of Levi's from Company A, who was also on the pension rolls for a Cedar Mountain wound, testified that "I have known him to pay to his mother all his earnings toward her support except a small amount he retained for common clothing for himself and during his service in the army he remitted sums of money to his mother for her support."[21]

The localism of the volunteer regiments had ramifications in the pension application process. Veterans who remained in their communities after the war did not have to look far for comrades who could provide affidavits. It may have been advantageous for a veteran from a locally raised regiment to remain in the community, where soldier and civilian support networks were merged, and where local physicians, lawyers, and officials, who may even have been wartime comrades, could lend a helping hand.

Local support networks did not, however, always translate into rubber-stamp approval for disability claims. Some veterans had to appear before the local physicians' examining board. Lemuel Ayres, apparently something of a character, with a curiously checkered career, attested that in May 1862 as a private in Company A of the Sixty-sixth he had received an accidental spinal injury, following which he had seen detached service in various capacities—including the observation of Confederate operatives in Canada! His attempts, eventually successful, to obtain a pension were met with determined medical opposition, an examining physician concluding, "The claimant having been thoroughly examined three times within the last five years as no disability found I am convinced that he has none and is using a cane and making the fuss he does simply for effect. There are many of his comrades residing in and around Urbana O. but none of them that I could find knew anything of his injury."[22]

Veterans of the Sixty-sixth who were not residing in west central

Ohio—and as time wore on the former soldiers became more and more dispersed—might have to put some extra work into one of the most fundamental requirements for a pension claim, that of establishing one's identity. In the days before Social Security and the universal civil registration of births, this task could sometimes pose a problem. The pension file for Jasper O'Haver contains an affidavit dated October 13, 1916, and signed by Barney Brown, one of O'Haver's comrades from Company B:

> I knew claimant Jasper O'Haver (called Jap) was well acquainted with him for the reason that as boys we were not always the best of friends but am assured of the fact that this is the identical Jasper O'Haver of Co. B 66th OVI from the following incident of which he calls my attention in a letter written Oct. 1st 1916, which calls my attention to [an] incident that occurred at Bridgeport Alabama in 1864 viz. he says in his letter "Comrade do you remember the winter of 1864 which we were at Bridgeport, Alabama you had the mumps & bought a jar of pickles at the sutlers and ate them all at one time" from the above I am assured that he is the original Jasper O'Haver of Co. B 66 O.V.I.

O'Haver was living in Tampa, Florida, by this time, while Brown resided in Long Beach, California.[23]

Federal Civil War pensions, liberally sprinkled about the population well into the early twentieth century, probably constituted whatever "safety net" could be found in the United States in the years before the New Deal and widespread company retirement plans. Examining the pension files of many veterans, one might easily wonder what would have happened to them and their spouses without even this slender support. Augustus Tanner, who had "stood up to the rack and cut the hay" at Chancellorsville but had lost his arm in the Atlanta campaign, married shortly after the war and had children. In 1921, approaching his eightieth year, he several times requested pension increases only to be told that he was already receiving the maximum benefit of seventy-two dollars per month for a lost arm. He penned a letter, apparently over three or four months, to the secretary of the interior describing his difficulties making ends meet while having to pay for a road assessment:

> Secretary of the Interior. I address you to give you my difficulties and troubles which I ought to have done long ago. It is with difficulty that I can write at all. Mrs. Tanner died two years ago. She was

much younger than me consequently could administer to my many wants. . . . I have a grand daughter that has been living with me. I give her $40.00 each three months. She wants more. It seems I cannot give her any more. She wants more. I know it is not enough. When I drew my last quarter of which was $216 I had to pay $200 tax on this brick road in front of my house third assessment and they are still coming. I have to move. You see it does not leave me much. . . . I ought to have one hundred per month then I can pay assessments better. I am not going to stay here long. I have a brother 85 years. My grandfather lived to be 108 years 4 months and 4 days, grandmother was 88 [years] 4 months, 4 days. I don't want to live so long. In truth I don't want to live through another winter. Our coal bills and living [expenses] is great. All my close [clothes] have been given to me for years back by my neighbors. . . . I wrote this up in the month of June. My neighbors have been telling me you won't be here to draw your pension in September. Some encouragement for the old soldier but I am here yet. . . . There are people here that are glad to have us old soldiers die off as it will lower taxes (fools). . . . I will not be here very long. It matters not.

Augustus Tanner
Co. I 66th OVI
Attica, Seneca Co.
Ohio

Augustus Tanner lived for another year and a half, until March 23, 1923.[24]

The organization that accomplished the most in easing the plight of "old soldiers" like Tanner was the Grand Army of the Republic (G.A.R.), a Union veterans' group launched shortly after the war. It ultimately became a widespread and powerful organization that lobbied successfully for pension reform; however, it was not until the early 1880s that the local G.A.R. post became a given in most Northern communities. Urbana's post was "mustered" on July 8, 1881, with eighteen charter members; it was named after W. A. Brand. By 1893 it would carry 210 names on its membership rolls.[25]

The G.A.R. was a lobby for, in varying degrees, pension reform and political and cultural conservatism. In Champaign County, though, it was probably more than anything else a fraternal body, organized around a shared experience that had been the pivotal episode in its members' lives. The G.A.R. began as a ritualistic order, with initiation rites and grades reminiscent of the Masons and similar groups, by the time the

Brand post was established these trappings had been abandoned, and membership had become a far simpler matter.[26] The war, in a sense, was the primary initiation. G.A.R. members could gather periodically and discuss old campaigns. Aid would be collected for needy comrades, and when the final call came for an old soldier, his fellows would bear him to the cemetery.

Against the day of the "final roll call," the comrades compiled a biographical and historical record. Like many other Grand Army posts, Urbana's gathered brief memoirs detailing the experiences of its members and brought them together into a single ledger. It is an immense volume, gilded and elaborately embossed, and it survives today in the local public library. Compiled in 1895, it contains accounts of the service and lives of some 130 local veterans. The post's final meeting probably took place on December 4, 1933—with but six members remaining and a treasury of $11.88.[27]

The Woodstock post was named after another Sixty-sixth veteran, Lt. Harrison Davis, who had been killed at Ringgold. Although its volume of memoirs (assuming one was ever compiled) seems not to have survived, the post left behind a unique and somewhat curious monument to the war and the G.A.R. When a new Universalist church was erected in the village in 1894, the Harrison Davis post donated an elaborate stained-glass window. It depicted a Union artillerist and infantryman on the battlefield, above them military service medals, and over all an eagle and banners—and a portrait of Gen. John Logan, generally credited with being the G.A.R.'s founder. The donation was appropriate for at least one reason: a little more than fifty years before, the people of Woodstock had presented a sword to the newly commissioned Lieutenant Davis in the frame Universalist church which had stood on the site now occupied by the new house of worship.

The G.A.R. was not the only veteran's organization. As with many Union regiments, the Sixty-sixth's veterans organized a reunion association. It held its first meeting in 1877, with 168 veteran attendees, including Candy and Powell.[28] Meetings were usually held in Champaign County, where most of the soldiers had been recruited, although one reunion, the twenty-second, was wooed across the county line to Logan County, to be held at the West Liberty "mansion house" of Oliver P. Taylor. (Taylor had the dubious distinction of having become in April 1862 the Sixty-sixth's first casualty, when he had been accidentally shot by a New York trooper while on picket duty.) The twenty-second meeting,

Reunion of the Sixty-sixth Ohio Volunteer Infantry, Urbana, Ohio, early twentieth century. *Kyle Kelch Collection.*

in October 1907, attracted about a hundred veterans and their guests, a total of approximately five hundred people.

Perhaps not fully realizing what he was committing himself (and his wife) to, Taylor had risen at the previous reunion and promised the "boys" a turkey dinner if they would only agree to be his guests at the next gathering. When the group convened in West Liberty, Taylor got to his feet and explained that "the season has been wet and not good for turkeys" but that he had substituted "Plymouth Rock hens and roosters, mixed about right." (Later he acknowledged that his wife had been concerned that there might not be enough to eat.)

Entertainment consisted of brass bands and vocal solos. The entire crowd joined in a rendition of "America." Some of the veterans told wartime stories. A local physician recited "in swinging rhythmic style a short poem of [his] own authorship entitled 'Those Girls a-Raking Hay.'" There also appeared "a Mrs. Huling of Mechanicsburg, as a whistler, which performance, tho somewhat unique, was none the less welcome and enjoyed to the extent of an ovation and encore." The list of veterans who had died since the 1906 reunion was announced: among them was Eugene Powell, who had passed away the previous March.

The main speaker was a Gen. Robert P. Kennedy (not a Sixty-sixth veteran), who lauded the common soldier and recalled the Battle of Antietam, to which he attributed a greater deadliness than even that bloody day could rightfully claim, asserting that "over that field men charged back and forth seven times and at the close of the struggle 43,000 men lay dead." The newspaper article reporting the event noted that the speech was a "masterly effort" but "possibly a trifle long for a soldiers' reunion."[29]

The reunions continued for several more years. There was even a commemoration on January 17, 1912, of the fiftieth anniversary of the Sixty-sixth's departure from Urbana. Fourteen veterans attended.[30] Charles Candy was elected the association's president for life at its reunion on October 10, 1910—an honor that could have gratified him for but a short while, as he died on October 28. His third wife, Ella, whom he had married the previous year and was over thirty years his junior, became the regimental association's corresponding secretary, in which capacity she continued until what was probably the final reunion—the forty-sixth—in 1932.

By then the attendees were few. As their numbers declined, the Sixty-sixth's survivors sometimes held combined reunions with other regimental associations. Prior to each reunion Mrs. Candy obtained from the Vet-

Charles Candy as an older man. *Massachusetts Commandery Military Order of the Loyal Legion and USAMHI.*

erans Administration a list of Sixty-sixth pensioners and their places of residence. What was likely the penultimate list, that of 1931, revealed that of the twenty-eight men then on the rolls fourteen were still in Ohio, but only five lived in the immediate area.[31]

Many regimental reunion associations became vehicles for the compilation of official regimental histories. Among the survivors of the Sixty-sixth, the most obvious candidate for the role of regimental historian was W. A. Brand. At the 1878 reunion he rose to remind his comrades of the importance of "minor details in making up history," requesting that they furnish him with anecdotes from the war so that he "might weave them into and make complete a history of the 66th." Brand died the following year, and as matters transpired, any hope of a veteran-compiled regimental history died with him. He had apparently consulted with Eugene Powell, who drafted a preliminary manuscript; it was never published, although segments concerning particular battles found their way into print.[32]

In the decades following the conflict the racial issues at the heart of the Civil War were, of course, not resolved. Addison White, the escaped slave whose refuge in Mechanicsburg caused such mayhem and controversy in 1857, joined that famed black regiment, the 54th Massachusetts. He survived the war and lived out his days with his family in

Mechanicsburg. He was not the only African American to enlist from Champaign County; one can find several veterans' tombstones in Urbana's cemetery for enlisted men of the 54th and 55th Massachusetts, as well as from regiments in the United States Colored Troops. At least five thousand Ohio African Americans enlisted in the Union army.[33]

Blacks had long been present in the county. They were among Urbana's original settlers, and one early African American resident was reputed once to have been a slave of George Washington, set free by the conditions of the Founding Father's will. Despite their tenure in the state and their contributions to the war effort, however, Ohio's blacks faced significant prejudice. The state itself refused to approve black suffrage before the Fifteenth Amendment in 1869. For the next several decades, racism in Ohio and the Midwest erupted in violent episodes of kinds normally associated with the former slave states. Such was the case when in 1897 a Champaign County black was charged with assaulting a prominent local woman. The local militia had been called out to prevent a lynching and was holed up in the courthouse. Tensions rose, and the militia fired on the angry mob that had gathered outside, killing and wounding several. Horrified at what had transpired, the militia abandoned its post and allowed the mob to drag the suspect from his cell and hang him from a tree on the courthouse grounds. These events unfolded only a few days after Memorial Day and under the gaze of the bronze cavalryman who stood on his monument a block away from the courthouse.[34]

The lynching found its way into a novel entitled *J. Hardin and Son.* Its author was a local writer, Brand Whitlock (1869–1934), whose novels and short stories were often set in a small Ohio town named Macochee, a thinly disguised Urbana.[35] Whitlock was also a progressive lawyer and politician and served as U.S. ambassador to German-occupied Belgium during the first years of World War I.

He was also Joseph Carter Brand's grandson. For Whitlock the period of the Underground Railroad and the Civil War, in which his grandfather had figured so prominently, beckoned as a grand heroic age, though one whose legacy was ambiguous. Writing in 1910, he was clearly impatient with politicians "just awakening to the fact that history did not end with the Civil War." The wounded veteran officeholder also emerges briefly in *J. Hardin,* in the person of Captain Drumbaugh, the clerk of courts, who swings into the courtroom "on his crutches and the one leg on which he had gone farther in public life than ever he would have gone on two."[36]

Whitlock sometimes featured his grandfather's regiment in his work. His Sixty-sixth Ohio, recruited in and around the fictional town of Macochee, figures in some of his short stories. Although the setting is fictional, the allusion is clearly to the historical Sixty-sixth Ohio—with references to Port Republic, Cedar Mountain, and the transfer after Gettysburg to the Chattanooga campaign. In one story, "The Field of Honor," boyhood memories are evoked:

> The colonel had commanded the Sixty-Sixth Regiment during the Civil War. To me this was equivalent to saying that he had fought and won the war: For I could conceive of no larger military establishment than the old Sixty-Sixth, on which, as one might say, we were all reared in Macochee. I always wondered why the colonel's portrait did not appear in Bancroft's *History of the United States* which we used in public school. The omission impressed me as a mean and petty jealousy of the publishers, for if the Sixty-Sixth had not fought and won the war, who on earth had?

In the same story a veteran proclaims: "Now, we of the old Sixty-Sixth were excessively proud of our regiment. . . . We made the whole circuit of the southern states. Such events bind men together, you understand; we had all the esprit de corps of an old regiment of imperial guards."[37]

Nevertheless, "The Field of Honor" serves primarily as a vehicle for contrasting postwar glory with the realities of combat. A local man leaves his pregnant wife behind to volunteer in the Sixty-sixth and by the battle of Cedar Mountain attains the rank of captain. In a nighttime ambush following the battle he loses his nerve and turns tail, only to be shot by one of his corporals. The captain is presumed dead, his body left on the field, and the incident hushed up. His widow preserves his memory as a man who died bravely facing the foe at Cedar Mountain; many years later, however, her husband returns, having assumed a false identity and spent several years in Latin America. He decides not to return to his prewar identity, telling an officer of the Sixty-sixth who had helped to promulgate the legend of his death, "You have given me a personality far better than I could have developed for myself. . . . [F]or twenty years I have lived, lived to her, to my son, to this community, as a man who died heroically on the field of honor."[38]

Still, despite the embellishment of wartime memories, the Civil War remained a source of inspiration to many in Whitlock's generation. He recalled in 1918 how he "was brought up in the tradition of the Civil

War; it loomed large in my youth and it is natural that the sentiments and the emotions that the memories it used to inspire in us as boys should be renewed now in the midst of this greater war that has come to us in our manhood."[39]

In "The Orator of the Day," Whitlock presents J. Augustus Pennell, a jaded young city lawyer who travels to a small Ohio town to deliver the Memorial Day address. Impatiently sitting through the preliminary ceremonies, he is at first dismissive of the veteran who delivers a rambling introduction to the "orator of the day," but as the old man continues, Pennell gradually finds his presence and words compelling. What had motivated these men to risk all in the 1860s?

> Was it the madness, the glory of war, that profound mysterious current moving in the minds of vast bodies of men at the same time, that impels to deeds of daring and a kind of universal hysteria? Was it the glamor of flags and uniforms, the stirring music of martial bands, the love of strife and conflict, the race-old lust and love of conflict—all those peculiar elements that go to make up the glory of war?[40]

As the veteran recites the deaths of friends, family, and neighbors, Pennell decides against such an interpretation:

> Where was the glory in this? No; these men, if they had ever dreamed of glory, had been disillusioned; they had learned all the sorrow, all the shame, all the suffering all the cruel senseless waste of war. War to them was no dream of glory; it was a reality—and Pennell felt a swelling in his throat as the revelation came to him in a gasp—the reality of the ideal. It was an ideal for which they had done all this—these old, broken, almost grotesque figures; an ideal of unity and liberty and, though he did not see the paradox, an ideal of brotherhood. In their day they saw wrongs to be righted and they did not stand paltering; they did not hesitate or equivocate; they got up and righted them.[41]

They had been warriors in the eternal battle against injustice and privilege, concludes Pennell: "The war was not yet over, nor would it be over for ages yet to come; in other forms, in other phases, it must still be waged, that eons hence humanity in all its glory might ultimately realize itself." Echoing Whitlock's progressive politics, the young lawyer asks himself, "Could he dare, as these men, in their day and in like circumstances had dared?"[42]

Though it may have resonated with Whitlock's political beliefs, this interpretation of the war glosses over historical experience as much as had the evocations of martial glory his character Pennell considers and rejects. The implication that the war had been a crusade to free the slave and that all the veterans were crusaders was wishful thinking. Such an interpretation could not easily accommodate the opposition within ranks to the Emancipation Proclamation or the racism that found expression in many of the soldiers' letters. If it had been a crusade, it was a crusade that had been betrayed to Klan terrorism, with little protest in the North.

The Union had been preserved, but to what end? For most of the veterans the accomplished goal of a united country was probably sufficient unto itself, while for many the idea that it would be a union with a minimum of Democratic officeholders (and certainly none in Champaign County, if it could be helped) was also a reasonable expectation. The soldiers had also fought for one another. The veterans' war had formed a community of sorts, emerging from towns and villages and farms, generating its own hierarchies and relationships, in turn transmuting into G.A.R. posts, regimental reunions, and Memorial Day celebrations. The men had shared an experience that set them apart and defined them. Although the details of the definition were still open to interpretation, they knew that they, together with other Union veterans, had brought a momentous task to a victorious conclusion.

Four years of civil war presented them with life's extremes, its demands, its dangers, in a fashion that no civilian could likely understand or appreciate. T. G. Keller, an adjutant and captain from the Sixty-sixth, died in 1893 while commander of the W. A. Brand G.A.R. post. The post record summarized his experience in a fashion that might seem emblematic for all veterans and their self-images:

> . . . none but comrades in line of active service can ever tell or know the hardships and privations endured on the line of march, in the storm, the mud, snow, wading the rivers, holding accoutrements high over head to keep them dry, can never be told by the ordinary historian to impress on the minds of posterity the awfulness of the trials; and a continuance of such events for 4 long

The returning cavalryman atop the Civil War monument
in Urbana's town square.

years should make us realize the possibility of the slender thread
binding us to life being, as in the case of Com'd Keller, suddenly
snapped asunder.[43]

Today the returning cavalryman, the "man on the monument," still
stands in Urbana's square, an annoyance to the drivers of tractor-trailers
and a source of consternation for student drivers. His presence poses
the same question posed by any monument: it is a message from the
past to the present, but what is the message? Perhaps the message of this
monument concerns not so much the war he has won as the fact that he
has finally come home.

Appendix:
The Official Roster

*W*hat follows is a reproduction of the roster published for the Sixty-sixth Ohio Volunteer Infantry in the Ohio Adjutant General's Report. It is offered here as a point of reference for the reader and also as a service to interested descendants of those who served in the regiment. It is not accurate in all respects: some names are misspelled, and other errors of omission or commission can be found. Also note that this book's index does not include the roster listings.

The organization of the roster, following the listings for field and staff, is by company, beginning with the commissioned officers, followed by noncommissioned officers. Other enlisted men are then arranged in roughly alphabetical order. A single soldier may appear more than once in these lists, depending on promotions or transfers between companies or between field and staff. For soldiers carried on the rolls as deserters the "remarks" column is blank; enlistees listed as having been discharged by civil authority were released from service as underage.

SIXTY-SIXTH REGIMENT OHIO VOLUNTEER INFANTRY.

THREE YEARS' SERVICE

THIS Regiment was organized at Camp McArthur, Urbana, Ohio, in December, 1861, to serve three years. On the expiration of its term of service the original members (except veterans) were mustered out, and the organization, composed of veterans and recruits, retained in service until July 15, 1865, when it was mustered out in accordance with orders from the War Department.

The official list of battles, in which this Regiment bore an honorable part, is not yet published by the War Department, but the following list has been compiled, after careful research, during the preparation of this work :

PORT REPUBLIC, VA.,	JUNE 9, 1862.
CEDAR MOUNTAIN, VA.,	AUGUST 9, 1862.
ANTIETAM, MD.,	SEPTEMBER 17, 1862.
DUMFRIES, VA.,	DECEMBER 27, 1862.
CHANCELLORSVILLE, VA.,	MAY 1–4, 1863.
GETTYSBURG, PA.,	JULY 1–3, 1863.
RINGGOLD, GA. (Taylor's Ridge),	NOVEMBER 27, 1863.
RESACA, GA.,	MAY 13–16, 1864.
DALLAS, GA.,	MAY 25 to JUNE 4, 1864.
KENESAW MOUNTAIN, GA.,	JUNE 9–30, 1864.
PINE MOUNTAIN, GA.,	JUNE 14, 1864.
PINE KNOB, GA.,	JUNE 19, 1864.
CHATTAHOOCHEE RIVER, GA.,	JULY 6–10, 1864.
PEACH TREE CREEK, GA.,	JULY 20, 1864.
ATLANTA, GA. (Siege of),	JULY 28 to SEPTEMBER 2, 1864.
SAVANNAH, GA. (Siege of),	DECEMBER 10–21, 1864.

66th REGIMENT OHIO VOLUNTEER INFANTRY.

FIELD AND STAFF.

Mustered in at Camp McArthur, Urbana, O., by ——. Mustered out July 15, 1865, near Louisville, Ky., by Edward A. Wickes, Captain 150th New York Volunteers, and A. C. M. 14th Army Corps.

Names.	Rank.	Age.	Date of Entering the Service.	Period of Service.	Remarks.
Charles Candy	Colonel	....	Nov. 25, 1861	3 yrs.	Discharged Dec. 16, 1864, by order of War Department; Brevet Brig. General March 13, 1865.
James H. Dye	Lt. Col.	....	Sept. 28, 1861	3 yrs.	Resigned May 24, 1862.
Eugene Powell	do....	29	June 5, 1861	3 yrs.	Promoted from Captain Co. I, 4th O. V. I., Oct. 22, 1861; to Colonel 193d O. V. I. March 12, 1865.
John T. Mitchell	do....	18	Oct. 9, 1861	3 yrs.	Promoted to Major from Captain Co. I April 8, 1865; to Lieut. Colonel April 12, 1865; mustered out with regiment July 15, 1865.
Charles E. Fulton	Major	28	Oct. 9, 1861	3 yrs.	Promoted from Captain Co. A May 24, 1862; resigned Dec. 4, 1862.
Joshua G. Palmer	do....	32	Oct. 1, 1861	3 yrs.	Promoted from Captain Co. B Dec. 5, 1862; died July 10, 1863, of wounds received July —, 1863, in battle of Gettysburg, Pa.
Samuel H. Hedges	do....	23	Oct. 15, 1861	3 yrs.	Promoted from Captain Co. D April 12, 1865; mustered out with regiment July 15, 1865.
Thomas P. Bond	Surgeon	....	Sept. 26, 1861	3 yrs.	Discharged Sept. 13, 1862, on Surgeon's certificate of disability.
Jesse W. Brock	do....	32	Nov. 5, 1861	3 yrs.	Promoted from Asst. Surgeon Sept. 13, 1862; mustered out with regiment July 15, 1865.
B. F. Ludlum	As. Surg.	27	Mch. 12, 1863	3 yrs.	Mustered out with regiment July 15, 1865.
William McLean Gwynne	Adjutant	21	Sept. 5, 1861	3 yrs.	Promoted to Captain Co. F June 21, 1862.
William Hamilton	do....	....	Oct. 1, 1861	3 yrs.	Appointed from 1st Lieutenant Co. H Nov. 12, 1862; resigned Feb. 19, 1863.
T. G. Keller	do....	28	Oct. 15, 1861	3 yrs.	Promoted to Sergt. Major from private Co. H Dec. 17, 1862; to 2d Lieutenant Co. H Feb. 19, 1863; 1st Lieutenant and Adjutant July 20, 1863; to Captain Co H Nov. 12, 1864.
John R. Clayton	do....	21	Nov. 7, 1861	3 yrs.	Promoted to Q. M. Sergeant from private Co. G July 13, 1864; to 1st Lieutenant and Adjutant April 12, 1865; to Captain July 13, 1865, but not mustered; mustered out with regiment July 15, 1865; veteran.
Joseph C. Brand	R. Q. M.	....	Sept. 28, 1861	3 yrs.	Promoted to Captain April 2, 1864; declined; appointed Captain and Commissary of Subsistence April 12, 1864.
William A. Brand	do	24	Oct. 28, 1861	3 yrs.	Promoted to Q. M. Sergeant from private Co. G Dec. 8, 1863; to 2d Lieutenant May 9, 1864; 1st Lieutenant and Regt. Quartermaster June 27, 1864; resigned May 30, 1865; veteran.
Wilson R. Parsons	Chaplain	....	Dec. 12, 1861	3 yrs.	Discharged Aug. 13, 1864, by order of War Department.
Robert Murdock	Ser. Maj.	18	Dec. 28, 1861	3 yrs.	Promoted from private Co. F Jan. 1, 1862; to 2d Lieutenant Co. G to date Feb. 28, 1862.
Joseph W. Hitt	do....	17	Nov. 6, 1861	3 yrs.	Promoted from Corporal Co. A March 1, 1862; to 2d Lieutenant Co. C Dec. 5, 1862.
W. Wallace Cranston	do....	22	Oct. 10, 1861	3 yrs.	Promoted from Sergeant Co. D May 12, 1863; to 2d Lieutenant Co. I July 13, 1864; veteran.
Silas C. Shofstall	do....	19	Oct. 7, 1861	3 yrs.	Promoted from private Co. B Aug. 23, 1864; to 1st Lieutenant Co. D April 12, 1865; veteran.
Jacob Houtz	do....	19	Sept. 24, 1861	3 yrs.	Promoted from Sergeant Co. B May 3, 1865; mustered out with regiment July 15, 1865; veteran.
William R. Ross	Q. M. S.	20	Nov. 4, 1861	3 yrs.	Promoted from Sergeant Co. A March 16, 1862; discharged Dec. 7, 1863, on Surgeon's certificate of disability.
John L. Davis	do....	25	Oct. 28, 1861	3 yrs.	Promoted from Sergeant Co. B May 5, 1865; to 2d Lieutenant July 13, 1865, but not mustered; mustered out with regiment July 15, 1865; veteran.
John A. Purinton	Com. Ser.	31	Oct. 1, 1861	3 yrs.	Reduced to ranks and transferred to Co. C Dec. 31, 1862.
Aaron D. Riker	do....	31	Oct. 11, 1861	3 yrs.	Promoted from private Co. G Jan. 1, 1863; to 1st Lieutenant Co. E April 12, 1865; veteran.

Names.	Rank.	Age.	Date of Entering the Service.	Period of Service.	Remarks.
John C. Middleton	Com. Ser.	31	Oct. 15, 1861	3 yrs.	Promoted from private Co. H June 6, 1865; mustered out with regiment July 15, 1865; veteran.
Elisha Post	Hos. St'd	23	Oct. 18, 1861	3 yrs.	Promoted from private Co. E Nov. 31, 1861; no further record found.
Joseph H. Case	...do...	23	Nov. 7, 1861	3 yrs.	Promoted from private Co. E Dec. 13, 1862; to 1st Lieutenant Co. F April 12, 1865; veteran.
John W. Reid	...do...	20	Feb. 24, 1864	3 yrs.	Promoted from Corporal Co. A May 3, 1865; mustered out with regiment July 15, 1865.
Harry W. Shepherd	Prin.Mus	27	Jan. 24, 1862	3 yrs.	Promoted from private Co. I July —, 1862; mustered out June 12, 1865, at Columbus, O., by order of War Department.
Francis M. Williams	...do...	18	Nov. 14, 1861	3 yrs.	Promoted from Musician Co. D to date July —, 1863; mustered out with regiment July 15, 1865; veteran.

REGIMENTAL BAND.

Mustered in Oct. 23, 1861, at Camp McArthur, Urbana, O., by William Hamilton, 2d Lieutenant 66th O. V. I.
Mustered out July 5, 1862, at Washington, D. C., by John Elwood, Captain ——, U. S. A.

Names.	Rank.	Age.	Date.	Period.	Remarks.
William W. Vance	Ldr. B'nd	25	Oct. 23, 1861	3 yrs.	Mustered out July 5, 1862, by order of War Department.
David S. Abbott	Musician	41	Oct. 23, 1861	3 yrs.	Mustered out July 5, 1862, by order of War Department.
David Burnham	...do...	27	Oct. 23, 1861	3 yrs.	Mustered out July 5, 1862, by order of War Department.
Joseph Chamberlin	...do...	27	Oct. 23, 1861	3 yrs.	Discharged April 20, 1862, by order of War Department.
John L. Clark	...do...	25	Oct. 23, 1861	3 yrs.	Mustered out July 5, 1862, by order of War Department.
Mathew A. Hemphill	...do...	35	Oct. 23, 1861	3 yrs.	Mustered out July 5, 1862, by order of War Department.
John M. Hemphill	...do...	15	Oct. 23, 1861	3 yrs.	Discharged July 14, 1862, at Washington, D. C., by order of War Department.
Nicholas P. Hewitt	...do...	28	Oct. 23, 1861	3 yrs.	Mustered out July 5, 1862, by order of War Department.
William W. Hughes	...do...	22	Oct. 23, 1861	3 yrs.	Mustered out July 5, 1862, by order of War Department.
John B. Johnston	...do...	24	Oct. 23, 1861	3 yrs.	Mustered out July 5, 1862, by order of War Department.
John H. Morton	...do...	35	Oct. 23, 1861	3 yrs.	Mustered out July 5, 1862, by order of War Department.
William B. Shyrigh	...do...	23	Oct. 24, 1861	3 yrs.	Mustered out July 5, 1862, by order of War Department.
Birdett Shyrigh	...do...	21	Oct. 23, 1861	3 yrs.	Mustered out July 5, 1862, by order of War Department.
William W. Simpson	...do...	35	Oct. 23, 1861	3 yrs.	Died March 16, 1862, at Martinsburg, Va.
Philip A. Smith	...do...	23	Oct. 23, 1861	3 yrs.	Mustered out July 5, 1862, by order of War Department.
Christian Stout	...do...	19	Oct. 23, 1861	3 yrs.	Mustered out July 5, 1862, by order of War Department.
Joseph C. Vance	...do...	23	Oct. 23, 1861	3 yrs.	Mustered out April 25, 1862, by order of War Department.

COMPANY A.

Mustered in from Oct. 6 to Dec. 11, 1861, at Camp McArthur, Urbana, O., by Charles E. Fulton, 2d Lieutenant
66th O. V. I. Mustered out July 15, 1865, near Louisville, Ky., by Edward A. Wickes, Captain 150th
New York Volunteers, and A. C. M. 14th Army Corps.

Names.	Rank.	Age.	Date.	Period.	Remarks.
Charles E. Fulton	Captain	28	Oct. 9, 1861	3 yrs.	Appointed Nov. 7, 1861; promoted to Major May 24, 1862.
Thomas McConnell	...do...	23	Oct. 14, 1861	3 yrs.	Appointed 1st Lieutenant Nov. 20, 1861; promoted to Captain May 24, 1862; to Major July 20, 1863.
Richard E. Plunkett	...do...	21	Nov. 13, 1861	3 yrs.	Promoted to 1st Lieutenant from 1st Sergeant Co. E Nov. 12, 1864; to Captain April 12, 1865; resigned June 2, 1865; veteran.
Robert Simpson	...do...	23	Oct. 8, 1861	3 yrs.	Promoted to 1st Lieutenant Co. H June 14, 1865; mustered out with company July 15, 1865; veteran.

Names.	Rank.	Age.	Date of Entering the Service.	Period of Service.	Remarks.
Marshall L. Dempcy	1st Lieut.	23	Oct. 14, 1861	3 yrs.	Appointed 2d Lieutenant Nov. 20. 1861; promoted to 1st Lieutenant May 24, 1862; resigned March 23, 1863, at Dumfries, Va., on Surgeon's certificate of disability.
John T. Mitchell	do	18	Oct. 9, 1861	3 yrs.	Promoted to 2d Lieutenant from 1st Sergeant May 24, 1862; 1st Lieutenant Jan. 27, 1863; to Captain May 9, 1864; transferred to Co. I Sept. 17, 1864.
Henry Fraley	do	23	Nov. 5, 1861	3 yrs.	Appointed Corporal May 14, 1862; Sergeant March 24, 1863; 1st Sergeant Nov. 1, 1864; promoted to 1st Lieutenant April 12, 1865; to Captain Co. H June 14, 1865; veteran.
John H. Diltz	1st Sergt.	23	Oct. 14, 1861	3 yrs.	Appointed from Sergeant July 1, 1863; promoted to 1st Lieutenant Co. D Aug. 11, 1864; veteran.
William C. McClellen	do	25	Oct. 28, 1861	3 yrs.	Mustered as private; appointed 1st Sergeant ——; mustered out with company July 15, 1865; veteran.
Samuel H. Hedges	Sergeant	23	Oct. 15, 1861	3 yrs.	Promoted to 2d Lieutenant Co. D Nov. 27, 1862.
John R. Organ	do	18	Oct. 14, 1861	3 yrs.	Promoted to 2d Lieutenant Co. I Jan. 27, 1863; veteran.
William R. Ross	do	20	Nov. 4, 1861	3 yrs.	Mustered as private; appointed Sergeant ——; promoted to Q. M. Sergeant March 16, 1862.
Joshua C. Light	do	22	Oct. 14, 1861	3 yrs.	Mustered as private; appointed Sergeant ——; discharged April 22, 1863, at Acquia Creek, Va., on Surgeon's certificate of disability.
Henry Heller	do	20	Oct. 20, 1861	3 yrs.	Mustered as private; appointed Sergeant ——; mustered out Dec. 17, 1864, on expiration of term of service.
John F. Morgan	do	19	Oct. 14, 1861	3 yrs.	Mustered as private; appointed Sergeant ——; mustered out with company July 15, 1865; veteran.
William Stokes	do	19		3 yrs.	Mustered as private; appointed Sergeant ——; mustered out with company July 15, 1865; veteran.
Thomas Thompson	do	22	Nov. 26, 1861	3 yrs.	Mustered as private; appointed Sergeant ——; promoted to 2d Lieutenant July 13, 1865, but not mustered; mustered out with company July 15, 1865; veteran.
William Thompson	do	20	Oct. 16, 1861	3 yrs.	Mustered as private; appointed Sergeant ——; mustered out with company July 15, 1865; veteran.
Jonathan L. Guthridge	Corporal	24	Oct. 14, 1861	3 yrs.	Appointed Corporal ——; discharged Oct. 25, 1862, at Alexandria, Va., on Surgeon's certificate of disability.
Robert N. Rannals	do	26	Oct. 15, 1861	3 yrs.	Appointed Corporal ——; discharged Dec. 5, 1862, at Washington, D. C., on Surgeon's certificate of disability.
Zenas B. Jones	do	26	Oct. 12, 1861	3 yrs.	Appointed Corporal ——; discharged Nov. 23, 1862, at Bolivar Heights, Va., on Surgeon's certificate of disability.
Joseph W. Hitt	do	17	Nov. 6, 1861	3 yrs.	Appointed Corporal ——; promoted to Sergt. Major March 1, 1862.
James H. Brooks	do	21	Oct. 30, 1861	3 yrs.	Appointed Corporal ——; discharged Dec. 29, 1863, at Baltimore, Md., on Surgeon's certificate of disability.
Samuel F. Diltz	do	24	Oct. 14, 1861	3 yrs.	Appointed Corporal ——; died Feb. 20, 1862, in hospital at Cumberland, Md.
Granville M. Smith	do	24	Oct. 14, 1861	3 yrs.	Appointed Corporal ——; mustered out Dec. 17, 1864, on expiration of term of service.
Henry C. Layborn	do	19	Jan. 26, 1864	3 yrs.	Appointed Corporal ——; mustered out with company July 15, 1865.
John W. Reid	do	20	Feb. 24, 1864	3 yrs.	Appointed Corporal ——; promoted to Hospital Steward May 3, 1865.
Elisha B. Seaman	do	22	Oct. 22, 1861	3 yrs.	Appointed Corporal ——; mustered out with company July 15, 1865; veteran.
Isaac Chidester	do	26	Oct. 14, 1861	3 yrs.	Appointed Corporal ——; mustered out with company July 15, 1865; veteran.
George B. Light	do	23	Oct. 29, 1861	3 yrs.	Appointed Corporal ——; captured March 29, 1864, at Caperton Ferry, W. Va.; mustered out June 22, 1865, at Camp Chase, O., by order of War Department; veteran.
Joseph M. Wren	do	20	Oct. 18, 1861	3 yrs.	Appointed Corporal ——; mustered out June 20, 1865, at Camp Chase, O., by order of War Department; veteran.
Ambusty, George	Private	21	Sept. 27, 1864	1 yr.	Drafted; mustered out June 3, 1865, near Bladensburg, Md., by order of War Department.
Ayers, Lemuel M	do	24	Oct. 16, 1861	3 yrs.	Transferred to Veteran Reserve Corps June 27, 1863, by order of War Department.
Baldwin, Richard W	do	24	Oct. 14, 1861	3 yrs.	Discharged Aug. 4, 1862, at Columbus, O., on Surgeon's certificate of disability.
Benkley, James	do	19	Aug. 12, 1864	1 yr.	Substitute; mustered out with company July 15, 1865.
Best, William E	do	26	Oct. 14, 1861	3 yrs.	Died July 21, 1862, at Washington, D. C.

Names.	Rank.	Age.	Date of Entering the Service.	Period of Service.	Remarks.
Blair, William J	Private	19	Oct. 14, 1861	3 yrs.	Killed May 3, 1863, inb attle of Chancellorsville, Va.
Black, Andrew	..do....	17	Oct. 26, 1861	3 yrs.	Killed June 9, 1862, in battle of Port Republic, Virginia.
Blessing, John	..do....	18	Aug. 28, 1864	2 yrs.	Substitute; mustered out with company July 15, 1865.
Bobo, Garrot	..do....	18	Aug. 12, 1864	1 yr.	Substitute; mustered out with company July 15, 1865.
Briney, John K	..do....	20	Oct. 12, 1861	3 yrs.	Killed June 9, 1862, in battle of Port Republic, Virginia.
Brooks, John M	..do....	19	Aug. 8, 1862	3 yrs.	Mustered out June 3, 1865, near Bladensburg, Md., by order of War Department.
Bryan, Luke W	..do....	30	Aug. 11, 1862	3 yrs.	Died Feb. 25, 1863, at Annapolis, Md.
Bryan, Madison	..do....	27	Nov. 11, 1861	3 yrs.	Mustered out with company July 15, 1865; veteran.
Bryant, James S	..do....	22	Dec. 16, 1861	3 yrs.	Discharged April 28, 1862, at Strasburg, Va., on Surgeon's certificate of disability.
Burns, Thomas A	..do....	26	Nov. 6, 1861	3 yrs.	Transferred to Veteran Reserve Corps April 6, 1864, by order of War Department.
Campbell, William	..do....	18	Oct. 15, 1861	3 yrs.	Died June 15, 1862, in hospital at Luray, Va.
Chidester, Granville L	..do....	19	Oct. 18, 1861	3 yrs.	Killed June 9, 1862, in battle of Port Republic, Virginia.
Christ, William	..do....	18	Oct. 12, 1864	1 yr.	Substitute; mustered out with company July 15, 1865.
Clapsadle, Jacob M	..do....	19	Nov. 18, 1861	3 yrs.	Mustered ont with company July 15, 1865; veteran.
Clinton, William	..do....	50	Oct. 14, 1861	3 yrs.	Discharged April 28, 1862, at Urbana, O., on Surgeon's certificate of disability.
Clark, Samuel H	..do....	19	Nov. 15, 1861	3 yrs.	Discharged Feb. 6, 1863, at Baltimore, Md., on Surgeon's certificate of disability.
Colbert, Isaac H	..do....	22	Oct. 6, 1861	3 yrs.	Discharged April 28, 1862, at Urbana, O., on Surgeon's certificate of disability.
Conrad, John W. H	..do....	21	Dec. 11, 1861	3 yrs.	Discharged Aug. 12, 1862, at Alexandria, Va., on Surgeon's certificate of disability.
Cotrell, Robert	..do....	18	Aug. 15, 1864	1 yr.	Substitute; mustered out June 3, 1865, near Bladensburg, Md., by order of War Department.
Cranston, Wallace W	..do....	22	Oct. 10, 1861	3 yrs.	Mustered as private; appointed Sergeant and transferred to Co. D ——.
Davis, Charles M	..do....	18	Aug. 15, 1864	2 yrs.	Substitute; mustered out with company July 15, 1865.
Dodson, John A	..do....	19	Aug. 17, 1864	3 yrs.	Substitute.
Dolson, Isaac H	..do....	20	Oct. 26, 1861	3 yrs.	Mustered out with company July 15, 1865; veteran.
Dugan, Samuel	..do....	18	Aug. 15, 1864	1 yr.	Substitute; mustered out June 3, 1865, near Bladensburg, Md., by order of War Department.
Ebert, George F	..do....	30	Nov. 29, 1861	3 yrs.	
Emerich, William H	..do....	20	Oct. 26, 1861	3 yrs.	On detached service at Columbus, O.; mustered out July 15, 1865, at Columbus, O., by order of War Department; veteran.
Estabrook, Isaac H	..do....				Mustered out May 29, 1865, at Camp Dennison, O., by order of War Department.
Forsyth, Newton	..do....	21	Oct. 22, 1861	3 yrs.	Discharged Aug. 6, 1862, at Columbus, O., on Surgeon's certificate of disability.
Forsyth, James R	..do....	25	Oct. 6, 1864	1 yr.	Substitute; died Jan. 3, 1865, in hospital at Savannah, Ga.
Forey, Michael	..do....	18	Jan. 3, 1862	3 yrs.	Mustered out Dec. 17, 1864, by order of War Department.
Ganson, Jasper N	..do....	19	Oct. 23, 1861	3 yrs.	Discharged Jan. 27, 1863, at Philadelphia, Pa., on Surgeon's certificate of disability.
Ganson, John G	..do....	18	July 2, 1862	3 yrs.	Discharged Jan. 27, 1863, at Philadelphia, Pa., on Surgeon's certificate of disability.
Gladden, Levi	..do....	20	Oct. 29, 1861	3 yrs.	Killed June 9, 1862, in battle of Port Republic, Va.
Glendening, John	..do....	17	Nov. 5, 1861	3 yrs.	Discharged Nov. 27, 1861, at Urbana, O., by civil authority.
Gray, Newton	..do....	23	Oct. 17, 1861	3 yrs.	Died Oct. 31, 1862, at Bedloe's Island, New York.
Gray, David	..do....	26	Jan. 2, 1862	3 yrs.	Mustered out Jan. 14, 1865, at Columbus, O., on expiration of term of service.
Graves, Austin	..do....	18	Oct. 12, 1864	1 yr.	Substitute; mustered out with company July 15, 1865.
Graham, John	..do....	18	Oct. 14, 1861	3 yrs.	Discharged Oct. 28, 1862, at Washington, D. C., on Surgeon's certificate of disability.
Graham, William	..do....	18	Oct. 11, 1864	1 yr.	Substitute; mustered out with company July 15, 1865.
Guthridge, William	..do....	17	Oct. 6, 1861	3 yrs.	Discharged Nov. 13, 1861, at Urbana, O., by civil authority.
Haynes, Andrew	..do....	18	Aug. 13, 1864	1 yr.	Substitute; mustered out July 11, 1865, at Tripler Hospital, Columbus, O., by order of War Department.
Heller, Amos	..do....	24	Oct. 18, 1861	3 yrs.	Discharged July 1, 1862, at Columbus, O., on Surgeon's certificate of disability.
Hoar, Hanson B	..do....	21	Dec. 5, 1861	3 yrs.	Mustered out Dec. 17, 1864, on expiration of term of service.

Names.	Rank.	Age.	Date of Entering the Service.	Period of Service.	Remarks.
Horn, James W.........	Private	22	Oct. 10, 1861	3 yrs.	Transferred to Veteran Reserve Corps Oct. 18, 1863.
Howard, Clark C	...do....	23	Aug. 9, 1862	3 yrs.	Discharged Jan. 2, 1863, at Baltimore, Md., on Surgeon's certificate of disability.
Howard, Patrick C	...do....	26	Oct. 31, 1861	3 yrs.	Discharged Oct. 29, 1862, at Washington, D. C., on Surgeon's certificate of disability.;
Howard, Perry C	...do....	17	Dec. 4, 1861	3 yrs.	Discharged Oct. 29, 1862, at Washington, D. C., on Surgeon's certificate of disability.
Humes, David M.........	...do....	26	Oct. 15, 1861	3 yrs.	Died Oct. 24, 1862, at Fort Delaware, Md.
Hust, M. W	...do....	17	Jan. 3, 1862	3 yrs.	Discharged Nov. 23, 1862, at Bolivar Heights, Va., on Surgeon's certificate of disability.
Johnson, Henry	...do....	25	Dec. 10, 1861	3 yrs.	Discharged Nov. 23, 1862, at Bolivar Heights, Va., on Surgeon's certificate of disability.
Johnson, Demetreo.......	...do....	18	Aug. 18, 1864	2 yrs.	Substitute; mustered out with company July 15, 1865.
Johnston, Stephen G	...do....	18	Aug. 17, 1864	2 yrs.	Substitute; killed Dec. 19, 1864, in siege of Savannah, Ga.
Jones, Thomas O	...do....	21	....	3 yrs.	On detached service at Columbus, O.; mustered out July 20, 1865, by order of War Department; veteran
Jones, Washington.......	...do....	20	Oct. 18, 1861	3 yrs.	Discharged Feb. 17, 1863, at Alexandria, Va., on Surgeon's certificate of disability.
Kerns, Martin A	...do....	17	Oct. 26, 1861	3 yrs.	Transferred to Veteran Reserve Corps July 1, 1863.
King, James L..........	...do....	18	Oct. 15, 1861	3 yrs.	Discharged June 23, 1863, at Cleveland O., on Surgeon's certificate of disability; veteran.
Kneal, John	...do....	18	Aug. 8, 1864	1 yr.	Substitute; mustered out May 24, 1865, at New York City, by order of War Department.
Knapp, John	...do....	18	Aug. 8, 1864	1 yr.	Substitute; mustered out July 22, 1865, at New York City, by order of War Department.
Laney, Joseph C	...do....	18	Aug. 11, 1864	1 yr.	Substitute; mustered out June 3, 1865, near Bladensburg, Md., by order of War Department.
Larue, John T..........	...do....	18	Mch. 4, 1864	3 yrs.	Mustered out with company July 15, 1865.
Linville, Howard........	...do....	19	Oct. 26, 1861	3 yrs.	Discharged March 9, 1863, at Alexandria, Va., on Surgeon's certificate of disability.
Little, Robert	...do....	25	Oct. 14, 1864	1 yr.	Substitute; mustered out July 11, 1865, by order of War Department.
Martin, John W.........	...do....	23	Oct. 16, 1864	1 yr.	Substitute; mustered out July 14, 1865, at Columbus, O., by order of War Department.
Mayes, Jacob...........	...do....	29	Oct. 18, 1861	3 yrs.	Mustered out with company July 15, 1865; veteran.
Mayes, Francis	...do....	37	Dec. 12, 1862	3 yrs.	Discharged Aug. 4, 1865, on Surgeon's certificate of disability.
Mayes, Andrew.........	...do....	28	Oct. 21, 1861	3 yrs.	Discharged Jan. 1, 1863, at Washington, D. C., by order of War Department.
McCamarcial, George....	...do....	18	Aug. 17, 1864	2 yrs.	Substitute.
McCullough, J. R........	...do....	41	Oct. 28, 1861	3 yrs.	Discharged Jan. 31, 1863, at Cincinnati, O., on Surgeon's certificate of disability.
McCulley, David	...do....	17	Oct. 17, 1861	3 yrs.	Died March 11, 1865, at Columbus, O.; veteran.
McDougal, James	...do....	18	Aug. 8, 1862	2 yrs.	Substitute; mustered out with company July 15, 1865.
McGill, James....... ...	...do....	18	Oct. 19, 1861	3 yrs.	Died Dec. 25, 1862, at Washington, D. C.
McGill, Cornell.........	...do....	19	Nov. 6, 1861	3 yrs.	Died Dec. 25, 1862, at Washington, D. C.
McNeal, James.........	...do....	24	Aug. 16, 1864	3 yrs.	Substitute; mustered out with company July 15, 1865.
McRoberts, William C	...do....	22	Oct. 11, 1861	3 yrs.	Discharged April 28, 1862, at Urbana, O., on Surgeon's certificate of disability.
Mercer, Louis A. J.......	...do....	18	Oct. 5, 1864	1 yr.	Substitute; mustered out May 29, 1865, at New York City, by order of War Department.
Meirheim, Max..........	...do....	35	Oct. 23, 1863	3 yrs.	Mustered out with company July 15, 1865.
Messer, Jacob	...do....	21	Oct. 29, 1861	3 yrs.	Mustered out Dec. 17, 1864, on expiration of term of service.
Moffitt, Owen..........	...do....	18	Oct. 26, 1861	3 yrs.	Died June 27, 1862, at Philadelphia, Pa.
Moore, Augustus E.......	...do....	19	Nov. 6, 1861	3 yrs.	Mustered out Dec. 17, 1864, on expiration of term of service.
Morr, Henry............	...do....	25	Sept. 26, 1864	1 yr.	Drafted; mustered out June 3, 1865, near Bladensburg, Md., by order of War Department.
Morgan, James W	...do....	24	Dec. 11, 1861	3 yrs.	Mustered out with company July 15, 1865; veteran.
Morrison, Charles W. T. F	...do....	40	Oct. 12, 1861	3 yrs.	Mustered out Dec. 17, 1864, on expiration of term of service.
Nagle, Ernst............	...do....	18	Oct. 26, 1861	3 yrs.	Mustered out June 13, 1865, at Camp Chase, O., by order of War Department; veteran.
Neal, Lemuel M.........	...do....	17	Oct. 25, 1861	3 yrs.	Discharged Nov. 17, 1861, at Urbana, O., by civil authority.
O'Flarerty, James........	...do....	23	Aug. 16, 1864	3 yrs.	Substitute.
Ogg, Wesley............	...do....	18	Oct. 12, 1864	1 yr.	Drafted; drowned June 14, 1865, in Ohio river, near Newport, Ky.

Names.	Rank.	Age.	Date of Entering the Service.	Period of Service.	Remarks.
Organ, Marion	Private	28	Oct. 9, 1861	3 yrs.	Discharged Oct. 31, 1862, at Urbana, O., on Surgeon's certificate of disability.
Outram, Timothy	do	17	Oct. 25, 1861	3 yrs.	Died April 25, 1862, at Winchester, Va.
Park, Thomas B	do	21	Oct. 19, 1861	3 yrs.	Discharged April 26, 1863, at Columbus, O., on Surgeon's certificate of disability.
Park, Thomas	do	19	Aug. 15, 1864	1 yr.	Substitute; appointed Corporal ——; reduced ——; mustered out June 3, 1865, near Bladensburg, Md., by order of War Department.
Poland, Jacob	do	29	Oct. 26, 1861	3 yrs.	Died July 9, 1862, at Washington, D. C.
Polack, Thomas	do	18	Jan. 2, 1864	3 yrs.	Mustered out with company July 15, 1865.
Porter, James C	do	31	Oct. 28, 1861	3 yrs.	Killed May 3, 1863, in battle of Chancellorsville, Va.
Price, Evan R	do	27	Oct. 15, 1861	3 yrs.	Discharged Nov. 22, 1862, at Alexandria, Va., on Surgeon's certificate of disability.
Price, Jacob S	do	17	Nov. 6, 1861	3 yrs.	Discharged Nov. 8, 1861, at Urbana, O., by civil authority.
Randall, Silvanus	do	30	Dec. 5, 1861	3 yrs.	Discharged Jan. 13, 1862, at New Creek, Va,, on Surgeon's certificate of disability.
Rafferty, William	do	18	Dec. 30, 1861	3 yrs.	Discharged April 28, 1862, at Strasburg, Va., on Surgeon's certificate of disability.
Reed, Thomas	do	18	Aug. 8, 1864	2 yrs.	Substitute; discharged June 12, 1865, at Fairfax Seminary, Va., on Surgeon's certificate of disability.
Reed, Jas. C	do	25	Jan. 2, 1862	3 yrs.	Discharged Sept. 20, 1863, at Washington, D. C., on Surgeon's certificate of disability.
Reid, James Calvin	do	21	Oct. 14, 1861	3 yrs.	Discharged Feb. 20, 1863, at Washington, D.C., on Surgeon's certificate of disability.
Reynolds, Lemuel	do	18	Nov. 7, 1861	3 yrs.	Discharged Feb. 24, 1863, at Baltimore, Md., on Surgeon's certificate of disability.
Risley, Marcus	do	23	Oct. 12, 1864	1 yr.	Substitute; mustered out with company July 15, 1865.
Runyon, John B	do	28	Oct. 6, 1861	3 yrs.	Died May 20, 1863, at Acquia Creek, Va.
Shaul, Joseph H. M	do	22	Oct. 17, 1861	3 yrs.	Discharged March 9, 1863, at Washington, D. C.
Sheldon, George	do	20	Aug. 13, 1864	3 yrs.	Substitute ——.
Sigman, John	do	20	Oct. 12, 1861	3 yrs.	
Sigman, Thomas B	do	18	Oct. 15, 1861	3 yrs.	
Smith, James W	do	21	Nov. 1, 1861	3 yrs.	Veteran.
Stokes, John H	do	18	Dec. 6, 1861	3 yrs.	Died July 6, 1862, at Washington, D. C.
Sullivan, Gabriel M	do	21	Nov. 6, 1861	3 yrs.	Discharged June 17, 1863, at Acquia Creek, Va., on Surgeon's certificate of disability.
Swaisgood, David	do	34	Sept. 27, 1864	1 yr.	Drafted; mustered out July 11, 1865, at Columbus, O., by order of War Department.
Teal, James	do	18	Aug. 15, 1864	1 yr.	Substitute; mustered out June 3, 1865, near Bladensburg, Md., by order of War Department.
Thatcher, Jonathan	do	23	Jan. 15, 1862	3 yrs.	Discharged Jan. 2, 1863, at Baltimore, Md., on Surgeon's certificate of disability.
Thompson, Samuel	do	35	Sept. 27, 1864	1 yr.	Drafted; died April 3, 1865, at Wilmington, North Carolina.
Tyrrel, Theodore	do	18	Oct 12, 1864	1 yr.	Substitute; mustered out with company July 15, 1865.
Uncles, Henry	do	18	Oct. 12, 1864	1 yr.	Substitute; mustered out with company July 15, 1865.
Weiderman, John	do	51	Nov. 5, 1861	3 yrs.	Died April 21, 1862, at Strasburg, Va.
Williams, John	do	34	Aug. 16, 1865	3 yrs.	Substitute; mustered out with company July 15, 1865.
Williams, Salames	do	18	Aug. 17, 1864	2 yrs.	Substitute; mustered out with company July 15, 1865.
Wilson, Elijah	do	18	Oct. 13, 1864	1 yr.	Substitute; mustered out with company July 15, 1865.
Wooley, Joseph J	do	24	Oct. 28, 1861	3 yrs.	Discharged Oct. 10, 1862, at Washington, D. C., on Surgeon's certificate of disability.
Wooley, John C	do	21	Oct. 15, 1861	3 yrs.	Discharged Oct. 13, 1863, at Alexandria, Va., on Surgeon's certificate of disability.
Worrell, Norris	do	27	Oct. 14, 1861	3 yrs.	Discharged June 28, 1862, at Alexandria, Va., on Surgeon's certificate of disability.
Wren, John	do	21	Jan. 26, 1864	3 yrs.	Died July 7, 1864, at Chattanooga, Tenn.

COMPANY B.

Mustered in Dec. 26, 1861, at Camp McArthur, Urbana, O., by Joshua G. Palmer, Robert Murdock and William A. Sampson, 2d Lieutenants 66th O. V. I. Mustered out July 15, 1865, near Louisville, Ky., by Edward A. Wickes, Captain 150th New York Volunteers, and A. C. M. 14th Army Corps.

Names.	Rank.	Age.	Date of Entering the Service.	Period of Service.	Remarks.
Joshua G. Palmer	Captain	32	Oct. 1, 1861	3 yrs.	Appointed Oct. 9, 1861; promoted to Major Dec. 5, 1862.
William McLean Gwynne	do	21	Sept. 5, 1861	3 yrs.	Transferred from Co. F Dec. 3, 1862; transferred to Co. H May 19, 1863.
B. F. Ganson	do	22	Oct. 3, 1861	3 yrs.	Appointed 1st Lieutenant Nov. 15, 1861; promoted to Captain April 16, 1863; mustered out Dec. 27, 1864, on expiration of term of service.

Names.	Rank.	Age.	Date of Entering the Service.	Period of Service.	Remarks
William W. Jackson....	Captain	21	Aug. 7, 1862	3 yrs.	Promoted to 1st Lieutenant from 1st Sergeant Co. H Nov. 12, 1864; to Captain April 12, 1865; mustered out with company July 15, 1865.
Archie Houston..........	1st Lieut.	24	Sept. 24, 1861	3 yrs.	Mustered as private; promoted to 2d Lieutenant Aug. 15, 1862; to 1st Lieutenant May 27, 1863; to Captain Aug. 19, 1864, but not mustered; resigned Sept. 30, 1864.
Ridgley P. Wilkins......... ..do....	do....	24	Oct. 3, 1861	3 yrs.	Mustered as private; appointed Sergeant ——; 1st Sergeant Oct. 1, 1864; promoted to 1st Lieutenant April 8, 1865; to Captain Co. I June 14, 1865; veteran.
Duncan A. McDonald....	2d Lieut.	24	Sept. 14, 1861	3 yrs.	Appointed Oct. 14, 1861; died Aug. 15, 1862, of wounds received Aug. 9, 1862, in battle of Cedar Mountain, Va.
James P. Conn ....do....	do....	19	Oct. 18, 1861	3 yrs.	Promoted from 1st Sergeant Co. I May 27, 1863; to 1st Lieutenant Co. F April 2, 1864; veteran.
William C. Flago........	1st Sergt.	18	Sept. 24, 1861	3 yrs.	Mustered as private; appointed 1st Sergeant ——; promoted to 2d Lieutenant April 16, 1863, but not mustered; killed May 3, 1863, in battle of Chancellorsville, Va.
James C. Bowe ....do....	do....	23	Nov. 9, 1861	3 yrs.	Mustered as private; appointed 1st Sergeant Dec. 16, 1863; promoted to 1st Lieutenant Co. E Aug. 11, 1864; veteran.
James M. Mitchell ....do....	do....	19	Oct. 10, 1861	3 yrs.	Mustered as private; appointed Sergeant ——; 1st Sergeant May 1, 1865; promoted to 1st Lieutenant July 13, 1865, but not mustered; mustered out with company July 15, 1865; veteran.
Elijah E. Weaver........	Sergeant	21	Oct. 28, 1861	3 yrs.	Mustered as private; appointed Sergeant ——; promoted to 1st Lieutenant July 13, 1865, but not mustered; mustered out with company July 15, 1865; veteran.
Peter Baker............... ..do....	do....	22	Oct. 10, 1861	3 yrs.	Appointed Corporal ——; Sergeant May 3, 1865; mustered out with company July 15, 1865; veteran.
John Gurnea.............. ..do....	do....	22	Nov. 9, 1861	3 yrs.	Appointed Corporal ——; Sergeant May 3, 1865; mustered out with company July 15, 1865; veteran.
John L. Davis............ ..do....	do....	24	Oct. 28, 1861	3 yrs.	Mustered as private; appointed Sergeant ——; promoted to Q. M. Sergeant May 5, 1865; veteran.
Jacob Houts.............. ..do....	do....	19	Sept. 24, 1861	3 yrs.	Appointed Corporal ——; Sergeant ——; promoted to Sergt. Major May 3, 1865; veteran.
Nathan D. Baker........	Corporal	27	Sept. 24, 1861	3 yrs.	Appointed Corporal ——; mustered out with company Dec. 22, 1864, at Savannah, Ga., on expiration of term of service.
George W. Parlett........ ..do....	do....	28	Oct. 10, 1861	3 yrs.	Appointed Corporal ——; discharged July 24, 1862, at Williamsport, Md., on Surgeon's certificate of disability.
Cyrus Gregg.............. ..do....	do....	18	Oct. 3, 1861	3 yrs.	Appointed Corporal ——; discharged May 22, 1862, at Winchester, Va., on Surgeon's certificate of disability.
John G. Miller............ ..do....	do....	22	Oct. 28, 1861	3 yrs.	Appointed Corporal ——; discharged Sept. 12, 1862, at Columbus, O., on Surgeon's certificate of disability.
William A. Powell........ ..do....	do....	19	Dec. 30, 1861	3 yrs.	Appointed Corporal ——; killed Aug. 9, 1862, in battle of Cedar Mountain, Va.
Harvey Vinyard.......... ..do....	do....	18	Sept. 24, 1861	3 yrs.	Appointed Corporal ——; died July 25, 1862, in Rebel Prison at Lynchburg, Va.
Barnard Harrigan........ ..do....	do....	22	Oct. 28, 1861	3 yrs.	Appointed Corporal ——; mustered out with company July 15, 1865; veteran.
Patrick Marks............ ..do....	do....	23	Oct. 28, 1861	3 yrs.	Appointed Corporal ——; mustered out with company July 15, 1865; veteran.
Henry Icinbarger........ ..do....	do....	19		3 yrs.	Appointed Corporal ——; mustered out with company July 15, 1865; veteran.
Allen, Ezra..............	Private	26	Oct. 16, 1861	3 yrs.	Discharged June 27, 1862, at Columbus, O., on Surgeon's certificate of disability.
Ambuster, George....... ..do....	do....	21	Sept. 24, 1864	1 yr.	Drafted; mustered out June 2, 1865, near Bladensburg, Md. by order of War Department.
Baker, Simon C........ ..do....	do....	36	Oct. 10, 1861	3 yrs.	Mustered out Dec. 3, 1864, at Columbus, O., on expiration of term of service.
Barnhouse, Morgan ....do....	do....	18	Oct. 14, 1864	1 yr.	Drafted; mustered out with company July 15, 1865.
Barley, Samuel.......... ..do....	do....	22	Oct. 8, 1861	3 yrs.	
Backman, Joseph........ ..do....	do....	24	Sept. 29, 1864	1 yr.	Drafted; mustered out June 2, 1865, near Bladensburg, Md., by order of War Department.
Bedell, Lewis............ ..do....	do....	18	Dec. 17, 1861	3 yrs.	Died Jan. 17, 1863, at Newark, O.
Boney, Simon L......... ..do....	do....	36	Sept. 28, 1864	1 yr.	Drafted; died Nov. 19, 1864, in hospital at Nashville, Tenn.
Boudry, Moses ....do....	do....	16	Jan. 22, 1864	3 yrs.	Mustered out with company July 15, 1865.
Bowe, John.............. ..do....	do....	19	Oct. 15, 1861	3 yrs.	Discharged Dec. 8, 1863, at Camp Dennison, O., on Surgeon's certificate of disability .

Names.	Rank.	Age.	Date of Entering the Service.	Period of Service.	Remarks.
Brown, Elias	Private	25	Oct. 3, 1861	3 yrs.	Discharged Oct. 21, 1862, at Washington, D. C., of wounds received Aug. 9, 1862, in battle of Cedar Mountain, Va.
Brown, John A...........	..do....	30	Oct. 10, 1861	3 yrs.	Discharged March 2, 1862, at Baltimore, Md., on Surgeon's certificate of disability.
Brown, Barnard..........	..do....	18	Jan. 20, 1864	3 yrs.	Mustered out with company July 15, 1865.
Branstetter, Elias........	..do....	27	Oct. 28, 1861	3 yrs.	Discharged Aug. 4, 1862, at Columbus O., on Surgeon's certificate of disability.
Brush, Stephen W	..do....	35	Oct. 14, 1861	3 yrs.	Mustered out with company July 15, 1865; veteran.
Bruffey, Bennett W	..do....	26	Sept. 24, 1861	3 yrs.	Mustered out Dec. 22, 1864, at Savannah, Ga., on expiration of term of service.
Bryan, Luke..............	..do....	33	Sept. 24, 1861	3 yrs.	Transferred to Co. A, 9th Veteran Reserve Corps, July 1, 1863; discharged ——, at Washington, D. C., on Surgeon's certificate of disability.
Byrne, Richard...........	..do....	29	Oct. 28, 1863	3 yrs.	Mustered out with company July 15, 1865.
Camp, Edward............	..do....	26	Oct. 4, 1861	3 yrs.	Died June 8, 1864, in Clark county, O., while on furlough; veteran.
Candy, John..............	..do....	41	Feb. 24, 1865	1 yr.	Mustered out with company July 15, 1865.
Chappel, William M.......	..do....	29	Dec. 26, 1861	3 yrs.	Discharged Dec. 28, 1862, at Washington, D. C., on Surgeon's certificate of disability.
Cleveland, Albert...... .	..do....	18	Sept. 24, 1861	3 yrs.	Mustered out with company July 15, 1865; veteran.
Collins, John............	..do....	45	Oct. 3, 1861	3 yrs.	
Coughlin, Martin.........	..do....	18	Oct. 10, 1861	3 yrs.	
Conover, James...........	..do....	18	Jan. 28, 1862	3 yrs.	Mustered out with company July 15, 1865; veteran.
Cutler, William B	..do....	23	Oct. 28, 1861	3 yrs.	Died April 16, 1862, at Martinsburg, Va.
Derrickson, Daniel......	..do....	45	Oct. 28, 1861	3 yrs.	Killed June 6, 1862, in action at Middletown, Virginia.
Desmier, Francis........	..do....	29	Oct. 30, 1863	3 yrs.	Died Dec. 1, 1863, at Chattanooga, Tenn., of wounds received Nov. 26, 1863, in action at Ringgold, Ga.
Dodds, Stephen D........	..do....	18	Jan. 14, 1864	3 yrs.	Mustered out with company July 15, 1865.
Dunkin, Michael........	..do....	22	Oct. 10, 1861	3 yrs.	Transferred to Co. D, 6th Veteran Reserve Corps, July 16, 1863.
Elson, Alexander.........	..do....	24	Sept. 28, 1864	1 yr.	Drafted; mustered out June 3, 1865, at Camp Dennison, O., by order of War Department.
Erwin, Joshua............	..do....	32	Oct. 3, 1861	3 yrs.	Mustered out with company July 15, 1865; veteran.
Faulkner, Charles M....	..do....	18	Nov. 4, 1861	3 yrs.	Mustered out with company July 15, 1865; veteran.
Fackler, Emanuel........	..do....	31	Sept. 29, 1864	1 yr.	Drafted; mustered out June 2, 1865, near Bladensburg, Md., by order of War Department.
Fisher, Cash M..........	..do....	18	Oct. 3, 1861	3 yrs.	Discharged Jan. 14, 1862, at Urbana, O., by civil authority.
Foster, George...........	..do....	18	Oct. 14, 1864	1 yr.	Drafted; mustered out with company July 15, 1865.
Frantz, Jacob............	..do....	21	Sept. 29, 1864	1 yr.	Drafted; mustered out June 2, 1865, near Bladensburg, Md., by order of War Department.
Geaheart, Henry.........	..do....	18	Jan. 9, 1864	3 yrs.	Mustered out with company July 15, 1865.
Gesner, Michael..........	..do....	34	Sept. 29, 1864	1 yr.	Drafted; mustered out June 2, 1865, near Bladensburg, Md., by order of War Department.
Groves, Israel............	..do....	17	Oct. 14, 1864	1 yr.	Substitute; mustered out with company July 15, 1865.
Groves, Isaac............	..do....	32	Sept. 15, 1862	3 yrs.	Discharged March 13, 1863, at Philadelphia, Pa., on Surgeon's certificate of disability.
Groves, John B...........	..do....	42	Oct. 8, 1861	3 vrs.	Discharged Sept. 12, 1862, at Columbus, O., on Surgeon's certificate of disability.
Gurnea, John B..........	..do....	45	Dec. 7, 1861	3 yrs.	Discharged Sept. 12, 1862, at Columbus, O.
Hartman, John O........	..do....	27	Oct. 28, 1861	3 yrs.	
Hesson, Elson............	..do....	35	Sept. 28, 1864	1 yr.	Drafted; absent, sick at Savannah, Ga., Jan. 27, 1865; no further record found.
Hennessy, Patrick........	..do....	30	Oct. 14, 1861	3 yrs.	Transferred from Co. C ——; discharged July 18, 1863, at Convalescent Camp, Va., on Surgeon's certificate of disability.
Hill, Samuel.............	..do....	44	Oct. 28, 1861	3 yrs.	Discharged July 31, 1862, at Columbus, O., on Surgeon's certificate of disability.
Horn, William B........	..do....	18	Oct. 4, 1861	3 yrs.	Transferred to Co. F, 17th Veteran Reserve Corps, Jan. 5, 1864.
Houtz, John W	..do....	18	Dec. 13, 1861	3 yrs.	Mustered out Dec. 22, 1864, at Savannah, Ga.; on expiration of term of service.
Hullinger, Ambrose......	..do....	28	Oct. 28, 1861	3 yrs.	Mustered out Dec. 22, 1864, at Savannah, Ga., on expiration of term of service.
Hubbard, Ross J..........	..do....	40	Sept. 28, 1864	1 yr.	Drafted; mustered out June 2, 1865, near Bladensburg, Md., by order of War Department.
Huston, Mahlon..........	..do....	21	Sept. 29, 1864	1 yr.	Drafted; mustered out June 4, 1865, by order of War Department.
Hunt, Benjamin C........	..do....	17	Dec. 13, 1861	3 yrs.	Mustered out with company July 15, 1865; veteran.

Names.	Rank.	Age.	Date of Entering the Service.	Period of Service.	Remarks.
Jackson, Oscar..........	Private	18	Oct. 12, 1861	3 yrs.	Discharged Aug. 6, 1862, at Columbus, O., on Surgeon's certificate of disability.
Jamison, Samuel..........	..do....	19	Oct. 3, 1861	3 yrs.	Died Oct. 6, 1862, at Washington, D. C.
Jennings, Edward........	..do....	20	Feb. 5, 1864	3 yrs.	Mustered out with company July 15, 1865.
Jenkins, James..........	..do....	19	Sept. 24, 1861	3 yrs.	Discharged July 24, 1862, at Columbus, O., on Surgeon's certificate of disability.
Kelsh, Abraham..........	..do....	21	Oct. 8, 1861	3 yrs.	Mustered out with company July 15, 1865; veteran.
Landis, Howard...........	..do....	18	Oct. 28, 1861	3 yrs.	Appointed Corporal ——; reduced ——; mustered out June 27, 1865, at Camp Dennison, O., by order of War Department.
Lahaie, Heiser............	..do....	21	Jan. 22, 1864	3 yrs.	Mustered out with company July 15, 1865.
Lashey, Harvey F........	..do....	18	Oct. 14, 1864	1 yr.	Substitute; died Dec. 18, 1864, in 2d Division, 20th Army Corps Hospital.
Lappin, Jacob............	..do....	18	Oct. 14, 1861	3 yrs.	Mustered out with company July 15, 1865; veteran.
Leclaire, Joseph..........	..do....	18	Oct. 29, 1863	3 yrs.	Mustered out with company July 15, 1865.
Lemen, Cyrus B..........	..do....	19	July 1, 1862	3 yrs.	Mustered out June 2, 1865, near Bladensburg, Md., by order of War Department.
Lesch, Trangott..........	..do....	35	Sept. 29, 1864	1 yr.	Drafted; mustered out June 2, 1865, near Bladensburg, Md., by order of War Department.
Malone, Michael..........	..do....	19	Oct. 10, 1861	3 yrs.	Mustered out with company July 15, 1865; veteran.
Mahan, William N........	..do....	19	Sept. 24, 1861	3 yrs.	Mustered out with company July 15, 1865; veteran.
Markley, John	..do....	19	Oct. 23, 1861	3 yrs.	Mustered out Dec. 22, 1864, at Savannah, Ga., on expiration of term of service.
Maxson, Silas	..do....	27	Oct. 10, 1861	3 yrs.	Discharged July 14, 1862, at Columbus, O., on Surgeon's certificate of disability.
McCarty, William........	..do....	23	Oct. 10, 1861	3 yrs.	
McCarty, John	..do....	19	....	3 yrs.	Mustered out with company July 15, 1865; veteran.
McCandless, Perry S	..do....	23	Oct. 27, 1861	3 yrs.	
McGill, William..........	..do....	18	Jan. 9, 1864	3 yrs.	Mustered out with company July 15, 1865.
Menges, James	..do....	21	Oct. 14, 1864	1 yr.	Substitute; mustered out with company July 15, 1865.
Mitchell, John S	..do....	26	Oct. 28, 1861	3 yrs.	Died March 13, 1865, in 2d Division, 20th Army Corps Hospital; veteran.
Morse, Elliott	..do....	25	Sept. 29, 1864	1 yr.	Drafted; discharged May 12, 1865, at Camp Dennison, O., on Surgeon's certificate of disability.
Murphey, Patrick	..do. ...	20	Nov. 2, 1863	3 yrs.	Killed June 15, 1864, in action at Pine Hill, Georgia.
Murphey, John E	..do.. ..	17	Oct. 23, 1861	3 yrs.	Mustered out with company July 15, 1865; veteran.
Murry, William	..do....	19	Sept. 24, 1861	3 yrs.	Mustered out with company July 15, 1865; veteran.
Newcomb, Charles	..do....	26	Dec. 9, 1861	3 yrs.	
Newcomb, Asa B.........	..do....	18	Dec. 14, 1861	3 yrs.	Mustered out with company July 15, 1865; veteran.
Oaky, Henry.............	..do....	25	Jan. 16, 1864	3 yrs.	Mustered out July 24, 1865, at Columbus, O., by order of War Department.
O'Haver, Jasper...........	..do....	18	Jan. 26, 1864	3 yrs.	Mustered out June 9, 1865, at Camp Dennison, O., by order of War Department.
O'Haver, Harvey	..do....	19	Oct. 8, 1861	3 yrs.	
Paine, Rufus..............	..do....	26	Sept. 28, 1864	1 yr.	Drafted; died Nov. 28, 1864, in Joe Holt Hospital at Jeffersonville, Ind.
Parlett, Matthew..........	..do....	18	Oct. 10, 1861	3 yrs.	Mustered out with company July 15, 1865; veteran.
Partland, Michael........	..do....	25	Oct. 28, 1863	3 yrs.	Mustered out with company July 15, 1865.
Pinder, George...........	..do....	18	Jan. 27, 1864	3 yrs.	Mustered out with company July 15, 1865.
Powell, Joseph	..do....	23	Sept. 24, 1861	3 yrs.	Killed Dec. 20, 1864, in siege of Savannah, Ga.; veteran.
Powell, John	..do....	18	Oct. 3, 1861	3 yrs.	Mustered out with company July 15, 1865; veteran.
Powell, William H	..do....	21	Oct. 3, 1861	3 yrs.	Died April 19, 1862, at Strasburg, Va.
Robbins, Silas............	..do....	19	Jan. 27, 1864	3 yrs.	Mustered out with company July 15, 1865.
Scanlon, Matthew........	..do....	24	Jan. 2, 1862	3 yrs.	Mustered out June 4, 1865, by order of War Department.
Shaffer, Silas	..do....	19	Jan. 20, 1864	3 yrs.	Mustered out with company July 15, 1865.
Shaffer, John.............	..do....	18	Oct. 10, 1861	3 yrs.	Mustered out with company July 15, 1865; veteran.
Shofstall, Silas C	..do....	19	Oct. 7, 1861	3 yrs.	Promoted to Sergt. Major Aug. 23, 1864; veteran.
Shofstall, Jacob	..do....	48	Dec. 24, 1861	3 yrs.	Discharged Feb. 19, 1862, at Regimental Headquarters, on Surgeon's certificate of disability.
Smith, Charles S	..do....	22	Jan. 18, 1864	3 yrs.	Absent; no further record found.
Stewart, Daniel...........	..do....	20	....	3 yrs.	Mustered out with company July 15, 1865; veteran.
Swartz, John.............	..do....	30	Oct. 28, 1861	3 yrs.	Mustered out with company July 15, 1865; veteran.
Swisher, John H	..do....	42	Oct. 8, 1861	3 yrs.	Died July 28, 1862, in Rebel Prison at Lynchburg, Va.

Names.	Rank.	Age.	Date of Entering the Service.	Period of Service.	Remarks.
Travis, George W........	Private	18	Oct. 10, 1861	3 yrs.	Mustered out with company July 15, 1865; veteran.
Tretch, Nicholas...........	...do....	37	Sept. 29, 1864	1 yr.	Drafted; mustered out June 2, 1865, near Bladensburg, Md., by order of War Department.
Tucker, Robert............	...do....	18	Oct. 27, 1861	3 yrs.	Mustered out with company July 15, 1865; veteran.
Waid, George R........	...do....	20	Oct. 3, 1861	3 yrs.	Mustered out with company July 15, 1865; veteran.
Walker, John W........	.do....	20	Sept. 24, 1861	3 yrs.	Killed Sept. 17, 1862, in battle of Antietam, Maryland.
Washington, James W..	....do....	22	Oct. 15, 1861	3 yrs.	Not mustered into service.
Wagner, Valentine......	....do....	27	Sept. 27, 1864	1 yr.	Drafted; mustered out June 4, 1865, by order of War Department.
Weaver, Charles..........	...do....	....	Dec. 26, 1861	3 yrs.	Mustered out with company July 15, 1865; veteran.
Weaver, William..........	....do....	21	Oct. 28, 1861	3 yrs.	Died April 8, 1862, at Martinsburg, Va.
Williams, A. M............	...do....	19	Oct. 8, 1861	3 yrs.	
Yeazel, Samuel...........	...do....	18	Dec. 27, 1861	3 yrs.	Captured June 9, 1862, at battle of Port Republic, Va.; mustered out March 4, 1865, at Columbus, O., on expiration of term of service.
Zombro, William H......	.do....	21	Sept. 24, 1861	3 yrs.	Discharged March 16, 1862, at Baltimore, Md., on Surgeon's certificate of disability.

COMPANY C.

Mustered in from Oct. 4 to Dec. 31, 1861, at Camp McArthur, Urbana, O., by Masten R. Wright, S. H. Wallace and Samuel T. McMorran, 2d Lieutenants 66th O. V. I. Mustered out July 15, 1865, near Louisville, Ky., by Edward A. Wickes, Captain 150th New York Volunteers, and A. C. M. 14th Army Corps.

Names.	Rank.	Age.	Date of Entering the Service.	Period of Service.	Remarks.
Samuel T. McMorran....	Captain	30	Oct. 1, 1861	3 yrs.	Appointed Nov. 19, 1861; discharged Jan. 27, 1863, by order of War Department.
Masten R. Wright........	...do....	....	Oct. 1, 1861	3 yrs.	Appointed 1st Lieutenant Nov. 19, 1861; promoted to Captain Jan. 27, 1863; discharged July 31, 1863, by order of War Department.
John N. Rathbun.........	...do....	30	Oct. 17, 1861	3 yrs.	Promoted from 1st Lieutenant Co. F March 3, 1864; resigned Oct. 17, 1864, at Atlanta, Ga.
James M. McIlroy........	...do....	22	Nov. 1, 1861	3 yrs.	Promoted from 1st Lieutenant Co. H Nov. 12, 1864; resigned April 3, 1865, at Goldsboro, N. C.; veteran.
Charles A. Poffenberger......	..do....	28	Oct. 1, 1861	3 yrs.	Mustered as private; promoted to 1st Lieutenant Aug. 19, 1864; to Captain April 12, 1865; resigned June 3, 1865, at Bladensburg, Md.; veteran.
James A. McClain........	...do....	22	Oct. 4, 1861	3 yrs.	Promoted to 1st Lieutenant from 1st Sergeant Co. E April 12, 1865; to Captain June 14, 1865; mustered out with company July 15, 1865; veteran.
Joseph W. Hitt..........	1st Lieut.	17	Nov. 6, 1861	3 yrs.	Promoted to 2d Lieutenant from Sergt. Major Dec. 5, 1862; to 1st Lieutenant April 16, 1863; killed May 25, 1864, in battle of Dallas, Georgia.
William A. Cavis.........	...do....	37	Nov. 8, 1861	3 yrs.	Promoted from 2d Lieutenant Co. F Aug. 11, 1864; resigned Oct. 20, 1864, on Surgeon's certificate of disability; veteran.
Samuel I. Croxton.......	...do....	25	Oct. 8, 1861	3 yrs.	Appointed 1st Sergeant from Sergeant Co. I Sept. 1, 1864; promoted to 1st Lieutenant June 14, 1865; mustered out with company July 15, 1865; veteran.
James K. Hurley.........	2d Lieut.	30	Oct. 2, 1861	3 yrs.	Appointed Nov. 19, 1861; resigned April 26, 1862.
William Overs...........	1st Sergt.	23	Oct. 9, 1861	3 yrs.	Mustered as private; appointed 1st Sergeant ——; promoted to 2d Lieutenant April 16, 1863, but not mustered; missing since July —, 1863; no further record found.
Joseph Christian.........	....do....	20	Nov. 7, 1861	3 yrs.	Mustered as private; appointed Sergeant April 1, 1864; 1st Sergeant June 24, 1865; mustered out with company July 15, 1865; veteran.
John T. Northcutt.......	Sergeant	31	Oct. 2, 1861	3 yrs.	Mustered as private; appointed Sergeant ——; promoted to 2d Lieutenant Sept 1, 1862; but not mustered; discharged Jan. 5, 1863, at Washington, D. C., for wounds received June 9, 1862, in battle of Port Republic, Va.
Squire H. Wallace........	...do...	37	Jan. 28, 1862	3 yrs.	Mustered as private; appointed Sergeant ——; discharged to date June 29, 1862, at Columbus, O., by order of War Department.

Names.	Rank.	Age.	Date of Entering the Service.	Period of Service.	Remarks.
Jacob Olewine	Sergeant	18	Nov. 7, 1861	3 yrs.	Mustered as private; appointed Sergeant ——; promoted to 2d Lieutenant July 13, 1865, but not mustered; mustered out with company July 15, 1865; veteran.
Peter Caylor	...do....	20	Oct. 2, 1861	3 yrs.	Mustered as private; appointed Sergeant ——; mustered out with company July 15, 1865; veteran.
August Subler	...do....	25	Oct. 19, 1861	3 yrs.	Mustered as private; appointed Sergeant ——; mustered out with company July 15, 1865; veteran.
Jacob Moss	...do....	31	Nov. 12, 1861	3 yrs.	Mustered as private; appointed Sergeant ——; died April 5, 1864, at Covington, O.; veteran.
Michael Alderman	Corporal	21	Oct. 21, 1861	3 yrs.	Appointed Corporal ——; killed June 9, 1862, in battle of Port Republic, Va.
Thomas Whalen	...do....	18	Dec. 16, 1861	3 yrs.	Appointed Corporal ——; died July 14, 1864, at Nashville, Tenn., of wounds received June 16, 1864, in action at Pine Mountain, Georgia.
Patrick Hannagan	...do....	22	Oct. 3, 1861	3 yrs.	Appointed Corporal ——; died July 24, 1862, at Alexandria, Va.
Levi Maggart	...do....	24	Oct. 2, 1861	3 yrs.	Appointed Corporal ——.
Lewis Caylor	...do....	21	Dec. 31, 1861	3 yrs.	Appointed Corporal ——; mustered out Jan. 2, 1865, on expiration of term of service.
Simon Ryan	...do....	20	Oct. 9, 1861	3 yrs.	Appointed Corporal ——; died July 2, 1864, at Chattanooga, Tenn., of wounds received June 15, 1864, in action near Kenesaw Mountain, Ga.; veteran.
Samuel Bigham	...do....	19	Nov. 20, 1861	3 yrs.	Appointed Corporal ——; mustered out with company July 15, 1865; veteran.
Reuben Humbert	...do....	20	Oct. 9, 1861	3 yrs.	Appointed Corporal ——; mustered out with company July 15, 1865; veteran.
Jacob Shappy	...do....	20	Oct. 19, 1861	3 yrs.	Appointed Corporal ——; mustered out with company July 15, 1865; veteran.
Frederick Batty	...do....	21	Dec. 7, 1861	3 yrs.	Appointed Corporal ——; mustered out with company July 15, 1865; veteran.
Frank Dapore	...do....	32	Dec. 7, 1863	3 yrs.	Appointed Corporal ——; mustered out with company July 15, 1865.
Abbott, John	Private	23	Oct. 4, 1861	3 yrs.	Mustered out Dec. 25, 1864, near Savannah, Ga., on expiration of term of service.
Amen, Mathias	...do....	22	Aug. 18, 1864	3 yrs.	Substitute; died Oct. 4, 1864, at Atlanta, Ga.
Anspach, Jonathan	...do....	50	Oct. 25, 1861	3 yrs.	Discharged June 1, 1862, at Williamsport, Md., on Surgeon's certificate of disability.
Ayatt, Nicholas	...do....	29	Dec. 7, 1861	3 yrs.	Discharged Nov. 25, 1862, at Bolivar Heights, Va., by order of War Department.
Barns, Henry	...do....	40	Oct. 14, 1861	3 yrs.	Discharged Oct. 6, 1862, at Washington, D. C., by order of War Department.
Batty, George	...do....	44	Nov. 5, 1861	3 yrs.	Transferred to Veteran Reserve Corps Aug. 30, 1863.
Benshoof, John F	...do....	26	Dec. 31, 1861	3 yrs.	Mustered out Jan. 2, 1865, on expiration of term of service.
Blackburn, George W	...do....	18	Aug. 15, 1864	1 yr.	Substitute; died Jan. 2, 1865, at Savannah, Georgia.
Blocher, Jeremiah	...do....	47	Nov. 8, 1861	3 yrs.	Died Oct. 1, 1862, at Annapolis, Md.
Blue, Gabriel	...do....	18	Oct. 7, 1861	3 yrs.	Discharged May 23, 1862, at Winchester, Va., by order of War Department.
Blue, Ezra	...do....	19	Oct. 7, 1861	3 yrs.	Discharged May 23, 1862, at Winchester, Va., by order of War Department.
Bowman, Thomas	...do....	23	Oct. 8, 1864	1 yr.	Drafted; mustered out with company July 15, 1865.
Bricker, Jacob	...do....	18	Oct. 20, 1861	3 yrs.	Mustered out with company July 15, 1865; veteran.
Brown, Amos	...do....	24	Nov. 6, 1861	3 yrs.	Died Oct. 1, 1862, at Annapolis, Md.
Brown, Enos	...do....	26	Oct. 11, 1861	3 yrs.	Died Oct. 15, 1862, at Alexandria, Va.
Brown, Patrick	...do....	27	Aug. 17, 1864	3 yrs.	Substitute.
Brush, Reed	...do....	49	Nov. 14, 1861	3 yrs.	Mustered out Oct. 26, 1864, on expiration of term of service.
Burkey, Christian	...do....	50	Oct. 26, 1861	3 yrs.	Discharged July 30, 1862, at Washington, D. C., by order of War Department.
Burton, Isaac	...do....	19	Oct. 6, 1864	1 yr.	Substitute; mustered out with company July 15, 1865.
Busch, Henry	...do....	40	Aug. 17, 1864	3 yrs.	Substitute; died June 3, 1865, at Bladensburg, Maryland.
Carpenter, Salem	...do....	18	Aug. 16, 1864	1 yr.	Substitute; mustered out June 1, 1865, by order of War Department.
Carrigan, Owen	...do....	18	Aug. 16, 1864	1 yr.	Substitute; mustered out June 1, 1865, near Bladensburg, Md., by order of War Department.
Christl, Sebastian	...do....	44	Aug. 16, 1864	3 yrs.	Substitute; discharged May 13, 1865, at Cincinnati, O., on Surgeon's certificate of disability.
Christy, Hugh	...do....	50	Oct. 18, 1861	3 yrs.	Mustered out Jan. 21, 1865, on expiration of term of service.
Corwin, Harvey B	...do....	40	Oct. 18, 1861	3 yrs.	Discharged Jan. 27, 1863, at Washington, D. C., by order of War Department.
Cox, Jacob	...do....	30	Dec. 19, 1861	3 yrs.	Killed June 9, 1862, in battle of Port Republic, Virginia.

Names.	Rank.	Age.	Date of Entering the Service.	Period of Service.	Remarks.
Davis, Curtis C..........	Private	19	Oct. 14, 1861	3 yrs.	Mustered out with company July 15, 1865.
Delaney, James............	...do....	19	Jan. 12, 1864	3 yrs.	
Dewitt, John T...........	...do....	23	Oct. 5, 1864	1 yr.	Substitute; mustered out with company July 15, 1865.
Demarst, Joseph..........	...do....	40	Oct. 19, 1861	3 yrs.	Discharged June 1, 1862, at Williamsport, Md., by order of War Department.
Dingey, Elijah.............	...do....	30	Oct. 5, 1864	1 yr.	Substitute; mustered out with company July 15, 1865.
Douglass, Samuel..........	...do....	21	Oct. 21, 1861	3 yrs.	
Drollsbough, John	...do....	40	Sept. 23, 1864	1 yr.	Drafted; mustered out June 1, 1865, near Bladensburg, Md., by order of War Department.
Durack, Patrick..........	...do....	28	Jan. 14, 1864	3 yrs.	Mustered out with company July 15, 1865.
Dunn, James.............	...do....	20	Aug. 17, 1864	2 yrs.	Substitute.
Dunn, John	...do....	18	Aug. 17, 1864	2 yrs.	Substitute.
Eckhart, Samuel	...do....	43	Oct. 26, 1861	3 yrs.	Mustered out with company July 15, 1865; veteran.
Elben, Levi..............	...do....	18	Oct. 8, 1861	3 yrs.	Transferred to Veteran Reserve Corps Aug. 30, 1863.
Elben, Rufus.............	...do....	18	Oct. 4, 1861	3 yrs.	Mustered out Dec. 25, 1864, near Savannah, Ga., on expiration of term of service.
Elben, John	...do....	28	Oct. 4, 1861	3 yrs.	
Elben, George	...do....	19	Oct. 8, 1861	3 yrs.	Transferred to 124th Co., 2d Battalion Veteran Reserve Corps, March 17, 1865; veteran.
Ellis, Nathan............	...do....	24	Oct. 14, 1861	3 yrs.	Discharged Oct. 25, 1864, at hospital, Camp Dennison, O., on Surgeon's certificate of disability.
Eury, Bazil..............	...do....	34	Dec. 26, 1863	3 yrs.	No further record found.
Evans Benjamin	...do....	37	Oct. 7, 1861	3 yrs.	Transferred to Veteran Reserve Corps Aug. 5, 1863.
Everett, Lewis	...do....	27	Oct. 12, 1861	3 yrs.	Died Nov. 3, 1864, at Atlanta, Ga.; veteran.
Fahey, Charles	...do....	26	Aug. 17, 1864	3 yrs.	Substitute.
Fell, John..............	...do....	33	Aug. 16, 1864	3 yrs.	Substitute; mustered out with company July 15, 1865.
Flowers, Amos	...do....	17	Oct. 12, 1861	3 yrs.	Discharged Nov. 24, 1861, at Urbana, O., by civil authority.
Fitz, George	...do....	25	Dec. 6, 1861	3 yrs.	Discharged July 7, 1862, on Surgeon's certificate of disability.
Ford, Richard............	...do....	44	Aug. 17, 1864	3 yrs.	Substitute; mustered out with company July 15, 1865.
Gabe, John J.............	...do....	19	Oct. 10, 1864	1 yr.	Substitute; died Nov. 30, 1864, in Rebel Prison at Andersonville, Ga.
Gearhart, Henry..........	...do....	17	Oct. 7, 1861	3 yrs.	
Giganded, John...........	...do....	40	Dec. 31, 1861	3 yrs.	Also borne as Joseph Giganded; discharged July 31, 1862, at Fredericks Md., on Surgeon's certificate of disability.
Goffany, Peter............	...do....	23	Oct. 19, 1861	3 yrs.	Discharged June 1, 1862, at Williamsport, Md., by order of War Department.
Grafton, Ezra............	...do....	25	Oct. 6, 1861	3 yrs.	Died March —, 1862, at St. Paris, Champaign county, O.
Groves, Joseph E.........	...do....	35	Oct. 18, 1861	3 yrs.	Transferred to Veteran Reserve Corps Aug. 9, 1863.
Hall, Fleming	...do....	43	Oct. 9, 1861	3 yrs.	Died July 25, 1862, in Rebel Prison at Lynchburg, Va.
Haley, John..............	...do....	42	Oct. 22, 1863	3 yrs.	Mustered out with company July 15, 1865.
Hannagan, Charles........	...do....	33	Aug. 29, 1864	1 yr.	Substitute; mustered out June 1, 1865, near Bladensburg, Md., by order of War Department.
Harrington, Giles.........	...do....	24	Jan. 9, 1862	1 yr.	
Harris, Frank	...do....	18	Aug. 17, 1864	1 yr.	Substitute; mustered out June 1, 1865, near Bladensburg, Md., by order of War Department.
Harmon, Benjamin........	...do....	45	Nov. 2, 1861	3 yrs.	
Harper, Charles..........	...do....	26	Oct. 29, 1861	3 yrs.	
Hennessy, Patrick........	...do....	30	Oct. 14, 1861	3 yrs.	Transferred to Co. B —.
Heckathorn, Francis M..	...do....	34	Oct. 22, 1864	1 yr.	Drafted; mustered out May 17, 1865, at Camp Dennison, O., by order of War Department.
Hogan, Archie............	...do....	29	Aug. 16, 1864	3 yrs.	Substitute; mustered out with company July 15, 1865.
Howard, John............	...do....	30	Aug. 16, 1864	1 yr.	Substitute; mustered out June 1, 1865, near Bladensburg, Md., by order of War Department.
Huffman, Reuben	...do....	34	Oct. 29, 1861	3 yrs.	Died Dec. 1, 1861, at Camp McArthur, O.
Jackson, William	...do....	25	Oct. 1, 1864	1 yr.	Substitute; mustered out June 1, 1865, near Bladensburg, Md., by order of War Department.
Jordan, Asa S............	...do....	31	Sept. 23, 1864	1 yr.	Drafted; mustered out June 1, 1865, near Bladensburg, Md., by order of War Department.
Joyce, Myron A..........	...do....	25	Nov. 25, 1861	3 yrs.	Mustered out Dec. 25, 1864, near Savannah, Ga., on expiration of term of service.
Koons, William...........	...do....	18	Oct. 9, 1861	3 yrs.	Discharged Sept. —, 1862, at Annapolis, Md., on Surgeon's certificate of disability.
Lakel, Charles......	..do....	18	Oct. 7, 1864	1 yr.	Substitute; mustered out with company July 15, 1865.

Names.	Rank.	Age.	Date of Entering the Service.	Period of Service.	Remarks.
Leo, Joseph	Private	28	Oct. 19, 1861	3 yrs.	
Lyons, Daniel W	...do....	21	Oct. 15, 1861	3 yrs.	Mustered out Dec. 25, 1864, near Savannah, Ga., on expiration of term of service.
Maggart, John	...do....	29	Oct. 2, 1861	3 yrs.	
Manger, John	...do....	52	Oct. 19, 1861	3 yrs.	Died Sept. 15, 1862, at Baltimore, Md.
Markel, Albert	...do....	24	Aug. 12, 1864	3 yrs.	Substitute; mustered out with company July 15, 1865.
Mahony, Jeremiah	...do....	51	Oct. 12, 1861	3 yrs.	Died July —, 1862, in Rebel Prison at Richmond, Va.
Martz, Martin	...do....	50	Oct. 9, 1861	3 yrs.	Discharged May 10, 1862, at New Market, Va., on Surgeon's certificate of disability.
McAlexander, William	...do....	56	Jan. 17, 1862	3 yrs	Discharged June 1, 1862, at Williamsport, Md., on Surgeon's certificate of disability.
McCabe, James	...do....	25	Jan. 5, 1864	3 yrs.	
McCarty, Cornelius	...do....	19	Oct. 4, 1864	1 yr.	Substitute; mustered out with company July 15, 1865.
McClary, Robert	...do....	52	Nov. 26, 1861	3 yrs.	Discharged Oct. 27, 1862, on Surgeon's certificate of disability.
McGale, Henry	...do....	22	Jan. 14, 1864	3 yrs.	Died June 8, 1864, at Chattanooga, Tenn., of wounds received May 25, 1864, in battle of Dallas, Ga.
McGinnis, Michael	...do....	42	Oct. 10, 1861	3 yrs.	Discharged Oct. 19, 1862, at Harper's Ferry, Va., by order of War Department.
McGuire, Michael	...do....	23	Jan. 27, 1864	3 yrs.	On detached service Oct. 4, 1864; mustered out July 12, 1865, at Columbus, O., by order of War Department.
Meyers, Frederick	...do....	29	Aug. 17, 1864	3 yrs.	Substitute; mustered out with company July 15, 1865.
Mitchell, David E	...do....	42	Oct. 4, 1864	1 yr.	Substitute; mustered out May 27, 1865, at McDougall Hospital, New York Harbor, by order of War Department.
Mitchell, Edward	...do....	28	Oct. 4, 1861	3 yrs.	Mustered out Dec. 25, 1864, near Savannah, Ga., on expiration of term of service.
Mosny, Martin	...do....	25	Oct. 6, 1861	3 yrs.	Discharged Sept. —, 1862, at Alexandria, Va., on Surgeon's certificate of disability.
Morly, William	...do....	21	Oct. 20, 1861	3 yrs.	
Muldowney, Richard	...do....	45	Oct. 12, 1861	3 yrs.	Discharged March 7, 1863, at Washington, D. C., by order of War Department.
Murry, Luke	...do....	38	Dec. 13, 1861	3 yrs.	Mustered out with company July 15, 1865; veteran.
Murphey, James	...do....	42	Aug. 17, 1864	3 yrs.	Substitute.
Nash, Thomas	...do....	45	Oct. 21, 1861	3 yrs.	
Nettle, Thomas	...do....	25	Nov. 20, 1861	3 yrs.	Discharged Dec. 13, 1863, at Philadelphia, Pa., by order of War Department.
Nibert, Harrison	...do....	36	Oct. 26, 1861	3 yrs.	
O'Brien, John	...do....	35	Jan. 13, 1864	3 yrs.	Mustered out with company July 15, 1865.
Oustatt, John	...do....	21	Oct. 12, 1864	1 yr.	Drafted, mustered out with company July 15, 1865.
Phillips, Samuel	...do....	21	Nov. 6, 1861	3 yrs.	
Platler, Charles	...do....	36	Aug. 17, 1864	3 yrs.	Substitute; mustered out with company July 15, 1865.
Pickering, Daniel	...do....	17	Oct. 12, 1861	3 yrs.	Discharged June 12, 1863, at Acquia Creek, Va., by order of War Department.
Purinton, John A	...do....	31	Oct. 1, 1861	3 yrs.	Reduced from Com. Sergeant Dec. 31, 1862; discharged Oct. 18, 1864, at Covington, Ky., on Surgeon's certificate of disability.
Quick, William	...do....	18	Oct. 14, 1861	3 yrs.	Mustered out Feb. 24, 1865, at Columbus, O., on expiration of term of service.
Quick, Moses	...do....	21	Oct. 14, 1861	3 yrs.	
Rebole, Celestian	...do....	48	Oct. 29, 1861	3 yrs.	Discharged Nov. 25, 1862, at Bolivar Heights, Va., by order of War Department.
Redding, James W	...do....	35	Sept. 23, 1864	1 yr.	Drafted; mustered out June 1, 1865, near Bladensburg, Md., by order of War Department.
Richey, John C	...do....	38	Oct. 12, 1864	1 yr.	Drafted; mustered out with company July 15, 1865.
Robinson, William	...do....	21	Jan. 2, 1862	3 yrs.	
Rowley, Samuel	...do....	18	Oct. 12, 1864	1 yr.	Substitute; mustered out with company July 15, 1865.
Ryan, Patrick	...do....	30	Oct. 12, 1861	3 yrs.	Mustered out with company July 15, 1865; veteran.
Saintgnon, Celestian	...do....	20	Oct. 14, 1861	3 yrs.	
Scaggs, Henry C	...do....	18	Dec. 9, 1861	3 yrs.	Died Feb. 3, 1862, at New Creek, Va.
Short, Pennal	...do....	18	Oct. 10, 1861	3 yrs.	
Smith, Abraham G	...do....	18	Oct. 19, 1861	3 yrs.	Discharged Nov. 25, 1861, at Urbana, O., by civil authority.
Stone, Winfield S	...do....	18	Oct. 7, 1864	1 yr.	Substitute; mustered out with company July 15, 1865.
Strawser, George W	...do....	29	Sept. 23, 1864	1 yr.	Drafted; died Feb. 16, 1865, at New Albany, Indiana.
Strong, Finney	...do....	19	Oct. 12, 1864	1 yr.	Substitute; mustered out with company July 15, 1865.
Sudsberger, Joseph	...do...	25	Aug. 17, 1864	3 yrs.	Substitute; prisoner of war; mustered out June 21, 1865, at Camp Chase, O., by order of War Department.

Names.	Rank.	Age.	Date of Entering the Service.	Period of Service.	Remarks.
Sullivant, William......	Private	50	Oct. 11, 1861	3 yrs.	Discharged Nov. 29, 1862, at Washington, D. C., by order of War Department.
Sullivant, Jeremiah......	....do....	35	Oct. 13, 1861	3 yrs.	
Sutton, Joseph...........	....do....	27	April 15, 1864	3 yrs.	Died June 17, 1864, of wounds received June 16, 1864, in action at Pine Hill, Ga.
Sparks, Henry............	....do....	40	Sept. 24, 1864	1 yr.	Drafted; mustered out June 1, 1865, near Bladensburg, Md., by order of War Department.
Speece, Charles...........	....do....	30	Sept. 23, 1864	1 yr.	Drafted; mustered out June 1, 1865, near Bladensburg, Md., by order of War Department.
Thume, Lawrence........	....do....	36	Oct. 21, 1861	3 yrs.	Transferred to Veteran Reserve Corps Aug. 9, 1863.
Whalen, Patrick..........	....do....	20	Nov. 1, 1861	3 yrs.	Discharged Sept. 15, 1862, at Washington, D. C., by order of War Department.
Whalen, Michael..........	....do....	41	....	3 yrs.	Mustered out with company July 15, 1865; veteran.
Whited, John F	....do....	46	Dec. 6, 1861	3 yrs.	Discharged Oct. 18, 1862, at Harper's Ferry, Va., by order of War Department.
Winter, Robert............	....do....	35	Aug. 10, 1864	3 yrs.	Substitute.
Wirick, John.............	....do....	47	Oct. 16, 1861	3 yrs.	Discharged Sept. 15, 1862, at Washington, D. C., by order of War Department.
Woodard, James.........	....do....	53	Oct. 5, 1861	3 yrs.	
Woolverton, David S....	....do....	25	Oct. 14, 1861	3 yrs.	Mustered out Dec. 25, 1864, near Savannah, Ga., on expiration of term of service.
Young, William..........	....do....	38	Oct. 29, 1861	3 yrs.	
Yutesler, Benjamin......	....do....	22	Oct. 9, 1861	3 yrs.	Mustered out with company July 15, 1865; veteran.

COMPANY D.

Mustered in from Oct. 2 to Dec. 22, 1861, at Camp McArthur, Urbana, O., by Robert Crockett and John O. Dye, 2d Lieutenants 66th O. V. I. Mustered out July 15, 1865, near Louisville, Ky., by Edward A. Wickes, Captain 150th New York Volunteers, and A. C. M. 14th Army Corps.

Names.	Rank.	Age.	Date of Entering the Service.	Period of Service.	Remarks.
Alvin Clark..............	Captain	48	Oct. 8, 1861	3 yrs.	Appointed Nov. 22, 1861; discharged Nov. 10, 1862, on Surgeon's certificate of disability.
John O. Dye	....do....	30	Oct. 1, 1861	3 yrs.	Promoted to 1st Lieutenant from 2d Lieutenant May 24, 1862; to Captain Nov. 10, 1862; discharged Aug. 13, 1864, on Surgeon's certificate of disability.
Samuel H. Hedges........	....do....	23	Oct. 15, 1861	3 yrs.	Promoted to 2d Lieutenant from Sergeant Co. A Nov. 27, 1862; to 1st Lieutenant April 16, 1863; to Captain Aug. 11, 1864; to Major April 12, 1865.
John H. Diltz..............	....do....	23	Oct. 14, 1861	3 yrs.	Promoted to 1st Lieutenant from 1st Sergeant Co. A Aug. 11, 1864; to Captain April 12, 1865; mustered out with company July 15, 1865; veteran.
Robert Crocket	1st Lieut.	45	Oct. 5, 1861	3 yrs.	Appointed Nov. 22, 1861; discharged May 25, 1862, at Fredericksburg, Va., by order of War Department.
Silas C. Shofstall..........	....do....	19	Oct. 7, 1861	3 yrs.	Promoted from Sergt. Major April 12, 1865; mustered out with company July 15, 1865; veteran.
Theodore Strausburg....	1st Sergt.	23	Nov. 5, 1861	3 yrs.	Mustered as private; appointed 1st Sergeant Jan. 4, 1862; discharged Oct. 10, 1862, at Columbus, O., on Surgeon's certificate of disability.
Charles W. Guy	....do....	18	Aug. 16, 1862	3 yrs.	Mustered as private; appointed Sergeant July 1, 1864; 1st Sergeant Aug. 31, 1864; promoted to 1st Lieutenant Co. G Nov. 12, 1864.
William Burnside	....do....	21	Aug. 15, 1862	3 yrs.	Mustered as private; appointed 1st Sergeant ——; mustered out June 2, 1865, near Bladensburg, Md., by order of War Department.
Sylvester H. Rock........	....do....	21	Oct. 21, 1861	3 yrs.	Mustered as private; appointed Sergeant April 30, 1865; 1st Sergeant July 1, 1865; promoted to 2d Lieutenant July 13, 1865, but not mustered; mustered out with company July 15, 1865; veteran.
Sylvanus Wilkins	Sergeant	27	Oct. 11, 1861	3 yrs.	Discharged July 24, 1862, on Surgeon's certificate of disability.
Cortland W. Dennis......	....do....	24	Oct. 8, 1861	3 yrs.	Died Aug. 28, 1862, in hospital at Washington, D. C.
William K. McCormick..	....do....	26	Oct. 26, 1861	3 yrs.	Mustered as private; appointed Sergeant Feb. 20, 1862; transferred to Veteran Reserve Corps ——.

Names.	Rank.	Age.	Date of Entering the Service.	Period of Service.	Remarks.
Peter Haidman	Sergeant	34	Oct. 2, 1861	3 yrs.	Mustered as private; appointed Sergeant March 15, 1862; discharged Feb. 14, 1863, at Columbus, O., on Surgeon's certificate of disability.
William Scott	do....	26	Oct. 25, 1861	3 yrs.	Mustered as private; appointed Sergeant Jan. 1, 1863; discharged Dec. 14, 1863, at Columbus, O., on Surgeon's certificate of disability.
W. Wallace Cranston	do....	21	Oct. 10, 1861	3 yrs.	Transferred from Co. A ——, as Sergeant; promoted to Sergt. Major May 12, 1863; veteran.
Peter Mitchell	do....	19	Oct. 14, 1861	3 yrs.	Mustered as private; appointed Sergeant ——; mustered out with company July 15, 1865; veteran.
Samuel A. Haines	do....	23	Nov. —, 1861	3 yrs.	Also borne as Adam S. Haines; mustered as private; appointed Sergeant ——; mustered out with company July 15, 1865; veteran.
Moses K. Morrow	Corporal	40	Oct. 10, 1861	3 yrs.	Killed Nov. 27, 1863, in battle of Taylor's Ridge, Ga.
St. Ledger James Rock	do....	24	Oct. 12, 1861	3 yrs.	Killed June 9, 1862, in battle of Port Republic, Virginia.
Sylvanus Tenny	do....	44	Oct. 11, 1861	3 yrs.	Appointed Corporal Feb. 25, 1862; discharged June 30, 1862, on Surgeon's certificate of disability.
Nathan J. Harrington	do....	38	Oct. 10, 1861	3 yrs.	Appointed Corporal ——; captured June 9, 1862, at battle of Port Republic, Va.; mustered out Jan. 16, 1865, at Columbus, O., on expiration of term of service.
James F. Baine	do....	19	Oct. 15, 1861	3 yrs.	Appointed Corporal ——; prisoner of war; mustered out June 13, 1865, at Camp Chase, O., by order of War Department; veteran.
George M. Hoover	do....	25	Oct. 15, 1861	3 yrs.	Appointed Corporal ——; mustered out with company July 15, 1865; veteran.
Thomas Sowell	do....	19	Oct. 11, 1861	3 yrs.	Appointed Corporal ——; mustered out with company July 15, 1865; veteran.
Henry Sphar	do....	18	Nov. 19, 1861	3 yrs.	Appointed Corporal ——; mustered out with company July 15, 1865; veteran.
Robert Blackwood	do....	38	Sept. 5, 1862	3 yrs.	Appointed Corporal ——; mustered out June 2, 1865, near Bladensburg, Md., by order of War Department.
Michael Hisey	do....	35	Oct. 16, 1861	3 yrs.	Appointed Corporal ——; discharged April 7, 1865, on Surgeon's certificate of disability; veteran.
Jeffery Williams	Musician	21	Nov. 11, 1861	3 yrs.	Discharged Jan. 29, 1863, at Columbus, O., on Surgeon's certificate of disability.
Francis M Williams	do....	18	Nov. 14, 1861	3 yrs.	Promoted to Principal Musician to date July —, 1863.
Anderson, John W	Private	18	Oct. 25, 1861	3 yrs.	Died Oct. 19, 1864, in Rebel Prison at Florence, S. C.; veteran.
Atkison, John H	do....	27	Sept. 12, 1864	1 yr.	Drafted; died Dec. 19, 1864, of wounds received ——, in siege of Savannah, Ga.
Arbuthnot, Joseph	do....	31	Aug. 16, 1864	3 yrs.	Substitute.
Bain, William P	do....	18	Dec. 11, 1861	3 yrs.	Killed June 9, 1862, in battle of Port Republic, Va.
Baker, Robert B. H	do....	29	Oct. 4, 1861	3 yrs.	Discharged Aug. 12, 1862, at Washington, D. C., on Surgeon's certificate of disability.
Belts, John	do....	19	Oct. 14, 1861	3 yrs.	Mustered out with company July 15, 1865; veteran.
Belts, Daniel	do....	18	Oct. 14, 1861	3 yrs.	Mustered out June 13, 1865, at hospital, Camp Dennison, O., by order of War Department; veteran.
Blair, Joseph	do....	18	Oct. 12, 1861	3 yrs.	Mustered out with company July 15, 1865; veteran.
Blakeley, John F	do....	25	Oct. 12, 1861	3 yrs.	Mustered out with company July 15, 1865; veteran.
Boggs, Milton P	do....	22	Oct. 21, 1861	3 yrs.	Discharged Aug. 11, 1862, at Fairfax Seminary Hospital, Va., on Surgeon's certificate of disability.
Boggs, William T	do....	25	Nov. 15, 1861	3 yrs.	Died July 20, 1864, near Atlanta, Ga.; veteran.
Boswell, William	do....	18	Oct. 8, 1861	3 yrs.	Mustered out with company July 15, 1865; veteran.
Boyd George	do....	18	Aug. 18, 1864	2 yrs.	Substitute ——.
Brunton, George	do....	19	Oct. 18, 1864	1 yr.	Substitute; mustered out with company July 15, 1865.
Brunstrap, William	do....	18	Aug. 13, 1864	3 yrs.	Substitute; mustered out with company July 15, 1865.
Burlew, Tobias	do....	23	Oct. 28, 1861	3 yrs.	Discharged May 10, 1862, on Surgeon's certificate of disability.
Cannon, Ebenezer D	do....	23	Nov. 19, 1861	3 yrs.	Discharged May 8, 1862, on Surgeon's certificate of disability.
Consuller, William	do....	18	Nov. 21, 1861	3 yrs.	Killed Aug. 9, 1862, in battle of Cedar Mountain, Va.
Crawford, Samuel	do....	38	Sept. 12, 1864	1 yr.	Drafted; mustered out June 2, 1865, near Bladensburg, Md., by order of War Department.

Names.	Rank.	Age.	Date of Entering the Service.	Period of Service.	Remarks.
Curny, Charles..........	Private	27	Oct. 6, 1864	1 yr.	Substitute; mustered out with company July 15, 1865.
Datster, Fletcher B.......	...do....	18	Jan. 2, 1864	3 yrs.	Mustered out with company July 15, 1865.
Dille, Josephus.............	...do....	29	Oct. 15, 1861	3 yrs.	Discharged Nov. 28, 1862, on Surgeon's certificate of disability.
Donnells, Milton..........	...do....	18	Aug. 14, 1864	1 yr.	Substitute; mustered out June 2, 1865, near Bladensburg, Md., by order of War Department.
Downs, Jacob W	...do....	20	Nov. 14, 1861	3 yrs.	Mustered out Dec. 28, 1864, on expiration of term of service.
Dunlap, James H..........	...do....	18	Aug. 16, 1864	1 yr.	Substitute; captured Feb. 17, 1865, in action at Lancaster C. H., S. C.; mustered out July 14, 1865, at Camp Chase, O., by order of War Department.
Earley, Jacob	...do....	17	Nov. 19, 1861	3 yrs.	Died Dec. 26, 1862, near Ridgeway, O.
Endsley, William..........	...do....	45	Nov. 18, 1861	3 yrs.	Discharged June 30, 1862, on Surgeon's certificate of disability.
Engle, Joseph	...do....	22	Oct. 20, 1861	3 yrs.	Discharged Oct. 14, 1862, at Fort McHenry, Md., on Surgeon's certificate of disability.
Epley, Samuel.............	...do....	27	Oct. 21, 1861	3 yrs.	Discharged Oct. 21, 1862, on Surgeon's certificate of disability.
Everett, Albert.............	...do....	27	Sept. 26, 1864	1 yr.	Drafted; mustered out July 15, 1865, by order of War Department.
Farris, Harvey R.........	...do....	23	Nov. 23, 1861	3 yrs.	Died April 23, 1862, at Strasburg, Va.
Frazier, Samuel	...do....	17	Nov. 19, 1861	3 yrs.	Discharged June 6, 1862, at Bellefontaine, O., by civil authority.
Fry, David	...do....	22	Oct. 27, 1861	3 yrs.	
Furguson, William A......	...do....	18	Nov. 23, 1861	3 yrs.	Killed June 9, 1862, in battle of Port Republic, Virginia.
Georgian, Thomas..........	...do....	36	Dec. 22, 1861	3 yrs.	
Gordon, John.............	...do....	28	Oct. 18, 1861	3 yrs.	
Griffin, Henry C..........	...do....	18	Aug. 16, 1862	3 yrs.	Mustered out June 25, 1865, at Washington, D. C., by order of War Department.
Hamilton, Samuel..........	...do....	33	Nov. 21, 1861	3 yrs.	Discharged Oct. 23, 1862, at Washington, D. C., on Surgeon's certificate of disability.
Hamden, John W	...do....	25	Nov. 19, 1861	3 yrs.	Mustered out with company July 15, 1865; veteran.
Hamden, Henry..........	...do....	18	Oct. 16, 1861	3 yrs.	Mustered out with company July 15, 1865; veteran.
Hammond, Robert	...do....	28	Mch. 11, 1862	3 yrs.	Appointed Corporal ——; reduced July 11, 1865; mustered out with company July 15, 1865.
Harmon, James	...do....	19	Jan. 8, 1862	3 yrs.	Died Aug. 10, 1862, in hospital at Alexandria, Virginia.
Hayes, John..............	...do....	18	Jan. 27, 1864	3 yrs.	Mustered out July 20, 1865, at Washington, D. C., by order of War Department.
Henry, Oliver............	...do....	17	Oct. 12, 1861	3 yrs.	Discharged Jan. 15, 1862, at Urbana, O., by civil authority.
Henry, Francis M	...do....	19	Oct. 14, 1861	3 yrs.	Discharged Oct. 27, 1864, at hospital, Columbus, O., on Surgeon's certificate of disability.
Hendershout, William H ....do....		27	Oct. 8, 1861	3 yrs.	Mustered out with company July 15, 1865; veteran.
Hogue, William Z..........	...do....	18	Nov. 23, 1861	3 yrs.	Discharged Nov. 18, 1862, at Washington, D. C., to enlist in Regular Army.
Houser, John.............	...do....	23	Oct. 6, 1864	1 yr.	Substitute; Mustered out with company July 15, 1865.
Howe, Chauncey S	...do....	42	Oct. 9, 1861	3 yrs.	
Howard, Noah	...do....	33	Dec. 9, 1861	3 yrs.	Discharged Jan. 15, 1863, at Columbus, O., on Surgeon's certificate of disability.
Howley, Edward	...do....	19	Aug. 17, 1864	3 yrs.	Substitute.
Hume, John	...do....	49	Oct. 12, 1861	3 yrs.	Discharged June 30, 1862, on Surgeon's certificate of disability.
Israel, Peter.............	...do....	31	Aug. 11, 1864	2 yrs.	Substitute; absent; no further record found.
Jacobs, William M.......	...do....	20	Nov. 23, 1861	3 yrs.	Discharged Nov. 27, 1862, at Washington, D. O., on Surgeon's certificate of disability.
Jenkins, Nicholas I........	...do....	18	Aug. 17, 1864	2 yrs.	Substitute; mustered out with company July 15, 1865.
Joiner, Arthur E.........	...do....	27	Nov. 19, 1861	3 yrs.	Discharged July 8, 1862, at Columbus, O., on Surgeon's certificate of disability.
Julian, John.............	...do....	43	Nov. 1, 1861	3 yrs.	Discharged May 8, 1862, on Surgeon's certificate of disability.
Kelley, John..............	...do....	24	Aug. 15, 1864	3 yrs.	Substitute; absent; no further record found.
Kessecker, John..........	...do....	18	Jan. 17, 1862	3 yrs.	Mustered out March 1, 1865, at Columbus, O., on expiration of term of service.
Knight, Hugh B..........	...do....	40	Nov. 18, 1861	3 yrs.	Discharged May 8, 1862, on Surgeon's certificate of disability.
Knight, Hugh B..........	...do....	43	Jan. 4, 1864	3 yrs.	Mustered out July 10, 1865, at Lincoln Hospital, Washington, D. C., by order of War Department.
Knight, William F	...do....	24	Dec. 29, 1863	3 yrs.	Mustered out with company July 15, 1865.
Krouskup, Solomon J	...do....	17	Nov. 4, 1861	3 yrs.	Discharged Jan. 16, 1862, at Bellefontaine, O., by civil authority.
Lease, Joseph M..........	...do....	27	Oct. 8, 1861	3 yrs.	Discharged Sept. 25, 1862, at Washington, D. C., on Surgeon's certificate of disability.

Names.	Rank.	Age.	Date of Entering the Service.	Period of Service.	Remarks.
Lidstone, George........	Private	28	Ang. 12, 1864	3 yrs.	Substitute; mustered out June 17, 1865, at Camp Chase, O., by order of War Department.
Leonard, John............	...do....	45	Oct. 18, 1861	3 yrs.	
Leophart, Jacob............	...do....	19	Oct. 8, 1861	3 yrs.	Mustered out Jan. 23, 1865, at Columbus, O., on expiration of term of service.
Long, Benjamin............	...do....	19	Nov. 19, 1861	3 yrs.	Discharged June 10, 1863, on Surgeon's certificate of disability.
Martin, William............	...do....	19	Aug. 17, 1864	3 ˙rs.	Substitute; mustered out June 2, 1865, near Bladensburg, Md., by order of War Department.
Mattucks, Edward........	...do....	29	Oct. 8, 1864	1 yr.	Substitute; mustered out with company July 15, 1865.
McCorkle, Alexander.....	...do....	36	Oct. 3, 1861	3 yrs.	Discharged Nov. 28, 1862, on Surgeon's certificate of disability.
McClary, John............	...do....	22	Oct. 16, 1861	3 yrs.	Killed July 4, 1863, in battle of Gettysburg. Pa.
McClain, James............	...do....	29	Nov. 18, 1861	3 yrs.	Transferred to Veteran Reserve Corps Oct. 30, 1863.
McGill, John............	...do....	18	Oct. 6, 1864	1 yr.	Substitute; absent; no futher record found.
Meyers, Jasper M........	...do....	26	Sept. 29, 1864	1 yr.	Substitute; mustered out June 2, 1865, near Bladensburg, Md., by order of War Department.
Miliner, Nathaniel.....	...do....	28	Oct. 21, 1861	3 yrs.	Discharged Oct. 27, 1862, at Columbus, O., on Surgeon's certificate of disability.
Minchell, John C..........	...do....	18	Nov. 14, 1861	3 yrs.	Mustered out with company July 15, 1865; veteran.
Morrow, James M........	...do....	16	Oct. 10, 1861	3 yrs.	Mustered out with company July 15, 1865; veteran.
Newcomb, Arian............	...do....	25	Oct. 12, 1861	3 yrs.	Transferred to Veteran Reserve Corps Sept. 24, 1863.
Owen, William H. H......	...do....	23	Jan. 1, 1864	3 yrs.	Died Jan. 11, 1865, at Jeffersonville, Ind.
Patten, Thomas............	...do....	18	Oct. 7, 1864	1 yr.	Substitute; mustered out with company July 15, 1865.
Phellis, Charles	...do....	18	Aug. 16, 1862	3 yrs.	Discharged Sept. 9, 1862, on Surgeon's certificate of disability.
Pullings, Samuel..........	...do....	18	Mch. 2, 1863	3 yrs.	Killed July 28, 1864, in action near Atlanta, Georgia.
Quinlan, Malachi..........	...do....	20	Aug. 16, 1862	3 yrs.	Transferred to Veteran Reserve Corps ——.
Raypole, John............	...do....	26	Sept. 2, 1864	1 yr.	Drafted; mustered out June 2, 1865, near Bladensburg, Md., by order of War Department.
Renmington, William H...	...do....	20	Aug. 16, 1864	1 yr.	Substitute ——.
Rish, Gideon............	...do....	28	Sept. 23, 1864	1 yr.	Drafted; mustered out May 29, 1865, at New York City, by order of War Department.
Robison, Enos............	...do....	43	Oct. 12, 1864	1 yr.	Drafted; mustered out May 29, 1865, at New York City, by order of War Department.
Rollins, James............	...do....	30	Oct. 21, 1861	3 yrs.	Discharged May 8, 1862, on Surgeon's certificate of disability.
Shade, Peter............	...do....	21	Oct. 21, 1861	3 yrs.	
Shourd, Reuben..........	...do....	20	Oct. 22, 1861	3 yrs.	
Sirks, David............	...do....	18	Nov. 12, 1861	3 yrs.	Mustered out with company July 15, 1865; veteran.
Smith, Hiram G..........	...do....	28	Oct. 8, 1861	3 yrs.	
Sowell, Clifton..........	...do....	46	Oct. 3, 1861	3 yrs.	Killed June 9, 1862, in battle of Port Republic, Virginia.
Southers, James............	...do....	36	Sept. 26, 1864	1 yr.	Drafted; mustered out June 2, 1865, near Bladensburg, Md., by order of War Department.
Stewart, William..........	...do....	57	Oct. 12, 1861	3 yrs.	Discharged Aug. 4, 1862, on Surgeon's certificate of disability.
Stewart, James............	...do....	23	Oct. 12, 1861	3 yrs.	Mustered out with company July 15, 1865; veteran.
Stevenson, Lewis..........	...do....	23	Oct. 25, 1861	3 yrs.	Died Dec. 7, 1862, in hospital at Alexandria, Virginia.
Stilwell, William H.....	...do....	29	Sept. 23, 1864	1 yr.	Drafted; mustered out May 17, 1865, at Camp Dennison, O., by order of War Department.
Summers, Perry..........	...do....	18	Oct. 15, 1861	3 yrs.	
Swallow, Riley	...do....	24	Oct. 12, 1861	3 yrs.	Discharged Jan. 30, 1863, on Surgeon's certificate of disability.
Taggart, Columbus	...do....	21	Sept. 23, 1864	1 yr.	Drafted; discharged April 6, 1865, at Raleigh, N. C., by reason of furnishing a suitable substitute.
Tenny, Paulus H........	...do....	22	Nov. 21, 1861	3 yrs.	Discharged Jan. 13, 1863, on Surgeon's certificate of disability.
Terrell, David............	...do....	28	Oct. 16, 1861	3 yrs.	Discharged Aug. 12, 1862, at Washington, D. C., on Surgeon's certificate of disability.
Thompson, James M	...do....	18	Aug. 11, 1864	1 yr.	Substitute; mustered out June 2, 1865, near Bladensburg, Md., by order of War Department.
Tupper, Gilbert	...do....	18	Aug. 13, 1864	1 yr.	Substitute; mustered out June 2, 1865, near Bladensburg, Md., by order of War Department.
Vickers, William............	...do....	21	Oct. 7, 1864	1 yr.	Substitute; mustered out with company July 15, 1865.
Wallace, George M........	...do....	25	Oct. 12, 1861	3 yrs.	Died May 20, 1864, in U. S. Hospital at Chattanooga, Tenn.; veteran.
Walsh, Edward............	...do....	40	Dec. 22, 1861	3 yrs.	

Names.	Rank.	Age.	Date of Entering the Service.	Period of Service.	Remarks.
Webb, Aden.............	Private	31	Oct. 7, 1864	1 yr.	Substitute; mustered out with company July 15, 1865.
Wherry, David..........	....do....	37	Sept. 23, 1864	1 yr.	Drafted; mustered out June 2, 1865, near Bladensburg, Md., by order of War Department.
Weller, George	....do....	23	Sept. 23, 1864	1 yr.	Drafted; mustered out June 2, 1865, near Bladensburg, Md., by order of War Department.
Wilkins, Amos	....do....	57	Oct. 11, 1861	3 yrs.	Discharged April 26, 1862, at Strasburg, Va., on Surgeon's certificate of disability.
Wilkins, Thomas J	....do....	22	Nov. 18, 1861	3 yrs.	Discharged Feb. 28, 1863, at Dumfries, Va., on Surgeon's certificate of disability.
Wilkins, Simon M........	....do....	18	Oct. 21, 1861	3 yrs.	Died April 5, 1862, at Bellefontaine, O.
Wilson, John L.............	....do....	25	Sept. 23, 1864	1 yr.	Drafted; mustered out June 2, 1865, near Bladensburg, Md., by order of War Department.
Williams Obediah	....do....	23	Nov. 11, 1861	3 yrs.	Mustered out with company July 15, 1865; veteran.
Williams, Elliott	....oo....	30	Nov. 12, 1861	3 yrs.	Killed June 9, 1862, in battle of Port Republic, Va.
Williams, Jesse.......	....do....	29	Oct. 2, 1861	3 yrs.	Appointed Sergeant ——; reduced to ranks to date July 1, 1865; mustered out with company July 15, 1865; veteran.
Williams, Ellis M.........	....do....	30	Dec. 3, 1861	3 yrs.	Discharged Dec. 3, 1862, on Surgeon's certificate of disability.
Williams, John M.........	....do....	23	Aug. 18, 1862	3 yrs.	Discharged Feb. 19, 1863, at Harper's Ferry, Va., on Surgeon's certificate of disability.
Williams, Garrett........	....do....	44	Oct. 18, 1861	3 yrs.	
Williams, Robert........	....do....	23	Aug. 18, 1862	3 yrs.	On detached service; mustered out June 15, 1865, at Columbus, O., on expiration of term of service.
Wooderson, Thomas P...	....do....	23	Oct. 16, 1861	3 yrs.	Discharged July 7, 1862, at Columbus, O., on Surgeon's certificate of disability.
Wren, John K..............	....do....	20	Dec. 12, 1861	3 yrs.	Discharged Dec. 16, 1863, at Fairfax Seminary Hospital, Va., on Surgeon's certificate of disability.
Young, John..............	....do....	21	Nov. 19, 1861	3 yrs.	Mustered out with company July 15, 1865; veteran.

COMPANY E.

Mustered in Dec. 26, 1861, at Camp McArthur, Urbana, O., by Thomas J. Buxton, 2d Lieutenant 66th O. V. I. Mustered out July 15, 1865, near Louisville, Ky., by Edward A. Wickes, Captain 150th New York Volunteers, and A. C. M. 14th Army Corps.

Names.	Rank.	Age.	Date of Entering the Service.	Period of Service.	Remarks.
Thomas J. Buxton.......	Captain	28	Oct. 15, 1861	3 yrs.	Appointed Nov. 30, 1861; resigned June 7, 1863.
John W. Watkins..........	....do....	23	Oct. 19, 1861	3 yrs.	Appointed 2d Lieutenant Nov. 30, 1861; promoted to 1st Lieutenant March 1, 1863; to Captain May 27, 1863; mustered out Dec. 27, 1864, at Savannah, Ga., on expiration of term of service.
Charles E. Butts..........	....do....	24	Oct. 21, 1861	3 yrs.	Appointed Sergeant from private Nov. 30, 1861; promoted to 2d Lieutenant April 16, 1863; to 1st Lieutenant Co. K April 2, 1864; to Captain April 12, 1865; detached as Act. Asst. Quartermaster June 8, 1865; promoted to Major July 13, 1865, but not mustered; mustered out Aug. 2, 1865, at Columbus, O., by order of War Department; veteran.
Lewellyn A. Powell.....	1st Lieut.	21	Oct. 15, 1861	3 yrs.	Appointed Nov. 30, 1861; resigned March 1, 1863.
Nelson Card...............	....do....	27	Oct. 30, 1861	3 yrs.	Appointed 1st Sergeant from Sergeant Nov. 1, 1862; promoted 2d Lieutenant March 1, 1863; 1st Lieutenant Jan. 1 1864.
James C. Bowe.............	....do....	23	Nov. 9, 1861	3 yrs.	Promoted from 1st Sergeant Co. B Aug. 11, 1864; to Captain April 12, 1865, but not mustered; discharged May 15, 1865, by order of War Department; veteran.
Aaron D. Riker..........	....do....	31	Oct. 11, 1861	3 yrs.	Promoted from Com. Sergeant April 12, 1865; mustered out with company July 15, 1865; veteran.
Thomas A. Davis........	1st Sergt.	23	Oct. 17, 1861	3 yrs.	Mustered as private; appointed 1st Sergeant ——; killed Aug. 9, 1862, in battle of Cedar Mountain, Va.
Richard E. Plunkett......	....do....	21	Nov. 13, 1861	3 yrs.	Mustered as private; appointed 1st Sergeant ——; promoted to 1st Lieutenant Co. A Nov. 12, 1864; veteran.

Names.	Rank.	Age.	Date of Entering the Service.	Period of Service.	Remarks.
Calvin Gibson	1st Sergt.	25	Nov. 1, 1861	3 yrs.	Mustered as private; appointed Sergeant ——; 1st Sergeant ——; promoted to 1st Lieutenant July 13, 1865, but not mustered; mustered out with company July 15, 1865; veteran.
James A. McClain	do	22	Nov. 4, 1861	3 yrs.	Appointed Sergeant from Corporal Jan. 1, 1863; 1st Sergeant Dec. 18, 1864; promoted to 1st Lieutenant Co. C April 12, 1865; veteran.
George W. Jones	Sergeant	22	Nov. 8, 1861	3 yrs.	Mustered as private; appointed Sergeant ——; mustered out March 14, 1865, at Camp Dennison, O., on expiration of term of service; veteran.
George W. Jamison	do	21	Oct. 18, 1861	3 yrs.	Mustered as private; appointed Sergeant ——; discharged Sept. 5, 1863, at Washington, D. C., on Surgeon's certificate of disability.
Edward M. Jones	do	21	Oct. 25, 1861	3 yrs.	Mustered as private; appointed Sergeant ——; discharged Jan. 2, 1863, at Baltimore, Md., on Surgeon's certificate of disability.
John M. Smith	do	25	Nov. 9, 1861	3 yrs.	Mustered as private; appointed Sergeant ——; mustered out with company July 15, 1865; veteran.
John W. Thomas	do	19	Nov. 9, 1861	3 yrs.	Mustered as private; appointed Sergeant ——; mustered out with company July 15, 1865; veteran.
David J. Williams	do	23	Oct. 19, 1861	3 yrs.	Mustered as private; appointed Sergeant ——; mustered out with company July 15, 1865; veteran.
Henry C. Olds	Corporal	30	Oct. 30, 1861	3 yrs.	Appointed Corporal ——; discharged Dec. 22, 1862, at Columbus, O., on Surgeon's certificate of disability.
Joshua J. Steckle	do	21	Oct. 21, 1861	3 yrs.	Appointed Corporal ——; discharged June 19, 1862, at Columbus, O., on Surgeon's certificate of disability.
Thomas C. Warren	do	20	Oct. 19, 1861	3 yrs.	Appointed Corporal ——; discharged Dec. 9, 1862, at Smoketown, Md., on Surgeon's certificate of disability.
Pell T. Couler	do	21	Oct. 29, 1861	3 yrs.	Also borne on rolls as Pell T. Courter; appointed Corporal ——; discharged Nov. 23, 1862, at Harper's Ferry, Va., on Surgeon's certificate of disability.
Van M. Pendleton	do	18	Nov. 13, 1861	3 yrs.	Appointed Corporal ——; mustered out with company July 15, 1865; veteran.
John S. James	do	18	Jan. 13, 1864	3 yrs.	Appointed Corporal ——; mustered out with company July 15, 1865.
Charles W. Fleming	do	20	Mch. 11, 1863	3 yrs.	Appointed Corporal ——; mustered out with company July 15, 1865.
Thomas Jenkins	do	20	Dec. 7, 1861	3 yrs.	Appointed Corporal ——; mustered out with company July 15, 1865; veteran.
Thomas C. Watson	do	19	Oct. 25, 1861	3 yrs.	Appointed Corporal ——; mustered out with company July 15, 1865; veteran.
Elias Kyle	do	21	Oct. 19, 1861	3 yrs.	Appointed Corporal ——; wounded Dec. 19, 1864, in siege of Savannah, Ga.; mustered out May 19, 1865, at Columbus, O., by order of War Department; veteran.
John Aller	do	19	Jan. 6, 1864	3 yrs.	Appointed Corporal to date June 30, 1865; mustered out with company July 15, 1865; veteran.
Daniel Williams	do	18	Jan. 18, 1864	3 yrs.	Appointed Corporal ——; mustered out May 17, 1865, at hospital, Camp Dennison, O., by order of War Department.
Adams, Demas	Private	17	Oct. 28, 1861	3 yrs.	Appointed Corporal ——; reduced ——; mustered out with company July 15, 1865; veteran.
Albright, John	do	35	Sept. 23, 1864	1 yr.	Drafted; died Dec. 15, 1864, in hospital at Savannah, Ga.
Albright, Samuel W	do	27	Sept. 23, 1864	1 yr.	Drafted; died Dec. 10, 1864, in hospital at Savannah, Ga.
Amdt, William D	do	17	Aug. 17, 1864	1 yr.	Substitute; mustered out June 16, 1865, at Washington, D. C., by order of War Department.
Armstrong, James W	do	23	Oct. 25, 1861	3 yrs.	
Bailey, David	do	19	Dec. 5, 1861	3 yrs.	Mustered out to date Dec. 22, 1864, near Louisville, Ky., on expiration of term of service.
Bartlett, Daniel	do	45	Oct. 21, 1861	3 yrs.	Discharged Nov. 27, 1862, at Georgetown, D. C., on Surgeon's certificate of disability.
Baker, Joseph	do	27	Oct. 19, 1861	3 yrs.	Mustered out to date Dec. 22, 1864, near Louisville, Ky., on expiration of term of service.
Belta, William H	do	16	Oct. 24, 1861	3 yrs.	Mustered out with company July 15, 1865; veteran.
Benadum, David	do	40	Sept. 23, 1864	1 yr.	Drafted; mustered out June 2, 1865, near Bladensburg, Md., by order of War Department.

Names.	Rank.	Age.	Date of Entering the Service.	Period of Service.	Remarks.
Boswell, James..........	Private	30	Sept. 28, 1864	1 yr.	Drafted; mustered out June 2, 1865, near Bladensburg, Md., by order of War Department.
Bower, Marquis..........	....do....	36	Nov. 19, 1861	3 yrs.	Killed July 22, 1862, by a Sentinel in Rebel Prison at Lynchburg, Va., while a prisoner of war.
Brown, Arstarcus W......	....do....	33	Sept. 30, 1864	1 yr.	Drafted; mustered out June 2, 1865, near Bladensburg, Md., by order of War Department.
Bump, William M........	....do....	19	Oct. 25, 1861	3 yrs.	
Cain, George W..........	....do....	17	Aug. 17, 1864	1 yr.	Substitute; mustered out June 2, 1865, near Bladensburg, Md., by order of War Department.
Canode, Henry..........	....do....	33	Sept. 23, 1864	1 yr.	Drafted; mustered out June 2, 1865, near Bladensburg, Md., by order of War Department.
Case, Dwight............	...do....	23	Oct. 30, 1861	3 yrs.	Discharged Feb. 13, 1863, at Baltimore. Md., on Surgeon's certificate of disability.
Case, Luke	....do....	24	Nov. 4, 1861	3 yrs.	Killed Aug. 9, 1862, in battle of Cedar Mountain, Va.
Case, Joseph H..........	....do....	23	Nov. 7, 1861	3 yrs.	Promoted to Hospital Steward Dec. 13, 1862.
Clark, Lewis J..........	....do....	30	Sept. 23, 1864	1 yr.	Drafted; mustered out May 17, 1865, at hospital, Camp Dennison, O., by order of War Department.
Clark, Lewis............	....do....	26	Oct. 13, 1864	1 yr.	Substitute; died Feb. 3, 1865, at Savannah, Georgia.
Conklin, William H......	...do....	22	Dec. 31, 1863	3 yrs.	Discharged Jan. 5, 1865, on Surgeon's certificate of disability.
Conklin, George	....do....	35	Dec. 31, 1863	3 yrs.	Died May 2, 1865, in hospital at Troy, N. Y.
Cox, David J	....do....	35	Oct. 30, 1861	3 yrs.	Discharged Jan. 30, 1863, at Philadelphia, Pa., on Surgeon's certificate of disability.
Davis, David	....do....	19	Nov. 19, 1861	3 yrs.	On detached service at Columbus, O.; mustered out July 12, 1865, at Columbus, O., by order of War Department; veteran.
Davis, John.............	....do....	18	Oct. 12, 1864	1 yr.	Drafted; absent; no further record found.
Denon, DeWitt C........	....do....	16	Jan. 29, 1862	3 yrs.	
Dowell, William H......	....do....	18	Feb. 26, 1862	3 yrs.	Transferred from Co. I to date Nov. 6, 1863; transferred to 20th Regiment Veteran Reserve Corps; mustered out July 26, 1865, at Philadelphia, Pa., on expiration of term of service.
Durfey, Jerome..........	....do....	18	Jan. 18, 1864	3 yrs.	Mustered out June 17, 1865, at Camp Chase, O., by order of War Department.
Estep, Levi.............	...do....	19	Oct. 16, 1861	3 yrs.	
Firtch, John............	...do....	31	Oct. 16, 1861	3 yrs.	Mustered out with company July 15, 1865; veteran.
Fleming, James Q.......	....do....	24	Oct. 18, 1861	3 yrs.	Killed June 9, 1862, in battle of Port Republic, Virginia.
George, Robert E........	....do....	17	Oct. 28, 1861	3 yrs.	Discharged Feb. 19, 1863, at Washington, D. C., on Surgeon's certificate of disability.
Gessner, John..........	....do....	29	Oct. 15, 1861	3 yrs.	Discharged May 10, 1862, at New Market, Va., on Surgeon's certificate of disability.
Gordon, Robert E........	....do....	16	Aug. 17, 1864	1 yr.	Substitute; captured April 6, 1865, at Goldsboro, N. C.; mustered out June 17, 1865, at Camp Case, O., by order of War Department.
Griffith, Thomas R.......	....do....	23	Nov. 8, 1861	3 yrs.	Absent, sick; mustered out July 22, 1865, at New York City, by order of War Department; veteran.
Griffith, John..........	....do....	23	Dec. 14, 1861	3 yrs.	Transferred to Veteran Reserve Corps Oct. —, 1863.
Griffith, Thomas..........	....do....	19	Feb. 9, 1864	3 yrs.	Died March 1, 1864, at Bridgeport, Ala.; veteran.
Haney, Albert..........	....do....	24	Oct. 25, 1861	3 yrs.	Mustered out with company July 15, 1865.
Harvey, John	....do....	18	Jan. 16, 1864	3 yrs.	
Higginbothom, Ezra......	....do....	24	Oct. 29, 1861	3 yrs.	Prisoner of war; discharged June 17, 1862, at Washington, D. C., by order of War Department.
Hodges, James B........	....do....	18	Nov. 18, 1861	3 yrs.	Mustered out to date Dec. 22, 1864, near Louisville, Ky., on expiration of term of service.
Hord, Bodiski M	....do....	16	Oct. 26, 1861	3 yrs.	Mustered out with company July 15, 1865; veteran.
Hord, Severus A........	....do....	18	Oct. 23, 1861	3 yrs.	Mustered out with company July 15, 1865; veteran.
Humphries, Edward........	....do....	35	Nov. 2, 1861	3 yrs.	Discharged Aug. 29, 1862, at Columbus, O., on Surgeon's certificate of disability.
Huntly, Oscar F.........	....do....	24	Oct. 25, 1861	3 yrs.	Transferred to Veteran Reserve Corps Oct —, 1863.
James, William B	....do....	18	Nov. 4, 1861	3 yrs.	Transferred to Veteran Reserve Corps Oct. —, 1863.
James, John S...........	....do....	18	Jan. 15, 1864	3 yrs.	Mustered out with company July 15, 1865.
Jenkins, Thomas L.......	....do....	20	Dec. 7, 1861	3 yrs.	Mustered out June 2, 1865, at Camp Dennison, O., by order of War Department; veteran.
Jones, David	....do....	19	Nov. 18, 1861	3 yrs.	Discharged May 10, 1862, at New Market, Va., on Surgeon's certificate of disability.
Jones, Isaac............	....do....	24	Oct. 21, 1861	3 yrs.	Died June 24, 1862, at Delaware, O.

Names.	Rank.	Age.	Date of Entering the Service.	Period of Service.	Remarks.
Jones, David L..........	Private	50	Dec. 8, 1861	3 yrs.	Discharged July 11, 1862, at Alexandria, Va., on Surgeon's certificate of disability.
Kanauss, Daniel A	....do....	16	Aug. 17, 1864	1 yr.	Substitute; mustered out June 2, 1865, near Bladensburg, Md., by order of War Department.
Keely, Patrick............	....do....	32	Nov. 11, 1861	3 yrs.	Discharged Jan. 30, 1863, at Washington, D. C., on Surgeon's certificate of disability.
Kirsting, Franklin	....do....	17	Mch. 17, 1863	3 yrs.	Discharged Nov. 26, 1863, at Cincinnati, O., on Surgeon's certificate of disability.
Lamb, Reuben A	....do....	44	Oct. 21, 1861	3 yrs.	Prisoner of war; discharged June 17, 1862, at Washington, D. C., by order of War Department.
Lawrence, Lee............	....do....	23	Oct. 30, 1861	3 yrs.	Mustered out to date Dec. 22, 1864, near Louisville, Ky., on expiration of term of service.
Lewis, Thomas............	....do....	22	Nov. 5, 1861	3 yrs.	Killed Jan. 23, 1862, in railroad accident at Bellaire, O.
Liston, John............	....do....	19	Oct. 7, 1864	3 yrs.	Mustered out May 12, 1865, at Columbus, O., by order of War Department.
Luke, Levi L............	....do....	17	Oct. 31, 1861	3 yrs.	Discharged June 23, 1862, at Columbus, O., on Surgeon's certificate of disability.
Martin, Adam............	....do....	18	Oct. 12, 1864	1 yr.	Substitute; mustered out July 7, 1865, at Tripler Hospital, Columbus, O., by order of War Department.
Miller, Joseph............	....do....	30	Sept. 25, 1864	1 yr.	Drafted; mustered out June 2, 1865, near Bladensburg, Md., by order of War Department.
Moore, John T..........	....do....	19	Nov. 8, 1861	3 yrs.	Died July 30, 1862, in Rebel Prison at Lynchburg, Va.
Morgan, James W........	....do....	18	Oct. 19, 1861	3 yrs.	Discharged Nov. 23, 1862, at Harper's Ferry, Va., on Surgeon's certificate of disability.
Morris, William............	....do....	19	Nov. 20, 1861	3 yrs.	On muster-in roll; no further record found.
Neling, William............	....do....	18	Nov. 20, 1861	3 yrs.	Mustered out with company July 15, 1865; veteran.
Oswaulth, Levi..........	....do....	25	Oct. 1, 1864	1 yr.	Drafted; mustered out June 2, 1865, near Bladensburg, Md., by order of War Department.
Pendleton, Samuel......	....do....	18	Jan. 19, 1864	3 yrs.	Died Sept. 5, 1864 at Chattanooga, Tenn.
Pierce, Milton............	....do....	28	Nov. 11, 1861	3 yrs.	Mustered out with company July 15, 1865; veteran.
Pooi, William H........	....do....	21	Nov. 9, 1861	3 yrs.	Discharged June 8, 1862, at Columbus, O., on Surgeon's certificate of disability.
Post, Elisha..	....do....	23	Oct. 18, 1861	3 yrs.	Promoted to Hospital Steward Nov. 31, 1861.
Post, Morton W..........	....do....	44	Oct. 24, 1861	3 yrs.	Discharged Nov. 23, 1862, at Harper's Ferry, Va., on Surgeon's certificate of disability.
Potter, Jerome	....do....	19	Nov. 3, 1861	3 yrs.	Transferred to 2d U. S. Infantry June 23, 1863.
Price, Thomas............	....do....	19	Oct. 21, 1861	3 yrs.	Died April 18, 1862, at Martinsburg, Va.
Putman, Philip............	....do....	21	Sept. 29, 1864	1 yr.	Substitute; died Jan. 10, 1865, at Savannah, Ga.
Quail, William B........	....do....	18	Sept. 29, 1864	1 yr.	Substitute; mustered out with company July 15, 1865.
Reese, William............	....do....	21	Jan. 19, 1864	3 yrs.	Mustered out with company July 15, 1865.
Richmond, Daniel M....	....do....	36	Jan. 25, 1864	3 yrs.	Mustered out to date July 15, 1865, at Columbus, O., by order of War Department.
Rowland, John T..........	....do....	55	Nov. 20, 1861	3 yrs.	Discharged Oct. 18, 1863, at Harper's Ferry, Va., on Surgeon's certificate of disability.
Rowland, William R.....	....do....	18	Jan. 19, 1864	3 yrs.	Mustered out with company July 15, 1865.
Rowland, Andrew........	....do....	18	Oct. 12, 1864	1 yr.	Substitute; mustered out with company July 15, 1865.
Rowland, William D....	....do....	18	Jan. 18, 1864	3 yrs.	Died Sept. 8, 1864, at Chattanooga, Tenn.
Sampson, Levi............	....do....	18	Oct. 30, 1861	3 yrs.	Killed June 9, 1862, in battle of Port Republic, Virginia.
Salsbury, Layfayette....	....do....	19	Nov. 8, 1861	3 yrs.	Discharged Sept. 23, 1862, at New York, on Surgeon's certificate of disability.
Shaffer, Smith J..........	....do....	20	Oct. 15, 1861	3 yrs.	Discharged Dec. 28, 1862, at Fort Delaware, Md., on Surgeon's certificate of disability.
Sherer, Elias S............	....do....	30	Sept. 23, 1864	1 yr.	Drafted; mustered out June 2, 1865, near Bladensburg, Md., by order of War Department.
Shindollar, Louis..........	....do....	25	Dec. 30, 1863	3 yrs.	Mustered out June 2, 1865, at Tripler Hospital, Columbus, O., by order of War Department.
Shindollar, Henry........	....do....	27	Oct. 16, 1861	3 yrs.	Died July 20, 1862, at Washington, D. C.
Sigfred, Jeremiah	....do....	19	Nov. 14, 1861	3 yrs.	Mustered out with company July 15, 1865; veteran.
Sigfred, Peter	....do....	21	Nov. 23, 1861	3 yrs.	On detached service; mustered out July 12, 1865, at Columbus, O., by order of War Department; veteran.
Silverwood, Isaac N......	....do....	21	Oct. 23, 1861	3 yrs.	Mustered out Nov. 15, 1864, at Columbus, O., on expiration of term of service.
Smith, John L............	....do....	21	Oct. 16, 1861	3 yrs.	Mustered out with company July 15, 1865; veteran.
Snook, Henry	...do....	35	Sept. 26, 1864	1 yr.	Drafted; mustered out July 7, 1865, at Tripler Hospital, Columbus, O., by order of War Department.
Snider, Levi	....do....	18	Sept. 24, 1864	1 yr.	Drafted; mustered out July 13, 1865, at David's Island, New York Harbor, by order of War Department.
Stephens, Thomas	....do....	24	Oct. 17, 1861	3 yrs.	Mustered out to date July 15, 1865, at Columbus, O., by order of War Department; veteran.

Names.	Rank.	Age.	Date of Entering the Service.	Period of Service.	Remarks.
Swartz, Jacob	Private	25	Nov. 7, 1861	3 yrs.	Mustered out to date Dec. 22, 1864, near Louisville, Ky., on expiration of term of service.
Speny, Truman	..do...	28	Sept. 30, 1864	1 yr.	Drafted; mustered out June 2, 1865, near Bladensburg, Md., by order of War Department.
Tallman, William	...do...	21	Oct. 16, 1861	3 yrs.	Mustered as private; appointed Sergeant ——; reduced to ranks ——; mustered out with company July 15, 1865; veteran.
Thomas, Joseph E	...do...	23	Sept. 23, 1862	3 yrs.	Discharged March 4, 1864, at Camp Dennison, O., on Surgeon's certificate of disability.
Tipton, George W	...do...	22	Oct. 21, 1861	3 yrs.	Discharged Sept. 9, 1863, at Washington, D. C., on Surgeon's certificate of disability.
Tipton, George W	...do...	22	Dec. 30, 1863	3 yrs.	Mustered out with company July 15, 1865; veteran.
Tipton, David R	...do...	19	Oct. 15, 1861	3 yrs.	
Turner, Wesley	...do...	30	Sept. 23, 1864	1 yr.	Drafted; died Dec. 15, 1865, at Chattanooga, Tennessee.
Van Horn, Oliver	...do...	17	Dec. 7, 1861	3 yrs.	Captured June 9, 1862, in battle of Port Republic, Va.; transferred to 18th U. S. Infantry Oct. 21, 1862; discharged to date Nov. 21, 1862, to enlist in 18th Infantry, U. S. A.
Vogleson, John W	...do...	25	Aug. 17, 1864	1 yr.	Substitute; mustered out June 2, 1865, near Bladensburg, Md., by order of War Department.
Wallin, John T	...do...	25	Oct. 30, 1861	3 yrs.	Mustered out with company July 15, 1865; veteran.
Watkins, Edward J	...do...	29	Oct. 25, 1861	3 yrs.	Died April 7, 1862, in hospital at Martinsburg, Virginia.
Webster, George P	...do...	19	Oct. 21, 1861	3 yrs.	Discharged Jan. 19, 1863, at Washington, D C., on Surgeon's certificate of disability.
Webster, George P	...do...	20	Jan. 23, 1864	3 yrs.	Mustered out with company July 15, 1865.
Webster, William B	...do...	19	Jan. 9, 1864	3 yrs.	Mustered out with company July 15, 1865.
Wells, Robert A	...do...	24	Nov. 13, 1861	3 yrs.	Discharged Oct. 14, 1862, at Fort Wood, N. Y., on Surgeon's certificate of disability.
Wells, Robert A	...do...	26	Jan. 1, 1864	3 yrs.	Mustered out May 17, 1865, at hospital, Camp Dennison, O., by order of War Department.
Williams, Morris	...do...	42	Nov. 19, 1861	3 yrs.	Discharged Feb. 13, 1863, at Dumfries, Va., on Surgeon's certificate of disability.
Wood, Isaac	...do...	19	Oct. 30, 1861	3 yrs.	Mustered out with company July 15, 1865; veteran.

COMPANY F.

Mustered in Dec. 26, 1861, at Camp McArthur, Urbana, O., by John Cassil, 2d Lieutenant 66th O. V. I. Mustered out July 15, 1865, near Louisville, Ky., by Edward A. Wickes, Captain 150th New York Volunteers, and A. C. M. 14th Army Corps.

Names.	Rank.	Age.	Date of Entering the Service.	Period of Service.	Remarks.
John Cassil	Captain	59	Oct. 16, 1861	3 yrs.	Appointed Dec. 11, 1861; resigned June 21, 1862.
William McLean Gwynne	....do...	21	Sept. 5, 1861	3 yrs.	Promoted from 1st Lieutenant and Adjutant June 21, 1862; transferred to Co. B Dec. 3, 1862.
Lemuel W. Smith	...do...	32	Oct. 17, 1861	3 yrs.	Appointed 1st Lieutenant Dec. 11, 1861; promoted to Captain Dec. 3, 1862; mustered out Dec. 29, 1864, at Savannah, Ga., on expiration of term of service.
James P. Conn	...do...	19	Oct. 18, 1861	3 yrs.	Promoted to 1st Lieutenant from 2d Lieutenant Co. B April 2, 1864; to Captain April 12, 1865; mustered out with company July 15, 1865; veteran.
John N. Rathbun	1st Lieut.	30	Oct. 17, 1861	3 yrs.	Mustered as private; promoted to 2d Lieutenant April 21, 1862; to 1st Lieutenant Dec. 5, 1862; to Captain Co. C March 3, 1864.
Joseph H. Case	..do...	23	Nov. 7, 1861	3 yrs.	Promoted from Hospital Steward April 12, 1865; mustered out with company July 15, 1865; veteran.
James O. Carter	2d Lieut.	29	Oct. 17, 1861	3 yrs.	Appointed Dec. 11, 1861; resigned April 21, 1862.
William A. Cavis	....do...	37	Nov. 8, 1861	3 yrs.	Mustered as private; appointed 1st Sergeant ——; promoted to 2d Lieutenant July 30, 1864; to 1st Lieutenant Co. C Aug. 11, 1864; veteran.
William C. Porter	1st Sergt.	24	Oct. 17, 1861	3 yrs.	Mustered as private; appointed 1st Sergeant ——; died Dec. 10, 1862, at Washington, D. C., of wounds received Aug. 9, 1862, in battle of Cedar Mountain, Va.

Names.	Rank.	Age.	Date of Entering the Service.	Period of Service.	Remarks.
William Scott...........	1st Sergt.	21	Nov. 13, 1861	3 yrs.	Mustered as private; appointed Sergeant Dec. 12, 1863; 1st Sergeant Sept. 1, 1864; promoted to 1st Lieutenant Co. K May 31, 1865; veteran.
Daniel Griffin..............	...do....	23	Oct. 23, 1861	3 yrs.	Mustered as private; appointed 1st Sergeant ——; mustered out to date June 28, 1865, by order of War Department; promoted to 2d Lieutenant July 13, 1865, but not mustered; veteran.
George Richey...........	Sergeant	23	Oct. 17, 1861	3 yrs.	Mustered as private; appointed Sergeant ——; killed June 9, 1862, in battle of Port Republic, Va.
James H. Newhouse........	...do....	21	Oct. 17, 1861	3 yrs.	Mustered as private; appointed Sergeant ——; discharged June 24, 1862, at Columbus, O., on Surgeon's certificate of disability.
William H. Loveless.....	...do....	21	Oct. 25, 1861	3 yrs.	Mustered as private; appointed Sergeant ——; wounded June 9, 1862, at battle of Port Republic, Va.; discharged Sept. 12, 1862, on Surgeon's certificate of disability.
George McGregor.........	...do....	20	Dec. 7, 1861	3 yrs.	Mustered as private; appointed Sergeant ——; mustered out Dec. 22, 1864, at Savannah, Ga., on expiration of term of service.
James Guy.................	...do....	18	Oct. 17, 1861	3 yrs.	Mustered as private; appointed Sergeant ——; mustered out June 28, 1865, by order of War Department; veteran.
Albert P. Orahood........	...do....	23	Oct. 19, 1861	3 yrs.	Mustered as private; appointed Sergeant ——; mustered out June 28, 1865, by order of War Department; veteran.
Daniel Beighler.........	Corporal	18	Nov. 27, 1861	3 yrs.	Appointed Corporal ——; mustered out June 28, 1865, by order of War Department; veteran.
James Brewster...........	...do....	23	Aug. 14, 1862	3 yrs.	Appointed Corporal ——; mustered out June 2, 1865, near Bladensburg, Md., by order of War Department.
Edward Cody..............	...do....	20	Oct. 17, 1861	3 yrs.	Appointed Corporal ——; mustered out June 28, 1865, by order of War Department; veteran.
Francis Cooledge.........	...do....	24	Oct. 21, 1861	3 yrs.	Appointed Corporal ——; discharged Jan. 31, 1863, at Washington, D. C., on Surgeon's certificate of disability.
William C. Dines........	...do....	25	Aug. 20, 1862	3 yrs.	Appointed Corporal ——; mustered out June 2, 1865, near Bladensburg, Md., by order of War Department.
John Freshwater.........	...do....	24	Nov. 20, 1861	3 yrs.	Appointed Corporal ——; killed June 9, 1862, in battle of Port Republic, Va.
Francis M. Gibson........	...do....	18	Nov. 29, 1861	3 yrs.	Appointed Corporal ——; mustered out June 28, 1865, by order of War Department; veteran.
James McGlynn............	...do....	27	Nov. 18, 1861	3 yrs.	Appointed Corporal ——; transferred to Veteran Reserve Corps March ——, 1865; veteran.
Delmore Robinson.........	...do....	18	Nov. 13, 1861	3 yrs.	Appointed Corporal ——; died July 10, 1862, at Alexandria, Va.
William Sharp...........	...do....	22	Dec. 6, 1861	3 yrs.	Appointed Corporal ——; killed June 9, 1862, in battle of Port Republic, Va.
Mathias Smith...........	...do....	19	Dec. 5, 1861	3 yrs.	Appointed Corporal ——; mustered out June 28, 1865, by order of War Department; veteran.
Amarine, John W........	Private	20	Nov. 20, 1861	3 yrs.	Mustered out June 28, 1865, by order of War Department; veteran.
Amarine, Alfred......	...do....	18	Nov. 27, 1861	3 yrs.	Mustered out June 13, 1865, at Camp Chase, O., by order of War Department; veteran.
Amarine, Rodney P	...do....	18	Jan. 25, 1864	3 yrs.	Prisoner of war; mustered out June 13, 1865, at Camp Chase, O., by order of War Department.
Arnold, Jasper	...do....	24	Aug. 9, 1862	3 yrs.	Mustered out June 19, 1865, at Tripler Hospital, Columbus, O., by order of War Department.
Bancroft, William.......	...do....	33	Jan. 22, 1864	3 yrs.	Mustered out June 28, 1865, by order of War Department.
Bassell, Adam.............	...do....	21	Jan. 11, 1864	3 yrs.	Died June 28, 1864, at Bridgeport, Ala.
Battees, William S.......	...do....	19	Nov. 6, 1861	3 yrs.	Killed June 9, 1862, in battle of Port Republic, Virginia.
Beck, Jesse K	...do....	23	Nov. 19, 1861	3 yrs.	
Beck, Alfred.............	...do....	18	Jan. 5, 1864	3 yrs.	Mustered out May 17, 1865, at Camp Dennison, O., by order of War Department.
Bell, William H.........	...do....	18	Jan. 23, 1864	3 yrs.	Mustered out June 28, 1865, by order of War Department.
Berrian, William.........	...do....	36	Nov. 1, 1861	3 yrs.	Discharged June 30, 1862, at Columbus, O., on Surgeon's certificate of disability.
Bethard, Albert G........	...do....	20	Oct. 17, 1861	3 yrs.	Discharged Oct. 14, 1862, at Philadelphia, Pa., on Surgeon's certificate of disability.
Bethard, James H	...do....	19	Oct. 17, 1861	3 yrs.	Discharged July 21, 1862, at Washington, D. C., on Surgeon's certificate of disability.
Billiter, Noah C	...do....	22	Dec. 7, 1861	3 yrs.	Discharged Nov. 24, 1862, on Surgeon's certificate of disability.

Names.	Rank.	Age.	Date of Entering the Service.	Period of Service.	Remarks.
Black, Thomas	Private	27	Dec. 9, 1861	3 yrs.	Discharged Dec. 16, 1862, at Baltimore, Md., on Surgeon's certificate of disability.
Black, James M	...do....	18	Oct. 12, 1864	1 yr.	Substitute; mustered out May 15, 1865, at Louisville, Ky., by order of War Department.
Brown, Albert	...do....	22	Nov. 21, 1861	3 yrs.	Discharged Nov. 15, 1862, at Harrisburg, Pa., on Surgeon's certificate of disability.
Burris, Martin	...do....	27	Nov. 19, 1861	3 yrs.	Mustered out June 28, 1865, by order of War Department; veteran.
Burris, Enoch	...do....	....	Aug. 9, 1862	3 yrs.	Discharged Nov. 29, 1862, at Harper's Ferry, Va., on Surgeon's certificate of disability.
Burkhart, Edward	...do....	27	Oct. 18, 1864	1 yr.	Substitute; mustered out June 28, 1865, by order of War Department.
Cassell, James M	...do....	20	Feb. 21, 1862	3 yrs.	Discharged Aug. 12, 1862, at Columbus, O., on Surgeon's certificate of disability.
Columber, Jesse..........	...do....	40	Jan. 27, 1864	3 yrs.	Mustered out June 28, 1865, by order of War Department.
Cole, James R..............	...do....	24	Mch. 29, 1864	3 yrs.	Died July 8, 1864, at Nashville, Tenn.
Constant, William J	...do....	23	Aug. 9, 1862	3 yrs.	Mustered out June 2, 1865, near Bladensburg, Md., by order of War Department.
Cooledge, Theophilus......	...do....	18	Oct. 19, 1861	3 yrs.	Died April 10, 1862, at Winchester, Va.
Cummings, James	...do....	33	Nov. 28, 1861	3 yrs.	
Dasher, John..............	...do....	33	Jan. 18, 1864	3 yrs.	Mustered out June 28, 1865, by order of War Department.
Deary, George...........	...do....	33	Sept. 23, 1864	1 yr.	Drafted; absent, sick; no further record found.
Dockum, Harvey..........	...do....	33	Nov. 8, 1861	3 yrs.	Discharged Oct. 24, 1862, at Columbus, O., on Surgeon's certificate of disability.
Dolbear, Edward C.......	...do....	18	Nov. 13, 1861	3 yrs.	Discharged Dec. 31, 1861, by civil authority.
Dulan, John..............	...do....	26	Dec. 10, 1861	3 yrs.	Not mustered into service.
Draper, Henry............	...do....	19	Nov. 29, 1861	3 yrs.	Died Aug. 24, 1864, at Nashville, Tenn.; veteran.
Edgington, Jeremiah......	...do....	18	Nov. 28, 1861	3 yrs.	Died July 18, 1864, at Marysville, O.; veteran.
Elliott, Felix	...do....	21	Dec. 9, 1861	3 yrs.	Mustered out June 28, 1865, by order of War Department; veteran.
Endris, Paul T...........	...do....	25	Oct. 14, 1864	1 yr.	Substitute; mustered out June 28, 1865, by order of War Department.
Filler, Benjamin F.......	...do....	26	Aug. 11, 1862	3 yrs.	Transferred to Veteran Reserve Corps July 1, 1863.
Freshwater, William C....	...do....	22	Jan. 17, 1862	3 yrs.	Died June 17, 1862, at Washington, D. C., of wounds received June 9, 1862, in battle of Port Republic, Va.
Gannurd, Belandis.......	...do....	33	Sept. 22, 1864	1 yr.	Drafted; mustered out June 2, 1865, near Bladensburg, Md.
Gray, James..............	...do....	22	Dec. 3, 1861	3 yrs.	Mustered out June 28, 1865, by order of War Department; veteran.
Gray, Stephen...........	...do....	18	Nov. 13, 1861	3 yrs.	Died Nov. 21, 1863, at Columbus, O., of wounds received July 2, 1863, at battle of Gettysburg, Pa.
Graham, Silas	...do....	28	Mch. 14, 1864	3 yrs.	Mustered out June 28, 1865, by order of War Department.
Gregory, Jason............	...do....	45	Oct. 26, 1861	3 yrs.	Discharged June 16, 1862, at Washington, D. C., on Surgeon's certificate of disability.
Griffith, John H..........	...do....	....	Aug. 11, 1862	3 yrs.	Discharged March 2, 1863, on Surgeon's certificate of disability.
Griffith, Tillman R.......	...do....	18	Mch. 10, 1864	3 yrs.	Mustered out to date June 30, 1865, by order of War Department.
Grow, George.............	...do....	18	Nov. 30, 1861	3 yrs.	Mustered out June 28, 1865, by order of War Department; veteran.
Grow, Henry	...do....	18	Dec. 2, 1861	3 yrs.	Discharged Jan. 26, 1863, at Washington, D. C., on Surgeon's certificate of disability,
Grow, Henry	...do....	20	Jan. 10, 1864	3 yrs.	
Guy, William.............	...do....	19	Oct. 17, 1861	3 yrs.	Mustered out June 28, 1865, by order of War Department; veteran.
Heastand, Enoch..........	...do....	36	Sept. 23, 1864	1 yr.	Drafted; mustered out June 1, 1865, at McDougall Hospital, New York Harbor, by order of War Department.
Heselden, Jacob..........	...do....	24	Nov. 16, 1863	3 yrs.	Mustered out June 28, 1865, by order of War Department.
Hoddy, Henry.............	...do....	26	Sept. 29, 1864	1 yr.	Substitute; mustered out June 2, 1865, near Bladensburg, Md., by order of War Department.
Holoway, William J......	...do....	24	Jan. 10, 1862	3 yrs.	Wounded Aug. 9, 1862, in battle of Cedar Mountain, Va.; transferred to Veteran Reserve Corps ——— 1863; mustered out as Sergeant Jan. 11, 1865, at Johnson Island, O., by order of War Department.
Horney, Johiel	...do....	18	Nov. 28, 1861	3 yrs.	Killed June 16, 1864, in action near Pine Mountain, Ga.; veteran.
Huffman, John T........	...do....	24	Oct. 17, 1861	3 yrs.	Discharged April 26, 1862, at Strasburg, Va., on Surgeon's certificate of disability.
Huffman, John T........	...do....	26	Mch. 28, 1864	3 yrs.	Mustered out July 27, 1865, at Washington, D. C., by order of War Department.
Huffman, Aaron W.......	...do....	20	Feb. 18, 1864	3 yrs.	Mustered out June 28, 1865, by order of War Department.
Humes, Alonzo...........	...do....	18	Nov. 13, 1861	3 yrs.	Discharged Jan. 7, 1863, at Washington, D. C., on Surgeon's certificate of disability.

Names.	Rank.	Age.	Date of Entering the Service.	Period of Service.	Remarks.
Ingram, Benjamin P	Private	19	Mch. 10, 1864	3 yrs.	
Jackson, Monroe	...do....	24	Oct. 14, 1864	1 yr.	Substitute; mustered out June 28, 1865, by order of War Department.
Jamison, Francis M......	...do....	44	Sept. 29, 1864	1 yr.	Substitute; died March 1, 1865, at Bedloe's Island, N. Y.
Kelly Daniel..............	...do....	45	Nov. 30, 1861	3 yrs.	Discharged Oct. 9, 1862, at New York, on Surgeon's certificate of disability.
Kelsey, William J........	...do....	20	April 1, 1864	3 yrs.	Mustered out June 28, 1865, by order of War Department.
Kelleher, Daniel..........	...do....	24	Oct. 15, 1864	1 yr.	Substitute; mustered out May 17, 1865, at Camp Dennison, O., by order of War Department.
Kent, Thomas	...do....	19	Oct. 17, 1861	3 yrs.	Mustered out June 28, 1865, by order of War Department: veteran.
Laird, Samuel D..........	...do....	18	Nov. 12, 1861	3 yrs.	Mustered out Dec. 22, 1864, at Savannah, Ga., on expiration of term of service.
Lannon, James A..........	...do....	18	Jan. 29, 1864	3 yrs.	Mustered out Jan. 28, 1865, by order of War Department.
Levemier, Francis........	...do....	30	Sept. 6, 1864	1 yr.	Substitute; mustered out June 2, 1865, near Bladensburg, Md., by order of War Department.
Lewellen, Andrew J.....	...do....	24	Aug. 9, 1862	3 yrs.	Died Dec. 14, 1862, at Harper's Ferry, Va.
Little, John	...do....	25	Dec. 6, 1861	3 yrs.	Died July 28, 1862, at Alexandria, Va.
Loats, Lewis H..........	...do....	33	Jan. 18, 1864	3 yrs.	Mustered out June 28, 1865, by order of War Department.
Loring, Emery...........	...do....	18	Oct. 17, 1861	3 yrs.	Wounded June 9, 1862, in battle of Port Republic, Va.; discharged March 5, 1863, on Surgeon's certificate of disability.
Luty, Jacob	...do....	19	Sept. 21, 1863	3 yrs.	Discharged Dec. 20, 1864, at Murfreesboro, Tenn., on Surgeon's certificate of disability.
Maggs, James F	...do....	28	Feb. 1, 1862	3 yrs.	Promoted to 1st Lieutenant April 12, 1865, but not mustered; mustered out June 28, 1865, by order of War Department; veteran.
Marks, Andrew..........	...do....	29	Nov. 28, 1861	3 yrs.	Mustered out Dec. 22, 1864, at Savannah, Ga., on expiration of term of service.
Mathers, John..........	...do....	26	Mch. 7, 1864	3 yrs.	Mustered out June 28, 1865, by order of War Department.
Mapes, Thomas A	...do....	36	Nov. 20, 1861	3 yrs.	Discharged Dec. 30, 1862, at Annapolis, Md., on Surgeon's certificate of disability.
McBride, Thomas	...do....		Sept. 15, 1862	3 yrs.	Died May 12, 1864, at Bridgeport, Ala.
McCarty, William.......	...do....	39	Dec. 7, 1861	3 yrs.	
McGlee, Andrew	...do....	34	Sept. 21, 1864	1 yr.	Drafted; discharged May 18, 1865, at Covington, Ky., on Surgeon's certificate of disability.
McGrath, David..........	...do....	25	Jan. 29, 1864	3 yrs.	Mustered out June 28, 1865, by order of War Department.
McGregory, Morris M...	...do....	18	Oct. 21, 1863	3 yrs.	Discharged May 24, 1865, at New York City, on Surgeon's certificate of disability.
McKitrick, James H	...do....	...	....	3 yrs.	Mustered out June 28, 1865, by order of War Department; veteran.
Michael, David..........	...do....	18	Oct. 10, 1864	1 yr.	Substitute; mustered out June 28, 1865, by order of War Department.
Mills, James.............	...do....	19	Nov. 28, 1861	3 yrs.	Mustered out June 28, 1865, by order of War Department; veteran.
Monroe, David B	...do....	19	Oct. 29, 1861	3 yrs.	Mustered out June 28, 1865, by order of War Department; veteran.
Murdock, Robert........	...do....	18	Dec. 28, 1861	3 yrs.	Promoted to Sergt. Major Jan. 1, 1862.
Myers, Joseph K	...do....	20	Oct. 21, 1861	3 yrs.	Mustered out June 28, 1865, by order of War Department; veteran.
Myers, James H..........	...do....	19	Jan. 26, 1864	3 yrs.	Transferred to Co. C, 8th Regiment Veteran Reserve Corps, Feb. 2, 1865; mustered out July 15, 1865, near Gainesville, Ky., by order of War Department.
Nicholson, Jeremiah......	...do....	34	Nov. 1, 1861	3 yrs.	Killed June 9, 1862, in battle of Port Republic, Va.
Ongram, Benjamin P....	...do....	19	Mch. 10, 1864	3 yrs.	
Orahood, Milton.........	...do....	21	Nov. 13, 1861	3 yrs.	Discharged Aug. 8, 1862, at Columbus, O., on Surgeon's certificate of disability.
Orahood, Amos..........	...do....	23	Dec. 6, 1861	3 yrs.	Died June 11, 1862, at Marysville, O.
Parmeter, Samuel.......	...do....	21	Nov. 16, 1861	3 yrs.	Discharged April 9, 1862, at Strasburg, Va., on Surgeon's certificate of disability.
Parmeter, Hiram D	...do....	29	Nov. 27, 1861	3 yrs.	Transferred to Veteran Reserve Corps July 1, 1863.
Peck, John O.............	...do....	18	Oct. 27, 1864	1 yr.	Mustered out June 28, 1865, by order of War Department.
Powers, William M......	...do....	19	Nov. 20, 1861	3 yrs.	Discharged Feb. 19, 1863, at Baltimore, Md., on Surgeon's certificate of disability.
Redding, William W	...do....	24	Nov. 6, 1861	3 yrs.	Discharged July 5, 1862, at Columbus, O., on Surgeon's certificate of disability.
Reid, Theodore..........	...do....	18	Jan. 5, 1864	3 yrs.	Mustered out June 28, 1865, by order of War Department.
Rider, Christopher.......	...do....	27	Nov. 5, 1861	3 yrs.	Discharged Dec. 15, 1862, at Providence, R. I., on Surgeon's certificate of disability.
Rice, Francis M..........	...do....	25	Aug. 11, 1862	3 yrs.	Mustered out June 28, 1865, by order of War Department.
Rice, Edward R..........	...do....	42	Sept. 22, 1864	1 yr.	Drafted; died Nov. 20, 1864, at Madison, Ga.

Names.	Rank.	Age.	Date of Entering the Service.	Period of Service.	Remarks.
Ryan, James H	Private	19	Nov. 15, 1861	3 yrs.	Wounded June 9, 1862, in battle of Port Republic, Va.; discharged Dec. 30, 1862, at Philadelphia, Pa., on Surgeon's certificate of disability.
Severn, Matthew	...do....	22	Nov. 28, 1861	3 yrs.	Killed June 9, 1862, in battle of Port Republic, Va.
Sharp, Russel B	...do....	18	Dec. 5, 1861	3 yrs.	Mustered out June 28, 1865, by order of War Department; veteran.
Shular, William A	...do....	19	Mch. 8, 1864	3 yrs.	Mustered out June 28, 1865, by order of War Department.
Shout, Isaiah	...do....	23	Oct. 28, 1861	3 yrs.	Discharged June 18, 1862, at Washington, D. C., on Surgeon's certificate of disability.
Shout, Isaiah	...do....	25	Sept. 26, 1863	3 yrs.	Mustered out May 29, 1865, at hospital, New York City, by order of War Department.
Sherborn, George	...do....	24	Feb. 20, 1862	3 yrs.	
Shoemaker, Andrew	...do....	42	Sept. 26, 1864	1 yr.	Substitute; mustered out June 2, 1865, near Bladensburg, Md., by order of War Department.
Shoemaker, John	...do....	42	Sept. 29, 1864	1 yr.	Substitute; died Nov. 25, 1864, at Millen, Ga.
Smith, Israel T	...do....	32	Nov. 28, 1861	3 yrs.	
Smith, Jacob H	...do....	39	Nov. 28, 1861	3 yrs.	Discharged March 27, 1863, at Alexandria, Va., on Surgeon's certificate of disability.
Smith, James F	...do....	20	Dec. 7, 1861	3 yrs.	Died Oct. 16, 1862, at Washington, D. C., of wounds received Aug. 9, 1862, in battle of Cedar Mountain, Va.
Smith, William M	...do....	37	Feb. 1, 1862	3 yrs.	Wounded June 9, 1862, in battle of Port Republic, Va.; discharged March 1, 1863, on Surgeon's certificate of disability.
Smith, John	...do....	20	Nov. 7, 1861	3 yrs.	Discharged Nov. 20, 1862, at Columbus, O., on Surgeon's certificate of disability.
Smith, John	...do....	22	Jan. 1, 1864	3 yrs.	Mustered out June 28, 1865, by order of War Department.
Smith, John T	...do....	18	Nov. 28, 1861	3 yrs.	Mustered out June 28, 1865, by order of War Department; veteran.
Sterlin, Darius	...do....	20	Dec. 9, 1861	3 yrs.	Died Dec. 6, 1862, at Fort Delaware, Md.
Stephens, William	...do....	47	Jan. 9, 1862	3 yrs.	
Stithern, Leonard	...do....	18	Nov. 30, 1861	3 yrs.	Died Jan. 20, 1862, at Urbana, O.
Stillings, William	...do....	18	Oct. 17, 1861	3 yrs.	Discharged Dec. 10, 1861, at Marysville, O., by civil authority.
Spain, Philander	...do....	39	Oct. 25, 1861	3 yrs.	Discharged Jan. 30, 1862, at Columbus, O., on Surgeon's certificate of disability.
Spain, Marshall	...do....	18	Feb. 29, 1864	3 yrs.	Mustered out June 28, 1865, by order of War Department.
Thayer, Joseph	...do....	45	Dec. 6, 1861	3 yrs.	Discharged March 2, 1863, at Washington, D. C., on Surgeon's certificate of disability.
Turner, Stephen	...do....	20	Jan. 5, 1864	3 yrs.	Killed May 25, 1864, in action near Dallas, Ga.
Turner, Sampson	...do....	19	Jan. 5, 1864	3 yrs.	Killed Aug. 31, 1864, in action near Chattahoochee River, Ga.
Turner, Emery	...do....	21	April 4, 1864	3 yrs.	Mustered out June 28, 1865, by order of War Department.
Warner, James B	...do....	19	Feb. 25, 1864	3 yrs.	Mustered out June 28, 1865, by order of War Department.
Welsh, Michael	...do....	33	Sept. 27, 1864	1 yr.	Drafted; mustered out June 2, 1865, near Bladensburg, Md., by order of War Department.
Welsh, Nathan C	...do....	18	Nov. 13, 1861	3 yrs.	On detached service at Columbus, O.; promoted to 2d Lieutenant Co. D, 187th O. V. I., March 1, 1865; veteran.
Wilcox, Richard	...do....	19	Nov. 22, 1861	3 yrs.	Discharged Feb. 12, 1863, at Baltimore, Md., on Surgeon's certificate of disability.
Wilcox, Richard	...do....	21	Jan. 18, 1864	3 yrs.	Died June 26, 1864, at Chattanooga, Tenn.
Wilcox, Charles E	...do....	21	Nov. 20, 1861	3 yrs.	Mustered out June 28, 1865, by order of War Department; veteran.
Wilmoth, John`	...do....	26	Nov. 8, 1861	3 yrs.	Killed June 9, 1862, in battle of Port Republic, Virginia.
Williams, Cyrus C	...do....	20	Mch. 8, 1864	3 yrs.	Mustered out June 28, 1865, by order of War Department.
Witter, Noah	...do....	28	Oct. 10, 1864	1 yr.	Drafted; mustered out Aug. 2, 1865, to date July 15, 1865, at Columbus, O., by order of War Department.
Wolford, Levi	...do....	18	Dec. 6, 1861	3 yrs.	Killed June 9, 1862, in battle of Port Republic, Va.
Worley, David	...do....	22	Mch. 28, 1864	3 yrs.	Killed July 1, 1864, in action near Kenesaw Mountain, Ga.
Worley, William L	...do....	18	Oct. 24, 1861	3 yrs.	Discharged Nov. 25, 1862, on Surgeon's certificate of disability.
Wyant, John J	...do....	18	Nov. 27, 1861	3 yrs.	Mustered out June 28, 1865, by order of War Department; veteran.

COMPANY G.

Mustered in Dec. 26, 1861, at Camp McArthur, Urbana, O., by James Q. Baird, James W. Christie and Joshua G. Palmer, 2d Lieutenants 66th O. V. I. Mustered out July 15, 1865, near Louisville, Ky., by Edward A. Wickes, Captain 150th New York Volunteers, and A. C. M. 14th Army Corps.

Names.	Rank.	Age.	Date of Entering the Service.	Period of Service.	Remarks.
James Q. Baird	Captain	32	Oct. 3, 1861	3 yrs.	Appointed Dec. 14, 1861; discharged May 30, 1863, on Surgeon's certificate of disability.
Robert H. Russell	do	24	Oct. 4, 1861	3 yrs.	Promoted to 2d Lieutenant from 1st Sergeant Aug. 25, 1862; to 1st Lieutenant Feb. 3, 1863; to Captain May 31, 1863; mustered out Dec. 28, 1864, on expiration of term of service.
W. Wallace Cranston	do	22	Oct. 10, 1861	3 yrs.	Promoted from 1st Lieutenant Co. I April 12, 1865; mustered out with company July 15, 1865; veteran.
James W. Christie	1st Lieut.	32	Oct. 5, 1861	3 yrs.	Appointed Dec. 14, 1861; discharged Feb. 3, 1863, on Surgeon's certificate of disability.
Elhannan Zook	do	22	Nov. 7, 1861	3 yrs.	Appointed Sergeant from Corporal Jan. 1, 1863; 1st Sergeant Jan. 2, 1863; promoted to 2d Lieutenant Feb. 3, 1863; to 1st Lieutenant May 31, 1863; discharged July 27, 1864, on Surgeon's certificate of disability.
William V. Taylor	do	22	Oct. 4, 1861	3 yrs.	Mustered as private; appointed 1st Sergeant — ; wounded July 20, 1864, in battle of Peach Tree Creek, Ga.; promoted to 1st Lieutenant to date July 27, 1864; discharged Dec. 15, 1864, by order of War Department.
Charles W. Guy	do	18	Aug. 16, 1862	3 yrs.	Promoted from 1st Sergeant Co. D Nov. 12, 1864; to Captain Co. K May 31, 1865.
Daniel D. Davidson	do	31	Nov. 7, 1861	3 yrs.	Promoted from 1st Sergeant Co. I May 31, 1865; mustered out with company July 15, 1865; veteran.
Charles H. Rhodes	2d Lieut.	21	Oct. 8, 1861	3 yrs.	Appointed Dec. 14, 1861; discharged Feb. 28, 1862, on Surgeon's certificate of disability.
Robert Murdock	do	18	Dec. 28, 1861	3 yrs.	Promoted from Sergeant Major Feb. 28, 1862; died Aug. 24, 1862, in hospital at Washington, D. C.
Frank Baldwin	1st Sergt	20	Oct. 15, 1861	3 yrs.	Appointed Corporal Dec. 15, 1862; Sergeant Jan. 1, 1863; 1st Sergeant Oct. 1, 1864; promoted to 1st Lieutenant Co I April 12, 1865; veteran.
Noah Minnich	do	19	Dec. 8, 1861	3 yrs.	Appointed Corporal Sept 1, 1863; Sergeant April 8, 1865; 1st Sergeant May 2, 1865; mustered out June 28, 1865, by order of War Department; veteran.
John K. Baldwin	Sergeant	22	Oct. 17, 1861	3 yrs.	Mustered as private; appointed Sergeant — ; died June 18, 1862, in hospital at Washington, D. C.
James H. McBeth	do	21	Oct. 22, 1861	3 yrs.	Mustered as private; appointed Sergeant — ; died Aug. 20, 1862, in hospital at Falls Church, Va.
John B. McGowen	do	43	Dec. 4, 1861	3 yrs.	Mustered as private; appointed Sergeant — ; killed June 9, 1862, in battle of Port Republic, Va.
A. B. Rumley	do	22	Dec. 2, 1861	3 yrs.	Mustered in as Emanuel B. Rusnler; mustered as private; appointed Sergeant — ; killed Aug. 9, 1862, in battle of Cedar Mountain, Virginia.
William W. Wilson	do	19	Oct. 4, 1861	3 yrs.	Mustered as private; appointed Sergeant — ; wounded June 9, 1862, in battle of Port Republic, Va.; discharged Jan. 7, 1863, at Columbus, O., on Surgeon's certificate of disability.
Henry H. Hanger	do	20	Oct. 22, 1861	3 yrs.	Mustered as private; appointed Sergeant — ; wounded June 16, 1864, in action at Pine Knob, Ga.; mustered out Jan. 19, 1865, at Columbus, O., on expiration of term of service.
John D. Outhart	do	23	Mch. 4, 1862	3 yrs.	Mustered as private; appointed Sergeant — ; mustered out April 8, 1865, on expiration of term of service.
Harrison Mayes	do	19	Nov. 4, 1861	3 yrs.	Mustered as private; appointed Sergeant — ; mustered out June 17, 1865, at Camp Chase, O., by order of War Department; veteran.
Thomas H. Gibbs	do	20	Oct. 22, 1861	3 yrs.	Appointed Corporal March 1, 1863; Sergeant April 8, 1865; mustered out June 28, 1865, by order of War Department; veteran.
Andrew J. Pitts	do	20	Oct. 24, 1861	3 yrs.	Appointed Corporal Oct. 29, 1862; Sergeant Nov. 1, 1864; mustered out June 28, 1865, by order of War Department; veteran.
Raymond Williams	do	26	Feb. 19, 1864	3 yrs.	Appointed Corporal Nov. 1, 1864; Sergeant May 2, 1865; mustered out June 28, 1865, by order of War Department; veteran.

Names.	Rank.	Age.	Date of Entering the Service.	Period of Service.	Remarks.
Miles W. Davis	Corporal	30	Nov. 9, 1861	3 yrs.	Appointed Corporal ——; discharged Nov. 16, 1862, at Columbus, O., for wounds received Aug. 9, 1862, in battle of Cedar Mountain, Virginia.
Abe Heflebower	do	21	Oct. 4, 1861	3 yrs.	Appointed Corporal ——; discharged Oct. 9, 1862, at Washington, D. C., on Surgeon's certificate of disability.
William Hulsizer	do	17	Nov. 22, 1861	3 yrs.	Appointed Corporal Nov. 1, 1864; mustered out June 28, 1865, by order of War Department; veteran.
Edward Lemon	do	21	Dec. 4, 1861	3 yrs.	Appointed Corporal ——; discharged March 20, 1863, on Surgeon's certificate of disability.
Darius Pike	do	18	Aug. 31, 1862	3 yrs.	Appointed Corporal ——; mustered out June 3, 1865, near Bladensburg, Md., by order of War Department.
John W. Russel	do	22	Oct. 28, 1861	3 yrs.	Appointed Corporal ——; discharged Aug. 26, 1863, on Surgeon's certificate of disability.
Samuel W. Taylor	do	21	Sept. 15, 1862	3 yrs.	Appointed Corporal ——; mustered out June 3, 1865, near Bladensburg, Md., by order of War Department.
John R. Wilson	do	18	Oct. 4, 1861	3 yrs.	Appointed Corporal ——; wounded Aug. 9, 1862, in battle of Cedar Mountain, Va.; May 4, 1863, in battle of Chancellorsville, Va.; Nov. 27, 1863, in battle of Ringgold, Ga.; mustered out Dec. 31, 1864, at Columbus, O., on expiration of term of service.
Able, Hiram	Private	19	Oct. 8, 1864	1 yr.	Substitute; mustered out June 28, 1865, by order of War Department.
Archer, Elisha	do	36	Sept. 28, 1864	1 yr.	Drafted; mustered out May 29, 1865, at McDougal Hospital, New York Harbor, by order of War Department.
Archer, Vincent	do	28	Sept. 28, 1864	1 yr.	Drafted; mustered out June 3, 1865, near Bladensburg, Md., by order of War Department.
Auborn, Addison	do	32	Nov. 12, 1861	3 yrs.	Discharged July 15, 1862, on Surgeon's certificate of disability.
Baird, William W	do	31	Oct. 14, 1861	3 yrs.	Killed Nov. 27, 1863, in battle of Ringgold, Georgia.
Bair, Frank	do	18	Nov. 3, 1861	3 yrs.	Mustered out July 12, 1865, to date Dec. 22, 1864, near Louisville, Ky., on expiration of term of service.
Baldwin, William	do	26	Nov. 5, 1861	3 yrs.	Promoted to 2d Lieutenant Co. D, 26th O. V. I., Dec. 23, 1861.
Barger, Joseph M	do	25	Oct. 10, 1861	3 yrs.	Discharged Nov. 5, 1864, at Columbus, O., on Surgeon's certificate of disability.
Barger, Samuel J	do	23	Oct. 4, 1861	3 yrs.	Discharged Feb. 17, 1863, for wounds received Aug. 9, 1862, in battle of Cedar Mountain, Virginia.
Barger, Philander K	do	26	Oct. 21, 1861	3 yrs.	Discharged Jan. 28, 1863, at Philadelphia, Pa., on Surgeon's certificate of disability.
Bartlett, E. B	do	20	Mch. 28, 1862	3 yrs.	Died Dec. 26, 1862, in hospital at Harper's Ferry, Va.
Blaylock, James	do	29	Nov. 9, 1861	3 yrs.	Discharged Dec. 21, 1864, at Marion Hospital, Cincinnati, O., on Surgeon's certificate of disability.
Boon, Daniel	do	22	Oct. 5, 1861	3 yrs.	
Brand, William A	do	24	Oct. 28, 1861	3 yrs.	Promoted to Q. M. Sergeant Dec. 8, 1863.
Brandon, James	do	19	Nov. 14, 1861	3 yrs.	Mustered in as John O. Branden; mustered out to date Dec. 22, 1864, near Louisville, Ky., on expiration of term of service.
Briggs, Samuel B	do	34	Nov. 1, 1861	3 yrs.	Discharged Jan. 7, 1863, at Georgetown, D. C., on Surgeon's certificate of disability.
Butler, William L	do	18	Jan. 2, 1862	3 yrs.	Killed May 3, 1863, in battle of Chancellorsville, Va.
Carothers, Thomas	do	18	Oct. 13, 1864	1 yr.	Substitute; mustered out June 28, 1865, by order of War Department.
Cawood, James B	do	21	Oct. 25, 1861	3 yrs.	Discharged July 3, 1862, at Columbus, O., for wounds received Aug. 9, 1862, in battle of Cedar Mountain, Va.
Cave, Francis P	do	23	Aug. 11, 1862	3 yrs.	
Clayton, John R	do	21	Nov. 7, 1861	3 yrs.	Promoted to Q. M. Sergeant July 13, 1864; veteran.
Cole, Joseph C	do	23	April 11, 1864	3 yrs.	Mustered out June 28, 1865, by order of War Department.
Cook, William H. H	do	26	Oct. 22, 1861	3 yrs.	Killed Aug. 9, 1862, in battle of Cedar Mountain, Va.
Cox, Peter	do	38	Oct. 18, 1861	3 yrs.	Died Sept. 20, 1864, at Nashville, Tenn., of wounds received May 25, 1864, in battle of Dallas, Ga; veteran.
Crim, William	do	42	Nov. 22, 1861	3 yrs.	Transferred to Veteran Reserve Corps Aug. 8 1863.
Cronan, Jeremiah	do	30	Dec. 12, 1861	3 yrs.	Discharged Nov. 23, 1862, for wounds received Aug. 9, 1862, in battle of Cedar Mountain, Virginia.

Names.	Rank.	Age.	Date of Entering the Service.	Period of Service.	Remarks.
Crooks, Jacob...........	Private	26	Oct. 10, 1864	1 yr.	Substitute; mustered out June 28, 1865, by order of War Department.
Davis, James G............	...do....	19	Oct. 14, 1864	1 yr.	Mustered out June 28, 1865, by order of War Department.
Deuel, Lee.................	..do....	16	Nov. 6, 1861	3 yrs.	Discharged June 6, 1865, at hospital, Louisville, Ky., on Surgeon's certificate of disability; veteran.
Dier, Israel.................	...do....	23	Oct. 15, 1861	3 yrs.	Mustered out June 28, 1865, by order of War Department; veteran.
Dow, Oscar H.............	...do....	26	Oct. 22, 1861	3 yrs.	Died Sept. 8, 1862, in hospital at Alexandria, Virginia.
Dow, William D.........	...do....	23	Oct. 22, 1861	3 yrs.	Mustered out to date Dec. 22, 1864, near Louisville, Ky., on expiration of term of service.
Downs, William W.........	...do....	17	Oct. 28, 1861	3 yrs.	Mustered out to date Dec. 22, 1864, near Louisville, Ky.. on expiration of term of service.
Espy, David H.............	...do....	27	Nov. 7, 1861	3 yrs.	Died Sept. 13, 1862, in hospital at Alexandria, Virginia.
Ford, Maley...............	...do....	22	Jan. 1, 1862	3 yrs.	Discharged Jan. 11, 1863, at New York City, for wounds received Aug. 9, 1862, in battle of Cedar Mountain, Va.
Furry, William.............	...do....	30	Jan. 18, 1864	3 yrs.	Mustered out June 28, 1865, by order of War Department.
Funston, Eugene...........	...do....	19	Nov. 5, 1861	3 yrs.	Mustered out to date Dec. 22, 1864, near Louisville, Ky., on expiration of term of service.
Gessell, Jacob..............	...do....	25	Sept. 28, 1864	1 yr.	Drafted; mustered out June 3, 1865, near Bladensburg, Md., by order of War Department.
Gilla, Lewis A.............	...do....	18	Aug. 1, 1862	3 yrs.	Mustered out June 3, 1865, near Bladensburg, Md., by order of War Department.
Golden, Thomas...........	...do....	44	Aug. 1, 1862	3 yrs.	Discharged Feb. 18, 1863, at Dumfries, Va., for wounds received Aug. 9, 1862, in battle of Cedar Mountain, Va.
Hall, John C..............	...do....	19	Jan. 12, 1865	3 yrs.	Mustered out June 28, 1865, by order of War Department.
Hannah, Elijah J.........	...do....	18	Oct. 4, 1861	3 yrs.	Discharged Feb. 21, 1863, at Fort Delaware, Md., for wounds received Aug. 9, 1862, in battle of Cedar Mountain, Va.
Harris, David M..........	...do....	37	Sept. 28, 1864	1 yr.	Drafted; mustered out June 3, 1865, near Bladensburg, Md., by order of War Department.
Henager, Hiram...........	...do....	18	Oct. 10, 1864	1 yr.	Substitute; mustered out June 28, 1865, by order of War Department.
Henesy, Edward...........	...do....	40	Jan. 2, 1862	3 yrs.	Transferred to Veteran Reserve Corps Feb. 28, 1863.
Hill, Scott.................	...do....	18	Dec. 6, 1861	3 yrs.	Died Feb. 16, 1862, in hospital at Cumberland, Maryland.
Hundly, William.........	...do....	42	Oct. 23, 1861	3 yrs.	Transferred from Co. H ——; discharged July 9, 1862, at Columbus, O., for wounds received Aug. 9, 1862, in battle of Cedar Mountain, Va.
Huffman, Henry...........	...do....	21	Aug. 1, 1862	3 yrs.	Discharged Dec. 5, 1864, at Columbus, O., for wounds received Aug. 9, 1862, in battle of Cedar Mountain, Va.
Hunter, Newton P.........	...do....	18	Mch. 4, 1864	3 yrs.	Absent, sick at Nashville, Tenn.; transferred to Co. B, 8th Veteran Reserve Corps, Dec. 3, 1864.
Ingles, Abram.............	...do....	39	Aug. 11, 1862	3 yrs.	Transferred to Veteran Reserve Corps Dec. 2, 1864.
Irwin, John R.............	...do....	20	Nov. 14, 1861	3 yrs.	Killed Aug. 9, 1862, in battle of Cedar Mountain, Va.
Johnson, William M.........	...do....	21	Oct. 18, 1861	3 yrs.	Mustered out June 28, 1865, by order of War Department; veteran.
Jordan, Michael A.........	...do....	30	Aug. 28, 1862	3 yrs.	Mustered out June 14, 1865, at Columbus, O., by order of War Department.
Justine, Samuel............	...do....	18	Jan. 28, 1864	3 yrs.	Mustered out June 28, 1865, by order of War Department.
Kettle, John W.............	...do....	40	Oct. 6, 1861	3 yrs.	Died July 9, 1862, in Rebel Prison at Lynchburgh, Va.
Kiser, James A.............	...do....	20	Dec. 8, 1861	3 yrs.	Mustered in as James M. Kiger; discharged Aug. 21, 1863, for wounds received Aug. 9, 1862, in battle of Cedar Mountain, Va.
Kirkwood, Thomas J.....	...do....	22	Oct. 22, 1861	3 yrs.	Discharged Nov. 29, 1862, at Philadelphia, Pa., for wounds received Aug. 9, 1862, in battle of Cedar Mountain, Va.
Kunkle, David	...do....	21	Dec. 9, 1861	3 yrs.	Mustered out July 12, 1865, at Columbus, O., by order of War Department; veteran.
Lafallette, Isaac............	...do....	18	Oct. 12, 1864	1 yr.	Substitute; mustered out June 28, 1865, by order of War Department.
Layton, Robert.............	...do....	24	Oct. 19, 1861	3 yrs.	Killed Aug. 9, 1862, in battle of Cedar Mountain, Va.
Lemon, Cyrus B...........	...do....	16	Nov. 30, 1861	3 yrs.	On muster-in roll; no further record found.
Licklider, David E	...do....	32	Aug. 1, 1862	3 yrs.	Discharged Dec. 5, 1864, at Columbus, O., for wounds received Aug. 9, 1862, in battle of Cedar Mountain, Va.

Names.	Rank.	Age.	Date of Entering the Service.	Period of Service.	Remarks.
Lineecun, William	Private	34	Sept. 28, 1864	1 yr.	Drafted; mustered out June 3, 1865, near Bladensburg, Md., by order of War Department.
Madden, Nelson	..do....	20	Oct. 13, 1864	1 yr.	Substitute; mustered out June 28, 1865, by order of War Department.
McClaskey, John H	..do....	24	Oct. 8, 1864	1 yr.	Substitute; mustered out June 29, 1865, New York Harbor, on expiration of term of service.
McClaskey, Thomas	..do....	19	Oct. 12, 1864	1 yr.	Substitute; mustered out June 2, 1865, at David's Island, New York Harbor.
McCullough, John S	..do....	19	Oct. 13, 1864	1 yr.	Substitute; mustered out June 28, 1865, by order of War Department.
Meny, Benson	..do....	44	Oct. 13, 1864	1 yr.	Substitute; mustered out May 27, 1865, at McDougal Hospital, New York Harbor, as Benson Wary.
Moore, Henry C	..do....	18	Oct. 12, 1864	1 yr.	Substitute; mustered out June 28, 1865, by order of War Department.
Morrow, Isaac L	..do....	45	Oct. 23, 1861	3 yrs.	Discharged Jan. 30, 1862, at Camp Candy, Md., for wounds received ——, in action.
Mowser, Casper	..do....	18	Dec. 8, 1861	3 yrs.	Died Oct. 10, 1862, in hospital at Smoketown, Maryland.
Mowser, Irvin	..do....	17	Jan. 17, 1862	3 yrs.	Died Feb 25, 1862, in hospital at Cumberland, Maryland.
Murphy, James	..do....	42	Aug. 25, 1862	3 yrs.	Absent, sick; mustered out July 17, 1865, at hospital, Camp Dennison, O., by order of War Department.
Near, William A	..do....	23	Oct. 22, 1861	3 yrs.	Killed Jan. 18, 1862, on cars near Bellaire, O.
Nickels, John	..do....	19	Oct. 19, 1861	3 yrs.	Mustered out June 28, 1865, by order of War Department; veteran.
Niles, Lewellyn	..do....	23	Oct. 22, 1861	3 yrs.	Mustered out July 12, 1865, to date Dec. 22, 1864, near Louisville, Ky., on expiration of term of service.
Ove uls, Jesse	..do....	34	Aug. 11, 1862	3 yrs.	Mustered out June 3, 1865, near Bladensburg, Md., by order of War Department.
Overh , William	..do....	33	Aug. 7, 1862	3 yrs.	Mustered out June 23, 1865, at Columbus, O., by order of War Department.
Owens, i ury C	..do....	21	Oct. 24, 1861	3 yrs.	Mustered out June 28, 1865, by order of War Department; veteran.
Patton, Sa. el	..do....	29	Dec. 4, 1861	3 yrs.	Mustered out June 28, 1865, by order of War Department; veteran.
Patton, Jame S	..do....	19	Dec. 3, 1861	3 yrs.	Mustered out June 28, 1865, by order of War Department; veteran.
Perigo, Richard	..do....	40	Oct. 12, 1861	3 yrs.	Discharged March 14, 1865, at hospital, Louisville, Ky., on Surgeon's certificate of disability.
Pitman, A. M	..do....	23	July 25, 1862	3 yrs.	Killed Aug. 9, 1862, in battle of Cedar Mountain, Virginia.
Pond, Able E	..do....	27	Aug. 1, 1862	3 yrs.	Transferred to Veteran Reserve Corps Nov. 13, 1863; mustered out July 17, 1865, at Washington, D. C., by order of War Department.
Porter, Francis M	..do....	21	Nov. 14, 1861	3 yrs.	Discharged July 3, 1862, at Columbus, O., for wounds received ——, in action.
Purcell, John	..do....	21	Nov. 26, 1861	3 yrs.	Discharged June 26, 1862, at Alexandria, Va., for wounds received ——, in action.
Randolph, George	..do....	27	Nov. 12, 1861	3 yrs.	Mustered out to date Dec. 22, 1864, near Louisville, Ky., on expiration of term of service.
Riker, William J	..do....	30	Aug. 1, 1862	3 yrs.	Mustered out June 3, 1865, near Bladensburg, Md., by order of War Department.
Riker, Aaron D	..do....	31	Oct. 11, 1861	3 yrs.	Promoted to Com. Sergeant Jan. 1, 1863.
Rizer, Benjamin	..do....	31	Nov. 3, 1861	3 yrs.	Mustered in as Benjamin Rider; discharged July 1, 1862, at Columbus, O., for wounds received ——, in action.
Roth, William M	..do....	22	Nov. 14, 1861	3 yrs.	Mustered out June 28, 1865, by order of War Department; veteran.
Russell, Perry	..do....	18	Oct. 12, 1864	1 yr.	Substitute; absent; no further record found.
Scott, Nicholas D	..do....	45	Nov. 2, 1861	3 yrs.	Discharged June 26, 1862, at Alexandria, Va., for wounds received ——, in action.
Shyrigh, Michael	..do....	36	Oct. 12, 1861	3 yrs.	Discharged July 9, 1862, at Columbus, O., for wounds received ——, in action.
Slater, Samuel	..do....	20	Aug. 18, 1862	3 yrs.	Mustered out June 3, 1865, near Bladensburg, Md., by order of War Department.
Smith, Andrew R	..do....	20	Oct. 28, 1861	3 yrs.	Mustered out June 28, 1865, by order of War Department; veteran.
Smith, Josiah	..do....	22	Oct. 28, 1861	3 yrs.	On detached service at Tod Barracks, O.; mustered out July 12, 1865, by order of War Department; veteran.
Sparrow, John W	..do....	19	Dec. 3, 1861	3 yrs.	Mustered out June 28, 1865, by order of War Department; veteran.
Stevens, James W	..do....	18	Nov. 3, 1861	3 yrs.	Transferred to Veteran Reserve Corps March 2, 1864.
Stevens, Abram	..do....	20	Aug. 11, 1862	3 yrs.	Mustered out June 3, 1865, near Bladensburg, Md., by order of War Department.
Steelman, Henry B	..do....	25	Dec. 9, 1861	3 yrs.	Transferred to Veteran Reserve Corps Aug. 8, 1863.

Names.	Rank.	Age.	Date of Entering the Service.	Period of Service.	Remarks.
Swisher, John H. C......	Private	18	Oct. 15, 1861	3 yrs.	Discharged Feb. 26, 1863, at Dumfries, Va., for wounds received ——, in action.
Talley, Nathan R..........	...do....	19	Oct. 24, 1861	3 yrs.	Mustered out June 28, 1865, by order of War Department; veteran.
Taylor, Oliver P...........	...do....	19	Oct. 22, 1861	3 yrs.	Discharged July 5, 1862, at Columbus, O., for wounds received ——, in action.
Taylor, John	...do....	17	Nov. 4, 1861	3 yrs.	Mustered out June 28, 1865, by order of War Department; veteran.
Thatcher, Henry C	...do....	20	Mch. 3, 1864	3 yrs.	Mustered out June 28, 1865, by order of War Department.
Tingley, Isaac..........	...do....	21	Dec. 2, 1861	3 yrs.	Discharged July 9, 1862, at Columbus, O., for wounds received ——, in action.
Vaughn, William E	...do....	26	Sept. 12, 1864	1 yr.	Substitute; mustered out June 3, 1865, near Bladensburg, Md., by order of War Department.
Vincent, Perry D..........	...do....	20	Nov. 5, 1861	3 yrs.	Discharged April 28, 1862, at Strasburg, Va., for wounds received ——, in action.
Wallace, George C.........	...do....	19	Oct. 4, 1861	3 yrs.	Died July 15, 1862, in hospital at Alexandria, Virginia.
Warren, Floyd	...do....	19	Sept. 13, 1864	1 yr.	Substitute; mustered out June 3, 1865, near Bladensburg, Md., by order of War Department.
Whitley, John...........	...do....	27	Jan. 20, 1864	3 yrs.	Killed June 16, 1864, in action at Pine Mountain, Ga.
Wilson, John T..........	...do....	25	Oct. 20, 1861	3 yrs.	Mustered out June 28, 1865, by order of War Department; veteran.
Willis, John M..........	...do....	25	Sept. 28, 1864	1 yr.	Drafted; mustered out June 3, 1865, near Bladensburg, Md., by order of War Department.
Yohn, Isaac	...do....	23	Jan. 1, 1862	3 yrs.	Mustered out Jan. 5, 1865, on expiration of term of service.

COMPANY H.

Mustered in Dec. 22, 1861, at Camp McArthur, Urbana, O., by William McAdams, William Hamilton and Jonas Drury, 2d Lieutenants 66th O. V. I. Mustered out July 15, 1865, near Louisville, Ky., by Edward A. Wickes, Captain 150th New York Volunteers, and A. C. M. 14th Army Corps.

Names.	Rank.	Age.	Date of Entering the Service.	Period of Service.	Remarks.
William McAdams......	Captain	47	Oct. 3, 1861	3 yrs.	Appointed Dec. 17, 1861; resigned April 11, 1863.
William McLean Gwynne	....do....	21	Sept. 5, 1861	3 yrs.	Transferred from Co. B May 19, 1863; discharged Dec. 16, 1864, by order of War Department.
T. G. Keller	...do....	28	Oct. 15, 1861	3 yrs.	Promoted to Sergt. Major from private Dec. 17, 1862; to 2d Lieutenant Feb. 19, 1863; 1st Lieutenant and Adjutant July 20, 1863; Captain Nov. 12, 1864; resigned May 30, 1865.
Henry Fraley..............	...do....	23	Nov. 5, 1861	3 yrs.	Promoted from 1st Lieutenant Co. A June 14, 1865; mustered out with company July 15, 1865; veteran.
William Hamilton.......	1st Lieut.	../.	Oct. 1, 1861	3 yrs.	Appointed Dec. 17, 1861; appointed Adjutant Nov. 12, 1862.
Harrison Davis..........	...do....	28	Oct. 2, 1861	3 yrs.	Mustered as private; appointed Sergeant ——; promoted to 2d Lieutenant Nov. 10, 1862; 1st Lieutenant Feb. 19, 1863; killed Nov. 27, 1863, in action at Taylor's Ridge, Ga.
James McIlroy............	...do....	22	Nov. 1, 1861	3 yrs.	Promoted from Sergeant Jan. 1, 1864; to Captain Co. C Nov. 12, 1864; veteran.
Robert Simpson	....do....	23	Oct. 8, 1861	3 yrs.	Appointed 1st Sergeant from Sergeant Dec. 21, 1864; promoted to 1st Lieutenant April 8, 1865; to Captain Co. A June 14, 1865; veteran.
James H. Corbin	...do....	19	Oct. 12, 1861	3 yrs.	Promoted from 1st Sergeant Co. K June 14, 1865; mustered out with company July 15, 1865; veteran
Monroe Elliott	2d Lieut.	20	Oct. 16, 1861	3 yrs.	Appointed Dec. 21, 1861; resigned Nov. 27, 1862, at Falmouth. Va.
John A. Gunn..........	1st Sergt.	31	Dec. 27, 1861	3 yrs.	Mustered as private; appointed Sergeant ——; discharged June 15, 1863, at Baltimore, Md., on Surgeon's certificate of disability.
William W. Jackson.....	:...do....	21	Aug. 7, 1862	3 yrs.	Appointed from private Jan. 1, 1863; promoted to 1st Lieutenant Co. B Nov. 12, 1864.
Orra Fairchilds..........	...do....	28	Nov. 1, 1831	3 yrs.	Mustered as private; appointed 1st Sergeant ——; promoted to 2d Lieutenant July 13, 1865, but not mustered out with company July 15, 1865; veteran.
Samuel Kenedy..........	Sergeant	23	Oct. 7, 1861	3 yrs.	

Names.	Rank.	Age.	Date of Entering the Service.	Period of Service.	Remarks.
Ross Colvell............	Sergeant	28	Oct. 2, 1861	3 yrs.	Mustered as private; appointed Sergeant ——; died Nov. 17, 1862, in hospital at Harper's Ferry, Va.
George W. Poling.........	....do....	24	Oct. 1, 1861	3 yrs.	Appointed Corporal April 25, 1862; Sergeant March —, 1863; promoted to 2d Lieutenant Co.G, 181st O. V. I., Sept. 7, 1864; veteran.
Jesse W. Good.............	....do....	23	Nov. 12, 1861	3 yrs.	Mustered as private; appointed Sergeant ——; mustered out with company July 15, 1865; veteran.
William Herron...........	....do....	38	Oct. 4, 1861	3 yrs.	Mustered as private; appointed Sergeant ——; mustered out with company July 15, 1865; veteran.
Samuel R. Smith........	....do....	24	Oct. 19, 1861	3 yrs.	Mustered as private; appointed Sergeant ——; mustered out with company July 15, 1865; veteran.
Orvill Stokes...............	....do....	21	Oct. 8, 1861	3 yrs.	Mustered as private; appointed Sergeant ——; promoted to 2d Lieutenant July 13, 1865, but not mustered; mustered out with company July 15, 1865; veteran.
William Apple..........	Corporal	18	Oct. 26, 1861	3 yrs.	Appointed Corporal ——; transferred to Veteran Reserve Corps June 21, 1865; veteran.
George B. Black..........	....do....	18	July 28, 1862	3 yrs.	Appointed Corporal May 14, 1865; mustered out June 3, 1865, near Bladensburg, Md., by order of War Department.
William Daily.............	....do....	31	Oct. 15, 1861	3 yrs.	Appointed Corporal ——; mustered out with company July 15, 1865; veteran.
Oliver P. Devore.........	....do....	18	Oct. 8, 1861	3 yrs.	Appointed Corporal ——; died Aug. —, 1862, at Alexandria, Va.
Thomas Good..	....do....	31	Oct. 24, 1861	3 yrs.	Appointed Corporal ——; discharged June 27, 1863, at Baltimore, Md., on Surgeon's certificate of disability.
Daniel W. Harris.........	....do....	18	Nov. 12, 1861	3 yrs.	Appointed Corporal ——; mustered out July 12, 1865, to date Dec. 22, 1864, near Louisville, Ky., on expiration of term of service.
John Hollingsworth........	....do....	18	Oct. 9, 1861	3 yrs.	Appointed Corporal ——; mustered out with company July 15, 1865; veteran.
Jacob Hudson..............	....do....	18	Dec. 1, 1861	3 yrs.	Appointed Corporal ——; killed Aug. 9, 1862, in battle of Cedar Mountain, Va.
Martin V. B. Kearns........	....do....	18	Nov. 27, 1861	3 yrs.	Mustered in as Martin C. Kearns; appointed Corporal ——; mustered out with company July 15, 1865; veteran.
John D. Kenedy............	....do....	25	Oct. 8, 1861	3 yrs.	
William H. Lease..........	....do....	18	Aug. 14, 1862	3 yrs.	Appointed Corporal ——; mustered out June 3, 1865, near Bladensburg, Md., by order of War Department.
Conrad B. Lepart	....do....	44	Oct. 15, 1861	3 yrs.	Appointed Corporal ——; discharged Sept. 24, 1862, on Surgeon's certificate of disability.
Daniel Poling..............	....do....	20	Dec. 10, 1861	3 yrs.	Appointed Corporal ——; mustered out with company July 15, 1865; veteran.
Isaac Robinson............	....do....	21	Oct. 9, 1861	3 yrs.	Appointed Corporal ——; mustered out with company July 15, 1865; veteran.
Townsend Walker	....do....	28	Oct. 23, 1861	3 yrs.	Appointed Corporal ——; discharged Oct. 11, 1862, at Lewisburg, O., on Surgeon's certificate of disability.
Apple, Harrison.........	Private	42	Aug. 5, 1862	3 yrs.	Mustered out July 10, 1865, at Louisville, Ky., by order of War Department.
Avery, William H	....do....	24	Sept. 29, 1864	1 yr.	Drafted; died June 19, 1865, in hospital at Jeffersonville, Ind.
Bastel, Martin	....do....	23	Oct. 15, 1861	3 yrs.	
Belty, William	....do....	20	Oct. 20, 1861	3 yrs.	Mustered in as William Bettz; died June 30, 1862, at Alexandria, Va.
Black, George............	....do....	18	Nov. 2, 1861	3 yrs.	
Blake, Byron............	....do....	18	Oct. 28, 1861	3 yrs.	Absent, sick; no further record found.
Bolman, Solomon........	....do....	21	Sept. 29, 1864	1 yr.	Drafted; died Nov. —, 1864, on the march from Atlanta to Savannah, Ga.
Bredlove, Thomas H......	....do....	26	July. 16, 1862	3 yrs.	Mustered out June 3, 1865, near Bladensburg, Md., by order of War Department.
Brolier, William..........	....do....	28	Sept. 29, 1864	1 yr.	Drafted; died Sept. 2, 1865, at Savannah, Ga.
Buckhart, William........	....do....	35	Sept. 29, 1864	1 yr.	Drafted; mustered out June 3 1865, near Bladensburg, Md., by order of War Department.
Callender, Elisha S.........	....do....	18	Oct. 22, 1861	3 yrs.	Mustered out to date Dec. 22, 1864, near Louisville, Ky., on expiration of term of service.
Campbell, George W........	....do....	18	Oct. 19, 1861	3 yrs.	Mustered out with company July 15, 1865; veteran.
Campbell, William	....do....	23	Aug. 5, 1862	3 yrs.	Died Dec. 24, 1862, in hospital at Philadelphia, Pennsylvania.
Campbell, Arthur....'......	....do....	20	Aug. 1, 1862	3 yrs.	Mustered out June 15, 1865, at Columbus, O., by order of War Department.
Carter, James H..........	....do....	29	Oct. 4, 1861	3 yrs.	Mustered out to date Dec. 22, 1864, near Louisville, Ky., on expiration of term of service.
Chatfield, John..............	....do....	20	Nov. 16, 1861	3 yrs.	Died March 22, 1862, in hospital at Martinsburg, Va.

Names.	Rank.	Age.	Date of Entering the Service.	Period of Service.	Remarks.
Click, Michael............	Private	20	Sept. 23, 1864	1 yr	Drafted; mustered out June 3, 1865, near Bladensburg, Md., by order of War Department.
Colvell, William V.......	...do....	35	Nov. 13, 1861	3 yrs.	Died April 8, 1862, at Urbana, O.
Cooksey, tJohn............	...do....	25	Jan. 14, 1864	3 yrs.	Mustered out with company July 15, 1865.
Curtis, Isaiah...........	...do....	27	Jan. 22, 1864	3 yrs.	Mustered out with company July 15, 1865.
Cushman, George W.....	...do....	36	Sept. 13, 1862	3 yrs.	Died May 12, 1864, at Nashville, Tenn.
Darling, Charles W......	...do....	21	Aug. 7, 1862	3 yrs.	Mustered out June 3, 1865, near Bladensburg, Md., by order of War Department.
Davis, William L........	...do....	18	Oct. 16, 1861	3 yrs.	Died April 12, 1862 in hospital at Winchester, Virginia.
Devore, Rollin J........	...do....	18	Aug. 1, 1862	3 yrs.	Mustered out June 15, 1865, at Columbus, O., by order of War Department.
Deroine, Nelsie.........	...do....	18	Feb. 2, 1864	3 yrs.	Also borne on rolls as Nelson Derwin; died July 3, 1865, at Tripler Hospital, Columbus, Ohio.
Eaten, Daniel............	...do....	19	Aug. 7, 1862	3 yrs.	Killed Nov. 27, 1863, at Taylor's Ridge, Ga.
Eccles, Thomas G........	...do....	36	Oct. 2, 1861	3 yrs.	Died Aug. 27, 1864, in U. S. Hospital at Nashville, Tenn.
Eichenbarger, David....	...do....	31	Oct. 8, 1861	3 yrs.	Discharged April 24, 1862, on Surgeon's certificate of disability.
Engle, Samuel...........	...do....	19	Jan. 17, 1862	3 yrs.	
Evans, William E.......	...do....	35	Aug. 15, 1862	3 yrs.	Mustered out June 3, 1865, near Bladensburg, Md., by order of War Department.
Faulkner, Norton........	...do....	26	Oct. 2, 1861	3 yrs.	Transferred to Veteran Reserve Corps ——, at Cleveland, O.
Faust, Joseph...........	...do....	20	Sept. 26, 1864	1 yr.	Drafted; mustered out June 3, 1865, near Bladensburg, Md., by order of War Department.
Faulkner, William H....	...do....	21	Oct. 19, 1861	3 yrs.	Discharged Jan. 14, 1863, at New York City, on Surgeon's certificate of disability.
Foley, John.............	...do....	35	Dec. 11, 1861	3 yrs.	Never mustered into service.
Foster, James S........	...do....	50	Oct. 6, 1861	3 yrs.	Discharged Nov. 27, 1862, at Washington, D. C., on Surgeon's certificate of disability.
Gleason, William........	...do....	25	Nov. 12, 1861	3 yrs.	
Glendening, John........	...do....	18	July 1, 1862	3 yrs.	Mustered out with company July 15, 1865; veteran.
Glick, David............	...do....	30	Sept. 29, 1864	1 yr.	Drafted; discharged June 3, 1865, at McDougal Hospital, New York Harbor, on Surgeon's certificate of disability.
Gilbert, George.........	...do....	18	Oct. 20, 1861	3 yrs.	Discharged June 26, 1862, at Columbus, O., on Surgeon's certificate of disability.
Green, George W. C.....	...do....	18	Jan. 4, 1864	3 yrs.	Mustered out July 13, 1865, at Washington, D. C., by order of War Department.
Grubbs, William J......	...do....	18	Mch. 15, 1864	3 yrs.	Mustered out with company July 15, 1865.
Grubbs, William S......	...do....	18	April 13, 1864	3 yrs.	Discharged June 13, 1865, at David's Island, New York Harbor, on Surgeon's certificate of disability.
Gunn, William A........	...do....	23	Oct. 8, 1861	3 yrs.	Mustered out July 12, 1865, to date Dec. 22, 1864, near Louisville, Ky., on expiration of term of service.
Guy, Levi C............	...do....	40	Sept. 29, 1864	1 yr.	Drafted; absent, sick; mustered out June 5, 1865, at New York City, by order of War Department.
Hamar, John............	...do....	18	Jan. 27, 1864	3 yrs.	Mustered out with company July 15, 1865.
Harris, Jobe............	...do....	27	Sept. 29, 1864	1 yr.	Drafted; mustered out June 3, 1865, near Bladensburg, Md.; by order of War Department.
Hemminger, Andrew.....	...do....	45	Jan. 14, 1862	3 yrs.	
Hollingsworth, Charles...	...do....	21	Aug. 12, 1862	3 yrs.	Mustered out June 23, 1865, at Columbus, O., by order of War Department.
Hunter, William O......	...do. .	45	Oct. 4, 1861	3 yrs.	Died April 11, 1862, in hospital at Martinsburg, Va.
Hundley, William........	...do....	42	Oct. 23, 1861	3 yrs.	Transferred to Co. G ——.
Jackson, Charles L......	...do....	18	Oct. 18, 1861	3 yrs.	Mustered out with company July 15, 1865; veteran.
Jacobs, Frank M	...do....	18	Aug. 7, 1862	3 yrs.	Discharged Feb. 18, 1863, at Dumfries, Va., on Surgeon's certificate of disability.
Johnson, Ira C..........	...do....	18	Feb. 1, 1864	3 yrs.	Mustered out with company July 15, 1865.
Keimes, David	...do....	18	May 4, 1864	3 yrs.	Mustered out May 29, 1865, at New York City, by order of War Department.
Keimes, Albert..........	...do....	18	Jan. 4, 1864	3 yrs.	Mustered out May 29, 1865, at New York City, by order of War Department.
Kernes, Joseph..........	...do....	52	Dec. 27, 1861	3 yrs.	Discharged Feb. 18, 1863, at Dumfries, Va., on Surgeon's certificate of disability.
King, Lester............	...do....	28	Jan. 25, 1864	3 yrs.	Mustered out with company July 15, 1865.
King, Sylvester.........	...do....	30	Jan. 25, 1864	3 yrs.	
Kimber, Enoch G........	...do....	33	Oct. 5, 1861	3 yrs.	Discharged Oct. 12, 1862, near Sandy Hook, Md., by order of War Department.
Lecampt, Charles H	...do....	42	Oct. 14, 1861	3 yrs.	Transferred to Veteran Reserve Corps ——, at Louisville, Ky.
Lilly, Armiger B........	...do....	20	Oct. 8, 1861	3 yrs.	Discharged July 29, 1863, at Baltimore, Md., on Surgeon's certificate of disability.
Limes, Wesley..........	...do....	32	Aug. 5, 1862	3 yrs.	Mustered out June 3, 1865, near Bladensburg, Md., by order of War Department.
Malia, Martin..........	...do....	20	Oct. 9, 1861	3 yrs.	Discharged July 20, 1862, by civil authority.

Names.	Rank.	Age.	Date of Entering the Service.	Period of Service.	Remarks.
Martin, John B.........	Private	24	Oct. 8, 1861	3 yrs.	Discharged June 30, 1863, at Baltimore, Md., on Surgeon's certificate of disability.
Martin, David.............	...do....	25	Dec. 11, 1861	3 yrs.	Never mustered into service.
Marks, Jonah S...........	...do....	19	Oct. 25, 1861	3 yrs.	Mustered out with company July 15, 1865; veteran.
Marks, James E............	...do....	24	Aug. 28, 1862	3 yrs.	Mustered out June 3, 1865, near Bladensburg, Md., by order of War Department.
Marks, Isaac..............	...do....	22	Aug. 28, 1862	3 yrs.	Mustered out June 3, 1865, near Bladensburg, Md., by order of War Department.
March, Samuel............	...do....	49	Oct. 16, 1861	3 yrs.	
Mattox, James............	...do....	19	Nov. 11, 1861	3 yrs.	Mustered out with company July 15, 1865; veteran.
McClish, John............	...do....	35	Sept. 29, 1864	1 yr.	Drafted; mustered out June 3, 1865, near Bladensburg, Md., by order of War Department.
McIlroy, John M.........	...do....	18	Aug. 12, 1862	3 yrs.	Mustered out May 17, 1865, at Camp Dennison, O., by order of War Department; veteran.
McMullen, William.......	...do....	23	Oct. 19, 1861	3 yrs.	Discharged June 15, 1863, at Fortress Monroe, Va., on Surgeon's certificate of disability.
Meeks, Zacharias	...do....	19	Jan. 14, 1862	3 yrs.	Died Nov. 12, 1862, in hospital at Harper's Ferry, Va.
Middleton, John C.........	...do....	31	Oct. 15, 1861	3 yrs.	Promoted to Com. Sergeant June 6, 1865; veteran.
More, Abraham	...do....	18	Oct. 10, 1864	1 yr.	Substitute; mustered out with company July 15, 1865.
Morgan, John W..........	...do....	18	Jan. 28, 1862	3 yrs.	Mustered out to date April 3, 1865, on expiration of term of service.
Murry, Joseph W	...do....	26	Aug. 18, 1862	3 yrs.	Transferred to Veteran Reserve Corps ——, at Point Lookout, Md.
Myers, David..............	...do....	35	Sept. 29, 1864	1 yr.	Drafted; mustered out June 3, 1865, near Bladensburg, Md., by order of War Department.
Overfield, John............	...do....	25	Dec. 1, 1861	3 yrs.	Mustered out with company July 15, 1865; veteran.
Paden, Ross..............	...do....	25	Oct. 7, 1861	3 yrs.	Discharged April 24, 1862, on Surgeon's certificate of disability.
Paden, James E	...do....	22	Dec. 19, 1861	3 yrs.	Discharged Nov. 23, 1862, on Surgeon's certificate of disability.
Pence, Andrew	...do....	20	Sept. 29, 1864	1 yr.	Drafted; mustered out June 3, 1865, near Bladensburg, Md., by order of War Department.
Petee, John................	...do....	20	Sept. 29, 1864	1 yr.	Drafted; mustered out June 3, 1865, near Bladensburg, Md., by order of War Department.
Poling, Ruben..............	...do....	20	Jan. 17, 1862	3 yrs.	Mustered out to date April 3, 1865, on expiration of term of service.
Renyolds, Hugh...........	...do....	28	Jan. 25, 1864	3 yrs.	Died June 24, 1864, at Chattanooga, Tenn.
Reames, Abraham........	...do....	22	Aug. 7, 1862	3 yrs.	Mustered out June 3, 1865, near Bladensburg, Md., by order of War Department.
Reames, Isaac..............	...do....	22	Aug. 7, 1862	3 yrs.	Mustered out June 3, 1865, near Bladensburg, Md., by order of War Department.
Reames, Caleb B............	...do....	20	Dec. 12, 1861	3 yrs.	Killed June 10, 1862, accidentally at Furrow's Furnace, Va.
Ruhl, John S	...do....	18	Oct. 14, 1864	1 yr.	Substitute; mustered out with company July 15, 1865.
Saygrover, George..........	...do....	18	Oct. 19, 1861	3 yrs.	Mustered out to date Dec. 22, 1864, near Louisville, Ky., on expiration of term of service.
Sembler, Peter........	...do....	35	Sept. 26, 1864	1 yr.	Drafted; mustered out July 6, 1865, at Columbus, O., by order of War Department.
Seitze, Phileman..........	...do....	40	Sept. 29, 1864	1 yr.	Drafted; mustered out June 3, 1865, near Bladensburg, Md., by order of War Department.
Shinamon, David..........	...do....	23	Oct. 14, 1861	3 yrs.	Died ——, in hospital at Cumberland, Md.
Smith, Julius D..........	...do....	18	Nov. 1, 1861	3 yrs.	
Smith, George W..........	...do....	22	Oct. 8, 1861	3 yrs.	Died Feb. 2, 1862, at Camp Candy, Md.
Spain, Leroy..............	...do....	20	Oct. 14, 1861	3 yrs.	Discharged June 26, 1862, at Columbus, O., on Surgeon's certificate of disability.
Spain, Emory.............	...do....	18	Nov. 12, 1861	3 yrs.	Discharged Feb. 21, 1863, at Baltimore, Md., on Surgeon's certificate of disability.
Spain, Newton S...........	...do....	38	Aug. 13, 1862	3 yrs.	Mustered out Aug. 23, 1865, at hospital, Alexandria, Va., by order of War Department.
Steiner, Calvin W..........	...do....	22	Nov. 11, 1861	3 yrs.	Discharged April 24, 1862, on Surgeon's certificate of disability.
Sweet, James C............	...do....	26	Dec. 17, 1861	3 yrs.	
Talbott, John H...........	...do....	37	Oct. 5, 1861	3 yrs.	Discharged March 16, 1862, by order of War Department.
Thomas, William J.........	...do....	19	Dec. 12, 1861	3 yrs.	Killed June 9, 1862, in battle of Port Republic, Virginia.
Thompson, Samuel........	...do....	27	Aug. 5, 1862	3 yrs.	Mustered out June 3, 1865; near Bladensburg, Md., by order of War Department.
Tonra, William............	...do....	28	Oct. 17, 1861	3 yrs.	Died June 21, 1864, of wounds received same day in action at Kenesaw Mountain, Ga.; veteran.
Trimble, William..........	...do ..	18	Oct. 14, 1861	3 yrs.	Killed June 9, 1862, in battle of Port Republic, Va.

Names.	Rank.	Age	Date of Entering the Service.	Period of Service.	Remarks.
Ward, Cornelius.........	Private	20	Dec. 2, 1861	3 yrs.	Killed June 9, 1862, in battle of Port Republic, Va.
Waitmon, Willie.........	...do....	18	Jan. 28, 1862	3 yrs.	Mustered out Feb. 15, 1865, at Columbus, O., on expiration of term of service.
Weld, Andrew............	...do....	28	Sept. 29, 1864	1 yr.	Drafted; died Jan. 20, 1865, at Savannah, Ga.
Wheeler, Leven D.......	...do....	18	Sept. 29, 1864	1 yr.	Drafted; mustered out June 3, 1865, near Bladensburg, Md.
Wilson, William.........	...do....	18	Nov. 21, 1861	3 yrs.	Killed June 9, 1862, in battle of Port Republic, Va.
Wilson, Matthew.........	...do....	23	Dec. 4, 1861	3 yrs.	Killed June 27, 1864, in battle of Kenesaw Mountain, Ga.; veteran.
Wilson, John.............	...do....	23	Nov. 26, 1861	3 yrs.	Discharged Nov. 14, 1862, at Annapolis, Md., on Surgeon's certificate of disability.
Wilson, Isaac.............	...do....	21	Dec. 1, 1861	3 yrs.	Never mustered into service.
Wilson, Joshua..........	...do....	18	Dec. 8, 1861	3 yrs.	
Wilson, Joshua D.......	...do....	18	July 26, 1862	3 yrs.	Discharged Feb. 28, 1863, at hospital, Philadelphia, Pa.,'on Surgeon's certificate of disability.
Williams, Milton H.,....	...do....	18	Dec. 11, 1861	3 yrs.	Mustered out with company July 15, 1865; veteran.
Williams, Octavo........	...do....	22	Dec. 12, 1861	3 yrs.	Never mustered into service.
Yetter, Christian........	...do....	35	Sept. 29, 1864	1 yr.	Drafted; mustered out July 7, 1865, at Tripler Hospital, Columbus, O., by order of War Department.

COMPANY I.

Mustered in Dec. 23, 1861, at Camp McArthur, Urbana, O., by Vesalius Horr and Andrew H. Yeazel, 2d Lieutenants 66th O. V. I. Mustered out July 15, 1865, near Louisville, Ky., by Edward A. Wickes, Captain 150th New York Volunteers, and A. C. M. 14th Army Corps.

Names.	Rank.	Age	Date of Entering the Service.	Period of Service.	Remarks.
Vesalius Horr...........	Captain	37	Oct. 2, 1861	3 yrs.	Appointed Dec. 17, 1861; discharged Oct. 27, 1862, on Surgeon's certificate of disability.
Andrew H. Yeazel........	...do....	22	Nov. 11, 1861	3 yrs.	Appointed 1st Lieutenant Dec. 17, 1861; promoted to Captain Nov. 1, 1862; discharged May 27, 1863, on Surgeon's certificate of disability.
John T. Morgan..........	...do....	19	Oct. 27, 1861	3 yrs.	Appointed Corporal ——; promoted to 1st Lieutenant Nov. 1, 1862; Captain July 20, 1863; discharged July 23, 1864, on Surgeon's certificate of disability.
John T. Mitchell........	...do....	18	Oct. 9, 1861	3 yrs.	Transferred from Co. A Sept. 17, 1864; promoted to Major April 8, 1865.
Ridgely Wilkins.........	...do....	24	Oct. 3, 1861	3 yrs.	Promoted from 1st Lieutenant Co. B June 14, 1865; mustered out with company July 15, 1865; veteran.
John R. Organ...........	1st Lieut.	18	Oct. 14, 1861	3 yrs.	Promoted to 2d Lieutenant from Sergeant Co. A Jan. 27, 1863; to 1st Lieutenant Jan. 1, 1864; killed July 20, 1864, in battle of Peach Tree Creek, Ga.; veteran.
W. Wallace Cranston......	,do....	22	Oct. 10, 1861	3 yrs.	Promoted to 2d Lieutenant from Sergt. Major July 13, 1864; 1st Lieutenant Aug. 11, 1864; to Captain Co. G April 12, 1865; veteran.
Frank Baldwin...........	...do....	20	Oct. 15, 1861	3 yrs.	Promoted from 1st Sergeant Co. G April 12, 1865; mustered out with company July 15, 1865; veteran.
Abram L. Shepherd......	2d Lieut.	32	Oct. 22, 1861	3 yrs.	Appointed Dec. 17, 1861; resigned Jan. 9, 1863.
Henry Swisher............	...do....	28	Oct. 22, 1861	3 yrs.	Mustered as private; promoted to 2d Lieutenant Nov. 1, 1862; discharged May 22, 1863, on Surgeon's certificate of disability.
Stephen Baxter.........	1st Sergt.	45	Nov. 25, 1861	3 yrs.	Mustered as private; appointed 1st Sergeant ——; killed June 9, 1862, in battle of Port Republic, Va.
James P. Conn...........	...do....	19	Oct. 18, 1861	3 yrs.	Appointed 1st Sergeant from Sergeant March 4, 1862; promoted to 2d Lieutenant Co. B May 27, 1863; veteran.
Daniel D. Davidson.....	...do.,..	31	Nov. 7, 1861	3 yrs.	Appointed Sergeant from Corporal May 1, 1862; 1st Sergeant May 1, 1864; promoted to 1st Lieutenant Co. G May 31, 1865; veteran.
James W. Burns..........	...do....	19	Nov. 13, 1861	3 yrs.	Appointed Corporal Dec. 16, 1865; Sergeant May 1, 1865; 1st Sergeant July 1, 1865; mustered out with company July 15, 1865; veteran.
Henry Ames.............	Sergeant	21	Dec. 6, 1861	3 yrs.	Mustered as private; appointed Sergeant ——; died June 21, 1864, at Chattanooga, Tenn., of wounds received June 16, 1864, in action near Kenesaw Mountain, Ga.; veteran.

Names.	Rank.	Age.	Date of Entering the Service.	Period of Service.	Remarks.
Samuel J. Croxton.......	Sergeant	25	Oct. 8, 1861	3 yrs.	Mustered as private; appointed Sergeant May 1, 1863; appointed 1st Sergeant Co. C Sept. 1, 1864; veteran.
William W. McCorkle...	...do....	24	Nov. 12, 1861	3 yrs.	Appointed Corporal Dec. 1, 1862; Sergeant Oct. 30, 1864; promoted to 2d Lieutenant July 13, 1865, but not mustered; mustered out with company July 15, 1865; veteran.
James W. Hoyt............	...do....	18	Nov. 16, 1861	3 yrs.	Mustered as private; appointed Sergeant Dec. 18, 1864; mustered out July 7, 1865, at Camp Dennison, O., by order of War Department; veteran.
Aaron Owens.............	...do....	29	Jan. 30, 1864	3 yrs.	Appointed Corporal Aug. 31, 1864; Sergeant May 1, 1865; mustered out with company July 15, 1865; veteran.
John Tucker.............	...do....	25	Oct. 8, 1861	3 yrs.	Mustered as private; appointed Sergeant —; mustered out Dec. 12, 1865, at Columbus, O., by order of War Department.
Marcus W. Cilley.. ...	Corporal	22	Oct. 15, 1861	3 yrs.	Appointed Corporal —; died Sept. 6, 1862, at Alexandria, Va., of wounds received —,;in action.
Joseph Coffey......	...do....	23	Oct. 14, 1861	3 yrs.	Appointed Corporal —; mustered out July 12, 1865, to date Dec. 22, 1864, near Louisville, Ky., on expiration of term of service.
Thomas E. Berry..........	...do....	26	Aug. 12, 1862	3 yrs.	Appointed Corporal —; mustered out June 5, 1865, near Bladensburg, Md., by order of War Department.
Robert Dook.............	...do....	25	Oct. 8, 1861	3 yrs.	Appointed Corporal —; mustered out to date Dec. 22, 1864, near Louisville, Ky., on expiration of term of service.
Daniel M. Hendrix.......	...do....	20	Oct. 8, 1861	3 yrs.	Appointed Corporal May 1, 1863; mustered out with company July 15, 1865; veteran.
Wilton Hutchinson.......	...do....	18	Oct. 10, 1861	3 yrs.	Appointed Corporal Aug. 31, 1864; mustered out with company July 15, 1865; veteran.
Samuel McClimans.......	...do....	21	Jan. 5, 1863	3 yrs.	Appointed Corporal May 1, 1865; mustered out with company July 15, 1865.
George Milledge..........	...do....	20	Oct. 15, 1861	3 yrs.	Appointed Corporal —; killed May 27, 1864, in action at Dallas, Ga.; veteran.
James Riddle.............	...do....	25	Aug. 1, 1862	3 yrs.	Appointed Corporal —; mustered out June 5, 1865, near Bladensburg, Md., by order of War Department.
George R. Taylor..........	...do....	22	Aug. 16, 1862	3 yrs.	Appointed Corporal —; mustered out June 5, 1865, near Bladensburg, Md., by order of War Department.
Arkalon Turney.*........	...do....	21	Oct. 13, 1861	3 yrs.	Appointed Corporal —; discharged July 23, 1862, at Columbus, O., on Surgeon's certificate of disability.
Levi Tyler...............	...do....	18	Dec. 15, 1861	3 yrs.	Appointed Corporal May 1, 1865; mustered out with company July 15, 1865; veteran.
William Saxbe...........	...do....	22	Oct. 14, 1861	3 yrs.	Appointed Corporal —; discharged Aug. 12, 1862, at Washington, D. C., on Surgeon's certificate of disability.
Adcock, Samuel.........	Private	20	Oct. 12, 1864	1 yr.	Substitute; mustered out with company July 15, 1865.
Apt, John F..............	...do....	25	Nov. 27, 1861	3 yrs.	
Baker, William..........	...do....	26	Oct. 25, 1861	3 yrs.	Mustered out with company July 15, 1865; veteran.
Barnes, William..........	...do....	19	Oct. 14, 1861	3 yrs.	Discharged May 23, 1862, at Winchester, Va., on Surgeon's certificate of disability.
Baxter, William H.......	...do....	19	Aug. 5, 1862	3 yrs.	Discharged March 11, 1864, at Caperton Ferry Ala., by order of War Department.
Baxter, Edward W.......	...do....	25	Aug. 3, 1862	3 yrs.	Mustered out June 5, 1865, near Bladensburg, Md., by order of War Department.
Black, William	...do....	20	Oct. 14, 1864	1 yr.	Substitute; died Jan. —, 1865, in hospital at Savannah, Ga.
Born, Jacob..............	...do....	31	Sept. 24, 1864	1 yr.	Drafted; mustered out June 17, 1865, at Washington, D. C., by order of War Department.
Boulton, James..........	...do....	21	Oct. 26, 1861	3 yrs.	Died Aug. 9, 1862, at Alexandria, Va.
Bowen, Webster.........	...do....	21	Oct. 14, 1861	3 yrs.	Discharged Sept. 23, 1862, at Washington, D. C., on Surgeon's certificate of disability.
Braun, John..............	...do....	45	Nov. 25, 1861	3 yrs.	Died May 15, 1862, at Martinsburg, Va.
Brittin, Wilson...........	...do....	21	Oct. 25, 1861	3 yrs.	Died Oct. 22, 1862, at Harper's Ferry, Va.
Brittin, Wilson S.........	...do....	20	Oct. 8, 1861	3 yrs.	Mustered out Jan. 7, 1865, at Columbus, O., on expiration of term of service.
Brittin, Francis M.......	...do....	20	Aug. 28, 1862	3 yrs.	Died Nov. 20, 1864, of wounds received —, in action near Atlanta, Ga.
Brinin, Samuel...........	...do....	25	Feb. 24, 1863	3 yrs.	Killed July 20, 1864, in battle of Peach Tree Creek, Ga.
Brillhart, Samuel........	...do....	19	Oct. 4, 1864	1 yr.	Substitute; mustered out with company July 15, 1865.
Canady, Joseph...........	...do....	45	Dec. 24, 1861	3 yrs.	Died May 14, 1862, at Strasburg, Va.
Chidester, Jacob..........	...do....	33	Aug. 11, 1862	3 yrs.	Transferred to Co. H, 10th Regiment Veteran Reserve Corps, Oct. 1, 1863, at New York, by order of War Department; mustered out June 27, 1865, at Washington, D. C., by order of War Department.

Names.	Rank.	Age.	Date of Entering the Service.	Period of Service.	Remarks.
Cheyney, Isaiah.........	Private	45	Oct. 12, 1861	3 yrs.	Mustered out to date Dec. 22, 1864, near Louisville, Ky., on expiration of term of service.
Conner, Bennet...........	....do....	33	Sept. 2, 1864	1 yr.	Drafted; mustered out June 5. 1865, near Bladensburg, Md., by order of War Department.
Cookes, James M.........	....do....	31	Dec. 14, 1861	3 yrs.	Killed June 9, 1862, in battle of Port Republic, Virginia.
Craig, Oliver..............	....do....	18	Oct. 12, 1861	3 yrs.	Discharged Aug. 26, 1862, at Columbus, O., for wounds received ——, in action, on Surgeon's certificate of disability.
Craig, William............	....do....	20	Oct. 12, 1861	3 yrs.	Mustered out with company July 15, 1865; veteran.
Craig, Andrew...........	..do....	19	Jan. 20, 1864	3 yrs.	Mustered out with company July 15, 1865.
Crabill, Wilson...........	..do....	32	Dec. 8, 1861	3 yrs.	
Crawley, Jonathan	...do....	32	Sept. 23, 1864	1 yr.	Drafted; mustered out June 5, 1865, near Bladensburg, Md., by order of War Department.
Dary, John...............	...do....	29	Sept. 23, 1864	1 yr.	Drafted; mustered out June 5. 1865, near Bladensburg, Md., by order of War Department.
Davis, Charles...........	...do....	18	Oct. 8, 1861	3 yrs.	Discharged Dec. 24, 1862, on Surgeon's certificate of disability.
Davis, Thomas B..........	...do....	22	Oct. 14, 1861	3 yrs.	Discharged July 5, 1862, at Columbus, O., on Surgeon's certificate of disability.
Diltz, Joseph	...do....	26	Dec. 27, 1861	3 yrs.	Prisoner of war; mustered out June 24, 1865, at Camp Chase, O., by order of War Department; veteran.
Doty, Hiram	...do....	33	Nov. 22, 1861	3 yrs.	Transferred to Veteran Reserve Corps Oct. 1, 1863, at Indianapolis, Ind., by order of War Department.
Dowell, William W......	...do....	20	July 26, 1862	3 yrs.	Transferred to Veteran Reserve Corps Nov. 18, 1863, by order of War Department.
Enoch, John	...do....	22	Sept. 4, 1864	1 yr.	Drafted; mustered out July 15, 1865, near Louisville, Ky., on expiration of term of service.
Forshay, Stephen...........	...do....	28	Sept. 28, 1864	1 yr.	Drafted; discharged March 14, 1865, at Tripler Hospital, Columbus, O., on Surgeon's certificate of disability.
Frankeberger, William......	...do....	34	Oct. 25, 1861	3 yrs.	Mustered out May 10, 1865, at hospital, Columbus, O., by order of War Department; veteran.
Freeman, Russell.........	...do....	24	Oct. 24, 1861	3 yrs.	Discharged Feb. 4, 1863, at Columbus, O., on Surgeon's certificate of disability.
Golliver, John............	...do....	29	Aug. 9, 1864	2 yrs.	Substitute; mustered out July 21, 1865, at Washington, D. C., by order of War Department.
Gove, Charles M...........	...do....	26	Nov. 15, 1861	3 yrs.	Discharged March 30, 1863, at Alexandria, Va., on Surgeon's certificate of disability.
Green, George W. C	...do....	18	Oct. 19, 1861	3 yrs.	Discharged May 29, 1862, on Surgeon's certificate of disability.
Guy, Cyrus	...do....	24	Nov. 5, 1861	3 yrs.	Discharged July 5, 1862, at Columbus, O., on Surgeon's certificate of disability.
Hall, Richard M...........	...do....	32	Oct. 16, 1861	3 yrs.	Mustered out with company July 15, 1865; veteran.
Hall, Erastus..............	...do....	32	Oct. 16, 1861	3 yrs.	Discharged July 23, 1862, at Columbus, O., on Surgeon's certificate of disability.
Hall, James	...do....	43	Oct. 12, 1864	1 yr.	Substitute; mustered out with company July 15, 1865.
Hammond, Daniel D	...do....	23	Dec. 20, 1861	3 yrs.	Discharged April 18, 1862, on Surgeon's certificate of disability.
Hanaman, William H......	...do....	18	Dec. 15, 1861	3 yrs.	Discharged Jan. 2, 1862, at Urbana, O., by civil authority.
Hartstone, Fred...........	...do....	45	Aug. 5, 1862	3 yrs.	Mustered out June 5, 1865, near Bladensburg, Md., by order of War Department.
Hess, William..............	...do ...	18	Dec. 10, 1861	3 yrs.	Died Oct. 11, 1862, at Washington, D. C.
Horn, Dwight	...do....	19	Oct. 1, 1861	3 yrs.	Died July 7, 1862, at Washington, D. C., of wounds received in action.
Irwin, Calvin C...........	...do....	18	May 1, 1862	3 yrs.	Wounded; discharged Oct. 10, 1862, at Washington, D. C., on Surgeon's certificate of disability.
Joiner, Joseph...............	...do....	20	Jan. 31, 1864	3 yrs.	Transferred to Veteran Reserve Corps Jan. —, 1865, by order of War Department.
Kearner, William	...do....	20	Jan. 15, 1864	3 yrs.	Mustered out with company July 15, 1865.
Kelch, Robert M	...do....	18	Nov. 11, 1861	3 yrs.	Died May 17, 1863, at Washington, D. C., of wounds received in action.
Keltner, Solonius...........	...do....	19	Aug. 3, 1864	1 yr.	Substitute; discharged June 30, 1865, at hospital, Camp Dennison, O., on Surgeon's certificate of disability.
Kinsey, Daniel	...do....	24	Sept. 24, 1864	1 yr.	Drafted; mustered out June 5, 1865, near Bladensburg, Md., by order of War Department.
Klingner, George...........	...do....	25	Sept. 27, 1861	1 yr.	Drafted; mustered out June 5, 1865, near Bladensburg. Md.
Klightlinger, Lewis.....	...do....	21	Dec. 14, 1861	3 yrs.	Mustered in as Lewis Keightlinger; killed June 9, 1862, in battle of Port Republic, Va.

Names.	Rank.	Age.	Date of Entering the Service.	Period of Service.	Remarks.
Knisely, John W........	Private	18	Oct. 23, 1861	3 yrs.	Discharged Oct. 26, 1862, on Surgeon's certificate of disability.
Koahler, John J............	...do....	31	Dec. 9, 1861	3 yrs.	Died Oct. 14, 1862, at Sharpsburg, Md., of wounds received in action.
Lanning, Lewis............	...do....	19	Aug. 5, 1864	1 yr.	Substitute; mustered out July 5, 1865, at Columbus, O., by order of War Department.
Legge, Samuel..............	...do....	40	Aug. 5, 1862	3 yrs.	Mustered out May 17, 1865, at Camp Dennison, O., by order of War Department.
Litzenburg, Joseph.......	...do....	19	Aug. 31, 1864	1 yr.	Substitute; mustered out June 5, 1865, near Bladensburg, Md., by order of War Department.
Locke, Joseph E..........	...do....	28	Nov. 19, 1861	3 yrs.	Mustered out with company July 15, 1865; veteran.
Loy, Martin A..........	...do....	19	Aug. 5, 1864	1 yr.	Substitute; mustered out June 5, 1865, near Bladensburg, Md., by order of War Department.
Maiers, Isaac..............	...do....	45	Oct. 26, 1861	3 yrs.	Discharged June 26, 1862, on Surgeon's certificate of disability.
Malone, John..............	...do....	19	Aug. 10, 1864	1 yr.	Substitute; mustered out June 5, 1865, near Bladensburg, Md., by order of War Department.
Mann, Azro..............	...do....	40	July 26, 1862	3 yrs.	Discharged Nov. 24, 1862, on Surgeon's certificate of disability.
McFall, Charles..........	...do....	26	Oct. 17, 1864	1 yr.	Substitute; mustered out with company July 15, 1865.
Meggle, Andrew..........	...do....	30	Sept. 21, 1864	1 yr.	Substitute; absent, sick; no further record found.
Metzler, Amos..........	...do....	19	Aug. 1, 1864	1 yr.	Substitute; mustered out Aug. 5, 1865, at Washington, D. C., by order of War Department.
Michael, Alexander......	...do....	44	Nov. 4, 1861	3 yrs.	Discharged March 28, 1863, at Alexandria, Va., on Surgeon's certificate of disability.
Miller, James	...do....	30	Dec. 3, 1861	3 yrs.	Discharged May 29, 1862, at Williamsport, Md., on Surgeon's certificate of disability.
Miller, Henry..........	...do....	22	Oct. 8, 1861	3 yrs.	Discharged Aug. 18, 1862, at Washington, D. C., on Surgeon's certificate of disability.
Milledge, Levi............	...do....	19	Jan. 19, 1864	3 yrs.	Mustered out with company July 15, 1865.
Milledge, John............	...do....	23	Aug. 8, 1862	3 yrs.	Mustered out June 5, 1865, near Bladensburg, Md., by order of War Department.
Moody, David............	...do....	19	Jan. 16, 1864	3 yrs.	Mustered out with company July 15, 1865.
Morris, Thomas R..........	...do....	29	Aug. 2, 1862	3 yrs.	Mustered out June 5, 1865, near Bladensburg, Md., by order of War Department.
Morris, William E........	...do....	20	Aug. 8, 1862	3 yrs.	Died Sept. 21, 1862, of wounds received in action.
Morris, Peter..........	...do....	23	Dec. 15, 1861	3 yrs.	Mustered out with company July 15, 1865; veteran.
Morey, Sylvanus B........	...do....	30	Nov. 9, 1861	3 yrs.	
Murmond, Jeremiah	...do....	42	Dec. 11, 1861	3 yrs.	
Nichols, James..........	...do....	19	Jan. 20, 1864	3 yrs.	Mustered out with company July 15, 1865.
Noonan, Patrick..........	...do....	18	Oct. 13, 1861	3 yrs.	Mustered in as Patrick Norman; mustered out with company July 15, 1865; veteran.
Noolan, John W..........	...do....	20	Dec. 11, 1861	3 yrs.	Mustered in James N. Nolan ——.
Owen, Joseph B..........	...do....	21	Aug. 11, 1862	3 yrs.	Mustered out June 19, 1865, at Tripler Hospital, Columbus, O., by order of War Department.
Owen, John W	...do....	24	Mch. 1, 1863	3 yrs.	Discharged May 17, 1865, at Camp Dennison, O., on Surgeon's certificate of disability.
Palmeter, Lafayette.....	...do....	24	Dec. 6, 1861	3 yrs.	Mustered out with company July 15, 1865; veteran.
Parker, Joseph	...do....	26	Oct. 14, 1861	3 yrs.	Mustered out to date Dec. 22, 1864, near Louisville, Ky., on expiration of term of service.
Parker, Frank J..........	...do....	23	Oct. 14, 1861	3 yrs.	Mustered out July 12, 1865, to date Dec. 22, 1864, near Louisville, Ky., on expiration of term of service.
Prottsman, John W........	...do....	30	Feb. 4, 1864	3 yrs.	Mustered out July 22, 1865, at New York City, by order of War Department.
Reed, William H..........	...do....	23	Nov. 19, 1861	3 yrs.	
Ritter, Levi H..........	...do....	19	Aug. 2, 1864	1 yr.	Substitute; died Dec. 18, 1864, at Chattanooga, Tenn.
Salmon, Joseph..........	...do....	43	Nov. 11, 1861	3 yrs.	On muster-in roll; no further record found.
Seaman, Henry M..........	...do....	22	Nov. 16, 1861	3 yrs.	Transferred to Veteran Reserve Corps at Baltimore, Md., Nov. 18, 1863.
Sergeant, David..........	...do....	25	Oct. 12, 1861	3 yrs.	Discharged May 22, 1862, at Winchester, Va., on Surgeon's certificate of disability.
Shepherd, Jasper C.......	...do....	39	Oct. 31, 1861	3 yrs.	Discharged Jan. 6, 1863, by order of War Department.
Shepherd, Harry W	...do....	27	Jan. 24, 1862	3 yrs.	Promoted to Principal Musician July —, 1862.
Smith, George..........	...do....	26	Nov. 21, 1861	3 yrs.	Discharged Jan. 21, 1863, on Surgeon's certificate of disability.
Smith, George..........	...do....	37	Nov. 22, 1861	3 yrs.	
Snodgrass, Henry M.......	...do....	38	Aug. 7, 1862	3 yrs.	Died Nov. 28, 1862, at Philadelphia, Pa.
Stone, A. J..........	...do....	27	Oct. 15, 1861	3 yrs.	Discharged, Jan. 30, 1862, at New Creek, Va., on Surgeon's certificate of disability.
Tanner, Augustus B.......	...do....	18	Dec. 6, 1861	3 yrs.	Mustered out Jan. 10, 1865, at Columbus, O., for wounds received in action; veteran.

Names.	Rank.	Age.	Date of Entering the Service.	Period of Service.	Remarks.
Taylor, Luther..........	Private	45	Nov. 2, 1861	3 yrs.	Discharged May 10, 1862, on Surgeon's certificate of disability.
Taylor, James E..........	...do....	43	Sept. 15, 1862	3 yrs.	Killed May 25, 1864, in battle of Dallas, Ga.
Timmons, James H......	...do....	22	Oct. 25, 1861	3 yrs.	Discharged Jan. 14, 1863, on Surgeon's certificate of disability.
Tyler, John W..............	...do....	23	Dec. 15, 1861	3 yrs.	Absent; no further record found; veteran.
Tyler, David..............	...do....	23	Feb. 1, 1864	3 yrs.	Mustered out with company July 15, 1865.
Vanfleet, Christopher B.	...do....	36	Nov. 19, 1861	3 yrs.	Discharged April 2, 1863, at Dumfries, Va., on Surgeon's certificate of disability.
Vanettie, Eli..............	...do....	24	Sept. 27, 1864	1 yr.	Substitute; mustered out June 5, 1865, near Bladensburg, Md., by order of War Department.
Welch, William A........	...do....	37	Sept. 27, 1864	1 yr.	Drafted; mustered out June 5, 1865, near Bladensburg, Md., by order of War Department.
Wenger, Jacob............	...do....	38	Sept. 25, 1864	1 yr.	Drafted; mustered out June 5, 1865, near Bladensburg, Md., by order of War Department.
White, Henry M............	...do....	23	Oct. 14, 1861	3 yrs.	Wounded ——; discharged Dec. 15, 1862, on Surgeon's certificate of disability.
Whitmier, Israel..........	...do....	30	Nov. 19, 1861	3 yrs.	
Winecup, Wesley..........	...do....	19	Jan. 28, 1864	3 yrs.	Died June 24, 1864, at Chattanooga, Tenn.
Wolf, Isaac..............	...do....	38	Sept. 27, 1864	1 yr.	Drafted; mustered out June 5, 1865, near Bladensburg, Md., by order of War Department.
Wynant, James............	...do....	17	Oct. 12, 1861	3 yrs.	Discharged Dec. 31, 1861, at Urbana, O., by civil authority.
Young, Robert............	...do....	21	Oct. 17, 1864	1 yr.	Substitute; mustered out June 3, 1865, at Camp Dennison, O., by order of War Department.

COMPANY K.

Mustered in Dec. 26, 1861, at Camp McArthur, Urbana, O., by Joseph H. Van Deman and William A. Sampson, 2d Lieutenants 66th O. V. I. Mustered out July 15, 1865, near Louisville, Ky., by Edward A. Wickes, Captain 150th New York Volunteers, and A. C. M. 14th Army Corps.

Names.	Rank.	Age.	Date of Entering the Service.	Period of Service.	Remarks.
Joseph Van Deman.....	Captain	32	Oct. 11, 1861	3 yrs.	Appointed Dec. 17, 1861; resigned Jan. 27, 1863.
William A. Sampson....	...do....	21	Oct. 1, 1861	3 yrs.	Promoted to 1st Lieutenant from 2d Lieutenant May 26, 1862; to Captain Jan. 27, 1863; discharged Jan. 12, 1865, on Surgeon's certificate of disability.
Charles W. Guy..........	...do....	18	Aug. 16, 1862	3 yrs.	Promoted from 1st Lieutenant Co. G May 31, 1865; mustered out with company July 15, 1865.
Wilson Martin..........	1st Lieut.	42	Nov. 14, 1861	6 yrs.	Appointed Dec. 17, 1861; resigned April 16, 1862.
Watson N. Clark........	...do....	22	Oct. 29, 1861	3 yrs.	Mustered as private; promoted to 2d Lieutenant May 26, 1862; to 1st Lieutenant to date Jan. 27, 1863; discharged April 14, 1863, on Surgeon's certificate of disability.
James Jacoby..............	...do....	22	Oct. 12, 1861	3 yrs.	Mustered as private; appointed Sergeant ——; promoted to 2d Lieutenant Jan. 27, 1863; 1st Lieutenant April 16, 1863; discharged May 5, 1864, on Surgeon's certificate of disability.
Charles E. Butts..........	...do....	24	Oct. 21, 1861	3 yrs.	Promoted from 2d Lieutenant to 1st Lieutenant Co. E April 2, 1864; to Captain Co. E April 12, 1865; veteran.
William Scott.,..........	...do....	21	Nov. 13, 1861	3 yrs.	Promoted from 1st Sergeant Co. F May 31, 1865; mustered out with company July 15, 1865; veteran.
James H. Corbin........	1st Sergt.	19	Oct. 12, 1861	3 yrs.	Appointed Corporal May 1, 1863; Sergeant Feb. 12, 1864; 1st Sergeant Dec. 17, 1864; promoted to 1st Lieutenant Co. H June 14, 1865; veteran.
Yelverton P. Berry	Sergeant	29	Oct. 29, 1861	3 yrs.	Mustered as private; appointed Sergeant ——; wounded ——; discharged Nov. 4, 1863, at Columbus, O., on Surgeon's certificate of disability.
Samuel Bowers............	...do....	24	Nov. 4, 1861	3 yrs.	Mustered as private; appointed Sergeant ——.
Philip Phillippi..........	...do....	22	Nov. 9, 1861	3 yrs.	Mustered as private; appointed Sergeant ——; mustered out June 28, 1865, by order of War Department; veteran.
Alva M. Rhoads..........	...do....	21	Nov. 11, 1861	3 yrs.	Mustered as private; appointed Sergeant ——; wounded ——; discharged ——, on Surgeon's certificate of disability.
Smiley J. Smith	...do....	24	Oct. 22, 1861	3 yrs.	Mustered as private; appointed Sergeant ——; mustered out Dec. 22, 1864, near Savannah, Ga., on expiration of term of service.

Names.	Rank.	Age.	Date of Entering the Service.	Period of Service.	Remarks.
Hilman P. Sweetland....	Sergeant	19	Nov. 6, 1861	3 yrs.	Mustered as private; appointed Sergeant ——; mustered out June 28, 1865, by order of War Department; veteran.
William Stokes...........	..do....	26	Nov. 30, 1861	3 yrs.	Mustered as private; appointed Sergeant ——; died April 6, 1862, at Martinsburg, Va.
Benjamin B. Wilson....)	..do....	....	Mch. 7, 1864	3 yrs.	Appointed Corporal Sept. 1, 1864; Sergeant Oct. 1, 1864; mustered out June 10, 1865, by order of War Department.
Robert W. Boyd.........	Corporal	19	Nov. 9, 1861	3 yrs.	Appointed Corporal ——; discharged Sept. 13, 1862, at Washington, D. C., on Surgeon's certificate of disability.
Wackerly Burnard	..do....	30	Oct. 1, 1864	1 yr.	Drafted; appointed Corporal ——; mustered out June 3, 1865, near Bladensburg, Md., by order of War Department.
Charles Custard	..do....	25	Jan. 17, 1862	3 yrs.	
James Foster............	..do....	38	Jan. 9, 1864	3 yrs.	Appointed Corporal ——; mustered out June 28, 1865, by order of War Department.
John W. Hoyt...........	..do....	21	Oct 2, 1861	3 yrs.	Appointed Corporal ——; discharged Aug. 13, 1862, at Columbus, O., on Surgeon's certificate of disability.
Cornelius D. Jones	..do....	32	Feb. 2, 1864	3 yrs.	Appointed Corporal ——; mustered out June 28, 1865, by order of War Department.
William F. Justice	..do....	24	Nov. 8, 1861	3 yrs.	Appointed Corporal ——; discharged April 24, 1862, at Strasburg, Va., on Surgeon's certificate of disability.
David L. Justice	..do....	20	Feb. 4, 1864	3 yrs.	Appointed Corporal ——; mustered out June 28, 1865, by order of War Department.
Elten Martin.............	..do....	22	Nov. 6, 1861	3 yrs.	Appointed Corporal ——; discharged April 23, 1862, at Strasburg, Va., on Surgeon's certificate of disability.
Daniel Miller.............	..do....	22	Jan. 18, 1864	3 yrs.	Appointed Corporal ——; mustered out June 28, 1865, by order of War Department.
Adam Mitchell...........	..do....	21	Nov. 18, 1861	3 yrs.	Appointed Corporal ——; died Aug. 22, 1862, at Alexandria, Va., of wounds received Aug. 9, 1862, in battle of Cedar Mountain, Va.
David Morrison...........	..do....	22	Nov. 29, 1861	3 yrs.	Appointed Corporal ——; discharged March 17, 1863, at Washington, D. C., on Surgeon's certificate of disability.
Benjamin Peak...........	..do....	25	Nov. 6, 1861	3 yrs.	Appointed Corporal ——; died Oct. 8, 1864, at Atlanta, Ga.; veteran.
Joseph B. Rhoades.......	..do....	18	Oct. 29, 1861	3 yrs.	Appointed Corporal ——; mustered out June 28, 1865, by order of War Department; veteran.
Charles A. Turner........	..do....	41	Oct. 23, 1861	3 yrs.	Appointed Corporal ——; discharged Dec. 7, 1862, on Surgeon's certificate of disability.
John Van Brimmer	..do....	19	Oct. 12, 1861	3 yrs.	Appointed Corporal ——; mustered out June 28, 1865, by order of War Department; veteran.
Frederick Hanger.......	Musician	18	Mch. 9, 1864	3 yrs.	Mustered out June 28, 1865, by order of War Department.
Adams, John............	Private	43	Aug. 16, 1864	3 yrs.	Substitute.
Alexander, Joseph C.....	..do....	45	Dec. 10, 1861	3 yrs.	Discharged Oct. 20, 1862, at hospital, Alexandria, Va., on Surgeon's certificate of disability.
Allen, Milton.............	..do....	19	Oct. 4, 1861	3 yrs.	Died Nov. 26, 1862, at David's Island, New York Harbor.
Anderson, William.......	..do....	18	Oct. 14, 1861	3 yrs.	Veteran.
Armstrong, J. Hamilton.	..do....	20	Oct. 3, 1861	3 yrs.	Mustered out June 28, 1865, by order of War Department; veteran.
Bacon, Charles W........	..do....	18	Oct. 14, 1861	3 yrs.	Discharged Nov. 24, 1862, at Bolivar Heights, Va., on Surgeon's certificate of disability.
Bancroft, Henry W.......	..do....	18	Aug. 1, 1864	1 yr.	Substitute; mustered out June 3, 1865, near Bladensburg, Md., by order of War Department.
Bailey, Solomon..........	..do....	21	Dec. 3, 1861	3 yrs.	Discharged Nov. 24, 1862, at Bolivar Heights, Va., on Surgeon's certificate of disability.
Beckman, Solomon W....	..do....	44	Oct. 28, 1861	3 yrs.	Discharged April 17, 1863, on Surgeon's certificate of disability.
Birk, George.............	..do....	31	Jan. 14, 1864	3 yrs.	Mustered out June 28, 1865, by order of War Department.
Bishop, James D..........	..do....	18	Dec. 2, 1861	3 yrs.	Mustered out June 28, 1865, by order of War Department; veteran.
Black, Henry.............	..do....	39	Dec. 1, 1861	3 yrs.	
Book, John...............	..do....	25	Oct. 14, 1861	3 yrs.	Discharged July 12, 1862, at Columbus, O., on Surgeon's certificate of disability.
Bower, Daniel............	..do....	19	Nov. 1, 1861	3 yrs.	Mustered as private; appointed Sergeant ——; reduced to ranks ——; mustered out June 28, 1865, by order of War Department; veteran.
Breedwell, Reuben........	..do....	34	Sept. 20, 1864	1 yr.	Drafted; mustered out June 3, 1865, near Bladensburg, Md., by order of War Department.
Burns, James.............	..do....	18	Oct. 4, 1861	3 yrs.	Died Feb. 29, 1864, at Columbus, O.
Burwell, James...........	..do....	33	Nov. 26, 1861	3 yrs.	Died April 14, 1862, at Winchester, Va.
Bumler, John.............	..do....	21	Aug. 15, 1864	2 yrs.	Substitute; mustered out June 28, 1865, by order of War Department.

Names.	Rank.	Age.	Date of Entering the Service.	Period of Service.	Remarks.
Chambers, William A....	Private	20	Aug. 15, 1864	1 yr.	Substitute; mustered out July 7, 1865, at Tripler Hospital, Columbus, O., by order of War Department.
Conner, Patrick..........	...do....	27	Feb. 26, 1864	3 yrs.	
Crawford, Thomas.........	...do....	13	Nov. 7, 1861	3 yrs.	Discharged Feb. 20, 1862, at Camp Chase, O., on Surgeon's certificate of disability.
Crawford, Silas............	...do....	36	Nov. 2, 1861	3 yrs.	Discharged July 12, 1862, at Columbus, O., on Surgeon's certificate of disability.
Crawford, George W.......	...do....	21	Nov. 29, 1861	3 yrs.	Discharged July 3, 1862, at Columbus, O., on Surgeon's certificate of disability.
Cunningham, William......	...do....	18	Aug. 12, 1864	1 yr.	Substitute; mustered out June 3, 1865, near Bladensburg, Md., by order of War Department.
Digmiller, John..........	...do....	42	Oct. 12, 1864	1 yr.	Substitute; mustered out June 28, 1865, by order of War Department.
Doran, Alexander........	...do....	18	Nov. 2, 1861	3 yrs.	Discharged May 12, 1862, at Winchester, Va., on Surgeon's certificate of disability.
Dupps, Christian..........	...do....	42	Aug. 15, 1864	3 yrs.	Substitute; mustered out June 28, 1865, by order of War Department.
Durfey, Jerome...........	...do....	18	Nov. 26, 1861	3 yrs.	
Duchen, Henry............	...do....	33	Oct. 1, 1864	1 yr.	Drafted; mustered out June 3, 1865, near Bladensburg, Md., by order of War Department.
Farrell, James............	...do....	25	Mch. 1, 1864	3 yrs.	Mustered out July 24, 1865, at Harrisburg, Pa., by order of War Department.
Finch, Crea...............	...do....	19	Oct. 17, 1861	3 yrs.	Died June 6, 1863, at Annapolis, Md.
Frankenfield, Joseph......	...do....	29	Nov. 2, 1861	3 yrs.	Died Dec. 24, 1862, at Dumfries, Va.
French, Charles W	...do....	18	Feb. 4, 1864	3 yrs.	Transferred to Co. D, 8th Veteran Reserve Corps, Oct. 22, 1864.
Gearing, Earnest.........	...do....	42	Sept. 26, 1864	1 yr.	Mustered out July 8, 1865, at Washington, D. C., by order of War Department.
Gibbs, Daniel W	...do....	36	Nov. 13, 1861	3 yrs.	Transferred to Veteran Reserve Corps ——.
Golliver, John F...........	...do....	18	Aug. 9, 1864	2 yrs.	Substitute.
Green, Henry.............	...do....	40	Sept. 21, 1864	1 yr.	Drafted; died May 11, 1865, on Hospital Transport S. R. Spaulding.
Green, Horace.............	...do....	29	Nov. 5, 1861	3 yrs.	Wounded May 3, 1863, in battle of Chancellorsville, Va.; mustered out Jan. 16, 1865, at Columbus, O., on expiration of term of service.
Hatch, Samuel............	...do....	18	Oct. 30, 1861	3 yrs.	Mustered out June 28, 1865, by order of War Department; veteran.
Helmig, Joseph............	...do....	33	Oct. 1, 1864	1 yr.	Drafted; mustered out June 3, 1865, near Bladensburg, Md., by order of War Department.
Hilbruner, Andrew........	...do....	25	Aug. 12, 1864	3 yrs.	Substitute; mustered out June 28, 1865, by order of War Department.
Himmelsbaug. John......	...do....	18	Oct. 30, 1861	3 yrs.	
Hoffman, Ferdinand.......	...do....	28	Aug. 15, 1864	3 yrs.	Substitute.
Jackson, Thomas..........	...do....	39	Aug. 15, 1864	3 yrs.	Substitute; mustered out June 17, 1865, at Washington, D. C., by order of War Department.
Johnson, James	...do....	42	Aug. 15, 1864	3 yrs.	Substitute.
Johnson, W. A............	...do....	32	Aug. 17, 1864	3 yrs.	Substitute; absent, sick; no further record found.
Justice, David...........	...do....	18	Oct. 26, 1861	3 yrs.	Discharged July 28, 1862, at Mount Pleasant General Hospital, Washington, D. C., on Surgeon's certificate of disability.
Kelch, David B............	...do....	23	Oct. 15, 1861	3 yrs.	Died Dec. 31, 1862, at Harper's Ferry, Va.
Kelley, Hiram C...........	...do....	26	Aug. 16, 1864	1 yr.	Substitute.
Kimble, George...........	...do....	18	Aug. 6, 1864	1 yr.	Substitute; mustered out June 3, 1865, near Bladensburg, Md., by order of War Department.
King, Jacob S.............	...do....	29	Sept. 27, 1864	1 yr.	Drafted; mustered out June 3, 1865, near Bladensburg, Md., by order of War Department.
Kinney, Andrew J.........	...do....	25	Sept. 27, 1864	1 yr.	Drafted; mustered out May 17, 1865, at Camp Dennison, O., by order of War Department.
Klee, Jacob...............	...do....	25	Aug. 16, 1864	3 yrs.	Substitute; mustered out June 28, 1865, by order of War Department.
Lawyer, L. C..............	...do....	18	Aug. 16, 1864	1 yr.	Substitute; mustered out June 3, 1865, near Bladensburg, Md., by order of War Department.
Levelle, Frank............	...do....	25	Aug. 17, 1864	1 yr.	Substitute.
Leslie, James S...........	...do....	31	April 15, 1864	3 yrs.	Mustered out with company July 15, 1865.
Long, Fowler H...........	...do....	30	Nov. 17, 1861	3 yrs.	Discharged April 23, 1862, at Strasburg, Va., on Surgeon's certificate of disability.
Maron, Jones.............	...do....	25	Dec. 3, 1861	3 yrs.	Mustered in as James Marron.
Martin, William..........	...do....	38	Aug. 17, 1864	1 yr.	Substitute.
Mattix, Isaiah	...do....	20	Nov. 28, 1861	3 yrs.	Discharged Dec. 18, 1862, at Convalescent Camp near Alexandria, Va., on Surgeon's certificate of disability.
Meeker, Robert E........	...do....	23	Nov. 13, 1861	3 yrs.	Discharged July 30, 1862, at Columbus, O., on Surgeon's certificate of disability.
Mills, Levi C.............	...do....	18	Aug. 16, 1864	1 yr.	Substitute; mustered out June 3, 1865, near Bladensburg, Md., by order of War Department.
Newhouse, James F......	...do....	18	Nov. 18, 1861	3 yrs.	Killed Nov. 27, 1863, in battle of Ringgold, Ga.

Names	Rank.	Age.	Date of Entering the Service.	Period of Service.	Remarks.
Newhouse, John........	Private	22	Oct. 30, 1861	3 yrs.	Mustered out June 28, 1865, by order of War Department; veteran.
Norris, Charles T........	...do....	20	Oct. 25, 1861	3 yrs.	Discharged Dec. 15, 1862, at Providence, R. I. on Surgeon's certificate of disability.
Oser, Earnest.............	...do....	36	Oct. 1, 1864	1 yr.	Drafted; mustered out June 3 1865, near Bladensburg, Md., by order of War Department.
Parker, James........	...do....	28	Nov. 20, 1861	3 yrs.	Discharged Nov. 23, 1862, at Bolivar Heights, Va., on Surgeon's certificate of disability.
Partridge, Almond......	...do....	18	Nov. 13, 1861	3 yrs.	
Penroy, Edward..........	...do....	44	Dec. 11, 1861	3 yrs.	Discharged Sept. 30, 1864, at Camp Chase, O., on Surgeon's certificate of disability.
Phifer, John..........	...do....	36	Aug. 13, 1864	1 yr.	Substitute.
Phillips, John............	...do....	18	Aug. 16, 1864	1 yr.	Substitute.
Phyres, Hiram..........	...do....	20	Oct. 11, 1864	3 yrs.	Substitute; also borne on rolls as Hiram Pyres; died Jan. 26, 1865, at Savannah, Ga.
Powell, William..........	...do....	18	Nov. 13, 1861	3 yrs.	Discharged March 23, 1863, at hospital, Antietam, Md., on Surgeon's certificate of disability.
Rice, Simon P............	...do....	18	Nov. 26, 1861	3 yrs.	Died Feb. 20, 1862, at Delaware, O.
Richt, Christian.........	...do....	42	Sept. 12, 1864	1 yr.	Drafted; mustered out June 3, 1865, near Bladensburg, Md., by order of War Department.
Robinson, James P.......	...do....	40	Nov. 16, 1861	3 yrs.	Discharged June 26, 1862, at Camp Chase, O., on Surgeon's certficate of disability.
Robins, Andrew...........	...do....	18	Aug. 11, 1864	1 yr.	Substitute; mustered out June 3, 1865, near Bladensburg, Md., by order of War Department.
Rodney, John.............	...do....	35	Aug. 15, 1864	3 yrs.	Substitute.
Rodes, Robert............	...do....	18	Nov. 16, 1861	3 yrs.	Discharged Oct. 19, 1862, by reason of being a minor.
Roll, William.............	...do....	16	Oct. 23, 1861	3 yrs.	
Saxton, Gilbert...........	...do....	44	May 9, 1864	3 yrs.	Drafted.
Sayre, William F..........	...do....	19	Oct. 12, 1861	3 yrs.	Mustered as Wm. M. Sayre; killed June 16, 1864, in action at Pine Knob, Ga.; veteran.
Secrist, Henry............	...do....	36	Jan. 25, 1864	3 yrs.	Mustered out June 26, 1865, at Camp Chase, O., by order of War Department.
Shaffer, James T..........	...do....	21	Oct. 25, 1861	3 yrs.	
Shaw, Francis C..........	...do....	18	Nov. 18, 1861	3 yrs.	Discharged Jan. 28, 1863, at Baltimore, Md., on Surgeon's certificate of disability.
Sheets, Joseph.............	...do....	23	Sept. 26, 1864	1 yr.	Drafted; mustered out May 17, 1865, at Camp Dennison, O., by order of War Department.
Short, John...............	...do....	32	Oct. 29, 1861	3 yrs.	Discharged June 16, 1862, at Washington, D. C., on Surgeon's certificate of disability.
Shooster, Frederick	...do....	36	Oct. 3, 1864	2 yrs.	Substitute; mustered out June 28, 1865, by order of War Department.
Smart, Joseph W	...do....	19	Nov. 28, 1861	3 yrs.	Mustered as private; appointed Sergeant ——; reduced to ranks ——; mustered out July 17, 1865, at David's Island, New York Harbor, by order of War Department; veteran.
Smith, Newton	...do....	19	Nov. 7, 1861	3 yrs.	
Smith, John	...do....	32	Aug. 16, 1864	3 yrs.	Substitute.
Snyder, William..........	...do....	22	Oct. 7, 1861	3 yrs.	Discharged Nov. 24, 1862, at Convalescent Camp near Alexandria, Va., on Surgeon's certificate of disability.
South, Joseph.............	...do....	18	Oct. 23, 1861	3 yrs.	Discharged Jan. 1, 1862, at Urbana, O., by civil authority.
Sourback, George	...do....	27	Oct. 1, 1864	1 yr.	Drafted; mustered out June 3, 1865, near Bladensburg, Md., by order of War Department.
Sprawl, George A........	...do....	34	Nov. 29, 1861	3 yrs.	Mustered out Dec. 22, 1864, near Savannah, Ga., on expiration of term of service.
Spees, Leander H........	...do....	18	Oct. 30, 1861	3 yrs.	Discharged July 5, 1862, at Columbus, O., on Surgeon's certificate of disability.
Spencer, William A	...do....	25	Sept. 20, 1864	1 yr.	Drafted; mustered out June 3, 1865, near Bladensburg, Md., by order of War Department.
Spencer, William P.......	...do....	18	Aug. 15, 1864	1 yr.	Substitute; mustered out June 3, 1865, near Bladensburg, Md., by order of War Department.
Spoots, Sylvester	...do....	37	Oct. 1, 1864	1 yr.	Drafted; mustered out June 3, 1865, near Bladensburg, Md., by order of War Department.
Stanley, Jacob A.........	...do....	38	Sept. 21, 1864	1 yr.	Drafted; mustered out June 3, 1865, near Bladensburg, Md., by order of War Department.
Straus, Frederick.........	...do....	29	Aug. 13, 1864	2 yrs.	Substitute; prisoner of war; mustered out June 10, 1865, at Camp Chase, O., by order of War Department.
Stokes, Benjamin F......	..do....	20	Nov. 30, 1861	3 yrs.	Mustered out June 28, 1865, by order of War Department; veteran.
Stokeley, Philip	...do....	19	Dec. 3, 1861	3 yrs.	Discharged Aug. 4, 1862, at Cumberland, Md., on Surgeon's certificate of disability.
Stockman, Elias G.	...do....	20	Oct. 19, 1861	3 yrs.	Wounded May 3, 1863, in battle of Chancellorsville, Va.; transferred to Veteran Reserve Corps ——.

Names.	Rank.	Age.	Date of Entering the Service.	Period of Service.	Remarks.
Stottlemyre, Daniel.....	Private	19	Oct. 29, 1861	3 yrs.	Discharged Oct. 13, 1862, at General Hospital, Fairfax Seminary, Va., on Surgeon's certificate of disability.
Sweet, Mark..............	....do....	26	Nov. 24, 1861	3 yrs.	Mustered out Dec. 22, 1864, near Savannah, Ga., on expiration of term of service.
Taylor, James E.........	....do....	38	Nov. 17, 1861	3 yrs.	Discharged July 22, 1862, at Columbus, O., on Surgeon's certificate of disability.
Taylor, Silas	....do....	25	Mch. 23, 1864	3 yrs.	Captured Nov. 19, 1864, at Madison, Ga.; mustered out June 23, 1865, at Camp Chase, O., by order of War Department.
Tittlebaugh, Edward....	....do....	20	Nov. 20, 1861	3 yrs.	Also borne as Edward Tiddlebaugh; discharged Jan. 5, 1863, at Baltimore, Md., on Surgeon's certificate of disability.
Trout, Amos..............	....do....	34	Dec. 10, 1861	3 yrs.	
Watson, Charles..........	....do....	26	Sept. 20, 1864	1 yr.	Drafted; mustered out June 3, 1865, near Bladensburg, Md., by order of War Department.
Webb, Martin	....do....	19	Dec. 10, 1861	3 yrs.	Mustered out June 28, 1865, by order of War Department; veteran.
Willis, William H	....do....	18	Oct. 16, 1861	3 yrs.	Discharged Dec. 31, 1861, by civil authority.
Williams, Isaac	....do....	30	Nov. 18, 1861	3 yrs.	Discharged June 30, 1862, at Columbus, O., on Surgeon's certificate of disability.
Wine, Charles	....do....	19	Aug. 10, 1834	1 yr.	Drafted; mustered out June 3, 1865, near Bladensburg, Md., by order of War Department.
Witt, Thomas..............	....do....	18	Aug. 16, 1864	1 yr.	Substitute; mustered out June 3, 1865, near Bladensburg, Md., by order of War Department.
Yantz, Peter..............	....do....	18	Oct. 4, 1864	2 yrs.	Substitute; mustered out July 12, 1865, at Tripler Hospital, Columbus, O., by order of War Department.

UNASSIGNED RECRUITS.

Names.	Rank.	Age.	Date of Entering the Service.	Period of Service.	Remarks.
Brinkhard, Elijah.......	Private	25	Jan. 28, 1864	3 yrs.	Never joined regiment.
Coen, John..............	....do....	24	Jan. 18, 1864	3 yrs.	Assigned to regiment, but never reported for duty.
Conner, Michael..........	....do....	35	Feb. 26, 1864	3 yrs.	Assigned to regiment, but never reported for duty.
Gibson, William..........	....do....	19	Mch. 22, 1865	3 yrs.	
Hill, William.............	....do....	18	Jan. 9, 1864	3 yrs.	Assigned to regiment, but never reported for duty.
Lachapell, Gustis........	....do....	28	Nov. 12, 1863	3 yrs.	
Lawrence, Edward	....do....	38	Jan. 22, 1864	3 yrs.	Assigned to regiment, but never reported for duty.
Meheo, Edward	....do....	39	Nov. 6, 1863	3 yrs.	Assigned to regiment, but never reported for duty.
Rogers, Sampson Andrew	...do....	39	Mch. 8, 1864	3 yrs.	No further record found.
Shaffer, Charles H.......	....do....	19	Jan. 20, 1864	3 yrs.	Also borne on rolls as Silas H. Shaffer; assigned to regiment, but never reported for duty.
Shields, Albert	....do....	20	Mch. 26, 1864	3 yrs.	
Watson, Robert H	....do....	18	April 7, 1865	3 yrs.	Mustered out May 15, 1865, at Hart Island, New York Harbor, by order of War Department.
White, William L	....do....	27	Feb. 1, 1864	3 yrs.	Never joined regiment.

Notes

PROLOGUE

1. *Union County Gazette* (hereafter *UCG*), 11 August 1887.

1. UDNEY HYDE AND ADDISON WHITE

1. This account of the Addison White case follows *The History of Champaign County, Ohio,* 606–10, and Ralph M. Watts, "History of the Underground Railroad in Mechanicsburg," *Ohio Archaeological and Historical Quarterly* 153 (1934).

2. A SPLENDID BANNER

1. *Population of the United States in 1860,* 364–65, 376.
2. Ibid.; Hubert G. H. Wilhelm, *The Origins and Distribution of Settlement Groups: Ohio, 1850,* Champaign County tables, Appendices A and B; David T. Thackery, "A Work in Progress: The Study of a Rural Immigrant Community," *Origins* 6 (1990): 2, 3.
3. *Ohio State Democrat* (hereafter *OSD*), 4 June 1857.
4. Ibid., 29 October 1857.
5. *UCG,* 11 October 1860.

6. Ibid., 25 October 1860.

7. Ibid., 15 November 1860.

8. Michael Shiery to wife and children, 17 April 1861, Michael Shiery pension file, RG 15, National Archives.

9. *History of Clark County, Ohio,* 274–75; 1860 census, Springfield, Clark County, Ohio, 201, RG 29, National Archives; Mark M. Boatner III, *The Civil War Dictionary,* 516.

10. *UCG,* 6 June 1861.

3. LET US DO NO MAN INJUSTICE

1. Wilhelm, *Origins and Distribution,* table of Champaign County regional origins (unnumbered page).

2. *UCG,* 1, 8 August 1861.

3. Ibid., 15 August 1861.

4. Ibid., 29 August 1861.

5. Brand Whitlock, *Forty Years of It,* 17.

6. *UCG,* 29 August 1861.

4. LEAVE THE CORN UPON THE STALK, JOHN

1. Noel Fisher, "Groping toward Victory: Ohio's Administration of the Civil War," *Ohio History* 105 (Winter–Spring, 1996): 29.

2. William E. Smith and Ophia D. Smith, *A Buckeye Titan,* 465.

3. James Dye pension file, RG 15.

4. *UCG,* 18 October 1861.

5. Ibid., 17 October 1861; 1860 U.S. census, Urbana, Champaign County, Ohio, 102.

6. *UCG,* 10 October 1862.

7. Ibid., 17, 31 October 1861.

8. Ibid., 17 October 1861.

9. Sarah E. Gladden, "Lines Composed on Levi Gladden, Who Enlisted Oct. 29th, 1861 under Capt. C. Fulton, Co. A, 66th Reg., O.V.I." (broadside).

10. Evan P. Middleton, *History of Champaign County, Ohio,* 2:577.

11. *UCG,* 16 January 1862.

12. Quoted in F. M. McAdams, *Every-day Soldier Life, or a History of the One Hundred and Thirteenth Ohio Volunteer Infantry,* 7.

13. W. A. Brand G.A.R. Post No. 98, "Soldiers Record Book," Champaign County Public Library, Urbana, Ohio.

14. Quoted in Smith and Smith, *Buckeye Titan,* 470–71.

15. *UCG,* 31, 24 October 1861.

16. 1860 U.S. census, Urbana, Champaign County, Ohio, 96; Ohio Adjutant General, *Official Roster of the Soldiers of the State of Ohio in the War of the Rebellion, 1861–1866,* 5:524.

17. *The History of Union County, Ohio,* 85.

18. Samuel B. Briggs diary, Charles Emory Collection, Springfield, Ohio.

19. J. Wilbur Jacoby, *History of Marion County, Ohio and Representative Citizens,* 249.

20. R. H. Russell to father, 15 December 1862, William S. Russell Collection, Urbana, Ohio.

21. Letter from "Marion boy," *UCG,* 7 April 1864.

22. *UCG,* 31 March 1881.

23. 66th Ohio Infantry Collection (MSS 842), Ohio Historical Society (OHS). This collection contains a draft history of the regiment by Eugene Powell, with comments by W. A. Brand.

24. See letters 1612 through 1631 (21–25 August 1861), Ohio Governors' Papers (MSS 306), OHS.

25. *History of Champaign County, Ohio,* 633–36.

26. Charles Candy pension, Union pension files, RG 15.

27. *Statement of Military Services, &c. of Charles Candy, (Late) Colonel 66th Ohio Vet. Vol. Infantry, Brevet Brigadier General, U.S. Vols.*

28. Candy pension file; 1860 U.S. census, Urbana, Champaign County, Ohio, 125. The pension file contains a copy of Candy's death certificate, giving Candy's father's name as John.

29. 66th Ohio Infantry Collection.

30. William H. H. Tallman manuscript memoir (photocopy), Charles Rhodes III Collection, United States Army Military History Institute (USAMHI), Carlisle Barracks, Carlisle, Pennsylvania.

31. *UCG,* 31 October, 7, 21 November 1861.

32. Ibid., 5 December 1861.

5. SO WE ARE SURE TO GO

1. *Urbana Free Press* (hereafter *UFP*), 8 January 1862.

2. Russell to parents, 11 January 1862, William Russell Collection.

3. *UCG,* 23 January 1862.

4. *Will Abstracts of Champaign County, Ohio: Books A thru F, 1810–1888,* 104 (Book C, 380).

5. Mary Diltz to Joseph Diltz, 26 January 1862; Joseph Diltz to Mary Diltz, 19 January 1862, Diltz Papers, Duke University, Durham, North Carolina.

6. *UFP,* 22 January 1862; *UCG,* 23 January 1862; James H. Dye pension file, RG 15.

7. Roll of Deserters from Ohio Regiments, 1861–1865 (Ohio Adjutant General, Series 108, BV 1936), OHS, Columbus, Ohio.

8. *UCG,* 30 January 1862.

9. 66th Ohio Infantry Collection.

10. Letter from "Bud," *UCG,* 30 January 1862.

11. Joseph Diltz to Benjamin F. Madden, 2 February 1862, Diltz Papers, Duke University.

12. Joseph Diltz to Mary Diltz, 24 January 1862, ibid.

13. Joseph Diltz to Benjamin F. Madden, 2 February 1862, ibid.

14. Augustus Tanner to father, 30 January 1862, OHS.

15. Ibid.

16. Tallman ms. memoir, USAMHI. The unlucky officer may have been 2d Lt. Charles H. Rhodes of Company G, whose election had been reported by Robert Russell in a letter to his parents only three months previously.

17. "WAB" letter, *UCG*, 20 February 1862.

18. Robert Russell to father, 5 February 1862, William Russell Collection.

19. Lawrence Wilson, *Itinerary of the Seventh Ohio Volunteer Infantry, 1861–1864*, 118–19.

20. Nathan Baker to family, 20 February 1862, Kyle Kelch Collection, Urbana, Ohio.

21. Samuel B. Briggs diary, Charles Emory Collection.

22. 66th Ohio Infantry Collection; George L. Wood, *Famous Deeds by American Heroes: A Record of Events from Sumpter to Lookout Mountain*, 87.

23. Record of Events, RG 94, National Archives; *UCG*, 20 February 1862; Whitelaw Reid, *Ohio in the War: Her Statesmen, Generals and Soldiers*, 2:387; Wilson, *Seventh Ohio*, 119; J. Hamp SeCheverell, *Journal History of the Twenty-Ninth Ohio Veteran Volunteers, 1861–1865*, 36.

24. U.S. War Department, *War of the Rebellion: A Compilation of the Official Records of the Union and Confederate Armies* (hereafter *OR*), ser. 1, vol. 5, 406.

25. *OR*, vol. 51, 1:531.

26. Ibid., 533.

27. Quoted by Richard Moe, *The Last Full Measure: The Life and Death of the First Minnesota Volunteers*, 87.

28. A. J. Riker diary (photocopy), St. Paris Public Library, St. Paris, Ohio.

29. John W. Elwood, *Elwood's Stories of the Old Ringgold Cavalry 1847–1865: The First Three Year Cavalry of the Civil War*, 85–90. Lander's bombast was also subject for comment by Gen. Alpheus Williams, who commanded Union troops in an adjoining sector. See Alpheus Williams to daughter, 19 February 1862, in *From the Cannon's Mouth*, ed. Milo M. Quaife, 59–60.

30. *UCG*, 27 February 1862.

31. Joseph Van Deman to Mrs. C. C. Chamberlin, Kyle Kelch Collection, Urbana, Ohio.

32. William Sayre to Ziba Sayre, 25 February 1862, William Sayre Collection, USAMHI; *UCG*, 27 February 1862; Joseph Diltz to Mary Diltz, 26 February 1862, Diltz Papers.

33. *OR*, vol. 12, 3:5.

34. *UCG*, 13 March 1862; *UFP*, 12 February 1862.

35. Robert Russell to father, 9 March 1862, William Russell Collection.

36. *UCG*, 27 March 1862.

37. Robert Russell to father, 8 and 9 March 1862, William Russell Collection.

38. Robert Russell to father, 10 March 1862, ibid.; William Sayre to Ziba Sayre, 10 March 1862, Sayre Collection.

39. *UCG*, 27 March 1862; Robert Russell to father, 10 March 1862, William Russell Collection; William Sayre to Ziba Sayre, 10 March 1862, Sayre Collection.

40. *UCG*, 27 March 1862.

41. Ibid.

42. Ibid., 10 April 1862.

6. DISTANCE LENDS ENCHANTMENT

1. *UCG*, 10 April 1862; Robert Russell to father, 31 March 1862, William Russell Collection.

2. Joseph Diltz to Mary Diltz, 30 March 1862, Diltz Papers.

3. Cornelia McDonald, *A Diary with Reminiscences of the War and Refugee Life in the Shenandoah Valley 1860–1865*, 45.

4. Ibid., 45–46.

5. Tallman memoir.

6. Robert Russell to father, 31 March 1862, William Russell Collection.

7. *UCG*, 17 April 1862.

8. Ibid., 20 February, 17 April 1862.

9. William Sayre to Ziba Sayre, 23 March 1862, Sayre Collection.

10. Augustus Tanner to father, 29 March 1862, Augustus Tanner Correspondence, OHS.

11. *UCG*, 29 April 1862.

12. Ibid., 17 April 1862; McDonald, *Diary*, 56.

13. McDonald, *Diary*, 56–57.

14. Tallman memoir.

15. McDonald, *Diary*, 59.

16. *UCG*, 15 May 1862.

17. William Sayre to Ziba Sayre, 15 April 1862, Sayre Collection.

18. Mary Diltz to Joseph Diltz, 8 April 1862, Diltz Papers.

19. *UCG*, 24 April 1862.

20. Robert Russell to father, 14 April 1862, William Russell Collection.

21. Record of Events 66th Ohio Infantry, Compiled Records Showing Service of Military Units in Volunteer Union Organizations, RG 94.

22. Tallman memoir.

23. William Sayre to Ziba Sayre, 20 May 1862, Sayre Collection; *Delaware (Ohio) Gazette*, 30 May 1862.

24. Wilson, *Seventh Ohio*, 150–51; *Delaware (Ohio) Gazette*, 30 May 1862; Joseph Diltz to Mary Diltz, 23 May 1862, Diltz Papers.

25. *UCG*, 17 July 1862.

26. Ibid., 13 June 1878.

27. Robert Russell to father, 24 May 1862, William Russell Collection.

28. A. J. Riker diary, St. Paris Public Library.

29. Wilson, *Seventh Ohio*, 153–54; *UCG*, 10 July 1862.

30. *UCG*, 13 June 1878.

7. PORT REPUBLIC: AND THEY SAY THE BATTLE RAGED

1. *UCG*, 26 June 1862.

2. Robert Krick, *Conquering the Valley: Stonewall Jackson at Port Republic*, 60–63.

3. *OR*, vol. 12, 1:695.

4. *UCG*, 26 June 1862.

5. *OR*, vol. 12, 1:696.

6. *Delaware (Ohio) Gazette*, 20 June 1862; Krick, *Conquering the Valley*, 420–21.

7. Terry L. Jones, *Lee's Tigers: The Louisiana Infantry in the Army of Northern Virginia*, 89.

8. *UCG*, 26 June 1862.

9. "A Young Hero. Private Calvin C. Irwin, Company I, Sixty-Sixth Ohio Volunteers," *The Soldier's Casket* 3 (March 1865). The style is reminiscent of that of W. A. Brand, who may well have been the author.

10. *UCG*, 26 June 1862.

11. Robert Simpson pension file, RG 15.

12. *Delaware (Ohio) Gazette,* 11 July 1862.

13. Richard Taylor, *Destruction and Reconstruction: Personal Experiences of the Late War,* 93.

14. Edward A. Moore, *The Story of a Cannoneer under Stonewall Jackson,* 77.

15. *OR,* vol. 12, 1:690; Reid, *Ohio in the War,* 2:387.

16. *UCG,* 20 November 1862.

17. Levi Gladden pension file, RG 15. Levi's mother, Eliza, applied for a pension, representing herself as partially dependent on her son.

18. Sarah E. Gladden, "Lines on the Death of Levi Gladden, Who Fell at the Battle of Port Republic June 9, 1862, Aged 21 Years, 3 Months, 3 Weeks and 5 Days" (broadside).

19. *UCG,* 29 January 1863.

20. Ibid., 17 July 1862.

21. Ibid., 26 June 1862; SeCheverell, *Twenty-Ninth Ohio,* 47; *OR,* vol. 12, 1:687; C. J. Rawling, *History of the First Regiment Virginia Infantry,* 95; Richard S. Skidmore, ed., *The Civil War Journal of Billy Davis from Hopewell, Indiana to Port Republic, Virginia,* 146.

22. John N. Rathbun to Lib Rathbun, 14 June 1862, John N. Rathbun Papers, USAMHI; *UCG,* 4 July 1878.

23. SeCheverell, *Twenty-Ninth Ohio,* 48–49.

24. *UCG,* 26 June 1862.

25. Ibid., 26 June 1862, 17 July 1862; Samuel T. McMorran Pension file, RG 15.

26. *History of Champaign County,* 614.

27. *UCG,* 4 July 1878.

28. Quoted in William Bart Saxbe, Jr., *Thomas Saxbe (1810–1868) and His Descendants,* 30.

8. PRISONERS OF WAR: I HAVE JUST BEEN TO SEE A MAN DIE

1. *UCG,* 20 November 1862–12 February 1863. This chapter follows this source unless otherwise noted.

2. *UCG,* 20 November 1862.

3. Thomas Buxton pension file, RG 15.

4. W. A. Brand G.A.R. Post No. 98, "Soldiers Record Book."

5. *UCG,* 27 November 1862.

6. Ibid., 25 December 1862.

7. Ibid., 11 December 1862.

8. Abstracts of Obituaries, Death Notices and Funeral Notices from *Delaware (Ohio) Gazette,* January 1858–December 1874, 24.

9. *UCG,* 1 January 1863.

10. Sandra V. Parker, *Richmond's Civil War Prisons,* 14–15; *Atlas to Accompany the Official Records of the Union and Confederate Armies,* plate 89.

11. Parker, *Richmond's Civil War Prisons,* 15.

12. *UCG,* 22 January 1863.

13. Ibid., 29 January 1863.

14. Ibid., 5 February 1863.

15. Ibid.

16. Parker, *Richmond's Civil War Prisons,* 14.

9. REGROUPING

1. *UCG,* 19 June 1862.

2. Joseph Diltz to Mary Diltz, 25 June 1862, Diltz Papers; Thomas Sigman service records, Compiled Military Service Records of Volunteers, RG 94; 1860 census, Mad River Twp., Champaign County, Ohio, 289; special schedules of the 1890 census enumerating Union veterans and widows, Mutual, Union Twp., Champaign County, Ohio. This is one of the few instances when desertion is admitted in the 1890 veterans census.

3. Roll of Deserters from Ohio Regiments, OHS.

4. Charles Newcomb service record, Compiled Military Service Records of Volunteers, RG 94.

5. Squire Wallace service record, ibid.

6. Quoted in Saxbe, *Thomas Saxbe,* 30.

7. *UCG,* 17 July 1862.

8. Ibid., 10 July 1862.

9. Ibid., 31 July 1862.

10. Ibid., 17 July 1862.

11. Ibid.

12. Ibid., 17, 24 July 1862.

13. Charles Candy to Governor David Tod, 3 July 1862, Ohio Governors' Papers (MSS 306).

14. Joseph Diltz to Mary Diltz, 25 June 1862, Diltz Papers.

15. *UCG,* 24 July 1862.

16. Ibid., 7 August 1862.

17. Joshua Saxton to Governor David Tod, 3 July 1862, Ohio Governors' Papers (MSS 306).

18. *UCG,* 24 July 1862.

19. Ibid., 11 August 1862.

20. Ibid.

21. Ibid.

22. Samuel P. Bates, *Martial Deeds of Pennsylvania,* 634.

23. William Sayre to Ziba Sayre, 6 August 1862, Sayre Collection.

10. CEDAR MOUNTAIN: THY WORK AND THY WARFARE DONE

1. Troop totals attributed to the battle of Cedar Mountain vary. The count of twenty-two thousand versus twelve thousand comes from Robert Krick's account in *The Civil War Battlefield Guide,* 70–73. Anyone researching Cedar Mountain will benefit from Robert Krick's masterful and detailed account, *Stonewall Jackson at Cedar Mountain.*

2. SeCheverell, *Twenty-Ninth Ohio,* 51; *UCG,* 28 August 1862.

3. *UCG,* 28 August 1862; *OR,* vol. 12, 2:165.

4. Charles Candy to H. A. Tripp, 29 June 1887, John Mead Gould Papers, Duke University.

5. *OR*, vol. 12, 2:165–66.

6. *UCG*, 28 August 1862.

7. *OR*, vol. 12, 2:165.

8. *UCG*, 28 August 1862.

9. *OR*, vol. 12, 2:166.

10. Ibid., 137.

11. *Delaware (Ohio) Gazette*, 22 August 1862; Samuel T. McMorran pension file, RG 15.

12. Charles E. Fulton service record, Compiled Military Service Records of Volunteers, RG 94.

13. Joseph Diltz to Mary Diltz, 11 August 1862, Diltz Papers.

14. *The Medical and Surgical History of the War of the Rebellion*, 1:402; *UCG*, 28 August 1862.

15. David Espy journal (on microfilm), Wright State University, Fairborn, Ohio.

16. *UCG*, 28 August 1862.

17. Ibid.

18. Ibid.

19. Ibid.

20. Ibid., 16 April 1863.

II. A LOOK OF HORROR AND OF DESOLATION

1. *UCG*, 28 August, 4 September 1862.

2. Ibid., 18 September 1862.

3. Celestian Saintignon pension file, RG 15.

4. Bates, *Martial Deeds*, 859; Boatner, *Civil War Dictionary*, 856.

5. Espy journal (26 May 1862); *UCG*, 2, 30 October 1862; James R. Lytle, ed., *20th Century History of Delaware County, Ohio and Representative Citizens*, 804–5.

12. ANTIETAM: JUST COVERED WITH DIRT AND THAT IS ALL

1. George A. McKay, in Wilson, *Seventh Ohio*, 204.

2. Alpheus Williams to daughters, 22 September 1862, in Quaife, ed., *From the Cannon's Mouth*, 125.

3. Eugene Powell to John M. Gould, 18 November 1893, Antietam Collection, Dartmouth College; D. Cunningham and W. W. Miller, eds., *Report of the Ohio Antietam Battlefield Commission*, 44–49. Powell's letters form the basis for much of this work's account of the Sixty-sixth at Antietam. Apparently they were also the starting point for the narrative in the battlefield commission's report.

4. Antietam Battlefield Commission, 47–48.

5. Bell Irvin Wiley, *The Life of Billy Yank, the Common Soldier of the Union*, 58.

6. Eugene Powell to John Mead Gould, 18 November 1893, Antietam Collection.

7. *OR*, vol. 19, 1:509.

8. Joseph Diltz to Mary Diltz, 21 September 1862, Diltz Papers.

{ *Notes to Pages 89–108* · 293 }

9. Joseph Diltz to Sidney Milledge, 10 October 1862, ibid.

10. William Sayre to Ziba Sayre, 25 September 1862, Sayre Collection.

13. STAND OFF MR. SECESH

1. Alpheus Williams to daughter, 28 October 1862, in Quaife, ed., *From the Cannon's Mouth*, 141.

2. *UCG*, 30 October 1862.

3. John Geary to Mary Geary, 2 November 1862, in *A Politician Goes to War: The Civil War Letters of John White Geary*, ed. William Alan Blair, 65.

4. *UCG*, 20 November, 4 December 1862.

5. Ibid., 4 December 1862.

6. Ibid., 18 December 1862.

7. Anne Baxter Knutson, ed., *Took a Notion: The Civil War Diaries of William Henry Baxter of Mechanicsburg, Ohio*, 1.

8. Charles Candy to Governor David Tod, 5 October 1862, Ohio Governors' Papers (MSS 306).

9. *UCG*, 9 October 1862.

10. Ibid., 11 December 1862.

11. Ibid., 6 November 1862.

12. Ibid., 13 November 1862.

13. Ibid., 20 November 1862.

14. Wilson, *Seventh Ohio*, 218.

15. Ibid., 219; *UCG*, 16 December 1862.

16. *UCG*, 16 December 1862.

17. Ibid., 1 January 1863.

18. Ibid., 1 January, 26 February 1863; Nate Welsh to "Johnny Raw" [John Rathbun?], 26 December 1862, Rathbun Papers.

19. This account of the fight at Dumfries is largely derived from Candy's official report and those of his subordinates, in *OR*, vol. 21, 2:723–31. Stuart's report and those of his subordinates are found in the *OR*, vol. 21, 2:731–42, and in some instances they supplement or clarify the Federal reports.

20. *UCG*, 8 January 1863.

14. I AM GETTING VERY TIRED OF SOLDIERING

1. Joseph and Mary Diltz are listed (p. 171) in the 1860 census as living in Union Township, Champaign County, Ohio, with a child, Isadora, aged four months; the enumeration date is July 19. Diltz's pension file lists a child born October 27, 1861, but none before that date. These discrepancies aside, it is clear that Joseph Diltz was a father; certainly, Joseph's letters to Mary refer to "children."

2. Joseph Diltz pension file, RG 15.

3. Joseph Diltz to Mary Diltz, 10 November, 25 December 1862, 30 December 1863, Diltz Papers.

4. Ibid., 7 January 1863.

5. Ibid., 9 January 1863.
6. Robert T. Pennoyer, ed., *Diaries of Pvt. John W. Houtz 66th Ohio Volunteer Infantry, 1863–1864*, 14.
7. *UCG*, 12 March 1863.
8. Ibid., 19 March 1863.
9. Ibid.
10. *The Crisis*, 21 January 1863.
11. *UCG*, 19 March 1863.
12. William J. Constant to John N. Rathbun, 20 April 1863, Rathbun Papers.
13. 1860 U.S. census, Rush Township, Champaign County, Ohio, 5.
14. *UCG*, 5 February 1863.
15. Ibid., 22 January 1863.

15. CHANCELLORSVILLE: I STOOD UP TO THE RACK AND CUT THE HAY

1. Knutson, ed., *Took a Notion*, 15.
2. Robert Russell to father, 1 February 1863, William Russell Collection.
3. Ibid., 4 March 1863.
4. Pennoyer, ed., *Houtz*, 15.
5. *UCG*, 21 March 1863.
6. Frederick Dyer, *A Compendium of the War of the Rebellion*, 1618.
7. Robert Russell to family, 23 April 1863, William Russell Collection; Pennoyer, ed., *Houtz*, 16.
8. Joseph Diltz to Mary Diltz, 26 April 1863, Diltz Papers.
9. *OR*, vol. 25, 1:734.
10. Washington A. Roebling to John Bigelow, 9 December 1910, Bigelow Papers, Library of Congress, cited by Ernest B. Fergurson, *Chancellorsville 1863: The Souls of the Brave*, 129–30.
11. Pennoyer, ed., *Houtz*, 17.
12. *UCG*, 14 May 1863.
13. 66th Ohio Infantry Collection.
14. *UCG*, 1 August 1878. One of a series of extensive, though anonymous, letters written while on a tour of Civil War battlefields. The author was probably Frank Baldwin, a sergeant in Company I at the time of the Chancellorsville battle.
15. *OR*, vol. 25, 1:734.
16. Walter Frederick Beyer and Oscar Frederick Keydel, eds., *Deeds of Valor from Records in the Archives of the United States Government: How American Heroes Won the Medal of Honor*, 1:144–45; Joseph P. Mitchell, *The Badge of Gallantry: Recollections of Civil War Congressional Medal of Honor Winners: Letters from the Charles Kohen Collection*, 178–79; *UCG*, 21 May 1863.
17. *UCG*, 14 May 1863; Augustus Tanner to mother, 8 May 1863, Tanner Correspondence, OHS; "Journal of a Soldier," *UCG*, 25 April 1864; Robert Russell to father, 12 May 1863, William Russell Collection.
18. *UCG*, 1 August 1878.
19. Tallman memoir.
20. *OR*, vol. 25, 1:730–31.

21. Three letters published in the *Urbana Citizen and Gazette*<m>from Joseph C. Brand and Joshua Palmer (14 May 1863) and from W. A. Brand ("D. N. Arbaw," 21 May 1863)<m>speak of the rescue of the 60th New York. Interestingly, a history of the 60th itself, Richard Eddy's *History of the Sixtieth Regiment New York State Volunteers,* makes no mention of the episode.

22. 66th Ohio Infantry Collection.

23. *OR,* vol. 25, 1:743; Robert Russell to parents, 12 May 1863, William Russell Collection.

24. *OR,* vol. 25, 1:731; Augustus Tanner to mother, 8 May 1863, Tanner correspondence.

25. 66th Ohio Infantry Collection; *UCG,* 14 May 1863.

26. *UCG,* 21 May 1863; George Milledge to Mary Diltz, 9 May 1863, Diltz Papers.

27. William Sayre to Ziba Sayre, 9 May 1863, Sayre Collection.

28. *OR,* vol. 25, 1:184; W. A. Sampson pension file, RG 15; *UCG,* 21 May 1863; "Journal of a Soldier," *UCG,* 21 May 1863; Knutson, ed., *Took a Notion,* 21–22.

29. *OR,* vol. 25, 1:184, 733.

30. Robert Russell to father, 12 May 1863, William Russell Collection; Augustus Tanner to mother, 8 May 1863, Tanner correspondence.

31. Tallman memoir.

16. GETTYSBURG: THE ENEMY WILL SIMPLY SWALLOW YOU

1. Quoted in Shelby Foote, *The Civil War: A Narrative,* 2:315.

2. Robert Russell to parents, 22 May 1863, William Russell Collection.

3. Pennoyer, ed., *Houtz,* 20–21; 66th Ohio Infantry Collection.

4. Pennoyer, ed., *Houtz,* 22.

5. Edwin B. Coddington, *The Gettysburg Campaign: A Study in Command,* 119.

6. Pennoyer, ed., *Houtz,* 23; Blair, ed., *A Politician Goes to War,* 93.

7. Tallman memoir; *UCG,* 16 July 1863.

8. Tallman memoir.

9. *UCG,* 16 July 1863.

10. Tallman memoir.

11. *OR,* vol. 27, 1:826.

12. Eugene Powell, "'Rebellion's High Tide': Dashed against the Immovable Rocks of Gettysburg," *National Tribune* 19 (5 July 1900): 39.

13. 66th Ohio Infantry Collection.

14. Powell's recollections of the position taken by the Sixty-sixth on Culp's Hill are unclear. We have five accounts by Powell: *OR,* vol. 27, 1:844–45; the *National Tribune* article; his account in the 66th Ohio Infantry Collection; and two letters published in *The Bachelder Papers,* 1:584–85, 2:1226–27; however, a coherent picture does not emerge from these accounts. Most problematic is Powell's confusion of his left and right in his official report, and his references in other accounts to retaking Federal works. Fortunately, a letter from three of the Sixty-sixth's officers<m>John Mitchell, Thomas McConnell, T. G. Keller<m>to John Bachelder clearly locates the regiment at the position of the monument and markers on the hill today. In addition, the Tallman memoir states that the Sixty-sixth attacked the right and rear of Johnson's troops. The author is indebted to Harry Pfanz for his assistance in dealing with the issues

associated with the regiment's position on Culp's Hill. See also Mr. Pfanz's excellent account of the action on Culp's Hill in his *Gettysburg: Culp's Hill and Cemetery Hill.*

15. *UCG,* 16 July 1863; Pennoyer, ed., *Houtz,* 1; John W. Busey, *These Honored Dead: The Union Casualties at Gettysburg,* 224.

16. *UCG,* 23 July 1863.

17. John W. Busey and David G. Martin, *Regimental Strengths at Gettysburg,* 94.

18. Powell, "'Rebellion's High Tide'"; William M. Scott pension file, RG 15; *History of Logan County and Ohio,* 811.

19. Tallman memoir.

20. *OR,* vol. 27, 1:858.

21. Tallman memoir; William Sayre to family, 5 July 1863, Sayre Collection; *OR,* vol. 27, 1:833.

22. Tallman memoir.

23. Ibid.

17. WE ALL ARE ANXIOUS TO LEAVE THIS PLACE

1. Joseph Diltz to Mary Diltz, 30 June 1863, Diltz Papers.

2. *UCG,* 16 July 1863.

3. Tallman memoir.

4. Blair, ed., *A Politician Goes to War,* 105; George Milledge to Mary Diltz, 15 August 1863, Diltz Papers.

5. Pennoyer, ed., *Houtz,* 34–35.

6. Ibid., 35.

7. Ibid., 36.

8. Tallman memoir.

9. Ibid.

10. Joseph Diltz to Mary Diltz, 18 September 1863, Diltz Papers; Pennoyer, ed., *Houtz,* 40; Wilson, *Seventh Ohio,* 264; Blair, ed., *A Politician Goes to War,* 115.

18. WHY, AIN'T I DISTRIBUTING THEM?

1. *UCG,* 8 October 1863; Wilson, *Seventh Ohio,* 266; Tallman memoir. Altercations between soldiers on troop trains and citizens could erupt for a number of reasons. One such incident, at Cambridge, between troops and shopkeepers, resulted in the death of a soldier. See William G. Wolfe, *Stories of Guernsey County, Ohio: History of an Average Ohio County,* 291–92.

2. *UCG,* 8 October 1863.

3. Ibid., 1 October 1863.

4. Ibid., 27 August 1863. Once again we are seeing the antiwar Democrats only through the lens of the local Republican newspaper. No other contemporary account has been located.

5. Abraham Ingalls Papers, Sharon Ware Collection, Fairfield, Ohio.

6. *OR,* vol. 30, 2:697–700; *UCG,* 22 October 1863; Robert Russell to father, 18 October 1863, William Russell Collection.

7. Robert Russell to father, 22 September 1863, William Russell Collection; *UCG*, 22 October 1863.
8. *UCG*, 4 December 1863.
9. Ibid., 22 October 1863.
10. Ibid., 20 November 1863.
11. Ibid.

19. A FLAG ON THE MOUNTAIN

1. Ulysses S. Grant, *Ulysses S. Grant: Memoirs and Selected Letters*, 413.
2. Eugene Powell, "An Incident of the Capture of Lookout Mountain," *Historical and Philosophical Society of Ohio Publications*, 2:47–48.
3. Ibid., 49.
4. Tallman memoir.
5. *UCG*, 11 December 1863; Powell, "An Incident," 51.
6. Robert Russell to father, 4 December 1863, William Russell Collection; *OR*, vol. 31, 3:412, 420–21; Robert Russell pension file, RG 15.
7. Powell, "An Incident," 51.
8. *OR*, vol. 31, 2:402.
9. Ibid., vol. 23, 2:403.
10. 66th Ohio Infantry Collection. Brand's charges seem never to have been aired in print.
11. *OR*, vol. 31, 2:420; 66th Ohio Infantry Collection; *UCG*, 11 December 1863.
12. *OR*, vol. 31, 2:410.
13. Pennoyer, ed., *Houtz*, 4; *UCG*, 11 December 1863; Tallman memoir.

20. REENLISTMENT AND FURLOUGH: REPRESENTATIVES OF ALL THAT IS BEST

1. Blair, ed., *A Politician Goes to War*, 144; *OR*, vol. 31, 2:406. The evidence is mixed as to what really happened, although it is clear that several buildings were burned, perhaps including a few houses. If the entire village was in fact burned, it is curious that there is no reference to it in Susie Blaylock McDaniel's *Official History of Catoosa County, Georgia 1853–1953*, a local history that takes a predictably dim view of the Union army. Robert Russell wrote to his father (4 December 1863) that the troops had burned six flour mills, two sawmills, two tanneries, a niter factory, a wagon shop, and a gun manufacture, but he makes no mention of burning houses. Yet in Eddy's *History of the Sixtieth Regiment, New York State Volunteers* we read that the White Stars "burned the village" (317). Albert R. Greene, son of General Greene, writes in "From Bridgeport to Ringgold by Way of Lookout Mountain" that the troops "moved away by the light of the burning houses, for it was said that Osterhaus' men had been fired on from the windows as they entered the town" (45). William Baxter noted in his diary that "we set fire to the town before we left" (Knutson, ed., *Took a Notion*, 32).
2. Wilson, *Seventh Ohio*, 290; Theodore Wilder, *The History of Company C, Seventh Regiment, O.V.I.*, 40.

3. Middleton, *Champaign County,* 1:790–91, 796; Joseph Holliday, "Relief for Soldiers' Families in Ohio during the Civil War," *Ohio History* 71 (July 1962): 99.

4. Tallman memoir.

5. Reid Mitchell, *The Vacant Chair: The Northern Soldier Leaves Home,* 158.

6. Joseph Diltz to Mary Diltz, 4 December 1863, Diltz Papers.

7. Ibid., 6 December 1863.

8. Ibid., 12 December 1863.

9. *UCG,* 1 January 1864; Middleton, *Champaign County,* 1:796.

10. *UCG,* 4 December 1863.

11. Middleton, *Champaign County,* 1:796.

12. The enlistment count is based on the rosters published in Ohio Adjutant General's Report.

13. Smith and Smith, *Buckeye Titan,* 473; Reid, *Ohio in the War,* 1:71.

14. *UCG,* 28 January 1864.

15. Wood Gray, *The Hidden Civil War: The Story of the Copperheads,* 141–42, 164–65; *Union County Democrat,* 3 February 1864.

21. PREPARATION FOR ATLANTA

1. *UCG,* 7 April 1864; Blair, ed., *A Politician Goes to War,* 150; Pennoyer, ed., *Houtz,* 42–44.

2. Pennoyer, ed., *Houtz,* 46.

3. Ibid., 49.

4. Ibid., 50, 58–59.

5. *UCG,* 18 February, 10, 24 March 1864; Middleton, *Champaign County,* 1:791.

6. George Milledge to Mary Diltz, 30 March 1864, Diltz Papers; *UCG,* 7 April 1864.

7. *UCG,* 3 March, 7 April 1864.

8. Tallman memoir.

22. OH!

1. William Sayre to Ziba Sayre, 8 May 1864, Sayre Collection.

2. *OR,* vol. 38, 2:114–17, 153–55; Jacob D. Cox, *Sherman's Battle for Atlanta,* 34–35.

3. *OR,* vol. 38, 2:188–89.

4. Pennoyer, ed., *Houtz,* 74.

5. Williams to daughter, 31 May 1864, in Quaife, ed., *From the Cannon's Mouth,* 312.

6. *OR,* vol. 38, 2:122–25, 155–56; Albert Castel, *Decision in the West: The Atlanta Campaign of 1864,* 221–26; *UCG,* 9, 30 June 1864; 66th Ohio Infantry Collection.

7. Pennoyer, ed., *Houtz,* 75; *UCG,* 30 June 1864.

8. 66th Ohio Infantry Collection.

9. *OR,* vol. 38, 2:125.

10. Pennoyer, ed., *Houtz,* 78.

11. *OR,* vol. 28, 2:127; Geary to wife, June 1864, Blair, ed., *A Politician Goes to War,* 180–81; Castel, *Decision in the West,* 275–79.

12. *OR,* vol. 38, 2:127–28, 156–57, 187.

13. W. A. Sampson to Ziba Sayre, 19 June 1864, Sayre Collection.
14. *OR,* vol. 38, 2:129; *History of Union County,* 638.
15. *OR,* vol. 28, 2:132–33.
16. *UCG,* 28 July 1864.
17. Ibid., 21 July 1864.
18. Douglas Southall Freeman, ed., *Lee's Dispatches: Unpublished Letters of General Robert E. Lee, C.S.A., to Jefferson Davis and the War Department of the Confederate States of America 1862–1865,* 282.

23. GENERAL SHERMAN HAS TAKEN ATLANTA

1. *OR,* vol. 38, 2:136–41, 158–59; 66th Ohio Infantry Collection.
2. Robert Russell pension file, RG 15; Robert Russell to father, 24 August 1864, William Russell Collection; Pennoyer, ed., *Houtz,* 89.
3. *OR,* vol. 38, 2:140.
4. Ibid., 141; *UCG,* 4 August 1864; Pennoyer, ed., *Houtz,* 89.
5. *UCG,* 21 July 1864.
6. Ibid., 22 September 1864; Jesse Brock pension file, RG 15.
7. James P. Conn pension file, RG 15.
8. *UCG,* 7, 28 July 1864.
9. Castel, *Decision in the West,* 381; Herman Hattaway and Archer Jones's *How the North Won: A Military History of the Civil War* estimates Confederate casualties to be much higher (609).
10. *OR,* vol. 38, 2:141; *UCG,* 4 August 1864.
11. Celestian Saintignon pension file, RG 15.
12. *OR,* vol. 38, 2:112–47.

24. TO THE SEA AND VICTORY

1. *UCG,* 22 September 1864; William Sampson pension file, RG 15.
2. Robert Russell pension file, RG 15; Robert Russell to father, 14 September 1864 and 5 October 1864, William Russell Collection; *UCG,* 22 September 1864; Lytle, *20th Century History of Delaware County, Ohio and Representative Citizens,* 805.
3. John N. Rathbun to Brig. Gen. William D. Whipple, 4 October 1864, Rathbun Papers.
4. Augustus Tanner to father, 6 September 1864, Tanner correspondence.
5. *UCG,* 15 September 1864.
6. Middleton, *Champaign County,* 1:797. These records have unfortunately eluded the author.
7. *OR,* vol. 28, 3:663–68.
8. Ohio Adjutant General, Roster, 5:519–61; Roll of Deserters from Ohio Regiments, 1861–1866, OHS; Pennoyer, ed., *Houtz,* 103, 111.
9. *OR,* vol. 79, 162.
10. Robert Russell to "Miss Delia," 26 December 1864, OHS.

11. Pennoyer, ed., *Houtz*, 118.

12. *OR*, vol. 44, 269–83. See especially his exacting tabulations of supplies seized and of materials and facilities destroyed (282). The impression conveyed is one of an exacting organization—but then, Geary was a master at conveying impressions.

13. *UCG*, 12 January 1865; *OR*, vol. 64, 290.

14. *OR*, vol. 47, 1:280; Geary to wife, 23 December 1864, Blair, ed., *A Politician Goes to War*, 219.

15. Pennoyer, ed., *Houtz*, 121–23.

16. Russell to mother, 18 January 1865; Russell to father, 13, 17 February 1865, William Russell Collection.

17. Tallman memoir.

18. Ibid.

19. *OR*, vol. 47, 1:682–83.

20. Tallman memoir.

21. *OR*, vol. 47, 1:687, 707; Fitz Hugh McMaster, *History of Fairfield County, South Carolina, from "Before the White Man Came" to 1942*, 156–57.

22. *OR*, vol. 47, 1:697.

23. Geary to wife, 19 April 1865, Blair, ed., *A Politician Goes to War*, 239.

24. *Cincinnati Gazette*, 30 April 1865, quoted in Middleton, *Champaign County*, 1:803.

25. HONOR AND POSITION

1. Tallman memoir.

2. Ibid.

3. Dyer, *Compendium*, 1555. The 193d was mustered out on August 3, 1865, but even so it lost twenty-nine men to sickness.

4. Ibid., 1528.

5. Frank Levelle service record, Compiled Military Service Records of Volunteers, RG 94.

6. Middleton, *Champaign County*, 2:847; Joseph Diltz pension file, RG 15.

7. *UCG*, 25 May 1865.

8. Middleton, *Champaign County*, 2:384–85; *Centennial Biographical History of Champaign County*, 609–11; *Champaign County*, 647–48.

9. "Surgical History," *Medical and Surgical History*, 2:478; *Champaign County*, 827; Middleton, *Champaign County*, 1:134.

10. Middleton, *Champaign County*, 1:135–36, 139.

11. *History of Delaware County and Ohio*, 752.

12. Felice A. Bonadio, *North of Reconstruction: Ohio Politics, 1865–1870*, 24–25.

13. Ezra J. Warner, *Generals in Blue: Lives of the Ohio Commanders*, 170.

14. Whitlock, *Forty Years of It*, 18–19.

15. Ibid., 19–20; Middleton, *Champaign County*, 2:820–21; *Urbana and Champaign County*, 64.

16. *Champaign County*, 633–34, 655–56.

17. *Urbana and Champaign County*, 53. Middleton noted that on September 1, 1862, the county's tally for men of military age came to 4,112 (*Champaign County*, 1:683).

18. Middleton, *Champaign County,* 1:803–6.

19. Statistics cited in Stuart McConnell, *Glorious Contentment: The Grand Army of the Republic, 1865–1900,* 153; Mary R. Dearing, *Veterans in Politics: The Story of the G.A.R.,* 400; Maris A. Vinovskis, "Have Social Historians Lost the Civil War? Some Preliminary Demographic Speculations," in *Toward a Social History of the American Civil War: Exploratory Essays,* ed. Maris A. Vinovskis, 23, 27.

20. Thomas Whalen pension file, RG 15; *List of Pensioners on the Roll, January 1, 1883,* 3:42.

21. Levi Gladden pension file, RG 15.

22. Lemuel Ayres pension file, RG 15; W. A. Brand G.A.R. Post No. 98, "Soldiers Record Book."

23. Jasper O'Haver pension file, RG 15. Punctuation has been added to the quotation.

24. Augustus Tanner pension file, RG 15. Punctuation has been added to the quotation.

25. *Proceedings of the Twenty-seventh Annual Encampment of the Department of Ohio, Grand Army of the Republic, Hamilton, Ohio, May 16th, 17th, and 18th,* 4.

26. McConnell, *Glorious Contentment,* 93–103.

27. W. A. Brand G.A.R. Post 98, Minutes, Champaign County Historical Society, Urbana, Ohio.

28. *UCG,* 8 February 1877.

29. Ibid., 11 October 1907.

30. Ibid., 18 January 1912.

31. Veterans Administration letter to Mrs. Charles Candy, 5 September 1931, 66th O.V.I. Reunion Association papers, Champaign County Historical Society, Urbana, Ohio.

32. *UCG,* 13 June 1878. The 66th Ohio Infantry Collection (MSS 842) at the Ohio Historical Society contains Powell's draft history, with W. A. Brand's sometimes critical annotations and comments.

33. *UCG,* 22 October 1863; *Champaign County, Ohio 1991,* 323; Fisher, "Groping Toward Victory," 35.

34. *Champaign County,* 326; *Champaign County, Ohio 1991,* 297–99; Middleton, *Champaign County,* 1:1143–46.

35. Brand Whitlock, "The Field of Honor," in *The Fall Guy,* 51, 56–57.

36. Allan Nevins, ed., *The Letters and Journal of Brand Whitlock,* 125; Brand Whitlock, *J. Hardin and Son,* 163.

37. Whitlock, "The Field of Honor."

38. Ibid., 70.

39. Nevins, ed., *Letters and Journal of Brand Whitlock,* 264.

40. Brand Whitlock, "Orator of the Day," in *The Fall Guy,* 137.

41. Ibid., 138–39.

42. Ibid., 140–41.

43. W. A. Brand G.A.R. Post No. 98, "Soldiers Record Book."

Bibliograhy

MANUSCRIPT SOURCES

Champaign County Historical Society, Urbana, Ohio
    66th Ohio Reunion Association scrapbook and papers
    W. A. Brand Post 98 (Grand Army of the Republic) miscellaneous papers
Champaign County Public Library, Urbana, Ohio
    W. A. Brand Post No. 98 (Grand Army of the Republic)
    Personal War Sketches
Dartmouth College, Hanover, New Hampshire
    Eugene Powell letters, Antietam Collection
Duke University, Durham, North Carolina
    John Mead Gould Papers
    Joseph Diltz Papers, 1861–65
    William G. McCreary Papers, 1864–65
Charles Emory Collection, Springfield, Ohio
    Samuel B. Briggs diary, 1862
Kyle Kelch Collection, Urbana, Ohio
    Joseph Van Deman correspondence
    Thomas P. Bond correspondence

Ohio Historical Society, Columbus, Ohio
    66th Ohio Infantry Collection (MSS 842), containing draft history of the
        regiment by Eugene Powell with comments by W. A. Brand
    Robert H. Russell letter, 1864 (OVS 131)
    Augustus Tanner correspondence, 1862–64 (VFM 1825)
    Ohio Adjutant General, Muster-in and Muster-out Rolls,
        1861–65 (Series 2440)
    ————. Roll of Deserters from Ohio Regiments, 1861–1865
        (Series 108, BV 1936)
    Ohio Governors' Papers (MSS 999)
William S. Russell Collection, Urbana, Ohio
    Robert H. Russell correspondence, 1861–65
Saint Paris Public Library, Saint Paris, Ohio
    A. J. Riker diary (photocopy)
United States Army Military History Institute, Carlisle Barracks, Pennsylvania
    John M. Rathbun Papers, 1862–64
    William M. Sayre Collection(photocopy transcript), 1862–64
    William H. H. Tallman memoir, manuscript
United States National Archives, Washington, D.C.
    Compiled Records Showing Service of Military Units in Volunteer Union
        Organizations. Record of Events 66th Ohio Volunteer Infantry (Record
        Group 94)
    Compiled Service Records of Union Veterans (Record Group 94)
    Union Pension Records (Record Group 15)
    Sharon Ware Collection, Fairfield, Ohio
    Abraham Ingalls Papers
Wright State University, Fairborn, Ohio
    David H. Espy journal, 1862 (microfilm)

GENERAL REFERENCE WORKS

Atlas to Accompany the Official Records of the Union and Confederate Armies.
    Reprint, New York: Fairfax Press, 1983.
Boatner, Mark Mayo, III. *The Civil War Dictionary.* Rev. ed. New York: Vin-
    tage, 1987.
Bosse, David. *Civil War Newspaper Maps: A Historical Atlas.* Baltimore: Johns
    Hopkins University Press, 1993.
The Civil War Battlefield Guide. Boston: Houghton Mifflin, 1990.
Cromie, Alice Hamilton. *A Tour Guide to the Civil War.* 2d ed., revised and
    updated. New York: E. P. Dutton, 1975.
Current, Richard N., ed. *Encyclopedia of the Confederacy.* New York: Simon and
    Schuster, 1993.

Dictionary of American Biography. New York: Scribner's, 1928–58.

Dyer, Frederick. *A Compendium of the War of the Rebellion.* Des Moines, Iowa: Dyer, 1908.

McPherson, James M. *The Atlas of the Civil War.* New York: Prentice Hall Macmillan, 1994.

Ohio Adjutant General. *Official Roster of the Soldiers of the State of Ohio in the War of the Rebellion, 1861–1866.* Akron and Cincinnati, Ohio, 1886–95.

Sifakis, Stewart. *Who Was Who in the Civil War.* New York: Facts on File, 1980.

U.S. Adjutant General. *Official Army Register of the Volunteer Force of the United States Army for the Years 1861, '62, '63, '64, '65.* Washington, D.C.: Adjutant General, 1867.

U.S. War Department. *The War of the Rebellion: A Compilation of the Official Records of the Union and Confederate Armies.* 128 vols. Ser. 1. Washington, D.C.: GPO, 1880–1901.

Warner, Ezra J. *Generals in Blue: Lives of the Union Commanders.* Baton Rouge: Louisiana State Univ. Press, 1964.

PUBLISHED PRIMARY SOURCES

Alexander, William L. *List of Ex-Soldiers, Sailors and Marines Living in Iowa.* Des Moines, 1886.

Baumgartner, Richard A., and Larry M. Strayer, eds. *Echoes of Battle: The Struggle for Chattanooga.* Huntington, W.Va.: Blue Acorn Press, 1996.

Beyer, Walter Frederick, and Oscar Frederick Keydel, eds. *Deeds of Valor from Records in the Archives of the United States Government: How American Heroes Won the Medal of Honor.* Detroit: Perrien-Keydel, 1907.

Blair, William Alan, ed. *A Politician Goes to War: The Civil War Letters of John White Geary.* University Park: Pennsylvania State Univ. Press, 1995.

Cryder, Marilyn M., and Sharlene Shoaf. *Abstracts of Obituaries, Death Notices and Funeral Notices from The Delaware Gazette, Delaware, Ohio January 1858–December 1874.* Delaware, Ohio: Cryder, 1993.

Cunningham, D., and W. W. Miller, eds. *Report of the Ohio Antietam Battlefield Commission.* Springfield, Ohio: Springfield Publishing, 1904.

Elwood, John W. *Elwood's Stories of the Old Ringgold Cavalry 1847–1865: The First Three Year Cavalry of the Civil War.* Coal Center, Pa.: John W. Elwood, 1914.

Forry, Michael. "'Enough to Make a Preacher Sware': A Union Mule Driver's Diary of Sherman's March." Transcribed by W. R. Johnson in *Atlanta History* 33 (Fall 1989): 3.

Freeman, Douglas Southall, ed. *Lee's Dispatches: Unpublished Letters of General Robert E. Lee, C.S.A. to Jefferson Davis and the War Department of The Confederate States of America, 1862–1865.* Baton Rouge: Louisiana State Univ. Press, 1994.

Grant, Ulysses S. *Memoirs and Selected Letters.* New York: Literary Classics of the United States, 1990.

Greene, Albert R. "From Bridgeport to Ringgold by Way of Lookout Mountain." In *Soldiers and Sailors Historical Society of Rhode Island Personal Narratives,* ser. 4, no. 7 (1890).

Knutson, Anne Baxter, ed. *Took a Notion: The Civil War Diaries of William Henry Baxter of Mechanicsburg, Ohio.* Afton, Minn.: A. B. Knutson, 1996.

Ladd, David L., and Audrey J. Ladd, eds. *The Bachelder Papers.* Dayton, Ohio: Morningside, 1994.

List of Pensioners on the Roll, January 1, 1883. Washington, D.C.: GPO, 1883.

McAdams, F. M. *Every-day Soldier Life, or a History of the One Hundred and Thirteenth Ohio Volunteer Infantry.* Columbus, Ohio: Chas. M. Cott, 1884.

McDonald, Cornelia. *A Diary with Reminiscences of the War and Refugee Life in the Shenandoah Valley 1860–1865.* Annotated and supplemented by Hunter McDonald. Nashville, Tenn.: N.p., 1934.

The Medical and Surgical History of the War of the Rebellion. Washington, D.C.: GPO, 1877.

Mitchell, Joseph B. *The Badge of Gallantry: Recollections of Civil War Congressional Medal of Honor Winners: Letters from the Charles Kohen Collection.* New York: Macmillan, 1968.

Moore, Edward A. *The Story of a Cannoneer under Stonewall Jackson.* Lynchburg, Va.: J. P. Bell, 1910.

Nevins, Allan, ed. *The Letters and Journal of Brand Whitlock.* New York: D. Appleton-Century, 1936.

Pennoyer, Robert T., ed. *Diaries of Pvt. John W. Houtz, 66th Ohio Volunteer Infantry 1863–1864.* Homer, N.Y.: Robert Pennoyer, 1994.

Pierson, Stephen. "From Chattanooga to Atlanta in 1864." *Proceedings of the New Jersey Historical Society* 16 (1931).

Population of the United States in 1860. Washington, D.C.: GPO, 1864.

Powell, Eugene. "An Incident of the Capture of Lookout Mountain." Part 2. *Historical and Philosopical Society of Ohio Publications* (1926).

———. "'Rebellion's High Tide.' Dashed Against the Immovable Rocks of Gettysburg. The Splendid Work on Culp's Hill by the Twelfth Corps." *National Tribune* 19 (5 July 1900): 38, 39.

Proceedings of the Twenty-seventh Annual Encampment of the Department of Ohio, Grand Army of the Republic, Hamilton, Ohio, May 16th, 17th, and 18th. Sandusky, Ohio: Ohio G.A.R., 1893.

Quaife, Milo M., ed. *From the Cannon's Mouth: The Civil War Letters of General Alpheus S. Williams.* Detroit: Wayne State Univ. Press, 1959.

SeCheverell, J. Hamp. *Journal History of the Twenty-Ninth Ohio Veteran Volunteers, 1861–1865.* Cleveland, 1883.

The Seventh Regiment: A Record. New York: James Miller, 1865.

Skidmore, Richard S., ed. *The Civil War Journal of Billy Davis: From Hopewell,*

Indiana, to Port Republic, Virginia. Greencastle, Ind.: Nugget Publishers, 1989.

Taylor, Richard. *Destruction and Reconstruction: Personal Experiences of the Late War.* New York: Appleton, 1879.

Whitlock, Brand. *Forty Years of It.* New York: D. Appleton, 1925.

Wilder, Theodore. *The History of Company C, Seventh Regiment, O.V.I.* Oberlin, Ohio: J. B. T. Marsh, 1866.

Will Abstracts of Champaign County, Ohio: Books A thru F, 1810–1888. Urbana, Ohio: Champaign County Genealogical Society, 1996.

Wilson, Lawrence. *Itinerary of the Seventh Ohio Volunteer Infantry, 1861–1864.* New York: Neale Publishing, 1907.

Wood, George L. *Famous Deeds by American Heroes: A Record of Events from Sumpter to Lookout Mountain.* New York: James Miller, 1865.

"A Young Hero. Private Calvin C. Irwin, Company I, Sixty-Sixth Ohio Volunteers." *The Soldier's Casket* 3 (March 1865).

SECONDARY SOURCES

20th Century History of Delaware County, Ohio and Representative Citizens. Ed. James R. Lytle. Chicago: Biographical Publishing, 1908.

Bates, Samuel P. *Martial Deeds of Pennsylvania.* Philadelphia: T. H. Davis, 1875.

Bigelow, John, Jr. *The Campaign of Chancellorsville: A Strategic and Tactical Study.* New Haven, Conn.: Yale Univ. Press, 1910.

Biographical Record of Clark County, Ohio. Chicago: S. J. Clarke, 1902.

Bonadio, Felice A. *North of Reconstruction: Ohio Politics, 1865–1870.* New York: New York Univ. Press, 1970.

Brand, William A. *Roll of Honor: The Soldiers of Champaign County Who Died for the Union.* Urbana, Ohio: Saxton & Brand, 1876.

Busey, John W. *These Honored Dead: The Union Casualties at Gettysburg.* 2d ed. Hightstown, N.J.: Longstreet House, 1996.

Busey, John W., and David G. Martin. *Regimental Strengths at Gettysburg.* Baltimore: Gateway Press, 1982.

Castel, Albert. *Decision in the West: The Atlanta Campaign of 1864.* Lawrence: Univ. Press of Kansas, 1992.

Centennial Biographical History of Champaign County. Chicago: Lewis Publishing, 1902.

Champaign County, Ohio 1991. Urbana, Ohio: Champaign County Genealogical Society, 1991.

Clark, Walter. *Histories of the Several Regiments and Battalions from North Carolina in the Great War 1861–'65.* Reprint, Wendell, N.C.: Broadfoot's Bookmark, 1982.

Coddington, Edwin B. *The Gettysburg Campaign: A Study in Command.* New York: Charles Scribner's Sons, 1968.

Collins, Darrell L. *The Battles of Cross Keys and Port Republic.* Lynchburg, Va.: H. E. Howard, 1993.

Cox, Jacob D. *Sherman's Battle for Atlanta.* Reprint, New York: Da Capo Press, 1994.

———. *Sherman's March to the Sea, Hood's Tennessee Campaign & the Carolina Campaigns of 1865.* Reprint, New York: Da Capo Press, 1994.

Cozzens, Peter. *The Shipwreck of Their Hopes: The Battles for Chattanooga.* Urbana: Univ. of Illinois Press, 1994.

Dearing, Mary R. *Veterans in Politics: The Story of the G.A.R.* Baton Rouge: Louisiana State Univ. Press, 1952.

Eddy, Richard. *History of the Sixtieth Regiment, New York State Volunteers.* Philadelphia: Richard Eddy, 1864.

Fisher, Noel. "Groping toward Victory: Ohio's Administration of the Civil War." *Ohio History* 105 (Winter–Spring 1996).

Fergurson, Ernest B. *Chancellorsville 1863: The Souls of the Brave.* New York: Vintage Books, 1993.

Freeman, Douglas Southall. *Lee's Lieutenants: A Study in Command.* 3 vols. New York: Scribner's, 1942.

Gaff, Alan D. *On Many a Bloody Field: Four Years in the Iron Brigade.* Bloomington: Indiana Univ. Press, 1996.

Glatthar, Joseph T. *The March to the Sea and Beyond: Sherman's Troops in the Savannah and Carolinas Campaigns.* New York: New York Univ. Press, 1986.

Gray, Wood. *The Hidden Civil War: The Story of the Copperheads.* New York: Viking Press, 1942.

Greene, A. Wilson. "'A Step All-Important and Essential to Victory': Henry W. Slocum and the Twelfth Corps on July 1–2, 1863." In *The Second Day at Gettysburg: Essays on Confederate and Union Leadership,* ed. Gary W. Gallagher. Kent, Ohio: Kent State Univ. Press, 1993.

Hattaway, Herman, and Archer Jones. *How the North Won: A Military History of the Civil War.* Chicago: Univ. of Illinois Press, 1983.

Hennessy, John J. *Return to Bull Run: The Campaign and Battle of Second Manassas.* New York: Simon & Schuster, 1993.

Historical Review of Logan County, Ohio. Chicago: S. J. Clarke, 1903.

History of Champaign County, Ohio. Chicago: W. H. Beers, 1881.

History of Clark County, Ohio. Chicago: W. H. Beers, 1881.

History of Delaware County and Ohio. Chicago: O. L. Baskin, 1880.

History of Hardin County, Ohio. Chicago: Warner, Beers, 1883.

History of Logan County and Ohio. Chicago: O. L. Baskin, 1880.

History of Marion County, Ohio. Chicago: Leggett, Conaway, 1883.

History of Union County, Ohio. Chicago: W. H. Beers, 1883.

Hitt, Michael D., comp. *First Lieutenant Joseph White Hitt 1844–1864.* N.p., 1994.

Holliday, Joseph E. "Relief for Soldiers' Families in Ohio during the Civil War." *Ohio History* 71 (July 1962): 2.

Jacoby, J. Wilbur. *History of Marion County, Ohio and Representative Citizens.* Chicago: Biographical Publishing, 1907.

Jones, Terry L. *Lee's Tigers: The Louisiana Infantry in the Army of Northern Virginia.* Baton Rouge: Louisiana State Univ. Press, 1987.

Krick, Robert. *Conquering the Valley: Stonewall Jackson at Port Republic.* New York: William Morrow, 1996.

———. *Stonewall Jackson at Cedar Mountain.* Chapel Hill: Univ. of North Carolina Press, 1990.

Linderman, Gerald F. *Embattled Courage: The Experience of Combat in the American Civil War.* New York: Free Press, 1987.

Lytle, James R. *20th Century History of Delaware County, Ohio and Representative Citizens.* Chicago: Biographical Publishing, 1908.

McConnell, Stuart. *Glorious Contentment: The Grand Army of the Republic, 1865–1900.* Chapel Hill: Univ. of North Carolina Press, 1992.

McDaniel, Susie Blaylock. *Official History of Catoosa County, Georgia 1853–1953.* Dalton, Ga., 1953.

McMaster, Fitz Hugh. *History of Fairfield County, South Carolina, from "Before the White Man Came" to 1942.* 1946. Reprint, Spartanburg, S.C.: Reprint Co., 1980.

McPherson, James M. *Battle Cry of Freedom: Civil War Era.* New York: Oxford Univ. Press, 1988.

The Medal of Honor of the United States Army. Washington, D.C.: U.S. Dept. of the Army, 1948.

Middleton, Evan P. *History of Champaign County, Ohio.* Indianapolis: Bowen, 1917.

Mitchell, Reid. *The Vacant Chair: The Northern Soldier Leaves Home.* New York: Oxford Univ. Press, 1993.

Moe, Richard. *The Last Full Measure: The Life and Death of the First Minnesota Volunteers.* New York: Henry Holt, 1993.

O'Brien, Kevin. "'A Perfect Roar of Musketry': Candy's Brigade in the Fight for Culp's Hill." *The Gettysburg Magazine* 9 (July 1993).

Parker, Sandra V. *Richmond's Civil War Prisons.* Lynchburg, Va.: H. E. Howard, 1990.

Pfanz, Harry W. *Gettysburg—Culp's Hill and Cemetery Hill.* Chapel Hill: Univ. of North Carolina Press, 1994.

Rankin, *Thomas M. Stonewall Jackson's Romney Campaign January 1–February 20, 1862.* Lynchburg, Va.: H. E. Howard, 1994.

Rawling, C. J. *History of the First Regiment Virginia Infantry.* Philadelphia: J. B. Lippincott, 1887.

Reid, Whitelaw. *Ohio in the War: Her Statesmen, Generals and Soldiers.* Columbus, Ohio: Eclectic, 1893.

Saxbe, William Bart, Jr. *Thomas Saxbe (1810–1860) and His Descendants.* Baltimore: Gateway Press, 1980.

Sears, Stephen W. *Chancellorsville.* Boston: Houghton-Mifflin, 1996.

————. *Landscape Turned Red: The Battle of Antietam.* New York: Ticknor & Fields, 1983.

Smith, Joseph P., ed. *History of the Republican Party in Ohio and Memoirs of Its Representative Supporters.* Chicago: Lewis Publishing, 1898.

Smith, William E., and Ophia D. Smith. *A Buckeye Titan.* Cincinnati: Historical & Philosophical Society of Ohio, 1953.

Statement of Military Services, &c. of Charles Candy, (Late) Colonel 66th Ohio Vet. Vol. Infantry Brevet Brigadier General, U.S. Vols. N.p., n.d.

Summers, Festus P. *The Baltimore and Ohio in the Civil War.* New York: G. P. Putnam's, 1939.

Sword, Wiley. *Mountains Touched with Fire: Chattanooga Besieged, 1863.* New York: St. Martin's Press, 1995.

Tanner, Robert G. *Stonewall in the Valley: Thomas J. "Stonewall" Jackson's Shenandoah Valley Campaign, Spring, 1862.* 2d ed. Mechanicsburg, Pa.: Stackpole Books, 1996.

Thackery, David T. "A Work in Progress: The Study of a Rural Immigrant Community." *Origins* 6 (1990): 2, 3.

Urbana and Champaign County. Urbana, Ohio: Gaumer Publishing, 1942.

Vinovskis, Maris A., ed. *Toward a Social History of the American Civil War: Exploratory Essays.* New York: Cambridge Univ. Press, 1990.

Watts, Ralph M. "History of the Underground Railroad in Mechanicsburg." *Ohio Archaeological and Historical Quarterly* 42 (1934).

Wiley, Bell Irvin. *The Life of Billy Yank, the Common Soldier of the Union.* Baton Rouge: Louisiana State Univ. Press, 1952.

Wilhelm, Hubert G. H. *The Origins and Distribution of Settlement Groups: Ohio, 1850.* Athens: Ohio Univ. Press, 1982.

Wolfe, William G. *Stories of Guernsey County, Ohio: History of an Average Ohio County.* Cambridge, Ohio: William Wolfe, 1943.

FICTION AND POETRY

Gladden, Sarah E. "Lines Composed on Levi Gladden, Who Enlisted Oct. 29th, 1861, under Capt. C. Fulton, Co. A, 66th Reg., O.V.I." Broadside.

————. "Lines on the Death of Levi Gladden, Who Fell at the Battle of Port Republic June 9, 1862, Aged 21 Years, 3 Months, 3 Weeks, and 5 Days." Broadside.

Miller, Paul W., ed. *Brand Whitlock's The Buckeyes: Politics and Abolitionism in an Ohio Town, 1836–1845.* Athens: Ohio Univ. Press, 1977.

Whitlock, Brand. *The Fall Guy.* Indianapolis: Bobbs-Merrill, 1912.

————. *The Gold Brick.* Indianapolis: Bobbs-Merrill, 1910.

————. *J. Hardin and Son.* New York: D. Appleton, 1923.

NEWSPAPERS

The Crisis

Delaware (Ohio) Gazette

Ohio State Democrat

Union County Democrat

Union County Gazette

Urbana (Ohio) Citizen and Gazette

Urbana (Ohio) Daily Citizen

Urbana (Ohio) Daily Times Citizen

Urbana (Ohio) Free Press

Urbana (Ohio) Morning Tribune

Urbana (Ohio) Union

Index

Baldwin, William, 14
Balloons, reconnaissance, 130
Banks, Gen. Nathaniel P.: at Cedar
    Mountain, 88, 91–92; command of,
    44, 79, 98; and Pope's defeat, 97–98; at
    Strasburg and Winchester, 54–55
Baxter, Sgt. Stephen, 35, 67–68, 112–13
Baxter, William Henry, 112–13, 127, 223
Belle Isle, prisoners on, 73, 139
Bentonville, North Carolina, 217
Best, W., 80
Bond, Thomas, 43
Bower, Marquis, 72
Bragg, Braxton, 176; and Army of Ten-
    nessee, 159, 189; at Chattanooga, 167,
    172
Brand, Quartermaster Joseph Carter, 7,
    13, 16, 66, 143, 165, 225; at Chancellors-
    ville, 132–33; family of, 112, 236–37;
    and monument association, 226; in
    politics, 30–31, 224; as quartermaster,
    38, 48; support for war, 123
Brand, William Augustus, 13, 31, 51, 67,
    97, 156, 163, 169; after war, 224–26,
    235; on camps, 111, 164; on casualties,
    46, 205; on Chancellorsville, 132–33,
    138; on civilians, 38–39, 83–84, 143,
    160; on condition of Sixty-sixth, 115,
    124; on contraband slaves, 48–49; in
    currency exchange, 93–94; on enlist-
    ments, 111, 186–87; on foraging, 43–44,
    83–84, 112; on officers, 82, 84, 89, 99,
    114, 129, 174–75
Bridgeport, Alabama, 185–86; Sixty-sixth
    in, 164, 188; supply line from, 166–67,
    187
Briggs, Pvt. Samuel B., 40
Brock, Jesse, 204
Brough, Johnny, 161–63
Brown, Barney, 230
Brush, Pvt. Stephen, 93
Buford, John, 142
Bull Run, Battle of, 25
Burials: after battles, 68, 108, 153, 196,
    205; armistice for, 93–94; disinterment
    after, 198, 218; of prisoners, 72; ship-
    ping bodies home for, 94–96, 177, 204;
    tombstones of veterans, 226–27
Burnside, Gen. Ambrose, 116, 128

Butterfield, Daniel, 194
Butts, Lt. Charles E., 125–26, 152
Buxton, Capt. Thomas J., 27, 67, 71

Camp Chase (Paw Paw), 41–43
Camp Lander (Camp Chase), 41–43
Camp McArthur (Urbana, Ohio), 20,
    33–37
Camps, 188; of Army of the Potomac,
    140–41; life in, 38, 40, 43, 79–81, 111–
    12, 127; winter, 112, 121, 127–29, 164
Candy, Bvt. Brig. Gen. Charles, 31–32,
    49, 113, 125, 129, 186, 235; abilities ques-
    tioned, 82–83; at Atlanta, 200–205; at
    Cedar Mountain, 89–92; at Chancel-
    lorsville, 131, 133, 135; at Chattanooga,
    169–70; and civilians, 47–48, 50–51;
    commands of, 94, 99, 111, 116, 188, 205,
    220; at Duck River, 163; at Dumfries,
    117–18; at Gettysburg, 144–47; injuries
    of, 170, 209; at New Hope Church,
    192–95; at Pine Knob, 197–98; at Port
    Republic, 63; at reunions of Sixty-
    sixth, 232, 234; and troops, 37, 52–53,
    81
Candy, Ella, 234–35
Careysville, Ohio, 162
Carroll, Col. Samuel S., 57–59
Cassill, Capt. John, 27, 33, 67, 125
Casualties: at Antietam, 105, 107–8; at
    Atlanta, 201, 204; at Bridgeport, 164;
    at Cedar Mountain, 89–94; at Chan-
    cellorsville, 132, 137–38; at Chattanoo-
    ga, 170, 173; Confederate, 213, 217; at
    Dug Gap, 192; at Dumfries, 118; at
    Gettysburg, 144, 152–53; at Kennesaw
    Mountain, 199; at New Hope Church,
    194–96; at Pine Knob, 197–98; rate of
    Sixty-sixth's, 64–65, 79–80; and reen-
    listment, 177–78; at Ringgold, 175–76;
    at Savannah, 213; in Sixty-sixth, 107–8,
    124, 205, 219–20
Cavalry: at Antietam, 106; at Cedar
    Mountain, 89; in Champaign County
    monument, 226; Confederate, 114–16;
    at Dumfries, 117; at Port Republic, 58, 64
Cedar Mountain, Virginia, 88–95; map, 91
Champaign County, Ohio, 186, 217. (See
    also Urbana, Ohio); divisiveness about

Williams, Alpheus S., 98–99, 102–3, 110,
142, 188; at Antietam, 106; at Atlanta,
201–2; at Gettysburg, 144–47; at Kolb's
Farm, 198; at New Hope Church, 194
Williams, Milo G., 183
Wilson, William W., 221–22
Winchester, Virginia, 39–40, 45–50, 54,
114–15
Winder, Charles S., 59
Wives, joining officer husbands, 111–12
Women: in recruitment, 21–22; and

Union soldiers, 48. *See also* Civilians;
Ladies Aid/Relief Societies
Woodstock, Ohio, 17, 27
Wounded, 208–9; at Antietam, 107–8; at
Atlanta, 204–5; at Cedar Mountain,
90–94; at Chancellorsville, 133–34,
138–39; at Chattanooga, 170; effects of,
124–25, 220, 227–28; at Gettysburg,
152; at Ringgold, 175–77

Yeazel, Lt. Andrew H., 29, 115

A Light and Uncertain Hold

was designed and composed by Will Underwood in 10.5/13.5 Adobe
Garamond with Snell Roundhand Bold Script display on a Power
Macintosh using Adobe PageMaker at The Kent State University Press;
printed by sheet-fed offset lithography on 50-pound Glatfelter Supple
Opaque natural stock (an acid-free, recycled paper), Smyth sewn and
bound over binder's boards in Arrestox B cloth, and wrapped with dust
jackets printed in four-color process on 100-pound enamel stock coated
with polyester gloss film lamination by Thomson-Shore, Inc.; and
published by

The Kent State University Press

KENT, OHIO 44242